Maldives

the Bradt Travel Guide

Royston Ellis

www.bradtguides.com

Bradt Travel Guides Ltd, UK
The Globe Pequot Press Inc, USA

edition
4

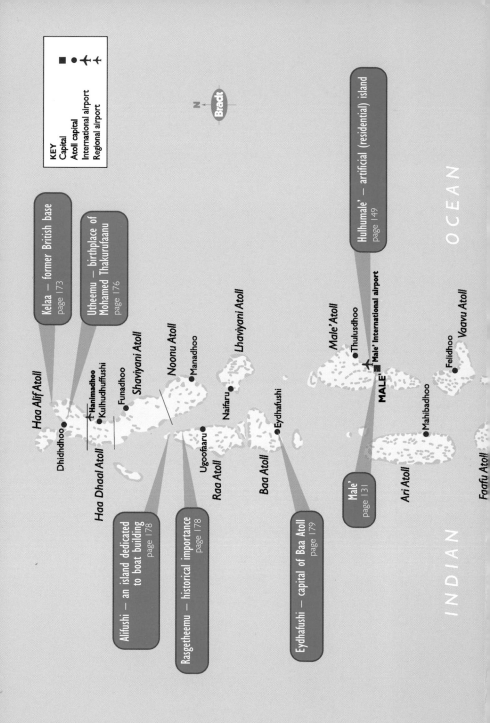

KEY
■ Capital
● Atoll capital
✈ International airport
✦ Regional airport

N
Bradt

INDIAN OCEAN

Haa Alif Atoll

Kelaa — former British base
page 173

Utheemu — birthplace of Mohamed Thakurufaanu
page 176

Dhidhdhoo

Hanimadhoo
Kulhudhuffushi
Funadhoo

Haa Dhaal Atoll

Shaviyani Atoll

Alifushi — an island dedicated to boat building
page 178

Manadhoo

Noonu Atoll

Lhaviyani Atoll

Rasgetheemu — historical importance
page 178

Ugoofaaru
Naifaru

Raa Atoll

Baa Atoll

Eydhafushi

Eydhafushi — capital of Baa Atoll
page 179

Hulhumale' — artificial (residential) island
page 149

Male' Atoll

Thulusdhoo

Male' International airport
MALE'
Male'
page 131

Mahibadhoo

Ari Atoll

Felidhoo

Vaavu Atoll

Faafu Atoll

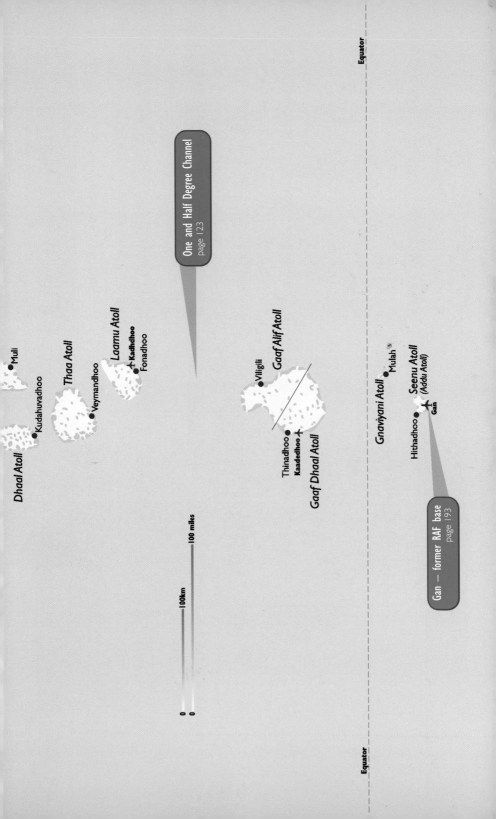

Muli

Dhaal Atoll

Kudahuvadhoo

Thaa Atoll

Veymandhoo

Laamu Atoll

Kadhdhoo ✈

Fonadhoo

One and Half Degree Channel
page 123

Viligili

Gaaf Alif Atoll

Thinadhoo

Kaadedhoo ✈

Gaaf Dhaal Atoll

Gnaviyani Atoll

Mulah

Seenu Atoll

(Addu Atoll)

Hithadhoo

✈

Gan

Gan — former RAF base
page 193

100km

100 miles

0

0

Equator

Equator

Maldives
Don't
miss…

Male'
Waterfront and
mosque by night
(GA) page 131

Pristine beaches
Angsana Ihuru
(GAR/Tips) page 154

above left **Seaplane anchored off the beach** (GA) page 79

above **Windsurfing is available at most resorts**
(EN/PCL) page 122

left **Colourful cocktails are served in the resorts**
(PF/PCL)

below **Coco Palm Boduhithi, North Male' Atoll**
(GAR/Tips) page 156

Clear turquoise
waters, one of
thousands of lagoons
in the Maldives (GA)

AUTHOR

Royston Ellis is a travel writer, novelist and biographer based in Sri Lanka who first visited the Maldives on holiday in 1983. He spent several months there in 1994 and 1995 researching for the first edition of this book, and lived in Male' during 1998 when he was writing the biography of Maumoon Abdul Gayoom, the President of the Maldives. He has also written *A Hero In Time* based on the life of the Maldives national hero, Mohamed Thakurufaan. He visits the Maldives frequently, his most recent visit being in July 2008 for the final update of this edition.

Royston Ellis contributes features on Indian Ocean destinations to international newspapers and inflight magazines and lectures on the area on luxury cruise liners such as *Silverseas* and *Seabourn* ships and Scotland's own cruise liner, *Hebridean Spirit*. He is author of over 60 books including some best-selling historical novels written under the pseudonym of Richard Tresillian.

For Bradt Guides, he has written *Sri Lanka*, including the 2008 third edition, and is the pioneering author of *Mauritius, Rodrigues & Réunion*.

AUTHOR'S STORY

I can't believe I've been having an affair with the Maldives for over a quarter of a century. Looking back, as updating this fourth edition made me do, I realise it was inevitable: love at first sight.

When I was six years old I looked forward to a holiday in Clacton because I was told that the sea, which I had never seen, would be 'on the doorstep'. When I arrived with my parents at the boarding house I rushed to the back door and flung it open, only to see a garden of runner beans at the doorstep – no sea!

The Maldives delivers, not just the sea literally on one's doorstep, but also the perfect holiday package of sea, sun and sand. Over the 25 years I have been visiting the islands I have discovered so much more as well: a stirring history and a quietly determined people loyal to their friends and proud of their country. It was not surprising that it was a 15-year-old boy scout who jumped in to foil a knife attack on his country's president in January 2008.

When I told a friend who knows me well that I was going to the Maldives again, he was astonished. 'But there's nothing to do there!' he said. It is because there is always something to do, a place or a person to discover, that brought me to Bradt. I was in Mauritius writing a novel and couldn't find an up-to-date guidebook. I suggested to Hilary Bradt that I write one for her fledgling publishing house. She agreed immediately, although my idea of a guide to Maldives took longer to make the list – perhaps it was then too esoteric a destination.

Sitting on the balcony of a log cabin built on stilts over a tranquil lagoon in the Maldives, my childhood desire for the sea is fulfilled, without any disappointment. Even at home in Sri Lanka, where my veranda overlooks the Indian Ocean, I imagine I can see the lights of the islands twinkling on the horizon, beckoning me back. It's a dream, of course, and I hope this guide will make every reader's dream of the Maldives a blissful reality.

PUBLISHER'S FOREWORD — *Hilary Bradt*

The first Bradt travel guide was written in 1974 by George and Hilary Bradt on a river barge floating down a tributary of the Amazon. It was followed by *Backpacker's Africa*, published in 1979. In the 1980s and '90s the focus shifted away from hiking to broader-based guides to new destinations – usually the first to be published on those places. In the 21st century Bradt continues to publish these ground-breaking guides, along with guides to established holiday destinations, incorporating in-depth information on culture and natural history alongside the nuts and bolts of where to stay and what to see.

Bradt authors support responsible travel, with advice not only on minimum impact but also on how to give something back through local charities. Thus a true synergy is achieved between the traveller and local communities.

* * *

My association with Royston Ellis goes back to the mid-1980s, when he was one of only a handful of Bradt authors. Royston loves islands – he lives in Sri Lanka and wrote our Sri Lanka guide, although his first Bradt guide was to Mauritius. When he wrote the first edition of Maldives in 1994, the country was little known as a holiday destination. Now in its fourth edition, the guide covers the expansion of the Maldives into more than 150 tropical island resorts.

Fourth edition October 2008

First published 1995

Bradt Travel Guides Ltd, 23 High Street, Chalfont St Peter, Bucks SL9 9QE, England
www.bradtguides.com

Published in the USA by The Globe Pequot Press Inc, 246 Goose Lane,
PO Box 480, Guilford, Connecticut 06475-0480

Text copyright © 2008 Bradt Travel Guides Ltd

Maps copyright © 2008 Bradt Travel Guides Ltd

Illustrations copyright © 2008 Individual photographers and artists

Editorial Project Manager: Anna Moores

British Library Cataloguing in Publication Data
A catalogue record for this book is available from the British Library
ISBN-13: 978 1 84162 266 8

Photographs Gemunu Amarasinghe (GA), Jack Jackson (JJ), Pictures Colour Library: Picture Finders (PF/PCL), Edmund Nagele (EN/PCL), PhotoLocation Ltd (PLL/PCL), Clive Sawyer (CS/PCL); Tips Images: Reinhard Dirscherl (RD/Tips), Photononstop (P/Tips), Guido Alberto Rossi (GAR/Tips)
Front cover A resort island in the Maldives (Chad Ehlers/Alamy)
Back cover An Idyllic beach, Male' Atoll (PF/PCL), scuba diver looking for a lionfish, Meemu Atoll (RD/Tips)
Title page Dhoni in azure lagoon (P/Tips), crescent-tail bigcyc (RD/Tips), exotic cocktail (PF/PCL)

Illustrations Carole Vincer **Maps** Maria Randell and Dave Priestley
Typeset from the author's disc by Wakewing
Printed and bound in India by Nutech Photolithographers

Acknowledgements

A chance meeting with Ahmed Didi, a director of Universal Enterprises, when photographer Gemunu Amarasinghe and I were staying at the new Full Moon resort in 1994, led to enthusiastic support for the first edition of this guidebook from Mr M U Maniku, Chairman of Universal Enterprises and a pioneer of the tourist industry. Without his initial encouragement and help, this book could not have been written. I am grateful to Ibrahim Shakir (Charlie), Mohamed Firaq and my first contact in the 1980s, Mohamed Arif. To Mohamed Firaq of Inner Maldives Holidays I remain especially grateful for all the help and information he has given me for this book over the years, including organising my visits in 2007 and 2008 to update this edition.

I am grateful, too, to the Hon Ibrahim Hussain Zaki who, when he was Minister of Tourism, gave considerable encouragement for this and other book projects. To Mariyam Zulfa, editor of Explore Maldives, my special thanks for her dedicated reading of the first edition of this book and for her suggestions which greatly helped to strengthen the second edition. I am also grateful to B Kumarasiri for his company and assistance on several research visits to the islands.

Thanks, too, to Neel Jayantha, who accompanied me on my first visit to the Maldives in 1983 and has visited the country many times since then and helped in the research for the second edition.

Siân Pritchard-Jones and Bob Gibbons, updaters of the third edition, are grateful for the help and friendship offered by Mohamed Shahid of the Transit Inn in Male'. Thanks also to Ahmed Fiyaz of Universal Enterprises, who showed them around some resorts by speedboat. Also to the Novelty Bookshop in Fareedhee Magu, which helped them find what they were looking for at a good price – and for being interested enough to produce such fascinating books and posters on the Maldives.

'The Maldives,' they wrote in the third edition, 'is not an easy country to explore or to understand, and we are grateful to all the Maldivians we met for their help and the information they supplied.'

FEEDBACK REQUEST

Every effort has been made to ensure that the details contained within this book are as accurate and up to date as possible. Inevitably, however, things move on. Any information regarding such changes, or relating to your experiences in the Maldives – good or bad – would be very gratefully received. Such feedback is invaluable when compiling further editions. Send your comments to Royston Ellis at Bradt Travel Guides Ltd, 23 High Street, Chalfont St Peter, Bucks SL9 9QE, England; e info@bradtguides.com.

Contents

LIST OF MAPS

Spotted eagle ray

Introduction

Set like shining jewels in a turquoise blue sea are the islands of dreamers, romantics and beach lovers. The Maldives are a destination synonymous with sun worship, tranquillity, lazy days, good living, snorkelling in turquoise lagoons and diving to discover fascinating reefs. They epitomise all that one could imagine as paradise: a group of romantic islands ringed by glorious beaches, translucent warm waters and swaying coconut palms.

The islands have become the playground of the new jet-setters: celebrities, the incognito wealthy and those in search of a stylish vacation without having to compromise. As the tourism promotional headline declares, 'The Maldives are the sunny side of life.' But is this all?

The Maldives, a loop of islands in the Indian Ocean draped from north to south across the Equator, are home to an industrious people, long used to isolation and fending for themselves. They have been quick but cautious in embracing a modern world that means adapting to fast-changing and evolving new circumstances. The people of the Maldives have grasped these unfolding scenarios and made a dedicated effort to incorporate all that is new, productive, beneficial and useful to complement their time-honoured traditions.

Inevitably this fast-forwarding to the future has brought problems as a previously elementary people suddenly taste the fruit of progress and politics. It is not only the conveniences of the modern world that have arrived in the Maldives, inconveniences have slipped in too. Yet, for visitors, the island resorts are more seductive and desirable for a perfect holiday than they have ever been.

The Maldives consist of many atolls, geographical features that appear like bubbles on the ocean horizon. Each island invariably has a pristine white sandy beach. Each has a lagoon, a haven of calm, and surrounding most are colourful reefs of coral dropping into an infinite chasm. One of the many highlights of a visit to the islands, even for poor swimmers, is to dive and snorkel amongst these reefs.

The island resorts of the Maldives are designed for the holidaymaker arriving from overseas for a week or ten days. Most will be staying at one resort and hoping to top up a tan, swim in warm waters and explore the underwater world of the island. For an independent traveller hoping to explore the atolls, opportunities are gradually opening up with new regional airports and travellers' hotels. Male', the only easily accessible settlement for the independent traveller, is fascinating for its insight into island lifestyle. It is also possible to organise a trip by *dhoni*, or take a 'safari' cruising from atoll to atoll to see more of the islands.

The Maldives are the place for contemplation, relaxation and a pleasant lethargy induced by a warming sun, cool balmy evenings and moonlit starry nights. This edition is the first to cover the entire archipelago with all the new resorts and developments, making it of value to every visitor from backpacker to billionaire.

A BRIEF OUTLINE

The islands of the Maldives have attracted travellers for centuries. Curiously, the islands retain an image that is indefinable, neither Asian nor Middle Eastern. Even influences from neighbouring Sri Lanka and India are slight. Visiting the Maldives is going to spoil you for going anywhere else. For the visitor everything is simple, relaxed and stress-free. The Maldivians are a genuine, hospitable people, although reserved, so don't expect instant – and thus quick-dissolving – friendships.

Anyone who tells you the Maldives is boring may themselves be boring. However, since most visitors come on a pre-arranged holiday and stay on an island resort recommended by a travel agent (who has probably never been there), disappointments can occur.

Even if you do not want to laze in the tropical sun on a white, coral-sand beach, snorkel in turquoise lagoons, dive to discover fascinating reefs, go big-game fishing or windsurfing, be marooned on a real desert island or sip exotic cocktails before a gourmet-quality dinner, there is still much to see, do and enjoy, gaining an insight into a way of life that seems idyllic to visitors and of which Maldivians themselves are rather proud.

The island resorts do not offer the artificial razzle-dazzle of Mediterranean beach strips. The theme is holiday, pure and simple. But if you are adventurous and want to discover the secrets that make Maldivians such a self-confident, self-contained, pleasant people to be with, there are chances to do so.

At first, arriving travellers affected by the (at times unacknowledged) pressures of flying and the red tape of travel, may take a while to adjust to the unaffected, unconcerned attitude of the people and their lifestyle. Do not feel upset if your haste and priorities seem not to matter; survival techniques are different in the Maldives.

Whether your visit is cocooned by a tour operator's programme or arranged completely by yourself, this book aims to help you gain more than a suntan from experiencing one of the most enchanting and delightful places on earth.

The Maldives are not generally geared to those wishing to reach beyond the 'organised', but it is possible. *Dhonis*, the traditional Maldivian sailing and fishing boats, are the taxis of the islands. Most *dhonis* are now mechanical, and scheduled ones only operate from Male', the capital. Prices are dependent on the whim of the vessel's skipper, and on demand. To venture beyond the tourist zones, to discover more of the Maldives, needs some initiative and the help of Maldivians, especially an experienced travel agent like Mohamed Firaq, whose Inner Maldives Holidays was voted the Leading Indian Ocean Travel Agency at the World Travel Awards in 2007 (see page 50 for contact details). As more resorts are being opened in atolls previously unexplored by visitors, the opportunities for seeing intriguing aspects of the country have increased.

'Aren't the Maldives expensive?' people are sure to ask, especially if they usually go to a low-cost holiday destination in a less romantic part of the world. A holiday in the Maldives is not 'cheap' but, on the other hand, the 'holiday product' has become so good that guests are comfortable with the cost. And there is a wide range of resorts, from beachfront rooms at less than US$250 per night for two, all inclusive, to resorts at ten times that. The list of resorts in *Appendix 3*, pages 204–7, shows some 20 resorts in the low price range.

What about the extras? Since every resort is on an island and everything (food, staff and guests) is imported, extras can push up the price of the holiday. Enjoy fancy cocktails and you will need a fancy holiday budget.

Resort island food, if you are on a bed and breakfast basis, will vary in price according to the standard of the island as well as of the chef. Special theme dinners at upwards of US$50 a head are usual on a more upmarket island but, at the same resort, two could eat for less than that in the coffee shop. Speedboat hire, if you want to visit other resorts in a hurry, will cost considerably more than you usually pay for a 30-minute taxi ride at home.

Of course, there are ways to keep costs down and some ideas are suggested in this book. Not everyone wants to be cloistered among coconut palms where the only sign of inhabitants on the 'desert island' are fellow sun-worshippers from overseas being served by uniformed stewards.

The Maldives resorts thrive on repeat guests, visitors who return year after year. This book tries to help the first-time visitor gain the same knowledge and affection for the islands as these regulars. Visiting the Maldives as part of a package is probably the cheapest way of getting there from other continents, and you will have the security of a pre-paid island base. Be aware, though, if your chosen island doesn't appeal there are no local ferries which you can hop on and off and book into another resort. It is not practical to go on a whim from one island to another as an independent traveller as resorts are usually booked months in advance.

It is recommended that you let your travel agent or contact in the Maldives know exactly what you want from a holiday. The resorts' own websites will take you on a guided tour round their facilities with images of the rooms and bathrooms, so you can get an idea of what is in store before you make your reservation. The islands of the Maldives are unique, very special places with very special people; a visit there is a valuable experience to cherish and enjoy.

NOMENCLATURE

Is it 'the Maldives' or 'Maldives?' When people refer to the Maldives, it seems to be a convenient abbreviation for the Maldive Islands. Use of the word Maldives without the definite article indicates the nation. Just to add to the confusion, the word is pronounced Mol-deeves, not Mal-dives. The people are called Maldivians. The capital is pronounced Mar-lay.

Another puzzle is how to spell or write that name; is it Male, Male´, Malé or Male'? In *The Times*, 23 September 1989, Royston Ellis commented:

> Male' is written that way either because early printers lacked an acute accent, or it could be a contraction of Malei, referring to the dynasty which ruled the archipelago first as Buddhists and then as Muslims 800 years ago.

Even though acute accents are available to typesetters, Male' is never written with one. So although it causes headaches for typesetters and proofreaders, this guide follows the Maldivian tradition, and thus Male' is printed here the way it usually is in the Maldives. For the possessive, Male's is used.

SPELLING

A careful reader who consults various sources referring to the islands will notice that proper names in the Maldives can be spelt in several different ways when they are rendered in Roman script. In this guide I have tried to be consistent in the spellings I use, preferring those most often seen in official sources, rather than trying to follow a rigid system of translation. However, even in official sources a name may appear in two or more different ways, though fortunately the various spellings are usually phonetically similar. By way of further complication, some islands and atolls have very similar names but different spellings are used. Many islands and atolls have names ending in a '...doo' sound. Where this applies to an island it should be spelt '...dhoo', but for an atoll '...dhu' is correct; thus Felidhoo is an island in Felidhu Atoll. I hope that readers will bear all this in mind when consulting other sources and publications, and will not become too confused!

Unfortunately, to make matters worse, the atolls which make up the Maldives all have at least two names, a traditional one and a shorter alphabetical code name. This system is explained in *Chapter 3*, page 101, and the various names are summarised in the tables in *Appendix 2*, pages 200–3.

TELEPHONE NUMBERS

All telephone numbers in the Maldives were changed during 2005, with both landline and mobile numbers being switched from six to seven digits. Numbers given in this guide have been updated, but should you find yourself with an old six-digit number, it's worth knowing the basics.

For Dhiraagu mobile services, prefix six-digit numbers with a 7. Landlines vary, but all Male' numbers gain the prefix 3. Elsewhere, the first two digits of each number have been replaced by a three-digit code identifying the atoll. Details of these are available on www.visitmaldives.com/Media_center/numberchange.php. Emergency numbers remain unchanged.

Bougainvillea

Part One

GENERAL INFORMATION

MALDIVES AT A GLANCE

Location Indian Ocean, west of Sri Lanka, from 7°N to just south of Equator

Area 90,000km²; land area 298km²

Climate Warm and summer-like year round with occasional monsoon winds and rains. Wettest months May and November. Average temperature 23–32°C.

Status Republic

Population 338,000 (Est 2007)

Capital Male', population 100,000 (Est 2007)

Economy Tourism, fishing, shipping

Languages Dhivehi, English

Religion Islam

Currency Rufiyaa (Rf); 1Rf = 100 laari (L)

Exchange rate US$1 = 12.75Rf (fixed); £1 = 25.23Rf, €1 = 20.06Rf (July 2008)

International airports Male' and Gan

International telephone code +960

Time GMT+5

Electrical voltage 220–240V; UK-style three-pin plugs

Weights and measures Metric for weights; imperial for measurements

Flag Green rectangle with crescent in centre surrounded by red border

National flower Pink rose (*Rosa polyantha*)

National tree Coconut palm

Public holidays See page 83

Background Information

BASIC FACTS

COUNTRY The Maldives is an independent republic (formerly a sultanate) in the Indian Ocean, comprising an archipelago of 198 inhabited (200 for administrative purposes) and 991 uninhabited islands (the official count) in 26 natural atolls. In Dhivehi, the language of the Maldives, the country is known as Dhivehi Raajje (the Dhivehi Realm).

LOCATION AND SIZE The country is west of Sri Lanka (latitude 7° 6' 30"N to 0° 41' 48"S; longitude 72° 32' 30"E to 73° 45' 54"E) and comprises a slender chain of islands stretching from 7°N of the Equator to just south of it. Its nearest neighbours, to the north and east, are India, about 600km distant, and Sri Lanka, about 670km. To the west are the shores of Somalia, Africa; to the east, Indonesia, Singapore and Malaysia. To the southwest, the nearest country is the Seychelles, and further away is Madagascar. The republic covers a total area of 90,000km², about the size of Portugal, but that includes the sea. Land area is about 298km², roughly half the size of Singapore. The length of the archipelago is 822km and it is 130km at its widest. Few of the 1,190 or so islands are more than 1km² in area.

FEATURES The islands are small and low-lying with neither rivers nor mountains, the maximum height being about 2.4m above sea level. A shallow lagoon encircles each island. Every atoll is formed by different reefs, many of coral. The reefs, which are nature's protection from rough seas, are spectacular, home to a brilliant variety of tropical fish. Below the reefs the sea deepens to 365m. The islands have tropical castaway qualities, with tall coconut palms, white sandy beaches and crystal-clear lagoons. Some of the larger ones have ponds of brackish water.

TIME Maldives time is Greenwich Mean Time (GMT) plus five hours; it's nine hours ahead of Eastern Standard Time in the USA. Local time is 30 minutes behind that in India and Sri Lanka, three hours behind Singapore and five hours behind Australian Eastern Time. Some resorts, even those close to Male', declare their own time, setting their clocks from one to three hours ahead of Male' time. The managers say this is to give guests a later sunset. It also has the effect of confusing them so they don't realise that they are leaving their resort so far ahead of their flight's departure time. However, during the month of Ramazan, the staff on all islands stick to Male' time so they can observe the daylight hours of abstinence correctly. By Male' time, daybreak is between 05.00 and 06.00 and sunset between 18.00 and 19.00, all year round. The twilight is brief, with the sun slipping rapidly out of sight and invariably spreading an iridescent glow over the darkening sky (a great time for photographers). Maldivians are punctual for business meetings and generally respect other timings, helped by the strict observance of prayer times demanded by their religion. The influence of tourism – of planes leaving on

3

schedule, of meals expected on time – may also have helped to create an understanding of the need for punctuality.

GEOGRAPHY

The Republic of Maldives is not the smallest nation in the world, in either size or population, but it is unique in having the sea forming 99.6% of its 'territory'. The Maldive islands and atolls are actually part of the Laccadives–Chagos Ridge, which extends for 2,000km from latitude 14°N to 8°S. North of the Maldives are the Laccadives, also known as Lakshadweep, which are part of India. Access to them is by plane from Cochin (Kochi). The closest of those islands to the Maldives (about 130km) is Minicoy, whose inhabitants also speak Dhivehi, the language of the Maldives. South of Addu (the southernmost Maldives atoll) is the Chagos Archipelago. Formerly part of the Seychelles group, this now forms part of the British Indian Ocean Territory (BIOT). Diego Garcia in the archipelago used to belong to Mauritius but is now, as part of the BIOT, the main US military base in the Indian Ocean (see the Bradt guide *Mauritius, Rodrigues & Réunion* for the sorry story of how that happened). The Chagos Archipelago is 450km south of the Maldives.

PLATE TECTONICS AND ATOLL FORMATION To understand how the Maldives were formed, it is necessary to give a very brief outline of the theory of plate tectonics. The earth's crust is divided up into a number of huge plates, which move about above a generally molten sub-layer. Where the plates crash into each other, mountains are thrust upwards as one plate is pushed under the other. These areas are also the world's major earthquake zones. Under the main oceans are mid-ocean ridges, where new material erupts up through weak points and fault lines. It is these eruptions of basalt magma from deep in the earth that cause the movement of the plates. Above the plates are the continental land masses which ride along with the plates. At one time all the land mass was connected into one gigantic continent known as Gondwanaland or Pangea. The main ocean ridge in the Indian Ocean, which lies at a depth of 4,000–5,000m, is close to the island of Réunion, southwest of the Maldives. Around 200 million years ago, eruptions of volcanic basalt started to push Madagascar, Australia, the Antarctic and India away from Africa and the main land mass. India eventually drifted northeast and crashed into the Tibetan plate, about 50 million years ago, to form the Himalaya, Karakoram and Hindu Kush mountains.The Indian plate was subject to further eruptions of basalt and volcanic activity, which created the basalt Deccan plateau on which the Laccadive–Maldives–Chagos islands now sit. These volcanic events are widely believed to have resulted in the extinction of the dinosaurs. The atolls of the Maldives lie on this deep underwater ridge of volcanic basalt, which has come from the magma below the crust. Originally the eruptions formed volcanoes here above the sea. Fringing reef developed in the rocky zone surrounding each volcano. These volcanoes slowly subsided as the ocean floor settled. As they sank, the coral developing around their shores kept growing upwards. After the volcanoes had become completely submerged, lagoons were then left within these ring reefs (see diagrams opposite). This action is observed today around Hawaii. An exploration well dug in the North Male' Atoll seems to confirm this. It reached down to a volcanic basement at 2,100m colonised by coral dating from 53–38 million years ago.

The coral in the Maldives has grown upwards to great heights from the base plateau – at a maximum rate estimated at almost 1.25cm a year at times. During any temporary reduction in sea level, the coral dies and decays, forming hard levels that become the new foundation for any subsequent coral to develop above. Divers will

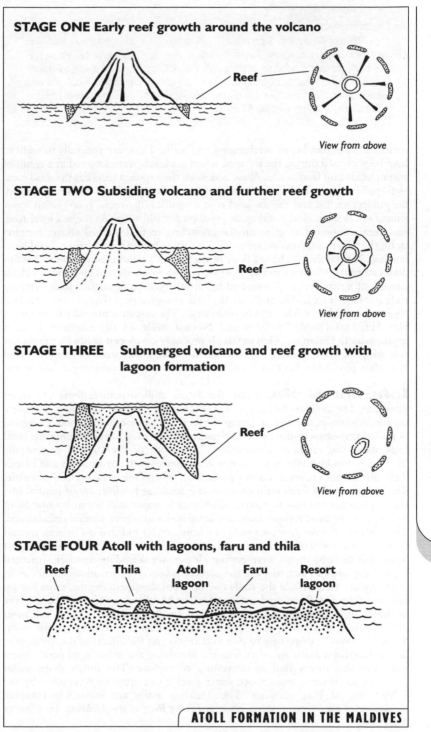

STAGE ONE Early reef growth around the volcano

Reef

View from above

STAGE TWO Subsiding volcano and further reef growth

Reef

View from above

STAGE THREE Submerged volcano and reef growth with lagoon formation

Reef

View from above

STAGE FOUR Atoll with lagoons, faru and thila

Reef   Thila   Atoll lagoon   Faru   Resort lagoon

ATOLL FORMATION IN THE MALDIVES

notice the large number of overhanging reef walls. These are generally thought to have been created during the ice ages, when sea levels were lowered as a result of water freezing on land masses. Wave action on the exposed reefs cut the dead coral reefs, producing eroded features such as the overhangs. When the ice age ended, the glaciers melted and the sea level rose, engulfing the reefs. Later, when water temperatures were ideal, coral again grew on the old reefs. As the sea level rose, new coral continued to grow on the encircling reefs described above, forming atolls, the ring formations we see today. The strata below the Maldives could be as much as 2,000m thick. The sea floor of the Indian Ocean is now around 2,500m deep east of the Maldives and up to 4,000m deep to the west. The Maldives chain consists of a twin series of atolls and has submerged reefs, surface reefs, fringing reefs and barrier reefs. The atolls are the large complex ring-shaped structures best observed from the air. They can be quite large. The vast structure which comprises Haa Alif, Haa Dhaal, Shaviyani and Noonu atolls, in the northern zone, is approximately 155km by 50km in size. It probably developed around a number of volcanic peaks. In the south, the Gaaf Alif and Gaaf Dhaal atolls collectively called Huvadhu, plus Addu Atoll, may have been two large, now submerged, volcanoes.

Kandus, farus and thilas Within the larger atoll structure, there are many variations. The atolls are formed generally as ring-shaped reef structures, but there are subdivisions in the type and shape of reefs with horseshoe, ribbon, elongated as well as ring-shaped structures. The main lagoons have formed within the coral reefs above the submerged volcanoes. The depth of the lagoons is generally 20–30m, but in Huvadhu is as much as 85m. Between the many atolls and islands there are deeper channels known as kandus, where the seawater can circulate. These rejuvenating fresh influxes allow the amazing biodiversity of natural life, corals, plankton and fish to survive. Within each major atoll are many islands, of which some become resorts, some are inhabited and others remain uninhabited. These islands all have their own reefs (the house reefs) and shallow lagoons around them. In time, some of the lagoons will eventually fill in to form other islands. Just when you thought things were getting clearer, we introduce another structural feature, the farus. In fact, many of the islands and smaller formations are not atolls at all, but are farus. While the atolls rise up from the ocean depths, farus rise up only from the atoll floors, and are found in the Maldives in great numbers. Many of the elongated, ringed, horseshoe-shaped small sub-islands within the main atolls are farus, as are many of the resorts that lie in the internal zones of the atolls. Their variations in shape may be due to currents and the effects of the monsoons. Within the major atolls are other features like thilas, the submerged coral towers and caves that divers find so interesting to explore. The thila's shape varies according to currents; from above water level it can often be recognised by the lighter ring of blue seawater. The Maldive atolls are incredibly complex formations. One recommended book is *Living Reefs of the Maldives*, by Charles Anderson.

THE GEOGRAPHY TODAY The word 'atoll' is probably a derivative of a local word, *atolhu*. The Oxford English Dictionary (OED) says the word is 'an adoption of the native name atollon'. It suggests that the word probably comes from the Malayalam (the language of the southwest coastal state of Kerala in India) word *adal* meaning 'closing, uniting'. The OED quotes a 17th-century author, Samuel Purchas, writing in 1625: 'Every atollon is separated from others and contaynes in itself a greate multitude of small Isles.' The Maldives chain of atolls was known to ancient mariners, being a particular hazard to ships sailing to and from India. Today supertankers plying between the Gulf and Japan plus cargo ships bound for Colombo and the Far East from Europe pass very close to the islands. A captain of a cruise liner confessed to passengers in 1994, 'I was surprised to see the Admiralty Charts for the Maldives, through which we passed in the dark, were printed in England in 1839.' It is a fact that the charts still in use today are essentially those surveyed and produced in 1835–39. Before then, the Maldives were marked on charts as a crudely drawn line of atolls, including islands which did not actually exist. Ibn Battuta, the Moroccan traveller, wrote:

> When a vessel arrives at any one of them [the atolls] it must needs take one of the
> inhabitants to pilot it to the other islands. They are so close set that on leaving one
> island the tops of the palms on another are visible. If a ship loses its course it is unable
> to enter and is carried by the wind to the Coromandel Coast [Malabar] or Ceylon.

So how many islands are there in the Maldives? Most sources give different answers. However, government publications seem to agree now on 1,190. H A Maniku provides a delightful account of the various estimates, ranging from the largest (12,700) suggested by Marco Polo (1254–1324) to volume VI of the *Encyclopaedia Britannica* which states 1,087 islands. Maldivians themselves insist on 2,000 islands, regarding anything less as an insult. Perhaps Dr Anderson has the right answer when he mentions that where sand accumulates on a reef flat it may form banks and islands. 'There are roughly 2,000 islands in the Maldives,' he writes in *Living Reefs of the Maldives*, 'but excluding unvegetated sand banks, the number is close to 1,200.' The official figure of inhabited islands for administrative purposes is currently 200, but that does not mean all the other islands are uninhabited, since tourist-resort islands (which are actually very densely inhabited) are classed as 'uninhabited'. This is the result of only genuinely uninhabited islands being leased for conversion to tourist-resort islands. They are deemed not to have permanent residents since the staff, whether Maldivian or expatriate, and, of course, the guests, do not actually have their homes on them. Similarly, other 'uninhabited' islands may have semi-permanent residents engaged in fish drying, coconut cultivation or other island pursuits.

The largest atoll is Huvadhu, in the south, with a lagoon area of 2,240km, making it among the largest atolls in the world. The smallest atolls are Kaashidhu, north of Male' Atoll, and Thoddhu, both just under 2km in diameter. The largest island is Fuvah Mulah (Fua Mulaku), 430km south of Male', which is 3.2km in length and 2km wide. The capital, Male', lies to the north of the centre of the atoll chain, at latitude 4° 10'N. It is the most heavily populated of all the islands (62,973 in the 1995 census; in 2007 estimated at 100,000 and growing) and is at the centre of all activity. The main tourism development began in the atoll in which Male' is located, and later in the neighbouring Ari Atoll. The opening up to tourism of other more distant atolls (Haa Alif, Haa Dhaal and Noonu in the north, and Thaa, Laamu, Gnaviyani and Gaaf Alif/Gaaf Dhaal in the south) has accelerated recently. The international airport is on Hulhule island, a ten-minute boat ride from the capital, with a newly opened one across the Equator on Gan, Addu Atoll. The surface area of Male' has increased, with land reclamation adding a third of its original size, but it is still only just over 2.5km². It is the least 'tropical' in appearance of all the islands, due to the density of construction. It has no natural beaches but now has an 'artificial beach' on the east side. Apart from Male', most of the islands have wonderful beaches galore. The sand is soft and sparkling white in the sun, with shell particles ground by the sea's constant wash into grains smaller than the stop at the end of this sentence. The beaches of the Maldives are hard to beat.

Every island supports vegetation of some kind, and it is remarkable how coconut palms manage to thrive in a small, sparse land area. Some islands boast venerable banyan trees. Careful nurturing on islands devoted to agriculture enables the growing of papaya, peppers, eggplants, melons, breadfruit and bananas. Because of the loose soil structure, cows cannot be reared, but chickens are to be found at village settlements. Although there are no forests, the vegetation can be lush and tangled enough to give privacy on those so-called Robinson Crusoe islands near resorts where honeymoon couples like to be marooned by day. The surface covering is usually a mixture of sand and organic matter, forming a layer of dark humus to about 15cm deep, sometimes with broken pieces of coral. Below is sandstone about 60cm deep, which changes to a layer of sand where fresh water can be found. Water is usually obtained by making shallow wells. Erosion is common, and a problem, especially on islands lying a few kilometres from windward reefs.

For local people, boat journeys between major atolls can be long, requiring at least one night on board. But with a modern speedboat it is possible to travel all the way from Helengeli, the northernmost resort in North Male' Atoll, to Kurumba, close to the airport, in just a morning. Tourists are transferred from the airport to the vacation resort by *dhoni*, speedboat or seaplane. No journey takes more than a few hours. Seas, however, are not always idyllically calm. The deep channels between atolls can make for rough crossings during bad weather, particularly during the May–October southwest monsoon season. Cloud structure is usually light and the climate well tempered by breeze.

CLIMATE AND SEASONS

The change in seasons is defined by the monsoon, which in the case of the Maldives refers to the wind rather than rain. It is tempting to think of the Maldives as always being sunny and that when winds blow they are usually no worse than a breeze to cool a summer's day. This is not actually true and the wind can whip up choppy seas quite quickly. However, there are no hurricanes or cyclones, and only occasional gales. There are hot days and cooler nights during the dry, northeast monsoon of January–March; the wet, southwest monsoon blows spasmodically May–December. Short, sharp stormy squalls can occur throughout the year but these rarely last long. Temperatures vary from 23°–32°C, with the daily average maximum temperature around 30.4°C/87°F, minimum 25.4°C/79°F. The average rainfall is 1,948mm a year. May (28cm) and November (27cm) are the wettest months. According to average figures, March has the most sunshine (over 9 hours a day), followed closely by April, February and January. June has the least sunshine (6.5 hours per day). Even when it is cloudy, the sun is so intense that it can affect fair skins even when it is out of sight. Tour operators always advise that care should be taken when sunbathing and that sunscreen protection should always be worn.

NATURAL HISTORY

SAVING THE ENVIRONMENT With 99.6% of its 'territory' being sea, the Maldives is the most watery nation on earth. Many scientists believe that global warming from the 'greenhouse effect' is going to cause the level of the sea to rise, threatening low-lying nations. Some experts predict a rise in the sea level of 6cm/2.4 inches per decade over the next century. In an impassioned plea to the rest of the world to help save the Maldives, President Gayoom told a news agency reporter in December 1994: 'Any rise in the sea level would be a catastrophe or a disaster for this country.' He pointed out that if Maldives is to be saved from a watery grave in the 21st century, industrialised nations must bring under control their emissions of the greenhouse gases that destroy the ozone layer and lead to the melting of mountain glaciers and polar ice caps, and consequent rises in the sea level. The president was quoted by Agence France Presse (AFP) as saying there is very little the Maldives can do about this. The islands do not emit the gases in any significant quantity. 'It is a worldwide problem, the whole world has to do something about it,' the president said. The Maldives government was very sensitive to the situation long before global warming became a universal concern. In 1987 the president highlighted the problem in speeches to the UN General Assembly and to the Commonwealth Heads of Government meeting in Vancouver. In 1989 the Maldives hosted a conference of small states to find joint efforts to save low-lying island nations from the consequences of global warming, climatic change and rises in sea level.

The threat of rising sea levels and the fragility of the country's marine environment became a national issue in April 1987, when unusually high waves struck the whole archipelago. On Male', a quarter of the island was inundated by water, 30% of newly reclaimed land was washed away, and the airport and many islands were flooded. During the 2004 tsunami, one third of Male' was flooded, but no permanent land damage resulted. Some eastern resorts suffered but the damage was less than expected as the sea rose up and washed over the islands then subsided, instead of battering down buildings in its way as happened in Sri Lanka. Over 21 years ago, in October 1987, the president told the UN General Assembly that

Man's action over many centuries has transmuted the natural order of his environment to the point where the whole world is ensnared in the consequences; as the scale of man's intervention in nature increased, the scope of nature's repercussions has multiplied.

Consequences of the actions of individual nations have reverberated globally and all humankind, present and future generations, may suffer the penalties for the errors of a few ... today the world is faced with risks of irreversible damage to the environment and threats to the very life support of the earth, the basis of survival and progress.

An Environment Action Plan was drawn up with the assistance of the United Nations Development Programme (UNDP) and the United Nations Environment Programme (UNEP). The thought behind the plan was the need for the prudent management of the islands' reefs and surrounding oceans to achieve sustainable development. Because of the lack of information, environmental assessment was to be carried out and action taken. The following fell under investigation:

- Health of the Maldivian coral reefs, coral bleaching, coral mining, sand dredging, coral reef growth rates, impacts of tourism, and sand production in natural systems
- Nature and volumes of marine pollution including hydrocarbons, solid waste and sewage around Male' and other populated centres
- Status of marine fisheries' stocks and of the aquaculture potential
- Status of aquifer resources outside Male'

- Current level of coastal erosion
- Future climatic patterns in relation to global warming and sea-level changes
- Wind and tidally generated current patterns
- Impact assessment for planned major developments
- Land resources including soils, vegetation, fuel and wood
- Energy consumption patterns and non-conventional energy sources
- Vulnerability of human settlements to storms and flooding
- Availability and suitability of energy-efficient building materials and designs
- Inter-island transport development

Maldives now has legislation for the protection of the environment as well as a national plan of action. The protection of coral reefs, to help prevent erosion, is a vital part of the plan. Because Maldivians traditionally used coral mined from the reefs to build their houses, the government has reduced duties on imported building materials, including cement, to make these less costly so that they would be used instead. The government has also restricted coral mining. President Gayoom is further quoted by AFP as saying:

> We are also carrying out programmes to create public awareness. We want everybody
> to co-operate, especially with regard to marine and reef pollution, throwing out of
> garbage and things like that onto our reefs.

The rules governing the operation of resorts are adamant in stating: 'garbage from tourist resorts should be disposed of in a manner that would not cause any damage to the environment'. Tourist resorts are required to have 'incinerators and compactors adequate in size to burn all flammable materials and crush all the cans respectively. Those who lack these facilities will not be allowed to operate'.

Visitors to the Maldives can see the results of land erosion on many islands, both tourist resorts and village islands, where the beaches are being washed away and the roots of the beachside vegetation and coconut trees are being exposed. The Universal Enterprises company is among resort operators taking steps to contain erosion by the sea. At some of its resorts, groynes have been built around the island as bastions against the rages of nature. Purists find them unsightly, but they have blended in with the seascape and also create translucent blue lagoons that are ideal for snorkelling. At Full Moon (in the boatyard away from the tourist area), tetrapods (four-sparred building blocks) are being manufactured, following the lead taken by the government in using them to stabilise reclaimed land. These are to replace the retaining walls, which have to be renewed every year, with a permanent structure to prevent erosion. President Gayoom's concern about the dangers of an angry environment to the fragile ecosystem of the Maldives, and to countries with low-lying land, has been the theme of many of his speeches. The major speeches can be read in his book, *The Maldives: A Nation In Peril* (see *Appendix 4*, page 209).

FLORA It is not all gloom about the environment; travellers expect desert islands, but in fact the country is unbelievably green. Even in Male', where most available land has been built on, trees peep through gaps and give shade to low rooftops. In village islands, coconut trees and tropical vegetation provide lush foliage that keeps the islands green and there are always plants in every garden and *gifili* (bathing area). Coconut palms and screwpines (*pandanus*), which do not have deep roots and thus do not reach down to the salt-water level, grow well. There are also mangroves where the conditions are right. The success of agricultural cultivation proves that, with proper care, plants of many kinds do grow. Cereals like millet and maize are cultivated widely. Colocasia (taro), alocasia, cassava and sweet potatoes are also grown. Chillies and small red onions flourish, as do pumpkins, drumsticks, beans, leaf cabbage, aubergines and gourds. A list of fruits includes bananas, papayas, watermelons, mangoes, limes (which grow well), oranges, breadfruit, screwpines, star-apples, guava, custard apples and locally named fruits like jujubes and jambos. Trees include those grown specifically for their timber, like dhiggaa (*Hibiscus tiliaceus*), funa (*Calophyllum inophyllum*), hirundhu (*Thespesia populnea*) and kanni (*Cordia subcordata*). Casuarina trees are planted to act as wind breaks and to protect other plants from the damaging effects of the sea as well as to provide firewood. Magoo (*Scaevola taccada*) plants are also grown for similar use. Bamboo grows and is in demand as the rod for pole and line fishing. While the village islands are green, they do not boast much in the way of colourful flowers, although the pink rose (*finifenmaa* in Dhivehi, botanically known as *Rosa polyantha*) is the national flower. Frangipani, hibiscus, bougainvillaea and poinsettia are seen, but the best places for brilliant flora are the resort islands. Some are deliberately left in cleared ground under the trees or in a jungly condition to create the rustic ambience their guests want. Others have gardens that are better than those in much lusher environments, like Sri Lanka. Soil and plants are imported, as are the gardeners, to create a setting of floral beauty that adds to the blissful atmosphere of a resort. Because of the efforts of some hoteliers, the environment has been enhanced, with consequent effect on the fauna, too. Some resorts resemble botanical gardens with their varieties of plants and trees, while others tend more to a tropical suburbia, with bougainvillaea screens to keep cabanas private, and frangipani walkways.

FAUNA There are no dangerous animals and poisonous reptiles in the Maldives; there are no dogs either because they are banned. Domestic animals include cats, although there don't seem to be very many, and poultry. Goats are found in small numbers in some islands, and increased rearing of goats is considered as a possibility with their meat as a diet supplement. There are no pigs, and cows are scarce because of lack of pasture. Fruit bats, or flying foxes, are to be seen, usually at sunset. Maldivians do not eat them, despite their being a delicacy further south in the Seychelles and Mauritius. There are rats.

Birds are plentiful, especially in the resorts which have been landscaped with gardens. Many of them are migrants. The common house crow hangs around fishing-village islands thriving on fish offal. Herons of various species are often seen wading or standing proudly on an island's shore. Seagulls, terns and other seabirds abound.

Even in the most luxurious resorts, you will see black ants scurrying around the bathroom, an unpleasant sight if you go to the bathroom half-awake. They are as long as the word 'ant' and crunch underfoot if you tread on them. Supposedly they do not bite. Mosquitoes and sandflies can be a nuisance in some resorts. They are not likely to be disease carriers, but be careful not to scratch any bite in case it festers. There are centipedes and scorpions which may inflict painful stings, but you will almost certainly only risk meeting those in jungly villages or uninhabited islands (where visitors are not supposed to go), not at resorts. Cockroaches exist, as everywhere, although the resort islands have vigorous spraying and fumigating programmes to keep out the creepy-crawlies. You will see some pretty lizards running around, tails up when you startle them. With gnarled but colourful faces, they have a resemblance to prehistoric creatures. They are harmless. Also harmless are the house geckos. Rain sometimes brings out frogs. There are actually two types of snake, both harmless to humans.

Turtles A reptile which was under threat of extinction is the turtle. It used to be killed by islanders for food and to satisfy a demand by visitors for turtleshell objects. However, all seven species of sea turtle are now protected from trade under the Convention on International Trade in Endangered Species (CITES), with further protection afforded under Maldives' own conservation laws: the government has banned the killing of turtles and also the possession of objects made from turtleshell. The chances now are that the turtle will survive, and turtle hatcheries have been set up on some resorts. The turtle species to be found in the Maldives are:

- Loggerhead (*Caretta caretta*) called locally *boabodu velaa* and named for its unusually large head
- Leatherback (*Dermochelys coriacea*) called locally *musinbee*
- Green sea turtle (*Chelonia mydas*) called locally *velaa*, so named because its fat is a greenish colour
- Olive ridley (*Lepidochelys olivacea*) called locally *vaavoshi velaa*
- Hawksbill (*Eretmochelys imbricata*) called locally *kahanbu*. Smaller than its cousins, it is regularly seen by divers and snorkellers. Its exquisite shell is the source of the traditional 'tortoiseshell', long coveted for ornamental purposes, but now outlawed in Maldives.

Turtles live largely in water, coming ashore only to nest. Unlike their landlubber cousins, sea turtles are unable to retract either their heads or their flippers into their shell for protection.

Nesting Turtles are cold-blooded animals, requiring warm water to survive. Even the sex of the hatchlings is determined by the temperature of the sand in which the eggs are laid: at 82°F (28°C), a balance between male and female is to be expected; cooler than that and males will dominate; hotter and there will be a predominance of females. Turtles do not nest until they are at least 15 years old, and they may be up to 30. The female lays her eggs deep in the sand, where they take around 60 days to hatch, at which time the hatchlings make their way towards the sea, attracted by the play of moonlight on the waves. If distraction from artificial lighting – for example from the torches of over-enthusiastic observers – leads them in the direction of a pool instead, then they will be trapped and will inevitably drown. In the wild, the green sea turtle lays between two and seven clutches per season, each containing around 100–150 eggs, which hatch from May to November. Nesting occurs at intervals of around two to five years. Monitoring of turtles in captivity has shown the hatchlings to grow up to 6lb (2.7kg) in their first year, and they can be expected to weigh up to 52lb (24kg) by the time they are three or four.

UNDERWATER LIFE You do not have to be a scuba diver or even a snorkeller to marvel at the underwater world. Some resorts have large fishponds fed by the tide, where fish, including sharks, can be viewed. At the jetties of most islands, fish gather whenever people pause, because they expect to be fed. Hundreds of species of multi-coloured tropical fish can be found, ranging from reef fish, and large filter feeders like manta ray, to whale shark, the largest fish in the world. There are said to be 5,000 species of shellfish in Maldivian waters.

Coral reefs Within the Maldives there are more than 250 differing types of coral. It can appear in an almost infinite number of forms, the more common of which are encrusting, plate-like, massive, boulder-like and tentacle. Coral reefs are composed of unimaginable millions of dead animals or polyps, beneath a living layer of the same creatures. During the day these live polyps appear dormant and tube-like. At night they unfold, with tentacles reaching out to feed on plankton. The polyps deposit calcium carbonate as a hard limestone at their bases, called calyx. The calyx is the tube part that the tentacles retreat into during the day to avoid predators. The limestone deposits are the base material for the reefs of the Maldives.

There are only limited numbers of coral reefs in the world, because they need three main conditions. No coral can be found in sea water below 20°C. This means that coral is found only in the tropics, and only where the currents are warm. Sea temperatures around the Maldives vary little between 28°C and 30°C. The recent higher temperatures caused by El Niño produced serious bleaching (and dying) of many coral reefs in the islands. Coral also needs shallow water to allow photosynthesis to occur. Since this is dependent on sunlight, the depth to which the process can function is up to only 20m, with poorer action sustainable only to a maximum depth of 45m. Finally, the water needs to be clear for the above process. In general, the waters are very clear around the islands, devoid of murky fine dirt and living material. However, without the organic detritus, the coral would not flourish. Organic nutrients from the vast numbers of reef dwellers are present, but are continually being filtered by the corals to maintain health and to recycle material to keep the water clear. Given these three prime conditions, the corals can grow quite fast. Some branch corals can achieve 25cm per year. On the other hand, some solid massive corals will add only a few millimetres per year.

The reefs in the Maldives, some 2,100m in depth, are built from the limestone skeletons of dead coral, detritus and coralline algae, plants found on the reef edges near the surface. The coralline algae help to bind the coral waste to build the reefs, and are also found in deep caves and lower in the reefs. Sponges, whose shapes vary with location and currents, also feed by filtering bacteria and fine particles. Those sponges that live at deeper levels of the reef attack the corals, which also helps to break down the coral. A lot of the finer coral material becomes sand, and some mixes into a soupy mess that remains *in situ*. Before the use of concrete was encouraged, coral was the basic building material of Maldivian dwellings. Few coral houses exist now in Male', but coral-stone walls remain in some of the quiet backstreets. Even the mortar between the blocks was derived from coral.

Coral zones As a general rule, there are four or five different zones between the pristine beaches of the atoll resorts and the deep drop-offs of the house reefs. Immediately adjacent to the beaches are zones of sand and invariably debris of old coral, dead coral and detritus of old coral beds. This, as any snorkelling or diving enthusiast will know, can be a little difficult to cross, with sharp, hard nodules of coral. After this zone one finds an area of mixed corals. This is characterised by massive lumps of stone-like corals, blue coral (Pocillopores) and corals called Acropora. These common Acropora have single polyps at the end of short finger-like branches. The next zone is where the corals have more extensive branches, often described as antler-shaped. This is staghorn coral, *Acropora formosa*.

Moving further out and into deeper water one finds the more massive brain corals and foliaceous coral. These structures, particularly the foliaceous corals, are unhappy in the presence of strong currents. Beyond this zone is the reef edge, where the most fertile area for coral development is found. Here are leaf-shaped corals, tabulate coral forms that have wide plates of short finger-like branches close together. Some of these have pink or blue edges, a common sight for divers at the reef edge. There are also laminar colonies, which have undulating edges and can appear bent. At the reef edge drop-off zone are massive honeycombed, clinging corals, many of them brain-shaped. The depth of the reef edge's drop down is normally around 10–15m, but it varies with currents and waves. Further down the reef walls are the fungal and discoid corals with more Acropora. The fungal or mushroom corals do not grow in colonies, but are more solitary. Invariably the base of the reef wall sinks into the sandy floor of the outer lagoon area and this can be up to 60–80m deep. Areas of reef close to the ocean side may be cut and intersected by clefts; these provide divers with exciting visions. Caves and channels are often found here.

Other reef features The reefs of the Maldives, however, are not made purely of dead coral. They are also composed of other materials derived from dead organic matter. These other materials are classed under the collective name of Cridaria or Coelenterates. The main organisms and creatures under this term are soft corals, fire coral (Millepora), sea fans, jellyfish and sea anemones. There are two main branches of organism within the term Cridaria, these being anthozoa and medusozoa.

Anthozoa The anthozoa are further divided into two subgroups. One branch are the octocorals: soft corals, gorgonians, blue corals and organpipe corals. The octocorals are corals whose polyps have eight tentacles. The fleshy bodies of the soft corals can support many polyps. However, they remain vulnerable and to counteract this they have developed primitive chemical defences. The gorgonians are the sea fans that can grow as large as 2m across and which bend with currents. The characteristic colouring of the blue corals and red organpipe corals is due to substances within the chemical composition. These corals leave hard limestone skeletons. Also under the anthozoa are the second branch, summarised as the hexacorals that can be both colonial and solitary. These hexacorals are the stony corals, anemones, black corals and palythoa. The sea anemones are found in shallow water, where they can be large; or lower down the reef, often in caves, as tube anemones that live in protective tubes. Black corals, found deeper on the reefs, can be seen in two predominant forms, as whip or wire corals. The palythoa are brown toxic corals.

Medusozoa Medusozoa are like inverted polyps. They come in two subgroups: hydrozoans and scyphozoa. The hydrozoans include creatures classed as hydroids and fire corals; they are all stinging creatures. Divers should beware of these organisms, particularly the colonial physalia or 'Portuguese man of war' and the feathery colonial hydroids that give a nasty burning sting. Fire corals also inflict pain that is not so severe. The scyphozoa are in the jellyfish family.

Other reef life The reefs are also home to sponges, worms, molluscs, crustaceans, echinoderms and sea squirts, as well as an incredible range of fish, large and small. Around and beyond the reef is the habitat for the large pelagic fish, silvertip and hammerhead sharks, etc. There are three types of worms: tongue, spoon or segment. Nearly all are strange, long and thin. There are said to be over 100,000 species of molluscs, which are invertebrates. Molluscs are found in three groups: gastropods, bivalves and cephalopods. The famous cowrie shells of the Maldives, which were used as money, belong to the gastropods. The bivalves, which feed by filtering, are mussels, oysters and clams with two shells. The cephalopods have fleshy bodies, such as the octopus and squid. Molluscs can secrete a calcareous shell, and have fleshy parts, despite the wide variation in their designs. Many have been preserved as fossils and are useful to geologists in determining the age of rock strata.

Crustaceans are, like their counterparts worldwide, creatures of the night such as shrimps and crabs. The echinoderms are marine invertebrates and occur in five groups: starfish, sea urchins, feather stars, brittle stars and sea cucumbers. The starfish are the most obvious. They digest externally, encasing their prey with their arms. The often-spiny sea urchins, feather stars and brittle stars are nearly all nocturnal creatures.

Sea cucumbers move along on their rows of tube feet, and most species digest sand in a search for food. Sea squirts are also found and have been given their name because they siphon water through their structures to gain nutrients.

Fish To attempt any detailed description of the incredible diversity of the fish that live around the Maldives is well beyond the scope of this book. Here follows a very brief outline of the main fish and their favourite haunts just to whet your appetite. Of course many have varying habitats and can be found in a myriad locations. Their sizes vary from the tiny, orange-spotted sand goby at 7cm to the massive whale sharks at 12m. The shapes are equally varied, from red spiny lionfish to hammerhead sharks and sailfish. Snorkellers need not necessarily venture any further than the lagoons and house reefs to see an amazing variety of extraordinarily vividly coloured fish of all shapes imaginable.

Lagoon fish The lagoons have quite a variety of fish. The more common are damselfish, surgeonfish and flame-parrotfish. These are often the younger ones. You may also see lizardfish, gobies, blue-green chromis, yellow goatfish, small spotted dart and black-spot emperor. It's not that uncommon to see spotted eagle rays and stingrays pass by at sunset and sunrise, having spent the night in the protected lagoons. These generally prefer the shallow areas less than 10m deep, and snorkellers amongst dead corals in the lagoons may see some. They may also inhabit the reef drop-off areas.

Reef-edge fish Some of the more common fish in these areas are hump-head wrasse, tuna fish, batfish, bluefin-trevally and spotted-sweetlips. The vivid luminescent blue-coloured, red-toothed trigger fish often swim in vast numbers at the reef edge. With the active currents of these zones, the fish are here to seek out the rich plankton. This is the zone where a big overlap of fish species can be found, often outside their traditional habitat. Larger fish here may include hammerhead sharks, silvertip reef sharks and great barracuda whitetip sharks. These reef edges are where snorkellers and divers can find the greatest variety and concentrations. The seabeds here will be teeming with fish from other habitats such as moray eels, soldier fish, stonefish, clownfish and scorpionfish. These will be in close proximity to some of the coral forms mentioned above like gorgonians, hard corals and the octocorals.

Coral dwellers Many fish spend the bulk of their lives closely entwined amongst the reefs. Among those that keep close to the protective reefs are various damselfish species, Indian butterflyfish, Clark's anemonefish, plus black-footed clownfish and yellowtail fairy-basslets. Other fish (most commonly the various butterflyfish) actively attack and chip away at the coral to find nutrients. The more common butterflyfish are threadfin, racoon, Bennett, triangular and the unusual long-nosed butterfly variety, with its strange nose for inserting into cracks. Some of the most brilliantly coloured fish are the parrotfish, which have sharper teeth to cut at the corals. The vivid green-and-purple steephead parrotfish, and the bicoloured, long-nosed and bullethead varieties, have amazing colouring in blue, greens, purple and fluorescent pink. If you encounter a small white cloud anytime, it could be the coral dust being blown out by these parrotfish after extracting any nutrients. Different features of the reef attract different fish. The emperor angelfish, royal and blue-faced angelfish and the butterflyfish seek out the narrow clefts and gaps. The strange, long, very thin alligator-like cornet fish and trumpfish look for sea fans. Wrasse come in many varieties, such as the red-breasted Maori, moon, yellowtail and green bird, with its longer nose. Cleaner wrasse actually live on parasites and nutrients from other fish's bodies. Some fish have spines and horns to protect themselves. The very common blue surgeonfish of the reefs is one such species. Others are black-spotted pufferfish, Bleeker's porcupinefish, orange-spine unicornfish and Moorish idol. A lot of triggerfish have sharp teeth: orange-striped triggerfish, clown, yellowmargin, titan, and boomerang triggerfish. Many are exceedingly colourful, with dorsal fins. They attack molluscs and sea urchins.

Kandus and thilas Fish found in the kandus and around the thilas (see *Kandus, farus and thilas* on page 6) are happy in the more active currents that occur in these zones, where seawater pours through gaps in the atoll between the farus and reefs. These channels can be up to 50m deep. Fish found in these areas, many of which are marine reserves, are bannerfish, blue-lined and chocolate surgeonfish, humpback and two-spot red snappers, wahoo and the unusual Vlaming's unicornfish. Larger fish here might include giant manta, grey reef shark, whale shark and blacktip reef sharks. Divers in these areas should be experienced and with guides. Sharks are called *miyaru* in Dhivehi; the larger ones have not been known to be predatory in the Maldives as yet. At the edges of these areas one can also find other reef fish.

Cave and grotto dwellers Although the accumulation of the dead coral polyps provides continuous material for the reefs to grow, other actions are also degrading them. Water action, as well as erosion by chemicals and predatory creatures and other forces, cuts out hollows, cracks, caves, gullies and grottoes. Fish that like these sheltered areas include crown and sabre squirrelfish, google-eye fish, oriental sweetlips and blue-striped snapper, as well as the morays: leopard, giant and honeycombed varieties. Many of these are nocturnal and some of the fish are a brilliant red colour.

Sand dwellers and reef fish Common fish in these areas include yellow-saddle goatfish, stellate rabbitfish, lizardfish, checkerboard wrasse, fire-fish and nurse sharks. Down on the sandy floor one may see the strange black-spotted garden eel. The sand dwellers find abundant food sources on the beds below the reefs, as well as cover.

Groupers Groupers often live in the regions below the diving zone, where they hunt out crustaceans, other fish and even octopus. Many are quite large. Common grouper varieties include lunar-tail, coral, peacock, four-saddle, black-saddle, small-toothed and red-mouth grouper.

Other fish There are some very strange fish lurking around the reefs, not easily seen and quite intimidating in appearance: for example, turkeyfish, long-nose hawk and pixy-hawk, as well as some scary-looking varieties like the leaf and devil scorpionfish. All these use their camouflage features for both defence and attack.

Underwater reference As well as photographic books by divers, there are some excellent guides to corals, fish, shells and reefs. Some are by Dr Charles Anderson; of special interest are *Common Reef Fishes of the Maldives* (in three volumes), *Living Reefs of the Maldives* and *Diver's Guide to the Sharks of the Maldives* (see *Appendix 4*, page 208). Also look out for two sets of three posters available in bookshops in Male' that display colourful illustrations of around 200 of the most common fish to be found. These are produced by the Novelty Bookshop (*Fareedhee Magu*) and MMI Bamboo (*Chandhanee Magu*). MMI Bamboo also produce three hard plastic sheets (roughly A4) illustrating the most common fish; divers can take these under water to use for identification purposes.

IN OUTLINE There were inhabitants in the islands over 3,500 years ago. Aryan immigrants seem to have started settlements around 500BC. Significant history dates from the conversion of the inhabitants to Islam from 1153, after which the islands were ruled by sultans of different dynasties, although there was a period of 15 years of Portuguese rule which ended in 1573. From 1887 until 1965 came a period of British protection, after which the islands reverted to full independence. The sultanate was abolished, actually for the second time, three years later in favour of a republic.

EARLIEST TIMES The Maldives are islands steeped in history, although the mists of time have obscured much of it, including the origins of the people. It is easy, though, to imagine how attractive the islands must have seemed to ancient mariners who sailed across the Indian Ocean and decided to settle there. Being seamen, they would have appreciated the calm waters of the lagoons and the tranquillity the deserted islands offered. With their knowledge of the sea, they were able to survive from it instead of, like pastorals, depending on the land for food. Whether they came by accident (and probably many who became settlers did so after being shipwrecked on the reefs) or design, perhaps as exiles, they joined other early inhabitants in making the Maldives their home. Where these settlers came from has been defined by historians anxious to categorise. Suffice it to accept that they came from many countries: those now known as India, Sri Lanka, Malaysia, Indonesia, Egypt and Greece and what was Arabia and the Roman Empire. The struggle for survival – however tranquil the islands – seems to have left little time for disputes and gradually an ad hoc nation of islanders came into being.

Historic architectural remains indicate that Buddhists and Hindus brought their own beliefs with them to the islands where they settled. Logically, Arab settlers would also have brought Islam with them, although there is no architectural or other evidence to support this prior to 1153, when Islam was officially adopted as the religion of all the Maldive islands. Maldivians are proud of their history, even if there is little visible evidence of the past, there being a scarcity of ancient buildings. For Maldivians, figures from history are surprisingly close. They share an intimacy with heroes of the past, as though they were respected relatives only recently passed away. While even the cannons and walls that within living memory marked a fort at Male' have gone, and sultans no longer hold sway under official umbrellas, links with the traditions of the past are preserved in the mind of every Maldivian.

CONVERSION TO ISLAM Every Maldivian schoolchild knows the legend of the circumstances which led to the embracing of Islam by the islands' ruler. This is how schoolchildren in grade seven (about 13 years old) learn it.

During Maha Kalaminja's reign a demon of the sea called Rannamarai threatened to destroy Male' unless it was offered a virgin girl on the first day of every month. The girl would spend the night in the temple and in the morning people would find her dead. The girl to be placed in the temple was chosen by drawing lots. This was being practised when Abu Barakaath Yoosuf Al-Barbari, a Moroccan trader and missionary, visited the Maldives. He stayed in a house where the daughter was chosen to go to the temple for sacrifice. Abu Barakaath promised to take the place of the girl that night. As soon as he went in, he started reciting the holy Koran. He was reciting verses when he saw the monster appearing. He did not stop the recitation. The monster came closer and closer, then suddenly sank into the water when it heard the recitation of the Koran. In the morning people were astonished to find Abu Barakaath alive and reciting the Koran. They took him to the sultan and he, too, was surprised. Abu Barakaath then and there preached and asked the sultan to accept Islam as a religion.

The government officially declared Islam as the religion of Maldives on the 2nd of Rabeeu al-Akhir 548AH: that is, in AD1153.

After conversion, the ruler became Sultan Mohamed Ibn Abdulla; there followed seven dynasties and a history that included several invasions and even a conquest. Always, though, the characteristic Maldivian tenacity enabled the nation to survive, progressing to the independent, unified republic of today. There is much legend and fantasy in the history of the Maldives, perhaps because the stories have been passed on by word of mouth rather than written down. Two leaflets ('History' and 'Constitutional History') have been produced by the Department of Information and Broadcasting to help sift fiction from fact.

Even so, there is not much information available on who were the rulers before the conversion to Islam. The ruler at that time was Dovemi Kalaminja of the Theemuge or Soamavansa dynasty which was also known as the Malei (Male') dynasty. There are records showing an embassy was sent from Divi (the Maldives, Dhivehi Raajje) and from Serendivi (Serendip, now Sri Lanka) to the court of the Roman Emperor Julian in AD362, eight centuries before the rule of Mohamed Ibn Abdulla. Legend conveniently provides a source for the rulers of the nation, although, at that stage, how much of a nation it was is a matter of conjecture. It suggests that a princess and her husband – Koemala Kaloa – arrived at Rasgetheemu island in North Maalhosmadulu (Raa) Atoll from what is now Sri Lanka. Being of royal blood, the couple were welcomed and settled as rulers in Male', even then the most important island in the archipelago.The oldest historical document of the Maldives is a collection of copper plates called Loamaafaanu (royal grants) dating from the 12th century. Recorded on these is a reference to the kings who were rulers in that century, prior to the conversion to Islam.

Conversion of the people from the cults they followed actually took close to 60 years. Islam was instrumental in unifying the inhabitants of the different atolls into a nation that was more than the few islands close to Male'. Ibn Battuta, the Moroccan traveller, visited 'Dhibat al Mahal', the Maldives, not long after 1342. He wrote:

> The inhabitants of the Maldives are all Muslims, pious and upright, sound in belief and sincere in thought; their bodies are weak, they are unused to fighting and their armour is prayer. The Indian pirates do not raid or molest them, as they have learned from experience that anyone who seizes anything from them speedily meets misfortune. In each island there are beautiful mosques, and most of their buildings are made of wood. They are very clean and avoid filth; most of them bathe twice a day to cleanse themselves because of the extreme heat there and their profuse perspiration. They make plentiful use of perfumed oils, such as oils of sandalwood.

There followed dynasties spanning eight centuries up to 1953, when the sultanate first became a republic. The post of sultan was never hereditary and a son succeeding his father as sultan purely because of natural succession seems to have been rare. There were sultanas as well, and women were always included on the ruling councils. The councils selected the sultan. The first dynasty (Malei) had 16 monarchs, whose reign spanned 169 years. The Veeru Umaru dynasty followed with two sultans and three sultanas ruling for 75 years. For the next 170 years, the Hilali dynasty of 24 sultans ruled, coming to an end with the death of Sultan Ali VI. Remembered as Ali the Martyr, he died while defending the country against the Portuguese.

PORTUGUESE ATTACKS Portuguese power came to the East with the arrival of Vasco da Gama in Calicut, India, in 1498. It was to bring an era of terror and repression unknown to Maldivians who, until then, had been able to live as mild-mannered, decent fishermen and maritime traders without causing problems, nor expecting any. The first contact Maldivians had with the Portuguese was in 1503, just five years after their arrival in the East. Their leader, Vicente Sodre, forbade traffic with the Maldives to the entrepreneurs of Calicut and enforced his order with the burning to death of 100 Moors. The atrocity was puzzling to the gentle Maldivians and a dire warning. Although it took 55 years, the inevitable invasion of the islands by the Portuguese came in 1558. There were two previous attempts by the Portuguese to win over the Maldives, which they considered important because of their location and the availability of shells (cowrie shells were currency in some countries), ropes of coconut fibre, and ambergris (a waxlike secretion of the sperm whale found in the sea and used in perfumery).

There was, however, another reason. The sultan at the time was a 20-year-old, Hassan IX. He disagreed with his elders, the council of ministers, and had to flee. He turned up in Cochin, India, where he was converted to Christianity by the Portuguese and became Don Emanuel. The young sultan was keen to return to Male' and sought Portuguese help. Two attempts by the Portuguese to take Male' were repelled, one of the Maldivian leaders being Ali Rasgefaanu, who was not yet sultan. When the Portuguese came the third time, it is said that the people of Male' were prepared to surrender but Ali Rasgefaanu was made of sterner stuff. With only a few supporters he was able to repel the invaders. He became Sultan Ali VI but was on the throne only a few months when he was killed in a further attempt to defend Male', which fell to the Portuguese. Until the western side of Male' was reclaimed, his tomb, built where he fell, could be visited by walking along the coral causeway from the shore. It is now surrounded by houses. Sultan Ali is a national hero whose heroism is commemorated by a public holiday every year on Martyr's Day. The Portuguese appointed 'Andrea Andreas' (probably the mixed-race Andre Andrade) as captain general and, as An'dhiri An'dhirin, he became ruler, claiming to rule in the name of the exiled Don Emanuel, and trying to convert the people to Christianity. The occupation has been described as 'the most cruel and humiliating period of Maldivian history' in an official publication. It lasted 15 years.

The leader of the resistance to the Portuguese came not from Male' but from an island to the north, Utheemu in North Thiladhunmathi. There, Mohamed Thakurufaanu, the son of a respected island chief, religious leader and trader, persuaded his two brothers, Ali and Hassan, to join him in guerrilla warfare against the Portuguese occupation and Christian conversion. He had contact with Maldivians in Maliku (Minicoy), the closest island to the Maldives (and probably once part of the Maldives) in the Laccadives group. History records, rather surprisingly, that it was with the help of the deputy of An'dhiri An'dhirin in the atoll that Thakurufaanu and his brothers were able to build a fast-moving vessel, called *Kalhuohfummi*. They took their families and others by this boat to Maliku, where two other Maldivians, Ali Haji and Hassan Haji, had been training for a possible rebellion. Classic guerrilla tactics of hit and run were employed by the brave band who would infiltrate an island at night, kill the sleeping Portuguese, then sail swiftly away. Ali was captured during a raid and beheaded.

After a few years, with the Portuguese increasingly vigilant, the surprise attacks were less successful and Thakurufaanu realised, following a secret visit to Male' to check the defences, that he would not be able to dislodge the Portuguese without help. He sought this from the rajah of Malabar, a favour that was to have unexpected consequences for the next 200 years. In 1573, on the night of the 1st of Rabeeu al-Awwal (now commemorated as National Day each year on the first

day of the third month of the lunar calendar), an attack was launched on Male'
and, with the help of its inhabitants, the capital was liberated. It had taken eight
years of guerrilla warfare to regain independence. (This stirring episode in
Maldivian history is the theme of Royston Ellis's novel *A Hero in Time*, see
Appendix 4, page 208.)

Thakurufaanu became Sultan Al Ghaazee Mohamed Thakurufaanu Al-Auzam
and reigned for 16 years. He founded the Utheemu dynasty, which ruled for 121
years. He also married the daughter of Ali Rasgefaanu. As sultan, he was
responsible for many reforms in the administration and judiciary of the nation, as
well as for setting up a well-organised standing militia. He introduced the first
coinage (instead of cowrie shells) and started trade relations with foreign countries.
His reign was a period of peace and prosperity. The tomb of this national hero,
after whom the Islamic Centre and the former waterfront Marine Drive are
named, is in Male'. His house still exists and a Memorial Centre has been
constructed in Utheemu, in the northernmost atoll. Visitors can fly to the airstrip
on Hanimadhoo and then take a *dhoni* for the 45-minute voyage to Utheemu, or
go by speedboat from neighbouring resort islands.

INVASIONS FROM INDIA The success of their venture in helping to liberate Male'
seems to have stirred ideas among the Malabars of south India about taking the
Maldives for themselves. In 1609 the Malabars descended on Male' and killed the
sultan, but they were repelled. Forty years later, the rajah of Cannanore twice
attacked the Maldives. The sultan at the time, Sultan Ibrahim Iskandhar (1648–87),
did something which seems alien to the placid Maldivian temperament: he went
on the offensive. (Perhaps he had been irked by two Portuguese attempts to invade,
in 1624 and 1648.) In 1650, the sultan's forces invaded territory of the rajah of
Cannanore and took some chiefs hostage. They were released on payment of a
nominal sum and the Maldives were undisturbed during the rest of the sultan's
long reign. He built the Friday mosque (Hukuru Miskiiy) and its landmark
minaret, still to be seen in Male', and founded the first public school, as well as
establishing many customs followed today.

The next Western power to move into the neighbourhood was the Dutch. Their
interest in the Maldives was mainly trade, especially cowrie shells. The sultans
maintained good relations with the Dutch governors of Ceylon (now Sri Lanka).
The Dutch actually surveyed the islands of the Maldives and Laccadives in 1671.
The Malabars tried again to invade in 1690, and a few years later the Utheemu
dynasty gave way to the Isdhoo dynasty. This lasted for five years and was followed
by the Dhiyamigili dynasty. Sultan Ibrahim Muzhiruddin (who reigned from 1701
until ousted in 1705) attacked the Maldives himself in 1711 and again in 1712 with
help from allies in India. There was another break of 40 years before invaders from
India tried again. In this they were aided by Maldivian opportunists (whom they
later drowned) and they mounted such a strong attack on Male' that they were able
to abduct the sultan. Their occupation lasted less than four months, thanks to the
wiles of Dhon Hassan Manikufaan, also known as Dhon Bandaaran, who came
from Huraa, in Male' Atoll. By a ruse, he was able to enter the palace and drive the
Malabars out. Huravee Day is celebrated every year to commemorate that defeat of
the invaders.

Expecting the Malabars to try again, Dhon Hassan Manikufaan was ready when
their fleet approached Male'. He tricked them into believing the capital was still
under Malabar control by flying the Malabar flag and dressing his soldiers as
Malabars. This ruse was also successful and the fleet was destroyed. The Malabars
attacked several times more, obliging Dhon Hassan Manikufaan to seek help from
the French fort at Pondicherry on India's southeast coast. A defence treaty was

agreed with the French, who were allowed to station forces in Male'. They did not stay long, but the tactic stopped the attacks. Dhon Hassan Manikufaan at first declined the role of sultan and ruled in the name of the daughter of the abducted sultan languishing in Minicoy. On the death of the sultan in 1759, he became Sultan Hassan Izzuddeen, founding the Huraage dynasty. The dynasty ruled, with an interruption in 1953–54 (when the country first became a republic), until 1968, the year the present republic was founded.

BRITISH INFLUENCE The Maldives had survived more than a dozen attacks during the previous two centuries, but, by the end of the 18th century, British power was becoming dominant in the Indian Ocean. The sultans maintained cordial relations with the British and permitted the survey of the islands which was begun in 1834 by Commander R Moresby, whose charts are in use even now. In 1887 an exchange of letters took place between the governor of Ceylon, representing Queen Victoria, and Sultan Mohamed Mueenuddeen II. The motive behind this for the Maldivians was to keep the British – who by then virtually controlled the Indian Ocean – out of the islands. The relationship was uneasy but enabled the Maldives to enjoy the status of a protected state, although not actually a protectorate, according to the 1994 Independence Day Memorial booklet. The statehood of the Maldives was recognised and Britain had no power to interfere in internal matters (although some say they tried), controlling only external affairs.

In 1932 the first written constitution was proclaimed, the islands having been governed since time immemorial by an unwritten one. Historical records show that a form of democracy did exist from early days. There were systems of taxation, national defence, discharge of public duties, and administration of justice. The sultan's role was similar to that of a constitutional monarch. When the necessity arose, the sultans deviated from normal procedures, with the advice and consent of the councils, thereby creating new precedents which in due course became new conventions. Even though sultans had supreme power, it seems they were never despotic or autocratic rulers. Their actions were constantly reviewed by the council of advisors and chiefs who voiced the views of the people at meetings of the councils, where the sultan was only a member. There were several instances of sultans being deposed by a decision of the councils on occasions when the sultan contravened the existing customs and conventions.

The sultan was assisted by three councils. One consisted of the nobles and included the mother or mother-in-law of the sultan, his wife and a sister or sister-in-law. The second council included the chief justice and chiefs representing the four wards of Male' and various officials in charge of such things as defence and public works. The third council combined the first two with lower-level officials such as gunners and exponents of martial arts. The written constitution was based on the customs, conventions and traditional administration that had evolved over the centuries. Various changes were incorporated up to the historic sixth constitution, which allowed for republican rule and was proclaimed on 1 January 1953. Mohamed Ameen Didi (formerly prime minister) became the first president and is regarded as the father of the modern Maldives, particularly for his reform of the education system, reviving Maldivian language and literature and giving women more of a place in society. After he died following unrest (he is buried at Kurumba), the sultanate was restored in 1954 and lasted under the reign of Sultan Mohamed Fureed Al-Awwal until 1968.

TRUE INDEPENDENCE By that time, full independence had come to the Maldives, on 26 July 1965, with an agreement signed by the then prime minister, Ibrahim Nassir, and the UK High Commissioner in Ceylon. The Maldives became a member of the United Nations on 21 September 1965 and a member of the Commonwealth in 1982. Following a referendum held on 1 April 1968, the sultanate was abolished. Ibrahim Nassir was elected president on 11 November 1968, the day now commemorated as Republic Day. Ibrahim Nassir was president for two terms. Maumoon Abdul Gayoom was elected president in November 1978 with a huge majority, 92.9% of the votes cast in the national referendum, after being nominated by the Citizens' Majlis. He was returned to office for a sixth term in November 2003, making him the longest-serving elected head of state in Asia. A new constitution, with many archaic anomalies removed, and reflecting a more democratic form of government, was introduced in 1998, after 17 years of discussion and debate, by a special majlis (council) of 103 delegates from Male' and the atolls.

President Gayoom was born in Male' in 1937 and was educated in Ceylon (where he developed a love of cricket). He received a university education in Egypt, obtaining a master's degree in Islamic studies. He also studied law and philosophy and did a post-graduate course at the American University of Cairo. Before entering government service in 1971, Mr Gayoom was a lecturer in Islamic Law and Philosophy in Nigeria in 1969–71. He held several important government posts and was then appointed the Maldives' first permanent representative to the United Nations in 1976. He was made Minister of Transport in 1977. In a policy statement in 1979 President Gayoom committed himself to a more open government, with greater freedom of the press, and the government run according to the principles of democracy. The decision-making process has been decentralised, with greater reliance on consultation within the cabinet and increased power for both the Citizens' Majlis and the judiciary. A threat to the established stability of the nation occurred in 1988 when a group of Tamil mercenaries from Sri Lanka attempted an invasion of Male', which led to several Maldivians being killed. President Gayoom sought help from India and the invaders were swiftly routed, arrested and then brought to trial. In his years of office since November 1978, President Gayoom has become acclaimed internationally for his championship of environmental causes and the concerns of small island states. He frequently makes eloquent and stirring speeches at world forums, including the Rio summit on the environment in 1992 and the follow-up five years later at the United Nations in New York. The then UN Secretary General, Kofi Annan, led the praise of the world community after his speech there by giving President Gayoom the headline-catching title of 'Godfather of Environmental Awareness'. Queen Elizabeth II created him a Knight Grand Cross of the Most Distinguished Order of St Michael and St George (GCMG) during the Commonwealth summit held in Edinburgh in 1997. Under President Gayoom, the Maldives has played a notable part in regional affairs. It has twice hosted summits of the leaders of the South Asian Association of Regional Co-operation (SAARC): Bangladesh, Bhutan, India, Pakistan, Sri Lanka, Nepal and the Maldives. As chairman on two occasions of SAARC, President Gayoom represented the interests of the governments of one-fifth of the world's population. More details of the recent history of the Maldives and of President Gayoom's influence on the islands for over 20 years can be found in Royston Ellis's book, *A Man for All Islands: The Biography of Maumoon Abdul Gayoom* (see *Appendix 4*, page 208).

Development, prosperity and constitutional changes have come to the Maldives during President Gayoom's terms of office. This has enabled the country to respond to, and assert, its political, social, economic and cultural uniqueness based on a history of zealously protected independence. However, criticism of the long regime of President Gayoom began to be publicly voiced, both in Maldives and overseas in 2004, and this resulted in some high-profile dissenters being jailed pending charges of high treason. They were released following the tsunami of 26 December 2004 as part of the president's effort to unite people in the recovery effort. After elections for representatives to the Citizens' Majlis were held in 2005 (having been postponed from December 2004 because of the tsunami), a Special Majlis was set up to formulate a multi-party democratic system and a new constitution. Political parties were legally allowed for the first time in 2005 and there were many changes in the president's cabinet of ministers with younger, reformist Maldivians playing a part.

In August 2007 an unusual referendum took place, with Maldivians given the chance to vote on whether they wanted a US-style executive president (as supported by the president's party, the DRP), or a parliamentary style of government like the Westminster system, as supported by the main opposition party, the MRP. The result was overwhelmingly in favour of a presidential system (62% to 38%) and President Gayoom announced his intention of standing for election under that system in the elections due before November 2008. He said, according to Reuters, 'I will step down after the first term. I have a young cabinet and they will take the development process forward.' He added: 'I want to see the reform programme through till it is finally settled. I want that to be my legacy for the nation.'

GOVERNMENT AND ADMINISTRATION

In the past, governing 90,000km² of sea and, perhaps, 2,000 islands must have presented considerable problems. But did it? Communication was always by sea and Maldivians did not have to wait for railway lines to be laid, motor cars to be invented or planes to fly to be able to travel to any part of their country. With the wind in a boat's sail and the ocean as a natural highway, getting around the island sultanate was easier than in a country with stagecoaches and cart tracks. Yet, even within living memory, it could take as long as three months to sail from Addu Atoll to Male' because of lack of the right wind, necessitating long stays at islands on the way.

Whatever happened before Islam was declared the religion seems to have been law-abiding, as history records no great upheavals in the administration. Since 1153 the basic laws have been the Islamic sharia. With religion and the state inextricably entwined, there has been clear authority, easily understood and known to all Maldivians from the day, as children, they begin to read the Koran. Thus atoll officials knew how to administer their islands without constant reference (as is possible now by email, fax and direct-dial telephone) to their head office in Male'.

The system of decentralised administration has developed because of geographical circumstances and serves the country well. There is a central system of government based in and administered from Male'. The country is divided into 20 administrative units. Nineteen of them are called atolls, although they do not conform with the geographical atolls, which amount to 26. Some geographical atolls are split into more than one unit, while other units embrace more than one atoll. To confuse you further, new names have been given to these units and both old and new ones are still in use (for instance Addu and Seenu Atoll are the same place). Each unit consists of uninhabited as well as inhabited islands, which are governed by an official appointed by the president as atoll chief. His role is similar to that of a governor of a province and he is known as the *atholhu varin*. He can consult the religious head, or *ghaazee*, on legal matters. The 19 atolls are also the constituencies of parliament and elect two members each. The 20th constituency and administrative unit is the capital, Male', which also sends two members to parliament. The atoll chief is aided by an official, called the *katheeb*, on every inhabited island. He is a government appointee, usually a distinguished island citizen, and is assisted by a number of full-time officials called *kuda katheeb*.

In a small island community, it is easy for the island chief to know what is happening and policing is done by the islanders themselves. Only when there is a major problem is it necessary for assistance to be sought from the police headquartered in Male'. An islander summoned to the chief's office would go immediately. There is also a magistrate or the *ghaazee* on each inhabited island who can deal with legal and criminal matters, with serious cases being referred to the courts in Male'.

The parliament, with chambers in Male', is unicameral and consists of the 40 elected members plus eight members nominated by the president. This system allows the appointment of qualified people and experts by the president to ministerial posts when necessary. Known as the Citizens' Majlis, the parliament came into being in its present form with the enactment of the 1932 constitution. The Majlis passes the laws and the budgets and also chooses the nominee for presidential candidate. Under the constitution in force until 2007, any Maldivian male wishing to become president may nominate himself for consideration by the Majlis. The presidential candidate had to win a majority in the presidential referendum, held every five years, to become president. Elections to the Citizens' Majlis are also held every five years, but not at the same time as the presidential referendum.

The general election in 1994 passed almost unnoticed by visitors, although the election process is not automatic since there are often several candidates for the two seats in each constituency. The 1999 general election was praised by overseas monitors for the peaceful manner in which it was held. The 2004 election was postponed and held early in 2005. After that a multi-party democratic system was introduced, with a US-style executive president form of government being approved by the majority of voters in a referendum held in 2007. The next presidential election is scheduled to be held before November 2008, the first under the new political system. The president is head of state and also the chief executive. Currently the cabinet comprises the president, vice president (if any), attorney general, and ministers with portfolios appointed by the president. Ministers and Majlis' members are easily accessible to their constituents and it is sometimes a surprise for visitors to find that the Maldivian sitting at the same shared table with them in a café is a government minister or a member of parliament. The bureaucracy, too, has a more human face than visitors from large countries are used to. Government offices are lively places without restrictive security, and are easy to visit. An interesting feature of civil service life is the hours of work: 07.30–13.30 Saturday–Thursday. This frees capable people to pursue their own interests (some civil servants actually own resort islands) in their spare time, which is considerable since commuting from a Male' residence to an office takes only a few minutes. The trend, however, is for qualified people to concentrate solely on their jobs and senior officials are often to be found in their offices in the evenings as well.

UNIFORMS The uniform of the military, known as the Maldives National Defence Force (MNDF), is a jungle green colour. Police wear a blue uniform while traffic police wear yellow waistcoats over their blue uniforms. At the airport, security staff wear a fawn uniform while immigration officials are in buff-coloured shirts. Customs officers wear white shirts and black trousers, or skirts.

NATIONAL EMBLEMS The national emblem (used as the logo on government documents) is an attractive design evocative of the Maldives, symbolising a proud, free spirit as well as alluding to island traditions and the state religion. The design depicts a coconut palm, a crescent surrounding a star and a national flag at each side, with a scrolled banner bearing the traditional title of the state. The coconut palm is a boldly stylised image and represents the importance of the palm in the livelihood of the nation. It is a tribute to the palm's many uses, not only as a food but also in construction. The crescent and star in between the two national flags signify respectively the Islamic faith of the state and its authority. Since the crescent is also carried on the flag, the importance of Islam to the republic is further emphasised. The inscription on the banner contains two phrases in Dhivehi, Ad Dawlat and Al Mahaldheebiyya, meaning the State of the Maldives, the traditional title of the republic first used by Sultan Al Ghaazee Mohamed Thakurufaanu Al-Auzam. When the emblem is reproduced in colour on a light-blue background with crescent and star of gold and the green palm tree, it evokes the importance of the ocean to Maldives.

NATIONAL FLAG The largest national flag of Maldives flies from the tall flagpole in the Jumhooree Maidan by the waterfront in Male'. It is an impressive sight when the breeze stretches it to maximum size. The flag is composed of a green rectangle with a crescent in the centre surrounded by a red border. In shape the flag is rectangular. The red border symbolises the blood of the nation's heroes who sacrificed their lives for independence. The green rectangle denotes life, progress and prosperity. The whole crescent represents the nation's Islamic faith. When the flag is hoisted, the curvature of the crescent should face outwards. The flag replaced the one withdrawn in 1965 which had a black-and-white strip on the hoist side. Paper flags can be bought from the supermarket in Orchid Magu in Male'.

NATIONAL TREE Dhivehi ruh is the national tree. Its botanical name is *Cocos nucifera* and it belongs to the Palmae (Arecaceae) family: enough clues for you to know that it is the coconut palm. The tree is to be found throughout the archipelago, growing densely on inhabited and uninhabited islands alike. It is economically important, not so much because its products are exported, but for its value in making certain imports unnecessary. A whole book could be (and probably has been) written on the many ways the coconut palm is of benefit in the tropics. Nowhere is this more evident than in the Maldives where its by-products range from rope made from the fibre (coir) harvested from the husk of the nut, branches used for brooms and roofing, and, of course, its essential role in the kitchen, especially in Maldivian recipes. It was declared the national tree in 1985.

NATIONAL FLOWER AND OTHER EMBLEMS It is a surprise to find that a very untropical flower, the rose, is the national flower of Maldives. Finifenma, commonly known as the pink rose (*Rosa polyantha*) is adored by Maldivians although not easily grown in island soil. Like the coconut palm, it was given the status of a national emblem in July 1985. Mariyam Zulfa, Maldivian editor and journalist, suggests that the rose was probably introduced to the Maldives by the British when they had a base on Gan in Addu Atoll. She finds it surprising that the jasmine did not come to be named as the national flower. 'Presentation by lovers of garlands made out of jasmine used to be a tradition, though this tradition is replaced by the giving of Western-style cut flowers today.' These have to be imported from Sri Lanka and India.

There is no national bird, but the heron (of which there are 13 different types) would be a likely candidate, especially as some species are unique to the islands. The national fish would surely be tuna. Breadfruit is grown wherever there are people and could qualify as the national vegetable through its popularity.

NATIONAL ANTHEM The national anthem, when played by one of the many bands which march through the streets of Male' on important state occasions, is a stirring tune. It has eight verses, but, at most gatherings where it is played, only three verses are sung. Translated from Dhivehi, these verses are:

> In National Unity we do salute our Nation
> In the National Language we do offer our prayers and salute our Nation.
>
> We bow in respect to the Emblem of our Nation
> And salute the Flag so exalted.
>
> We salute the colours of our Flag Green, red and white, which symbolise
> Victory, Blessing and Success.

ECONOMY

The principal economic activities in the Maldives Republic are tourism, fishing and shipping. In 2007 there was a US$940 million budget of which 45% was to be spent on building better infrastructure for people living in low-lying, far-flung atolls. The per capita income then was more than US$2,300, by far the highest in Asia. Using the skyline of Male' as an indicator, the economy of the Maldives is clearly booming. Where before there were one-storey, coral-stone warehouses, there are now the Maldivian version of mini-skyscrapers and one gets the impression of a Singapore in the making. Building is taking place throughout the capital, much of it on reclaimed land. In the streets, too, there is evidence of industry during the day as craftsmen, mechanics and carpenters can be glimpsed hard at work in compounds discovered unexpectedly down narrow alleys. Because of the difficulty of finding jobs on smaller islands, there is a migratory pull to Male'.

TRADING Marine products account for the majority of all exports, the major items being frozen and dried skipjack tuna. There are also some exotic fishy things such as dried shark fins, sea cucumber, cowrie shells and shark oil. Ambergris is exported, as are live reef and tropical fish. Other exports include apparel and scrap metal. Principal imports are consumer items such as manufactured goods; food, including rice, wheat and sugar and also tobacco and beverages; and petroleum products; as well as intermediate and capital goods (machinery, cement, etc). The influence of tourism on imports explains why over half of the nation's imports come from Singapore: not because the products originate there, but because of consignment convenience and business acumen (good credit facilities). India, Sri Lanka and the UAE also contribute imports of importance. Imported goods originate from over 60 countries, including the UK.

INDUSTRY While traditional industry struggles to survive, modern industries are giving a fillip to the nation's economy. The modern sector includes fish canning (much of it exported as English brand-name products to the UK), the manufacture of garments, production of PVC pipes, construction of fibreglass boats, washing powder and even a plant producing Coca-Cola. The traditional sector consists of boatbuilding (with a flourishing boatyard at Alifushi in Raa Atoll) and the cottage industries of mat weaving, rope making and a limited amount of local handicraft production. Tourism, transport and construction add to the industrial base.

Constraints on the increased development of various industries are the necessity of importing most of the raw materials and also the difficulty in finding labour for new enterprises since there is full employment, whether in industry or through self-employment with fellow islanders in fishing or agriculture.

AGRICULTURE When Ibn Battuta lived in the Maldives, he wrote:

> From these islands there are exported the fish, coconuts, cloths, and cotton turbans, as well as brass utensils, of which they have a great many, cowrie shells, and qanbur [a rope cord made from the hairy parts of the coconut shells]. . . The Indian and Yemenite ships are sewn together with them, for the Indian ocean is full of reefs, and if a ship is nailed with iron nails it breaks up on striking the rocks, whereas if is sewn with cords it is given a certain resilience and does not fall to pieces.

Today most of the islands are green, since even – or especially – uninhabited islands and islets have a wild growth of coconut palms, screwpines and some breadfruit and timber trees. Although the growing of crops and vegetables locally shows the essential part agriculture has played in the past, there have been gradual changes. Higher spending power to buy imported foods and the availability of imported rice have led to a reduction in demand for, and hence growth of, cereals and root crops. On the other hand, agricultural development is being vigorously encouraged by government programmes. It is estimated that, of the total land area of 298km², only about 10% is suitable for agriculture. This, of course, is shared among islands which are small, few having a land area in excess of 1km², and all being low lying with an average elevation of just 2m above sea level. Most of the soil is poor, with low water-retaining capacity, and is highly alkaline because of an excess of calcium from the basic coral rock.

All field crops are raised under natural rainfall during the southwest monsoon, which brings most of the rain. In addition, water is available from the underground water table which is only a few feet deep; 'a shallow lens of fresh water floating on seawater', according to one authority.

In 1997, 914 islands were leased out for agricultural or fisheries' purposes at an average annual rental of Rf1,503.09 (US$128.25). In 2007, the government announced an increase in the rent of uninhabited islands, based on an island's size. A rent of Rf1,200 (the equivalent of US$94.11) was to be charged for islands of one hectare (2.4711 acres) or less in area, with every additional hectare charged at Rf700 (US$54.90) a year. It was estimated that this would yield US$168,321 for the 683 island given on lease for agriculture. Agriculture is mostly a supplementary form of income, helped by the natural multiplicity of coconuts, the main crop. Coconut productivity is actually low because of poor genetic stock, close planting, lack of organic manure and fertilisers, and damage by beetles, rats and other pests. Nevertheless, production in 1997 amounted to 10,907,229 coconuts from the private sector and 5,876,978 from the government sector. (I have no idea who counted them.) The government has taken steps to encourage and improve agriculture in an effort to stop the outflow of foreign exchange on importing vegetables, fruits, meat and poultry products. Measures include coconut rehabilitation, pest control, provision of extension services, setting up nurseries and maximising the utilisation of uninhabited islands. Efforts are being made to create greater awareness among islanders of the country's agricultural potential.

A visit to a resort island where gardens and plants are painstakingly cared for proves that, given encouragement, crops will grow. Many islands import good-quality soil from Sri Lanka as well as plants. Biyadhoo, a resort island in South Male' Atoll, had experts employed in growing its own vegetables hydroponically. While the coconut has remained an essential part of the Maldivian diet, millet and maize, which used to be cultivated widely, have fallen out of favour. Yet millet flour is the best for making roshi, the kind of pancake that is a staple. Rice is imported and cannot be produced economically in the islands. Root vegetables such as cassava and sweet potato are grown in the south. If more of these and more millet could be grown, and people were to keep to the old eating habits, agriculture could flourish and imports would drop.

The market for fruit has great potential because of demand from the resorts. Bananas, papayas, watermelons, mangoes, limes, guavas and other tropical fruits are grown. Thoddoo island has become renowned for its watermelons, which are especially in demand in Male' during the Ramazan month of fasting; watermelon juice is eagerly sought at night. There does seem to be a lack of green vegetables in typical Maldivian meals, but vegetables are grown even if they are not common in the diet. Leaf cabbage, *brinjal* (aubergine or eggplant), gourds of various kinds and pumpkins are cultivated, along with green chillies and small red onions. Breadfruit is plentiful. A visit to the vegetable market in Male' gives an idea of the range of fruit and vegetables generally available. Hands of bananas hang by ropes from the rafters; also plentiful are heaps of chillies and the aromatic leaves used to flavour curries, handfuls of yams and piles of pumpkins.

Animal husbandry is a household activity, with chickens reared in back gardens for special treats, although eggs and poultry have to be imported in vast quantities for tourists. Some villagers rear goats for meat. Milk, another import, comes in powder form with many brands available. Given both local and tourist demand, the potential for agriculture is enormous. Government experts and private-sector entrepreneurs are taking a new interest in agriculture, which should lead to the lush greenery of the islands being profitable, not just pretty.

FISHING For an immediate impression of the importance of fishing in the Maldives, and to sense the vitality of the industry, go no further than the waterfront in Male' in the late afternoon when the fishing boats bring in their catch. *Dhonis* tie up on the sea side of Boduthakurufaanu Magu for a few hectic minutes while the fish they have caught are carried to the fishmarket. It is chaos as people stand around, other *dhonis* load up with cargo, cars ease past and short, wiry men with sarongs hoiked up to their thighs pull barrows stacked with whole skipjack tuna through the crowds.

Fishing is the main traditional occupation of the islands. Because of the country's vast marine resources, a 320km/200-mile Exclusive Economic Zone (EEZ) has been established by the government to protect and develop the fishing industry. The EEZ is patrolled by vessels of the MNDF (you'll see them moored in Male' harbour too) and they often arrest fishing boats from other countries (notably Sri Lanka), not only for fishing in the EEZ but for using nets to do so; trawling with nets is prohibited in the Maldives. Fishing in the Maldives is done with rod and line or by trolling with a line, or using a long line suspended from buoys. Any tuna caught in the Maldives is bound to be dolphin-friendly. Nets are used only to lift small live-bait fish from the sea.

To see the amazing technique practised by fishermen, walk westwards beyond the fish market, stop on the waterfront by the customs shed and look through the wire fence around the inner harbour any afternoon (except Fridays) about 17.00. A pack of rowing boats will be gathered near the wharf; each has a man at the oars, one sprinkling water on the sea to attract fish and another with a rod and line. The fisherman flicks his line in the sea and, as part of the same deft cast, withdraws it quickly. There is a fish on the end which he nimbly tosses off into the boat and casts again. The fish are so plentiful they take the hook without it even being baited, fooled by the sprinkled water into believing food is present.

Away from Male', fishermen use bait fish caught with a net in the reef waters around an island. The fish are stored in seawater at the bottom of the fishing *dhoni* to keep them alive. They are scattered alive on the sea in areas where the crew expect to find tuna. Attracted by the sudden supply of food, fish swarm around the *dhonis* and eagerly take the hooks – without bait – only to find themselves hauled on board. Bait fish not used are kept in large box-like containers with mesh sides in the waters off the home island where the *dhoni* anchors, so the bait can be used the next day.

While the percentage of the labour force involved in fishing is dropping, the efficiency is improving. Up to the 1970s, all fishing craft (called *masdhoni*) were sail-powered. Now most are mechanised. Since the masdhonis go where they want instead of at the whims of the wind, less time is spent looking for fish. And in the same time at sea, usually 12 hours, more fish can be caught.

Fishermen leave their island bases after dawn prayers and spend the whole day at sea. Night fishing (although popular with tourists for a couple of hours off the resort islands) and staying out at sea overnight is not usual. The fishing boats that go to sea for ten days at a time are the intruders, the deep-sea vessels from Sri Lanka. Four types of vessel are normally used. The mechanised masdhoni is 10–15m long, locally made with timber, open-decked and without a canopy. It carries a crew of eight or nine, of whom four or five do the actual pole-and-line fishing. The sailing *masdhoni* is a similar vessel, probably of older vintage than the mechanised one. It also stays at sea for 12-hour pole-and-line fishing trips but does not venture so far out. Trolling vessels (*vadhu dhoni*), which are 7.5–10m long, use troll lines with hooks. They fish mainly in reef waters and in the intra-island basins. Rowing boats are only 2–3m long and are used within the reef waters. Fishermen use hand lines for horse mackerel, sail fish and dog-tooth tuna.

There are three main areas for fishing. The reef waters include outer slopes of reefs and the channels between islands. Bait fish for catching tuna by pole and line can be caught in reef waters, as are lobsters. The intra-atoll basin means the area within atolls and is good for frigate mackerel, sail fish and seer fish. Nearshore waters are the waters outside the atolls but within 40km of the coast. Skipjack tuna are caught there. Until 1971 the Maldives exported dried and smoked tuna fish exclusively to Sri Lanka. Then the emphasis of the industry changed in response to export market demands and because of government infrastructural development. Mechanisation of power together with maintenance back-up was encouraged through loans. The sale of frozen fish to foreign companies, at atoll collection points, was initiated and a fish cannery set up on Felivaru in Lhaviyani Atoll. This was expanded in 1986 to a fish-processing plant with cannery, can-making plant and fishmeal plant, with water-purification and power-generating facilities. The capacity of the plant is 50 tonnes of canned tuna per day. The project, a government one with World Bank funding, includes refrigeration plants, cold storage, a quay and a slipway to cater for small fish-collector vessels.

There are four main methods of fish processing: freezing, canning, smoking and drying, and salting. Fresh tuna to be frozen is transferred to collecting vessels with freezers and immediately stored at freezing temperature for export or transportation to the canneries. In canning, fish is boiled at high temperatures before being hermetically sealed in the can. The traditional method of smoking

Background Information ECONOMY

and drying results in the product known as 'Maldive fish', and as such is hugely popular in Sri Lanka for adding flavour in the kitchen. After the fish is cleaned, gutted and filleted, it is boiled in water containing a lot of salt (an import from India). The boiled fish is then smoked by placing it on a wire or grooved plank shelf above a wood fire. This results in *walhoa mas*, smoked fish. To preserve it further, the smoked fish is put in the sun to dry. It is then Maldive fish and can keep for long periods.

In Male', colourful packs of Fisherman's dried tuna chips can be bought as an extraordinary souvenir. The pack describes how the tuna is 'caught on a traditional pole and line in the pollution-free waters of the Maldives, boiled, smoked and hygienically dried in the sun'. A panel contains impressive nutrition information detailing the fat (2.1%), protein (75.9%) and vitamins (A, E, B1, B2, B6, B12 and C). A few uninhabited islands are dedicated to processing fish that way, with the catch being gutted at night, when the sun is down, and dried on racks on the beach by day in the sun.

The sun also plays an important part in the processing of salt fish. At the waterside in village islands, fishermen gather to gut the day's catch and place the split fish into containers of salt. After a period of absorbing the salt (which prevents the growth of bacteria), the fish are sun-dried. The export market is increasing, with salt fish now going to Japan, USA, Thailand, Germany and Singapore, as well as to Sri Lanka. There is a collection centre for exporting smoked and salted fish at Thulusdhoo, which is also the main administrative island in Male' Atoll; it is called by some 'the Coca-Cola island' since the 'real thing' is bottled there.

The importance of fishing and fishermen to the nation's economy is commemorated every year on Fishermen's Day, 10 December.

TOURISM The welcome that tourists enjoy has, like the island resorts they visit, matured since tourism began as an industry in 1972. The welcome is no less genuine for being smooth and efficient. In fact, there is real warmth and enthusiasm for visitors, because the industry is recognised as having benefits that far outweigh the disadvantages. Disadvantages? At school, Maldivians are taught that 'cultural conflict is the most undesirable effect of mass tourism, as it upsets the harmony of life in the host country'. It is not hard to see that in a religious, conservative country like Maldives, freewheeling tourism could be disastrous. However, the designating of certain uninhabited islands as tourist resorts, thereby isolating the disruption to normal life, has worked.

The price in social and economic terms of a viable tourist industry that contributes much of the country's foreign currency earnings has proved low, especially when compared with neighbouring countries. It is a pleasant change to find that foreigners are not resented or harassed, but recognised as being a complementary part of the pattern of survival. The Maldives provide the right environment (now carefully protected); the world provides tourists who appreciate the good things in life available in the islands. Tourism began officially in 1972 when there were 1,097 visitors and the only resorts open were Kurumba (60 beds) and later Bandos (220 beds). In 1973, four more resorts opened (including Baros with 56 beds) and the number of visitors increased to 3,790. The industry boomed without any controls up to 1978 when there were 17 resorts and 29,325 visitors. Until 1978 tourism development was on an ad hoc basis, and giving cause for alarm. There was no policy, law or regulations governing the expansion and development of the industry. Uninhabited islands were being converted, sometimes by local entrepreneurs fronting for foreign investors, into resorts not much better than camping grounds with basic facilities. The danger to the survival of the fledgling industry was manifest: the Maldives were being ruined, not only

In 1971, an Italian entrepreneur, George Corbin, discovered the Maldives and decided he had found the perfect holiday destination, but there was nowhere to stay and no way to fly there. He entrusted a young man, Mohamed Umar Maniku, to make all the arrangements for a group of guests – many of them travel writers – he proposed to bring in 1972. There was only a small airstrip in Hulhule so the group, which numbered 22 Europeans, had to come by an Air Ceylon charter flight from Colombo. They stayed in three houses in Male' and M U Maniku took them to visit a different island every day. 'It was quite exciting,' Mr Maniku has recalled. 'We didn't know what to cook for them or how to deal with them.' They stayed ten days and were so enthusiastic, bookings from other visitors began to flow in.

Using local materials of coconut wood and palm thatch, 30 cabanas with makeshift bathrooms were put up on Kurumba. (The original *dhoni* which ferried the workers to Kurumba every day has pride of place in the main restaurant at Kurumba, as the buffet table.) 'I was cook, gardener and room boy. We had to do everything ourselves,' said Mr Maniku. 'We had nothing in the Maldives then, nothing. No banks, no airport, no telephone, only ham radio or Morse code with Colombo. Even the UNDP experts said tourism would never succeed because there were no facilities, no infrastructure.' Visitors loved it. 'They came on an extension of a holiday in Sri Lanka,' Mr Maniku recalled. 'We had to pay highly in commission to Sri Lanka travel agents to get them here, but we needed every cent to invest in the resorts. Tourists built the industry here. We listened to them and gave them what they wanted. At first it was *cadjan* (thatched) huts, which suited us as at the time it was all we could afford.'

Finding financing for the fledgling industry was difficult. 'We financed ourselves,' said Mr Maniku, who is now chairman of the Universal Enterprises group which operates several different resorts. Credit was given by Singapore suppliers but bank financing was not available until the industry was substantially developed. The momentum picked up in 1974, and in 1981, with the opening of the international airport at Hulhule, the Maldives became an independent destination. Aggressive marketing helped the Universal Enterprises group succeed as the pioneer of tourism in the Maldives. This was supported by developing resorts so that they were compatible with the environment, not by dumping dozens of concrete-block bungalows on a tiny island which becomes swamped with infrastructure.

Each Universal resort is distinguished by the lushness of its gardens and vegetation, nurtured by teams of gardeners and with soil and plants imported from Sri Lanka. To grow higher-yielding coconuts, and to combat soil erosion and eliminate pollution, experts were brought in.'We will never have mass tourism in the Maldives,' Mr Maniku said. 'Maldives must develop quality tourism, always giving tourists what they want. They used to come here with sandwiches, now they can eat gourmet meals in fine dining restaurants set in lush, tropical gardens.' As one of the largest operators in the Maldives, the Universal group caters for every segment of the market, from grand hotel luxury to beachcomber simplicity. Many of the group's staff have been in the same resort for years, climbing through the ranks from labourer to top posts. Maintaining high standards is seen as very important and each resort is personally run by a director, with a Maldivian manager as administrator and internationally trained professionals in charge of departments. 'If the owner of a resort isn't involved in everything, it will never succeed,' said Mr Maniku, remembering his early days. 'It's like caring for a baby.'

as a carefree home for the people but also as a holiday destination. And the country was not benefiting from the influx of tourist dollars, even if the foreign investors were.

President Gayoom, on his assumption of office in 1978, set out to transform the industry into something viable and worthwhile. A law on tourism which outlines the basic regulations of the industry was passed in 1979. A head tax (included in the room rate) was introduced, ensuring an immediate and direct contribution to the treasury on behalf of each tourist. In 1982 a separate department for tourism was created and this became a ministry in 1988. All resort islands, which were formerly under the Ministry of Agriculture, were brought under the Ministry of Tourism. A ten-year tourism plan was drawn up by a Danish consultancy firm funded by the Kuwait Fund; this identified tourism zones and strategies. Resort islands until then were concentrated in Male' Atoll, since it was close to the airport. This was itself upgraded in 1981 to international standards and made capable of taking long-haul jets, in response to the growth of tourism.

The commissioning of Ari Atoll Tourism Zone was begun in 1988, with the idea of having a central infrastructural island (for fuel storage, bulk handling of supplies, etc) serving the resort islands close to it. While resorts were developed by the private sector, there was little interest in, and hence no funding for, a supply island. From 1980 to 1990, 40 new island resorts opened and, with others increasing their bed capacity, 7,621 beds were available for visitors by the end of the decade. The bed count at the end of 1998 was 14,228. Bed capacity since then increased further to 15,044 on 84 resorts in 1999. Into the millennium figures rose to 16,444 on 87 resorts in 2003, while by the end of 2007 there were 89 resorts in operation with a bed count of 17,000. Visitor arrivals, which totalled 42,007 during 1980, had risen to 195,156 in 1990. The total number of visitors at the end of 1998 was 395,725. In 1999 the number of visitors was 429,666 (3,718,207 bed nights) and this increased to 563,593 (4,704,592 bed nights) in 2003, with an average of just over eight nights' stay each. Despite the effects of SARS and avian flu, as well as the Iraq conflict and the general perception of international terrorism, in 2004 over half a million visitors chose to visit the Maldives. The tsunami of course seriously affected the number of tourists visiting in January 2005. However, by June 2005 out of 87 resorts only 12 remained closed while repairing or upgrading following the tsunami and, except resorts like Fun Island which was being completely rebuilt, most reopened for the 2005/2006 season.

European countries have regularly provided the majority of visitors to the Maldives. Italy is the number-one source of guests to the islands from Europe, followed by Germany and the UK. France and Switzerland are the next-highest providers. The total number from Europe was more than 443,000 in 2003. The number of Asians over the same period was 101,800, mainly from Japan (42,000), China and India. Nearly 3,900 tourists came from Africa, 7,000 from Australia and 7,600 from America. Tourism contributed Rf37.5million to the economy in 2003. It was estimated that in 2008 the leasing of resorts for tourism would contribute 10.25% of the country's budget for that year. And in 2007 there was a record 675,889 tourists, an increase of 12.3% on 2006.

In 1997 several attractive uninhabited islands in atolls quite far from the airport were offered for tender for conversion into tourist resorts. Most of these have been designed to appeal to the upmarket nature-loving visitor and have long been opened. While the number of tourists was increasing, with visitors staying an average of more than eight nights each, standards were improving too, doubtless no coincidence. The idea was to break the seasonal pattern of tourism rather than simply to increase the number of rooms. Priority was given to upgrading the existing facilities at resorts, increasing average occupancy rate (in 1998 it reached

76% compared with 65.7% in 1994 and 40.5% in 1983), strengthening overseas promotion to win new markets and developing manpower for tourism. This has resulted in a change for the better. One resort manager, commenting on the tourism industry at the beginning of 2000, said that to remain competitive it was necessary to upgrade. 'Even a guest paying US$60 expects us to provide a US$200 service.' He explained that the honeymoon is over for tourism in the Maldives. 'It is no use opening a new resort and hoping people will come, as happened in the past. We have to provide quality service, modern infrastructure, good standards and aggressive marketing. The standard must be upmarket or we can't survive.'

This is bad news for those who want a cheap holiday in a bamboo shack by a deserted beach. Or is it? The resort operators know their market. Guests want sophistication even on a desert island; they seem to feel that if they are going to get back to nature they should do it in style, at least with a bathroom en suite. There are still low-cost islands, but the trend is for better facilities fitting in with, and not upsetting, the environment (desalination plants for constant fresh water, scientific garbage disposal units). That has to be paid for as part of the room rate. Preservation of the idyllic environment of a castaway image costs more. Incidentally, the local materials for building, such as palm thatch, are now more expensive (since regular maintenance and renewal is required) than imported roofing material. The rustic style of holiday for two guests on such an island as Cocoa – originally 16 beds in cabanas on the beach – actually costs a lot more than a holiday by the sea in a simpler but larger resort. Now Cocoa has itself moved further upmarket with overwater villas, but even these have palm thatched roofs.

Every effort is made to ensure the continued success of tourism because of its far-reaching consequences. While the number of employees directly involved in tourism is equivalent to one for every guest bed, there are thousands more who benefit indirectly. The construction industry is flourishing. The labour staff shortage is such that resort owners have been known to recruit labourers who were on an island during the building stage to stay on as waiters, laundrymen and gardeners. Engineers and maintenance men are in constant demand, and boat crews are needed, as are boats, which means the atoll boatbuilding yards are busy. The development of tourism has been so fast, parallel activity has yet to catch up.

Background Information ECONOMY

While handicrafts are produced in some islands, quality, product output and marketing have not matched potential. The shop owners in Male' push specially printed T-shirts and imported goods instead.

The tourism industry does not have a bad image in the Maldives and is seen as a good career for the young. The students at the Hotel and Catering Services Institute in Male' are sponsored by resorts which employ them after graduation. Some resorts have also set up their own training schools. Tourism is a male-dominated industry, even though some local women are taking jobs in resorts, especially those near Male' whence they can return home each night. Foreigners are currently employed as managers, chefs, accountants, diving instructors and tour guides. By law, all barmen too have to be foreigners (and even they have to undergo retraining to match the high standards of the resort bars). The advance in quality of the resorts has not been matched in experience by Maldivians and so even more expatriate (both Asian and European) hotel professionals are being employed, with some resorts having as many as 50% expatriate staff. Executive chefs and managers of the super luxurious resorts are usually European, guest relations staff Asian. The Ministry of Tourism sees the percentage of expatriates in the tourism industry as too high. It is hoped that as more school leavers join the industry as a career in years to come, the percentage will fall.

The number of resort islands operated by Maldivians has increased so that the majority are now operated by locals. Following changes in policy, resort islands are now owned by the government and leased (usually on 21-year leases, for which tenders are invited) to operators. They can be closed down, or penalties must be paid, if the resorts do not meet required standards. The future of the industry is being carefully considered, since expansion without due attention could result in a fall in average occupancy. The private sector is expected to play a greater role, while the government takes on the responsibility of delivering the basic infrastructure. New tourism zones are being opened up, particularly in Addu Atoll where on the large island of Viligili (or Villingili) there is a Shangri-La resort, and the intriguingly named island of Herethere opened as a 600-bed resort in December 2007.

The old airport at Gan, serving Addu Atoll, has been upgraded to international standards for long-haul flights direct from Europe. Maldives has great faith in, and great plans for, quality tourism. In 1997, which was promoted worldwide as 'Visit Maldives Year', there were nearly 400,000 tourists. In 2004 the number of tourists visiting the Maldives exceeded 500,000. With enough islands to absorb them and a policy of controlling development and safeguarding the natural environment (the attraction that lures visitors), the impact of tourism should continue to be beneficial to Maldivians and foreigners alike.

By 2007, over 600,000 tourists stayed at the resorts in a year. Plans were in hand to develop a further 44 uninhabited islands throughout the atolls to make the benefits of tourism more meaningful and apparent to those living far from the traditional tourist centre. There are also plans for a consortium of three state-owned companies, Maldives Airports, Island Aviation and Maldives Transport and Contracting Corporation, to build hotels linked with new regional airports on residential islands. A new master plan for tourism was launched in August 2007. According to the Ministry of Tourism:

> The thrust of the Maldives Third Tourism Master Plan is on expanding and
> strengthening the Maldives tourism as an instrument of economic and social
> development in a manner that benefits all Maldivians in all parts of the country. The
> Plan stresses the development of the industry along the lines of sustainability,
> adopting environmentally and socially responsible tourism practices. Accordingly, the
> Plan emphasises developing tourism in harmony with nature, facilitating and

CUSTOM-MADE FOR A MEMORABLE HOLIDAY

The then Minister of Tourism, Hassan Sobir, in an article in 1999 in *Serendib*, the inflight magazine of the then Air Lanka, reflected that Sri Lanka and the Maldives started out together as holiday destinations. 'Most people came here via Sri Lanka,' he said. 'Some visitors spent time in Sri Lanka for the culture and history, and then visited the Maldives for the beach part of their holiday.' His remarks on holidaying in Maldives are still valid, ten years later. He pointed out that the Maldives is almost custom-made for lovers of deserted island paradise. 'Each resort is built on an uninhabited island so there are no strangers on the beaches, only resort guests. Many resorts have facilities for children, so,' noted Sobir, 'parents can find time to play when their children are occupied.' He pointed out, too, that there are no cars at the resorts and no crime. 'People come here when they are looking for a safe holiday,' he said. He felt that part of the attraction of the Maldives was because, 'Visitors are more health conscious in exercise, even in the food they eat. There's an inclination towards using a holiday to regain fitness. They want a change from a hectic routine, they want to relax, get into shape, keep fit.'

Linda Miles-Pedler, then product manager of the major travel company Kuoni UK, stated in the same article: 'Sri Lanka and the Maldives make the perfect combination. Guests go to Sri Lanka for touring and then to Maldives for the beach.' She added that, in the Maldives, there is no sightseeing to feel guilty about not doing.

'We intend to keep Maldives as an exotic destination,' asserted Minister Hassan Sobir. 'We are lucky to have done things right from the beginning. Mass tourism leads to social problems and messing up of the environment. We have been receptive and are lucky to have responsible elements in tourism. Our people accept tourism as bringing benefits … The typical visitor is upper or middle class … There are resorts for low-income groups, but they're not cheap. They can't be, because islands are like stationary ships. Everything has to be brought in and that adds to expenses.' Contemplating the future for tourism, Sobir said that he sees the Maldives as continuing to appeal to an upmarket clientele. 'In five years, we expect potential growth in our favour,' he added. 'It will be gradual. We are different in many ways. Non-polluted atmosphere. One island, one resort. Very appealing to people for a memorable holiday.' He concluded: 'We feel we are recession proof. People earlier had the feeling that holidays were meant for rich people with a disposable income, which was used for their annual holiday. Things are changing now. Holidays are a vital part of life, seen more as a necessity rather than a luxury. People will reduce on something else and still take a holiday.'

enhancing private sector investment, developing human resources, creating greater employment opportunities and diversifying markets and products.

The Ministry claimed that, 'contrary to previous Plans, the Third Tourism Master Plan is formulated as a "living document" to ensure its responsiveness to rapid changes in the Maldivian economy and global trends in the industry'.

PEOPLE

Maldivians (Dhivehin) are of mixed race, and are a devout people. The sea and religion have moulded their personalities, and the individuality shows in every Maldivian you meet. They are not an excitable people given to ostentation. Perhaps it is the overpowering presence of the sea which humbles them while providing the resources that support their lightly worn self-assurance.

As a seafaring island nation, the Maldives has always been exposed to different cultural influences. These came mostly from the neighbouring maritime cultures of those countries bordering the Indian Ocean. So traces of Africa, Malaysia and Indonesia, as well as of Arabia and India, are to be seen in the features of the people. Whether it is from their lifestyle or from their ancestors, many Maldivians are strikingly attractive in appearance. They are not generally very tall and their features, however handsome, seldom reveal their emotions. It would be difficult for a visitor to know by a person's appearance which island he comes from. Some Maldivians claim they can tell by the way a person walks. The number of people who have settled in Male', having left the islands where they were born, means the capital's population has become very cosmopolitan in the local context. There are people who are fairer than others, but evidence of the Portuguese occupation in the 16th century has mostly disappeared (but see *North Thiladhunmathi*, page 173). More recently, the British presence (in Gan) is remembered for the English language, not English lineage.

In their social studies, Maldivian schoolchildren are taught that the people of the Maldives are of the Aryan race. Aryans were originally Indo-Europeans with Indo-Aryan subgroups who spread from south Russia and Turkistan about 2,000BC to Mesopotamia and Asia Minor, invading India about 1,500BC.Whether the Aryans who settled in the Maldives came directly from India or Sri Lanka is unclear. The school books state that Maldivians have a close resemblance to Arabs, Sinhalese and Indians in their appearance, language, physical traits, culture, traditions and behaviour. Professor Clarence Maloney, in his book *People of the Maldive Islands*, based on a visit in 1975, states:

> The cultural history of the Maldives is more complicated than has been thought, and beneath the Arab and Sinhala stratum there is a Tamil-Malayalam stratum, in addition to other early cultural influences in parts of the country.

Because of their geographical location, it is not difficult to envisage the islands attracting settlers (and ancient dropouts?) from the countries mentioned, as well as Phoenician, Egyptian, Chinese, Greek and Roman mariners, and to guess their influence on the evolution of the Maldivian people. However, there appears also to have been an aboriginal race involved. Some books repeat the legend of the Redin, a people folklore describes as having had light skin, brown hair and hooked noses. The people of Giraavaru are said to have been descendants of aboriginal inhabitants, but their ancestors are considered more likely to have been Tamils from southern India. Not a trace of them remains on Giraavaru [now a tourist resort 13km from the airport] since they were resettled in 1968 on Hulhule [the airport island], because of their dwindling numbers and the island's erosion. There were 131 of them in 14 households. Later they were moved to Male'. The women are said to have been extremely modest, never completely undressing themselves.

WOMEN Comprising the majority of the inhabitants in some atolls, and about 49% of the population nationwide – as well as making up a quarter of the public workforce – women have an importance and status which may not at first be apparent. Only in a few resorts will you find women working, and then usually in reception, not as room maids. You will not see them when you pop into a café for tea, yet you will see them in groups promenading the streets of Male' in the evenings. Women have been rulers in the Maldives in the past, the last one in the early 14th century. There is universal franchise for women.

They enjoy equal status with men, with equal access to education and to vocational and professional training, equal participation in community development, and equal opportunities in employment, remuneration and promotion as well as in commercial, social and cultural activities. This translates into reality rather curiously in non-Maldivian eyes. It does not mean a contest to oust men from the workplace and assert themselves nationwide. In Maldivian society, by tradition, women already exercise an independence in family matters. While a husband is head of the household, the wife has the greater influence on major decisions of the family. She retains her maiden name after marriage. A married woman can also acquire land or property; she can own, manage and sell a business in her own name. In the distribution of family property, a daughter gets half of what is inherited by the son (although this does not apply to land). In Maldivian society, according to Islamic law, men are responsible for the welfare of their female relatives, hence their larger share of the family fortune (but see *Family* on page 43).

Purdah, the tradition of secluding women of rank from public view, is not a tenet of life in the Maldives. In fact, by a recent law no-one is allowed to conceal his or her face in public. But some women in villages, not being as sophisticated as their sisters in the capital, are enchantingly shy and may hide their faces at the sight of a prying camera.

A stroll through the streets of Male' in the evening (or early morning before school starts) confirms the statistics about the large youth population. The young people seem refreshingly eager, grasping opportunities presented through various youth programmes designed to make them responsible citizens of the future.

MEETING MALDIVIANS The Maldivians to be met working in the holiday resorts are under the restraints of their employment but they will usually be relaxed enough to talk if they want to, and to give visitors an insight into their way of life. It is actually the best chance a visitor has of meeting Maldivians since, in the streets of the capital or in a fishing-village island during an excursion, people are likely to be reserved with strangers. Maldivians take time to get to know someone. By tradition, a stranger who arrives on an inhabited island will be given hospitality, but hearts will only be opened when the stranger has revealed what kind of person he is. It is hard for a stranger to win a Maldivian's respect simply because he or she is a stranger. They will be treated with the quiet courtesy typical of Maldivians, a façade that rarely erupts into something more demonstrative. Living on small islands, Maldivians are used to saying goodbye to strangers who come, win their hearts and then sail away, perhaps never to return. Emotions are kept under control because of that, avoiding the pain of close relationships which are bound to be broken. This apparent lack of feeling does not diminish the friendship of the Maldivian people, but only makes it more precious.

POPULATION STATISTICS The census population for 1995 was 244,644, with 125,089 males and 119,555 females; the 2000 census showed 269,010, and the latest figures available in December 2007 gave a total population of 338,000.There has been an annual increase of around 3% in the population since 1965. When tourism started in the Maldives in 1972 there were 122,673 inhabitants, up from 97,743 in 1965. The annual growth rate before that year fluctuated considerably with a decrease in some years. Figures available for 1921 show a population of only 70,413. In that year, men outnumbered women by 118.41 to 100. The ratio has changed gradually over the years and at the time of the 1995 census, there were 104.62 males for every 100 females. The 1995 census also showed that 25.7% of the country's population lived in Male'. Within the atolls, the population is spread unevenly since some islands, which have the space and easy access to good fishing, have a large number (some as many as 3,000) of inhabitants. Generally, however, the population of an inhabited island is between 200 and 800.

CITIZENSHIP The citizenship law has been revised to bring it in line with modern-day requirements. Citizenship is granted only to Muslims and then only to those who have lived in Maldives for several years. It is possible for foreigners to become Muslims and, in Maldives, this is usually done as a result of a foreigner wishing to marry a Maldivian, not to obtain residence or citizenship. A male foreigner wishing to marry a Maldivian woman can do so only if he converts to Islam. For 'People of the Book' (Christians and Jews), this is possible and is done by expressing in front of witnesses a belief in Allah and that Mohammed is the last prophet of God. The learning process, of course, takes much longer. The man's name is changed and registered. Maldivian men can, and do sometimes, marry foreign women.

LANGUAGE

Maldivian (Dhivehi) belongs to the Indo-Aryan group. Dhivehi is exclusive to the Maldives and to Minicoy, its northern neighbour in the Laccadives. It is a language peppered with derivations from Arabic (which influenced the maturing of the language), Hindi, Sinhala, Tamil, Parsee and English. English, being the medium for secondary education, is widely spoken. The literacy rate (in Dhivehi) is about 98%.

Listen casually to two Dhivehin (Maldivians) talking Dhivehi and you won't have a clue what they are talking about. The language is actually easy to listen to, without harsh, guttural sounds or explosive noises of command, but it is not soft and lilting either, and you get the impression that the way a word is said is as important as the actual word in conveying a meaning. Listen further and you will realise that some words are very familiar indeed: they are English, not exactly the same as in English but with a Maldivian flourish at the end. Such a word as *dhoru* sounds familiar, and it should be since it means 'door'. It transpires that English words can be converted into Dhivehi by adding a tail according to the meaning. This usually happens only with certain words in common use, not with spur-of-the-moment adaptations which would be lost on a Maldivian who does not understand English. For instance, key words have 'u' added to the end to signify the definite article. Thus teacher + u becomes *teacharu*, doctor + u becomes *daktaru*. I was delighted to find I could call myself *editaru*, much easier to say than *noos veriyaa* meaning 'journalist' (although that sounds vaguely familiar), and *liyun theriyaa* meaning 'writer'.

Maldivians delight in telling you that a Dhivehi word has been adopted by the English language as its own: atoll, which in Dhivehi is *atholhu*. Actually, Dhivehi is difficult to speak and, since there are different dialects, particularly in the south, even Dhivehin sometimes have problems. A foreigner who masters enough words to hold a conversation without confusing the various terms to use, according to a person's status, is clearly an accomplished linguist. Even if you are not, learning and trying out a few words in the right context will distinguish you as someone who is taking a little more trouble than usual to understand what is going on around about.

Dhivehi is the only native language of the Maldives and is flourishing, despite the adoption of some foreign words (Hindi, Arabic and Sinhala as well as English) for convenience. As a tongue, it has evolved with the Dhivehin themselves, possibly as a means of keeping communication among settled islanders private from newcomers, rather than to accommodate the newcomers so they, too, understood what was being said. The roots of Dhivehi are Indo-Aryan and, despite the influence of Sinhala, Hindi, Bengali, etc, the language has developed along its own lines, since it was spoken in isolation from the mainstream. One can imagine hardy and proud islanders a thousand years ago happily confusing intruders from Sri Lanka by speaking a language that was vaguely familiar but concealed real meanings by the use of words from other languages, unfamiliar to the Sri Lankans. This was part of the desire of Maldivians to fend for themselves, keeping aloof from people from over the seas who wanted to interfere. Experts say that, even today, the Dhivehi spoken in the south is more like Sinhala while that spoken in the north has words borrowed from Indian languages.

While spoken Dhivehi evolved easily over the centuries, the written word followed a slower, more convoluted course. In its archaic form it is known as Eveylaa Akuru or 'Ancient Letters', and a lot of its characters are similar to Sinhala, with sentences written across the page from left to right. The Arabic words in the Ancient Letters indicate that Arab influence existed long before the conversion of the nation to Islam. Conversion brought transformation in everything, although this took many years to be complete. The earliest Dhivehi writings date from the 12th century. The language – and literature – reflected the influence of a puritan religion by its addition of Arabic words to express ideas which up to then had no need to be expressed since they had not been thought of. Perhaps it was the shock of the brief Portuguese occupation of the country in the 16th century which led to a new script being adopted for written Dhivehi. Or it may simply have been the need to accommodate Arabic words more efficiently. Thaana, a version of the present-day script, written (as in Arabic) from right to left, replaced the Dhives Akuru ('Island Letters', in use from the 15th century) in the early 17th century. Gabulhi Thaana, adopted in the last century, is the present form of script. Incidentally, even a receipt in Dhivehi characters is printed from right to left with the quantity on the right and the price on the left. Books and local newspapers begin at what is the end for us, which is very confusing for browsers who flip through a book from the back, only to find it is the beginning.

Dhivehi, as the official language, is used unequivocally in the administration of the country. Until the 1960s it was also the medium of all education, but with the growing need for further education, English became the medium. Roman script has also been used to write Dhivehi but it is out of fashion now, except in the phrasebooks produced for foreigners. For words and phrases, see *Appendix 1*, page 198.

EDUCATION

There is great enthusiasm for education among the young people of the Maldives, a change from the days when a boy's ambition was to become a fisherman like his father, and a girl was likely to get married at 12. The aim is now the General Certificate of Education (Advanced Level), London syllabus. As school facilities have increased, so has the demand for education and it is now regarded by parents, even in the remotest island, as essential that their children should go to school. This has resulted in there being 246 government, private and community educational systems in the atolls, and a further 17 institutions (government, private and community) in Male'.

The first modern secondary school outside Male' was established in Addu Atoll in 1991, and this was followed by the opening in 1998 of the Northern Secondary school in South Thiladhunmathi Atoll. In addition to these two fully fledged secondary schools, secondary grades are currently offered in 50 schools in the atolls. During the past 20 years, Atoll Education Centres have been built in selected 'centre' islands, with relatively easy access for children from outer islands.

Education starts at home, and even on the beach or under a shady tree in the garden, with instruction in the Koran and arithmetic to children from the age of three, supplemented by attendance later at religious schools. The English-medium school system was begun in 1961 to provide primary and secondary education, both private and government, for students living in Male'. Students completing the tenth grade sit for the GCE O Level, and at the end of Grade 12 they take the GCE A Level examination of the University of London. Until 1977 education in the atolls was traditional, providing students with basic numeracy and literacy in addition to religious instruction. Now the traditional and English-medium system combine with a third system concentrating on the realities and culture of the country in an effort to equip pupils for the modern world.

The educational ladder begins with pre-school then primary for the first five grades, ages six to ten. Middle school is for children of 11 and 12, grades six and seven. Lower secondary consists of grades eight to ten for children of 13–15 years. The top of the ladder, high secondary level, consists of grades 11 and 12 and caters for those over 15. Some schools are mixed, although they may be laid out so that boys and girls who share the same classroom cannot see each other because of a dividing partition. Every inhabited island has a school of some sort and government primary schools are established in each of the 19 administrative atolls. Instruction in most of the island schools is in Dhivehi, but English is taught as a second language (often by teachers from Sri Lanka) from grade one. English-medium education in primary schools – and in secondary schools – is available in Male'.

University education has to be obtained abroad, but there are several specialist training institutes in Male'. Among them are the Maldives Institute of Technical Education (MITE), the Institute of Hotel and Catering Services, the Tertiary Institute for Open Learning, the Institute for Teacher Education, the Institute of Health Sciences and the Institute of Islamic Studies.

Non-formal education programmes exist – the Atoll Education Centres also provide non-formal education for adults – and there are many educational broadcasts by radio. The functional literacy rate in Dhivehi for ages 15–45 is 98%.

RELIGION

THE IMPORTANCE OF ISLAM Maldives is a 100% Sunni Muslim country. Islam is the religion of the state and the backbone of society. The president is the supreme authority, entrusted with the protection of the religion. No other religion is permitted and the religious paraphernalia of non-Muslims may be removed from visitors by customs officers at the airport and kept in bond until their departure. Religious observance is strict, with prayers five times a day at the mosques in Male' and on every inhabited island. The consumption of alcohol, drugs and pork is prohibited. Consequently, there are no liquor shops in the Maldives, except in the sterile duty-free area at the airport, although there are bars in the holiday resorts. There are no pigs (but pork is available in the resorts). Also forbidden are dogs, so don't try to smuggle in your favourite pooch (it's no joke, as a visitor who tried in 1994 found out).

The most impressive building in Male', with a dome of gold colour that reflects sunlight over the waterfront, is the Islamic Centre. This mosque was built in 1984 and is a building of grace both within and without. Non-Muslims are allowed to visit its galleries (09.00–17.00, except at prayer times) from where the carpeted floors of the mosque and the dark calligraphic wood carvings expounding the history of the religion can be viewed. It is an inspiring sight, significant of the strength that Islam brings to Maldivian society.

The only places of worship are mosques, since the Maldives is exclusively Muslim. There are over 20 mosques in Male', and every inhabited island, including the airport island and all resort islands, has at least one. The mosques are simple, gracious buildings lacking flamboyance but designed with dedication, often with wide arches and open windows to allow the breeze to cool worshippers. Even when empty, the spirit of reverence remains; for the Friday noon prayers the mosques are invariably full to overflowing, with worshippers who are late having to congregate outside. Praying is conducted facing the direction of Mecca, the holiest place in Islam. In some resort islands, like Kurumba, there is an arrow on the ceiling of every bedroom indicating which way Mecca lies. Women and men attend mosques and pray separately; there are separate mosques for women in the inhabited islands.

Children learn about Islam from the earliest age and can be heard reciting passages from the Koran at grandmother's knee in many houses in the evenings. The *kiyavaage* is the name given to a private home where children gather with the objective of learning to read the Koran and to read and write Dhivehi. A *makthab* is a separate building where they extend their studies of Islam and of the Koran into their teens. A feature of the faith of Maldivians is that it is traditional, an essential part of their life, an everyday affair. Visitors staying in resorts will barely notice its importance, but will benefit by taking the trouble to appreciate the strength Maldivians draw from its conventions.

Five main pillars of Islam

- **Witness (Shahadah)** Submission to God and acceptance that Mohammed is his prophet.
- **Prayer (Salat)** Five times a day, at sunrise, midday, afternoon, sunset and evening. Before praying, Muslims must wash head, hands and feet. They can pray in any place that is clean and not polluted, and they must face Mecca. On Fridays at midday, it is more beneficial to pray collectively at a mosque. Otherwise they may pray alone, wherever they may be. Men and women must pray separately.
- **Alms giving (Zakat)** According to the Koran, faith in God should be expressed by doing good to others.
- **Fasting (Sawm)** The month of Ramazan is a holy month, when all Muslims must fast from dawn till dusk. Those who are ill or travelling, or are pregnant, are permitted to postpone the fast until they are well. Elderly people and young children are excused from the fast, the purpose of which is to teach discipline to the soul. Eid al-Fitr is when the fast ends and all Muslims celebrate with a great feast, with hundreds of sheep and goats ritually slaughtered on this special day.
- **Pilgrimage (Hajj)** It is a sacred duty for every Muslim to go to the Ka'aba, the sacred mosque in Mecca, at least once. This should be done ideally between the seventh and tenth days of the month of Zuul-Hijja, the 12th month of the Muslim year. This is usually between March and July, depending on the moon. The Hajj includes, among other things, the tawaf, seven anticlockwise circuits of the Ka'aba, prostrations at the site of Abraham, and the sacrifice of either a sheep or camel, depending on one's wealth. This meat is given to the poor. The pilgrimage ends with another feast, the Eid al-Adha, after which the pilgrim must visit the tomb of the prophet in the holy city of Medina.

Other basic tenets of Islam The Koran (Quran) is the word of God. Mohammed is his prophet. The Sunna is the right way of life, which represents everything that the prophet Mohammed did or said. The books of Hadith record the Sunna, the way to live. Note that the Sunna is the guidance given by Mohammed; it is not the same as the Koran, which is the direct word of God. The Koran and the Sunna together are known as the al-Asl, the foundation of Islam. A madrasa is an Islamic school. Mohammed's daughter was Fatima. Ali was his cousin. Mohammed favoured Ali as his successor, and married Fatima to Ali. Those who follow Ali are known as Shi'a Muslims.

Prayer times Prayer times depend on the position of the sun. Maldivians pray five times a day and prayer has to be preceded by ablution, a ritual washing of the arms, legs, face, and behind the ears, and rinsing of the mouth. Shops in Male' close their doors for about 15 minutes during prayer times. The Post Shop and Dhiraagu (telephone company) remain open if you want somewhere to go. The morning prayer takes place just before dawn. The noon prayers are at midday, when the sun is at its height; the afternoon prayer (usually between 15.00 and 16.00) is when an object and its shadow are the same length. There is also the prayer time at sunset and the evening prayer a little while later, when red clouds begin to disappear.

Just in case you should forget, all television programmes are interrupted at prayer time, even BBC World and other foreign satellite channels.

OTHER BELIEFS For the primitive Maldivian, before the coming of Islam in the 12th century, there was a strong belief in superstitions. Even after the centuries that passed following the conversion to Islam, 'the conservative way of life, isolated nature of society and the bounds of island environs had made us reluctant to give up the old ways of life', wrote H A Maniku in *Dhevi*, a slim volume published in 1988 as the first issue of *Vanavaru* magazine. *Dhevi*, he explains, 'may be taken to convey the idea of an invisible, but sometimes visible, being [that is] capable of moving across the high seas, land and even through barriers. It may be helpful or harmful...' Maniku speculates that belief exists even today in dhevi and *fanditha* (which Clarence Maloney describes as 'a magic or religious "science" of any sort, white or black, curative or preventative, fertility ritual or divination'). Despite the condemnation under Islam of all practices of fanditha and the belief in dhevi, Maniku writes:

> There is no doubt that the belief in dhevi, what they cause and its cure through fanditha, are ingrained in the Maldivian psyche through generations of exposure to the elements that has made our society fearful of change – for fear of antagonising the spirits – that lurk at every turn in our environment. The sea, so fearful, so unknown, so violent and so overpowering yet that gives us the nourishment, that acts as our highway to the nearest community, surely was held in awe and respect.

The booklet is a treasure chest of folklore, an insight into the curiosities of societies isolated in a small-island world. Listed in it are as many as 170 types of dhevi, which the author calls some of the oldest terms preserved in the Dhivehi language. The small museum in the Sultan's Park in Male' contains perhaps the only indication that the islands were ever anything but compulsorily Muslim. Inside the only remaining old house are some fascinating exhibits, some up to 1m high, including a five-faced coral stele and various Buddha heads made of coral.

These are said to have links to Tantric Buddhism. Tantric ideas are thought to have originated in India before Buddhism, and possibly even before Hinduism. The Mahayana Buddhist sects later adopted Tantric practices, incorporating them into their regular beliefs. Many Tantric ideas have animistic elements. Such ideas are also part of the Tibetan Bon religion, which was incorporated into Tibetan Buddhism in the 7th century. Some of these ideas may well have migrated to the Maldives before they virtually disappeared in India under the swell of Hindu doctrines. Tantric influences are now found mainly in Nepal and Tibet, being classified under the term Vajrayana Buddhism. Buddhist exhibits, including the heads, were found in various places throughout the islands, but many of them were found in what is now Ameer Ahmed Magu, in the northern part of Male'. In particular, there is a striking Buddha head with moustache and long ears, which was discovered in Orchid Magu as recently as 1976. Some 10th-century heads were found in Horubadhoo island in Baa Atoll when excavating the Royal Island resort. At the Mundoo school in Laamu

Atoll, a 10th-century Buddha head and monkey head were found. And in Thaa Atoll a beautiful box was found, with Buddhist engravings both inside and outside. Warlike and dragon figures and coral elephants, as well as multi-level stupas, are among the fascinating objects on display there.

CULTURE

FAMILY, MARRIAGE, DIVORCE AND CHILDREN Despite its importance in Maldivian life, marriage is not celebrated lavishly. While some modern Maldivians might opt for marriage in Western dress with a reception, most people keep it traditionally simple. The father of the bride-to-be has to give his consent, while the bride states the amount of *mehir* (bride money) which the husband is expected to pay. The bride is then married by an authorised person. It does not result in the exchange of large financial contributions from either side of the families involved. There is no dowry system existing in any part of the country, and the parents of the bride do not have to bear the expenditure of the marriage. After marriage, the woman retains her maiden name.

Divorce is equally simple. For the man, it is done by saying 'I divorce you' to the wife and then reporting the deed to a magistrate. For the wife, a divorce can be obtained from the husband, or from the appropriate courts of the Ministry of Justice in situations where the husband refuses to divorce his wife. For three months after a divorce, a woman cannot marry again other than her immediate ex-husband. The time is to allow for reconciliation and for the establishment of paternity in case she is pregnant. During this period, the ex-husband has to support his former wife financially, and she should live in a place agreeable to him as well. After divorce, a woman is given half of all the property jointly owned with her husband, and any property acquired through her own efforts. The divorce rate is one of the highest in the world. There is no stigma attached to frequent marriage. A man may have more than one wife (up to four) at a time and each must be treated equally. However, the modern thinking is that one wife at a time is about all a husband can afford. In theory, with marriage and divorce so easy, a man could have as many wives as he fancies during his lifetime, but four marriages are typically the maximum. The custom is for a woman to marry young, 15 being the minimum legal age, but the age of first marriage is going up. The majority of marriages are between couples in the 20–24 years age group. This also constitutes the group with the highest number of divorces. In 1997, there were 2,450 marriages registered, and 1,277 divorces. There is a campaign to prevent the disintegration of families and family values. President Gayoom himself stresses in speeches that the partners in a marriage should resort to divorce only under certain conditions and when it is unavoidable, and that mere disagreements between two people do not warrant a divorce.

Couples are not allowed to live together without marriage and illegitimate children are rare. Adultery is an offence often punished by beating. Children of a finished marriage are provided for by the natural father, even when the mother remarries. Family units are large, with grandparents, parents and children living together, often with uncles, cousins and aunts in the same family compound. While many families have nearly a dozen children, the trend now is for smaller families. Family planning is encouraged by government-sponsored awareness programmes.

After the death of her husband, the widow is entitled by law to one-eighth of his property (see also *People*, page 35).

The marriage of foreign couples on special wedding holidays, such as takes place in some tropical countries like Barbados and Mauritius, does not happen in Maldives. There is no-one available to perform the ceremony for non-Muslims.

CIRCUMCISION This is a ritual for every Maldivian boy when he reaches six or seven years of age. The ceremony, with festivities that can last a week, takes place during the long school holiday beginning in December. It is held at the boy's home or at the home of a neighbouring boy since several boys are usually circumcised at the same time. There is lots of entertainment – games and music – while the boys lie with individual tent-like covers suspended over their private parts until recovered.

A lot of money – more than for a wedding – can be spent on this as it marks the most important moment in a boy's life. Female circumcision and coming-of-age rituals for girls are not practised.

BIRTH AND DEATH Birthdays are not usually commemorated or even remembered. By custom children are named when they are seven days old. On death, burial takes place within 24 hours. The traditional way is in a coffin which has a base of coir (coconut fibre) rope and wooden sides and top. On the 40th day after death, a special prayer is offered, followed by a feast. Every year after, prayer is observed on the anniversary of this day.

CLASS Maldivians are conservative. Although on the surface there is a constant state of change, with new buildings and new technologies, this as yet has had no effect on the fixed strata of society. There is no caste system but a complex class system does exist, and even the career opportunities in tourism have not opened up many channels for upward mobility.

DRESS The traditional dress of Maldivian women is both modest and attractive. Fashionable is the *faaskuri hedhun*, or *dhigu hedhun*, which is a long-sleeved dress reaching the ankles. It has a distinctive, wide scalloped collar. A headscarf, like a trailing veil and not covering the face, is worn with it. This is pinned to the hair and usually matches the hair's length. The dress is sometimes used as a uniform (such as by the airport check-in staff) or can be in discreetly patterned colours when used for recreation.

The modern man-about-Male' wears trousers and a shirt (with a tie if he is an office worker). Fishermen sport the traditional sarong (ankle-length cloth tied around the waist) which can be conveniently converted into a loincloth when necessary for fishing, wading in the water, etc.

According to a leaflet issued by the Department of Information and Broadcasting, older women prefer to wear a sarong-like wraparound skirt tucked around the waist and over it a long-sleeved dress of tropical colour that reaches just below the knee. The front and back of the neckline of this outfit are usually embroidered with fine lines of golden thread stitched in symmetrical form. The leaflet adds that the hair is combed in traditional style, to the right, 'wrapped in a piece of cloth and placed just above the right ear in the form of a bun'.

Returning again to Ibn Battuta (see above, page 27), he wrote during his travels of 1325–54:

> Their garments are simple aprons, one they tie round their waists in place of trousers, and on their backs they place other cloths resembling the pilgrims garments. Some wear a turban, others a small handkerchief instead. . . . Their women folk do not cover their hands, not even their queen does so, and they comb their hair and gather it at one side. Most of them wear only an apron from their waists to the ground, the rest of their bodies being uncovered. When I held the quadiship [local chieftain] there, I tried to put an end to this practice and ordered them to wear cloths, but I met with no success.

Women today are still to be seen very occasionally with their hair completely covered, with only the face peeping out of the Maldivian version of a wimple. The yashmak veil, concealing the whole of the face except the eyes, is not allowed as, by a recent law, people are prohibited from dressing in a manner that would conceal their identity.

Mostly nowadays, though, modern fashions are seen everywhere on the streets of Male': another sign of globalisation.

Footwear Sandals, thongs or rubber slippers are the best footwear on a resort island. In Male', too, footwear which can be removed easily is essential. Not only is it invariably removed before entering a mosque, the custom is to leave shoes outside before going into private houses or entering a carpeted office, to save tramping in lots of sand and mud. If there are a few pairs of sandals waiting outside a door, take that as a clue as to what to do. In village islands, sandal etiquette is very important. I have seen an island chief remove his sandals to walk across his linoleum-floored office and then put on another pair kept outside the door on the other side so he could walk straight out again. There are several shops in Male' specialising in footwear for both men and women, and the latest in sandals or formal footwear is readily (and reasonably) available.

Blue surgeonfish

Butterfly fish

2

Practical Information

WHEN TO GO

For brochure pictures of postcard-blue skies, go in the peak season months of mid December to mid March. The dry northeast monsoon (the islands, being on the Equator, are affected by monsoons, but not cyclones) of January–March is called *Iruvai* and, according to tradition, begins on 10 December and ends on 7 April. It brings hot days and cooler nights and usually clear skies. The atmosphere of the islands is noticeably balmier than during the southwest monsoon period.

The southwest monsoon (*Hulhangu*) brings some wet weather and blows from May to November. Tradition dates it from 8 April to 9 December. The good news is that it does not rain every day; the bad news is that strong winds and heavy rainfall can occur during those months.

To look on the bright side, summer in the Maldives is year long. If you have flown all that way to toast on the beach, a few hours of rain may briefly dampen your spirits, but there is something stimulating about a tropical shower, so count the experience as a bonus; without the rain there would be no lush vegetation. Be philosophical about it if you're marooned in a room at one end of an island, far from the bar at happy hour, and unable to get there because of a downpour. That's why there are umbrellas in each guestroom.

While many factors combine to create a holiday destination's peak season (weather at home is just as important as weather at the destination), the description 'peak season' obviously means that then is the best time to go. In the Maldives this is loosely defined by room rates as November–April. In May–October (except in August) room rates drop because demand is usually lower then.

In recent years, though, the pattern of occupancy has been changing. It used to be possible to arrive in the low season without a reservation and be assured of a room on the island of your choice. That is not necessarily so now. With the Maldives being marketed aggressively as a year-round destination, and with tourists from South Africa flocking there in their winter, the most popular resorts have full occupancy in the off-season too. The most popular month for tourists in 2007 was February when 65,224 visitor arrivals were logged; that's an average of almost 2,340 a day. Bookings at all resorts would be hard to get too at Christmas and in August, which encourages resorts to add a premium and a minimum stay requirement.

When to go? Whenever you feel like it.

HIGHLIGHTS

The obvious highlights of any trip to the Maldives are its underwater attractions and pristine beaches. Add to this the amenable climate for most of the year, speciality spas, good food, easy living and the grace of the people; what more do you need!

With over 90 resorts already open to choose from, there is something for everyone. Whether you are looking to relax or to join in the energetic pursuits in the water, the Maldives will have a place to suit your desires. The capital Male' is both a mellow town and an increasingly vibrant one. It is the only place where you will have a chance to meet and interact with the local people and their culture unless you fly on across the Equator to Gan.

For tourists staying at resorts far from Male', the missing link for the gregarious and curious will be the lack of a chance for independent interaction with non-tourist Maldivian culture.

TOUR OPERATORS

PACKAGE HOLIDAYS There are over 50 major tour operators throughout the world offering holidays in the Maldives. Before deciding to visit independently, check to see what is on offer, or let one of them arrange your holiday. If the tour operators in your home country do not have a holiday programme to suit you, you may prefer to deal directly with the resort or with tour operators in Male' (see below). At the time of writing, I couldn't find any travel operators in the USA or Canada who regularly organise tours or holidays in the Maldives so go through an experienced Male' agent.

Prices for package holidays naturally vary according to resort, grade of accommodation, whether meals and 'extras' are included, and the season chosen. Up-to-date prices will change; it is always worth shopping around.

Major tour operators
UK

Cosmos ✆ 0871 42 38 422; e cosmosairadmin@cosmos.co.uk; www.cosmos-holidays.co.uk
First Choice ✆ 0871 200 7799; www.firstchoice.co.uk
Hayes & Jarvis ✆ 0871 200 4422; e res@hayesandjarvis.co.uk; www.hayesandjarvis.co.uk
Kuoni ✆ 01306 747002; www.kuoni.co.uk
Maldive Travel ✆ 020 7352 2246; e maldives@dircon.co.uk; www.maldivetravel.com

Partnership Travel ✆ 0208 343 3446; www.partnershiptravel.co.uk
Somak ✆ 020 8423 3000; e holidays@somak.co.uk; www.somak.com
Thomas Cook ✆ 0870 750 5711; www.thomascook.com
Thomson ✆ 0871 231 4691; www.thomson.co.uk
Trailfinders ✆ 0845 050 5886; www.trailfinders.com

Elsewhere

Aitken Spence Sri Lanka; ✆ 011 2308021; www.aitkenspencetravels.com
Atitur Italy; ✆ 02 3041 2944; e info@aitur.com; www.atitur.com
Ceylon Tours Sri Lanka; ✆ 011 5531611, 2574589, 2565726; e info@ceylontours.com; www.ceylontours.com
ITS Reisen Germany; ✆ 02203 42 111; www.its.de
Grandi Viaggi Italy; ✆ 02 29046435, 06 85356850; e international@igrandiviaggi.it; www.igrandiviaggi.it
Hotelplan Italy; ✆ 02 721361; e info@hotelplan.it; www.hotelplan.it
Jet Tours France; ✆ 0 820 830 880; www.jettours.com
LTU Germany; ✆ 0211 9418 888; e serviceteam@airberlin.com; www.ltu.de

Neckermann Austria; ✆ 01 50 20 20; www.neckermann-reisen.at
Nouvelles Frontières France; ✆ 0825 000 747; www.nouvelles-frontieres.fr/nf
Qatar Airways ✆ +974 449 6000; www.qatarairways.com
Terres d'Aventure France; ✆ 0825 700 825; www.terdav.com
TUI Germany; ✆ 01805 884 266; e internet.service@tui.com; www.TUI.com
Vacanze Italy; www.vacanze.it
Valtur Italy; ✆ 02 300 99 811; e scrivi@valtur.it; www.valtur.it

Specialist dive operators A handful of UK-based tour operators run specialist diving tours to the Maldives, including the following:

Siân Pritchard-Jones and Bob Gibbons

Just a few days after our visit to update the third guide, the landscape of the Maldives was changed dramatically, and sadly fatally for some, by the tsunami which devastated much of southeast Asia and its beautiful coastlines. Despite being some 5,000km and three hours away from the epicentre of the earthquake that caused the tsunami, many of the tiny low-level islands were still seriously affected by the massive waves; around 100 people were killed and thousands were left homeless. Some islands disappeared under the sea, and nearly 40 of the then 198 inhabited islands were severely affected. Some suffered such serious damage to their infrastructure that it has been decided they are no longer habitable; their populations have been rehoused on other islands. It was estimated that the damage may be more than US$660 million, the country's annual GDP.

At the time there were 17,000 foreign tourists staying in the resorts, and 100 were injured, though more than half of the tourists remained to complete their holidays after the tsunami. Some British holidaymakers reported being up to their waists in the higher-level smoking area of a restaurant when the tsunami struck. Another reported being dragged down to 30m when out diving, but at least these people survived to tell the tale; others sadly lost their lives. When the tsunami first hit the most easterly island resorts, their management phoned the resorts further west and warned them, 'a big wave is on its way', so they were able to get their staff and guests to safety at a higher level. Nineteen resorts were damaged, and repairs and reconstruction took up to nine months; in several cases the resorts used the opportunity to upgrade their facilities. Four new resorts were under construction before the tsunami hit, so out of the 89 resorts in the Maldives then, 65 were in operation immediately after the tsunami. Politically the landscape changed too. Charges of treason against high-profile political dissenters were dropped soon after the tsunami struck, in an effort to unite people in the recovery effort. This was followed by the introduction of a multi-party democracy and proposals for major changes in the constitution.

Aquatours ℡ 020 8398 0505; e info@ aquatours.com; www.aquatours.com
Regal Dive Worldwide ℡ 01353 659 999; e info@regal-diving.co.uk; www.regal-diving.co.uk

Tony Backhurst Scuba Travel ℡ 0800 072 8221; e travel@scuba.co.uk; www.scuba.co.uk. Trips include exploring the wrecks of the Maldives.

Some local tour operators/travel agents *International dialling code: +960*

Maldives Tourism Promotion Board 3rd Floor, H Aage, 12 Boduthakurufaanu Magu, Male'; ℡ 3323228; f 3323229; e mtpb@visitmaldives.com; www.visitmaldives.com
AAA Travel & Tours Pvt Ltd STO Trade Centre, Male' 03 02; ℡ 3324933, 3322417; f 33314942; e trvlntrs@aaa.com.mv; www.aaatravel-maldives.com
Ace Travels Maldives H Agi, Male'; ℡ 3343510; f 3343511; e sales@acetravels.com.mv
Alhoa Maldives 2nd Floor, Ma Jawahiriyya Bldg, Chandhanee Magu, Male'; ℡ 3341951; f 3341953; e admin@alhoamaldives.com; www.alhoamaldives.com
Arrow Maldives Pvt Ltd Orchid Magu, Male'; ℡ 3336812; f 3323375; e info@ arrowmaldives.com; www.arrowmaldives.com

Capital Travel & Tours Pvt Ltd M Feylige/Iskandbaru Magu, Male'; ℡ 3315089; f 3320336; e capital@dhivehinet.net.mv; www.capitaltravel.com
Cross Asia Pvt Ltd H Threeklight, Sandhubaraka Goalhi, Male'; ℡ 3342960; f 3342961; e info@crossasiatravel.com; www.crossasiatravel.com
Crown Tours (Maldives) Pvt Ltd 6th Floor, Fasmeeru Bldg, Boduthakurufaanu Magu, Male'; ℡ 3322432; f 3312832; e ctours@dhivehinet.net.mv; www.crowntoursmaldives.com. Agents for Airtours & Trade winds.
Desire Maldives Travels & Tours Orchid Magu, Male'; ℡ 3331811; f 3318815; e info@desire-maldives.com; www.desire-maldives.com

Is the Maldives really a place for independent travel?

If all you want to do is sample the Maldives by visiting the capital Male', then the answer is yes. If you want to travel to inhabited islands freely and meet the local people, then the answer is no, unless you charter a safari vessel or spend a lot of money on internal flights.

The independent traveller in the Maldives is a rare creature and low-budget travellers can only visit as part of a low-cost holiday package, not independently. The lowest rate guest houses in Male' are occupied by expatriate labourers, while guest houses suitable for foreign tourists are in the range of US$65 a day for two, without meals. Food, however, in the cafés where locals eat is cheap – lunch could cost about US$2. Assuming you don't want to stay in a resort but would like to sample some tremendous underwater life, it is possible to go diving from Male'. Sea Explorers in Male' (page 120) can organise dives for independent visitors from around US$35–40 a dive, and there is no shortage of fascinating dive sites very close to the capital. The best way for an independent traveller to visit inhabited islands is to get in touch with someone like Mohamed Firaq of Inner Maldives Holidays (www.innermaldives.com) who can arrange it, at a cost.

Travellers willing to spend a bit more to stay on a resort island will need a minimum budget of US$65 per person sharing a double, for a room. The cost of meals and soft drinks even on the lowest rate resorts could add a further US$50 per person per day. Transfers to and from the resort islands closest to the airport will cost at least US$50 per person. The solution for the low-budget traveller is to pick a resort that has an 'all-inclusive' package. Visiting in high season, when resorts are often overbooked, seriously reduces the low-cost options and you simply cannot drop into a chosen resort unannounced. In any case, you need to have transport to the resorts and this has to be arranged with an advance reservation. The two local operators of seaplanes are contracted to resorts, and an individual cannot buy seats other than at the last minute, and then cannot stay at a resort without prior arrangement. Island Aviation fly independent passengers to the regional airports but accommodation needs to be booked in advance. Independent travellers can try hiring *dhonis* at the Male' waterfront but most

Dolphin Holidays Pvt Ltd 1st Floor, Maandhoo Villa, Bodufulha Goalhi, Male'; ℡ 9734989; f 3317239; e info@dolphin-holidays,com; www.dolphin-holidays.com

Ensis Cruise 5th Floor, M Westend, Handhuvaree Higun, Male'; ℡ 3331559; f 3331554; e cruise@ensistravel.com; www.ensiscruise.com

Floating Maldives M Dhon Alamaage, Shaheedh Ali Higun, Male'; ℡ 3342644; f 3342644; e info@floatingmaldives.com.mv; www.floatingmaldives.com.mv

Holidayplan Maldives Pvt Ltd H Lady Bird, Kasthoori Magu, Male'; ℡ 3320102; f 3313883; www.holidayp@dhivehinet.net.mv

Inner Maldives Holidays Pvt Ltd H Faalandhoshuge Aage, Ameer Ahmed Magu, Male'; ℡ 3315499; f 3330884; e intermal@dhivehinet.net.mv; www.innermaldives.com. Recognised by the world travel trade in 2007 with the award of 'The Indian Ocean's Leading Travel Agency.' Agents for Somak, Britannia, Thomson & Sri Lankan Airlines Holidays.

Intour Maldives Pvt Ltd 1st Floor, Gloryge, Fareedhee Magu, Male', Male'; ℡ 3339994; f 3339995; e info@intourmaldives.com; www.intourmaldives.com

Island Tours H Nooru, Violet Golbi, PO Box 20115, Male'; ℡ 3316232; f 3316325; www.islandtours.com.mv

Leisure Maldives 6th Floor, STO Aifaanu Bldg, PO Box 20111, Male'; ℡ 3314037; f 3314038; e info@leisure.com.mv; www.leisure.com.mv

Let's Go Maldives Pvt Ltd Male' 20 016; ℡ 3347755; f 3324513; e info@letsgomaldives.com; www.letsgomaldives.com

Marine Fauna Safari & Travel 2nd Floor, M Kurimaa, Sabudeli Magu, Male'; ℡ 3310941; f 3316153; e info@maldivescruise.com; www.maldivescruise.com

Moving International Pvt Ltd Ground Floor, Ma Aapiya, Kaaminee Magu, Male'; ℡ 3315798; f 3310264; e movinter@dhivehinet.net.mv; www.movinmaldives.com

will want to be paid for the whole day. Apart from islands very close to Male', it will take several hours by *dhoni* to reach most islands in North and South Male' atolls.

Although there might seem to be a deliberate, if unannounced, plan to discourage independent visitors and to keep things well ordered, there is not. Celebrities and the wealthy travel independently but they will have made advance arrangements for their preferred resort. Where 'independent traveller' means someone who wants a low-cost holiday, then the only way to do that is on a prepaid package holiday. Package tourists are the priority and everyone goes an extra mile to welcome such visitors to the Maldives.

'Although everyone we met in Male' was more than charming and friendly, actually finding ways to visit the islands other than through expensive options proved impossible,' write Siân and Bob. Don't expect to come to Male' and find people falling over to help you to get to inhabited islands in order to see normal villages and meet local people. Visiting Gan in the far south, for those willing to pay for the flights and to stay at the Equator Resort, is one way to see local life. However, Gan and its neighbouring islands, all linked by a magnificent new road, are not typical of the desert island image.

I maintain that the best way to meet Maldivians and find out independently about Maldives' society and lifestyle is to stay in Male'. There you can meet Maldivians from all the atolls. If the object is to see 'village' islands rather than interact with Maldivians, then I recommend chartering a safari boat which, since it costs from US$150 a day per person with accommodation, all meals, and cruising with local crew included, is a bargain. Safari boats anchor off designated village islands and visitors can go ashore. Be warned that inhabited islands are usually quite dull since the kids will be in school, the women inside and the men away working.

Independent travellers who make their own international flight arrangements can arrange through a local agent like Inner Maldives Holidays (see page 50) for accommodation in Male' and to stay at a few different resorts, with transfers included. The good news is that booking accommodation through a local agent is, incredibly, always cheaper than the rack rate a resort will quote an independent traveller.

Onboard Maldives 1st Floor, Gulfaam kuri, Keneree Magu, Male'; ☎ 3341608; f 3341609; e info@lastminutemaldives.com; www.lastminutemaldives.com

Paradise Holidays Pvt Ltd 1st Floor, 3/9 Star Bldg, Fareedhee Magu, Male'; ☎ 3312090; f 3312087; e parahol@dhivehinet.net.mv; www.parahol.com

Roomallot Pte Ltd Ma Kamini hiya, Kamini Magu, Male'; ☎ 3338621; f 3338622; e sales@roomallot.com; www.roomallot.com

Sea Dive (SEA) H Asfaam, Bodufunga du Magu, Male'; e seamaldives.com.mv; www.seamaldives.com.mv

Sea n See G Ocum Bldg, 2nd Floor, Hadheedhee, Male'; ☎ 3325634; f 3325633; e seansee@dhivehinet.net.mv; www.manthiri.com

Serena Spa Pvt Ltd M West End, Handhuvaree Higun, Male'; ☎ 3313866; f 3331083; e admin@serenaspa.com; www.serenaspa.com

Skorpion Travel Maldives H Hulhugalhi, 5th Floor, Karankaa Magu, Male'; ☎ 3327443; f 3327442;

e skorpion@dhivehinet.net.mv; www.skorpion-maldives.com

Star Tours Maldives 6th Floor, Moorithi Bldg, Chandhanee Magu, Male'; ☎ 3314595; f 3314617; e info@startoursmaldives.com.mv

Sultans Travel Ground Floor, Fasmeeru Bldg, 25 Boduthakurufaanu Magu, Male'; ☎ 3320330; f 3320440; e travel@sultansoftheseas.com; www.sultansoftheseastravel.com

Sunny Maldives H Haveeree Gulshan, Meheli Goalhi, Male'; ☎ 3338527; f 3338528; e sales@sunnymaldives.com; www.sunnymaldives.com

Sun Travel & Tours Pvt Ltd Meheli Goalhi, off Boduthakurufaanu Magu, Male'; ☎ 3325977; f 3320419; e info@sunholidays.com; www.sunholidays.com

Travellers World 2nd Floor, M Fahi Roalhi, Koarukendi Magu, Male'; ☎ 3343644; f 3328390; e info@travellersworld.com.mv; www.travellersworld.com.mv

Universal Enterprises Pvt Ltd 38/39 Orchid Magu, Male'; ☎ 3314873/4/5; f 3322678/3320274; e sales@unisurf.com; www.unisurf.com
Universal Resorts 39 Orchid Magu, PO Box 2015; ☎ 3323080/3322971; f 3325301; e sales@unient.com.mv; www.universalresorts.com. In UK ☎ 0845 230 0032.
Villa Hotels Villa Bldg, Ibrahim Hassan Didi Magu, PO Box 2073, 20–02 Male'; ☎ 3316161; f 3314565; e info@villahotels.com.mv; www.villahotels.com

Villa Travels & Tours H Siffa, Boduthakurufaanu Magu, Male'; ☎ 3330088; f 3312777; e info@villatravels.com; www.villatravels.com
Vista Company Pvt Ltd 4/3 Faamudheyrige, Faamudheyri Magu, Male'; ☎ 3320952; f 3318035; e vista@dhivehinet.net.mv; www.vistamaldives.com
Voyages Maldives Pvt Ltd Narugis Bldg, Chandhanee Magu, Male'; ☎ 3323617; f 3325336; e info@voyagesmaldives.com; www.voyagesmaldives.com

RED TAPE

ATTITUDE OF OFFICIALS This is so refreshing for anyone accustomed to officialdom in the region. Invariably I found officials prepared to help when approached with due respect and courtesy. Island chiefs were particularly hospitable. Since Maldivians generally lack the pomposity of self-importance and are not given to boasting, it is often a surprise to discover that the charming person you meet by chance is actually a local bigwig.

PASSPORTS AND VISAS It has only been necessary to have a passport to enter Maldives since 1978; now everyone must have one. Visas are not required in advance by any nationality, and a permit to stay for 30 days is issued to all arriving visitors free of charge. This takes the form of an entry stamp with date of entry, and an endorsement in red stating 'Employment Prohibited'.

VISA EXTENSIONS The Department of Immigration is in the Huravee Building on the left side heading east on Ameer Ahmed Magu, which is the road running parallel to the waterfront road in Male'. There is an information desk on the ground floor where they have the forms and details.

To apply for a visa extension, you need to pay Rf10 for a form, which must be stamped by your company or sponsor. Two photos are also required. The cost of the extension is then Rf750 for every three months (or less).

Extensions are granted to bona fide tourists, which is why it is helpful if a representative of the place (resort island or Male' guesthouse) where you are staying applies for the extension for you, as this is proof that you have accommodation. A valid airline ticket showing a confirmed date of departure is also required. Since most visitors hold credit cards, proof of funds (the minimum is US$25 per day) is rarely required, as long as your accommodation is assured. Your entry visa will be extended to the date 90 days after the date of arrival stamped in your passport, even if you only want a few extra days.

The issue of the extension visa can take five days but, in an emergency, it can be done in 24 hours. If you want to apply yourself, start early in the morning (08.00) but it really is better – and preferred by the immigration authorities – if a Maldivian does it for you.

In the same building, there is a post office counter with a fast post service and a photocopy booth on the ground floor.

WORK AND RESIDENCE PERMITS It is possible for a foreigner to work in the Maldives and some visitors do fulfil their dream of staying on a tropical island for longer than just a holiday. Of course, it's necessary to have a skill that is in demand and probably not available locally. One profession forbidden to Maldivians, and therefore open to foreigners, is that of barman. Most barmen come from Sri Lanka or India.

Windsurfing and diving instructors are mostly foreigners, from Europe or Japan, and there are many foreign tourist guides, although they are recruited overseas.

When a foreigner visits Maldives on holiday and manages to find a job, he or she has to leave the country (to Sri Lanka is the usual choice) while the prospective employer gets the work permit. Foreign nationals can be employed only with permission from the Ministry of Human Resources, Employment and Labour. The Department of Immigration and Emigration must be informed 48 hours in advance of the foreigner's impending arrival to work. An application for a resident visa must be submitted to the department within seven days of the work permit being issued.

The intended working resident has to undergo a medical, which includes a blood test. If this is passed successfully, an identification card, with the employee's photograph on it, is eventually issued, stating the job description, sometimes a little eccentrically. A friend of mine, employed as a cruise director on a small cruise ship, found he was designated as 'Hostess'.

The employer of a foreign national must be approved to employ a foreigner and 'must bear all costs relating to an expatriate employee's subsistence, sustenance and maintenance, additional costs included in the contract of employment, repatriation costs, forced or otherwise, and costs relating to the employee being deceased'.

The dependent spouse of an expatriate employee may also be allowed gainful employment. Any valid work permit must be officially cancelled if the holder leaves the Maldives before his term of contract has expired. If an employee goes on leave, he must present immigration with a letter from his employer saying he has permission to leave the island: rather demeaning if you are actually the foreign owner of your own company and, hence, your own employer. In that case you'll need a letter from a fellow director. Any expatriate who quits Maldives without the employer's consent cannot be re-employed in Maldives for a period of three years.

There are government-approved contracts of employment for skilled and unskilled workers, and for domestic servants, which include provision of board and lodging and 20 days' paid leave after 12 calendar months of employment. Tax, fees, and fines regarding work permit, visa and residence permit are paid by the employer. All expatriate employees must agree to a clause which states: 'The employee shall at all times confirm to obey, respect and not violate the laws and regulations, religion and customs of the Republic of Maldives.'

The potential for gainful self-employment for a foreigner with a needed skill does exist, but sponsorship by an established Maldivian partner for the work and residence permit is necessary. Since accommodation is in very short supply, a big problem would be finding somewhere affordable to live.

PERMITS TO VISIT VILLAGE ISLANDS The term 'village islands' is used to describe islands which are inhabited. There are 200 of them in the 19 administrative atoll units. Individual permits are not required to visit village islands as part of an organised day excursion from a neighbouring resort in the same atoll, nor as a passenger of a cruise/safari ship licensed to operate in Maldivian waters. But a permit is absolutely necessary for visiting any island 'off the beaten track', which means in the atolls which are not a tourist zone. A permit is not necessary to visit, or stay overnight in, Male', nor for Gan in Seenu Atoll. Permits should be obtained from the office of the Ministry of Atolls Administration which is on the waterfront in Male'.

It is only possible to get a permit if you have a local sponsor, so it is better to let your Maldivian contact apply on your behalf. To make such a contact, discuss your intentions with a local travel agent. It is no good going to where the inter-atoll vessels tie up opposite the fish market and trying to buy passage on one of them. The skipper will not take you without someone to vouch for you, and anyway, the vessel for your trip will be arranged by your local contact.

The easiest way to visit village islands is to take a cruise or to charter a vessel licenced by the Ministry of Tourism for diving or sightseeing safaris. Such vessels have berths, which solves the problem of where to sleep on a village island where you have no contacts. The vessels also levy the nightly head tax (US$8) payable by every tourist visiting the Maldives. The charter company will arrange the permit. The same permit is needed even if you only plan to visit genuinely uninhabited islands outside the tourist zones. For that, written permission must first be obtained from the owner or leaseholder of the uninhabited island, something the chartered vessel's skipper will arrange.

Although the penalty for travelling to the islands without a permit is only a relatively modest fine, it would be most irresponsible to take a chance, since the consequences for the local sponsor, including the skipper of any vessel in which the foreigner without a permit travels, could be severe.

The permit has to be produced to the island office immediately after arrival on each island. It becomes a wonderful souvenir of the trip as each island chief puts his seal, with the Maldives' crest and island name, and signature, all most beautifully scripted in Dhivehi, together with the date, on the back of the permit.

Permits can be obtained from the Faashanaa Building next to the police station in Male'. Let your sponsor do this since a letter from him will also be required, as well as a photocopy of your passport including the entry stamp pages. Permits are normally issued on the day of application.

FURTHER INFORMATION The tour operators who offer holidays in the Maldives have up-to-date information on the resorts they sell, as well as on general conditions in the Maldives. Specific questions about the resorts should be addressed to the general managers (best by fax or email), using the details given in the resort reports.

The **Maldives Tourism Promotion Board** (MTPB) has been set up to promote the Maldives as a holiday destination (see page 49). Information can be obtained by contacting the MTPB at Male' (*20–05, Maldives; ⟍ 3323228; f 3323229;* e *mtpb@visitmaldives.com; www.visitmaldives.com*). Personal visitors will find their questions answered eagerly there, and MTPB also has a good supply of attractive literature including an excellent (and free) book, *Maldives Visitor's Guide*, with photographs and details of all the resorts, together with extensive information on safari and local cruise ships.

Potential visitors to the Maldives who are in London during November could meet Maldivians during the public open days at the annual World Travel Market. Representatives of MTPB and resort managers, who attend the fair to promote the Maldives to the travel trade, are also available to members of the public who wish to learn more about the islands.

The MTPB maintains one office abroad, in Germany (*Maldives Tourist Promotion Board, Bethmannstrasse, 58, 60311 Frankfurt/Main, Germany; ⟍ +49 69 2740 4420; f +49 69 2740 4422;* e *maldivesinfo.ffm@t-online.de; www.visitmaldives.com*).

Information can also be obtained from individual travel agents in the Maldives (see pages 49–52) and from the offices of the honorary consuls and other representatives abroad (see below). The Maldives mission to the United Nations (also listed below) performs this function in North America.

Ⓔ EMBASSIES

HONORARY CONSULS IN MALE' Consular representatives do not exist as 'minders' or information bureaux, especially in Maldives, where many provide a country's representation on a part-time and informal basis. Consuls will help in an emergency, but repatriation to your home country at your government's expense is not one of the services you can expect them to provide.

Austria Mr Ali Noordeen, Universal Enterprises, 39 Orchid Magu, PO Box 20-15, Male'; ☎ 3322971; f 3322678; e sales@unient.com.mv

Bangladesh High Commission Hithah Finivaa Magu, Male'; ☎ 3315541

Denmark Mr Adbullah Saeed, 25 Boduthakurufaanu Magu, Male'; ☎ 3315175; f 3322523; e cyprea@dhivehinet.net.mv

Finland Mr Adbullah Saeed, 25 Boduthakurufaanu Magu, Male'; ☎ 3315176; f 3323523; e cyprea@dhivehinet.net.mv

France Mr Ismail Wafir, H Madhoo, 2nd Floor, Male'; ☎ 3320002; f 3317254; e galaxy@dhivehinet.mv

Germany Dr Ibrahim Maniku, Universal Enterprises, 39 Orchid Magu, PO Box 20-15, Male'; ☎ 3322971; f 3322678; e sales@unient.com.mv

India High Commission, Ameer Ahmed Magu, Male'; ☎ 3323015

Netherlands Mr Sanjay Bansal, 3rd Floor, STO Aifaanu Bldg, Boduthurufaanu Magu, Male'; ☎ 3323609; f 3322380; e dutchcon@klm.com.mv

New Zealand Mr Ahmed Saleem, 6th Floor, Fasmeeru Bldg, Boduthakurufaanu Magu, Male'; ☎ 3322432; f 3324009; e saleem@crowncompany.com

Norway Mr Abdullah Saeed, 25 Boduthakurufaanu Magu, Male'; ☎ 3315176; f 3323523; e cyprea@dhivehinet.net.mv

Pakistan High Commission, Lily Magu, Male'; ☎ 3323005

Russia Mr Mohamed Mahir Didi, Universal Enterprises, 39 Orchid Magu, PO Box 20-15, Male'; ☎ 3323080; f 3322678; e sales@unient.com.mv

Sri Lanka High Commission, Medhuziyaaraiy Magu, Male'; ☎ 3322845

Sweden Mr Abdullah Saeed, 25 Boduthakurufaanu Magu, Male'; ☎ 3315174; f 3323523; e cyprea@dhivehinet.net.mv

Turkey Mr Ismail Hilmy, 2nd Floor, H Aage, Boduthakurufaanu Magu, Male'; ☎ 3322719; f 3323463

UK c/o Dhiraagu Pvt Ltd, 19 Medhuziyaaraiy Magu, PO Box 2082, Male'; ☎ 3311218; f 3317981

MALDIVES REPRESENTATIVES ABROAD

Germany Maldives Tourism Promotion Board Bethmannstrasse 58, 60311 Frankfurt/Main, Germany; ☎ +49 69 2740 4420; f +49 69 2740 4422; e maldivesinfo.ffm@t-online.de; www.visitmaldives.com

India High Commission of Maldives in India, E-45 Greater Kailash – II, New Delhi – 110048; ☎ +91 1 51435701; f +91 11 51435709

Singapore Maldives Government Trade Representative, 10 Anson Rd, No 18–11 International Plaza, Singapore 079903; ☎ +65 6225 8955, 6225 6750; f +65 6224 6050; e Maldives@cyberway.com.sg

Sri Lanka High Commission of Maldives in Sri Lanka, 23 Kavirathna Pl, Colombo 6; ☎ +94 11 5516302; f +94 11 581200; e enquiries@maldiveshighcom.lk

UK High Commission of Maldives in UK, 22 Nottingham Pl, London W1U 5NJ; ☎ +44 207 224 2135; f +44 207 224 2157; e maldives.high.commission@virgin.net

United Nations Permanent Mission of Maldives to UN, 800 Second Av, Suite 400-E, New York, NY 10017; ☎ +1 212 599 6195; f +1 212 661 6405; e maldives@un.int; www.un.int/maldives

HONORARY CONSULS

Australia Mr Linton R Lethlean, Box 135, North Melbourne 3051; ☎ +61 3 9349 1473; f +61 3 9349 1119; e linton@austarmetro.com.au

Austria Mr Gerald Weidler, Weimarerstrasse 104, A-1190 Vienna; ☎ +43 1 369 664430; f +43 1 369 664430; e einkauf@weidler.com

Belgium Mr Frederic Edward Drion, Clos des Genets 17, 1325 Chaumont Gistoux; ☎ +32 1068 9212; f +32 1068 9213; e frederic.drion@euronet.be

France Dr Jacques Philipe Laboureau, 6 rue du Docteur Maret, BP 22290, 21022 Dijon, Cedex; ☎ +33 0 49 36 63 470; f +33 0 49 36 63 059; e jp.laboureau@wanadoo.fr

Germany Mr Gottfried Mucke, Immanuel Kant Strasse 16, D-61350, Bad Homburg; ☎ +49 61 72 867833; f +49 61 72 867833

Greece Mr Stavros C Galanakis, 167 Saronidas-Anavissou Av, Anavissos; ☎ +30 210 42 24 220; f +30 210 41 73 728; e stgalanakis@elvictor.com

Hong Kong Mr Bob P Harilela, 201-5 Kowloon Centre, Kowloon; ☎ +852 2376 2114; f +852 2376 2366

India Mumbai/Bombay Mr Asif Sultan Nathani, 212-A Maker Bhavan No 3, New Marine Lines, Mumbai 400 020; ☎ +91 22 2207 8041; f +91 22 2209 6507; e maldives@vsnl.com; Kolkata/Calcutta Mr

Chandra Shekhar Jaisal, Hastings Chambers, 7C Kiran Shankar Roy Rd, Kolkata 700 001; ✆ +91 33 248 5400; f +91 33 248 5750; e avksoat@ cal2vsnl.net.in; *Chennai/Madras* Mr Manikam Ramaswami, Loyal Textile Mills Ltd, 22 Anna Salai, Chennai 600 002; ✆ +91 44 841 4577; f +91 44 859 4454; e loyal@vsnl.com **Japan** Mr Isao Tsukamoto, Century Tower, Hongo 2-2-9 Bunkyo-Ku, Tokyo 113-85047; ✆ +81 3 4455 3144; f +81 3 3815 6757

Russia Dr Vladimir N Sautov, 23A-9 Povarskaya Street, Moscow 121069; ✆ +7 095 203 6854; f +7 095 203 6854; e fund@asean-russia.ru; www.asean-russia.ru
Thailand Mr Sanan Angubolkul, 355 Suksawat Rd, Soi 36, Rasburana, Bangkok 10140; ✆ + 662 428 9292; f +662 428 9293; e maldives_thailand@sritahi.co.th
Turkey Mr Nihat Boytuzan, Chumhuriyet Cad No 257/1, Harbiye 80230, Istanbul; ✆ +90 212 231 0189; f +90 212 230 3697; e nihatboytuzun@turk.net

For other Maldivian representation see www.presidencymaldives.gov.mv.

GETTING THERE AND AWAY

✈ **BY AIR** With the increasing popularity of the Maldives as a holiday resort, getting there by direct flight is becoming easier, and from many countries which do not have scheduled airline connections, a charter flight is included in the holiday package.

Scheduled services are offered by several international carriers. The main airlines are Emirates, Qatar, Sri Lankan, Malaysian and Singapore.

Sri Lankan operate non-stop scheduled flights to Male' from London at the weekends, otherwise carriers from Europe require a change of aircraft, usually somewhere in the Middle East. Sri Lankan also have regular flights from London, Paris, Frankfurt, Singapore and Tokyo to Colombo for onwards flights to Male'.

Qatar fly to Male' from Doha, with connections from London/Manchester/Paris/Frankfurt and Rome. **Emirates** has the most connections from Europe, Africa and the USA with a stopover of two or three hours and a change of aircraft in Dubai. **Aeroflot** flies from Moscow. **Austrian**, **Balkan**, **Lauda Air**, **Condor** and **LTU** have flights in season from Europe with non-stop (nine-hour) flights by LTU (from Berlin, Düsseldorf, Frankfurt, Hamburg, Hanover and Stuttgart) or by Condor (from Cologne, Frankfurt and Munich). Charter flights have recently been introduced from European cities direct to Gan, the new international airport serving the deep south of Maldives.

From India there are flights from several cities with Sri Lankan (with over 100 flights a week to/from India) via Colombo to Male'. Sri Lankan operates one or two flights a day between Colombo and Male' and there are also Emirates and low-cost Mihin Air flights linking Colombo and Male'. In January 2008, the Maldivian airline, Island Aviation, began flights linking Male' with Trivandrum in southern India. **From the Far East** and **Southeast Asia**, there are flights with Sri Lankan from Tokyo, Bangkok, Kuala Lumpur and Singapore, with a change of flight in Colombo. Singapore has a daily non-stop flight between Singapore and Male', which is a convenient way to reach the islands from the USA and the Orient. Bangkok Air, from Bangkok, Viva Macau from Macau and Jazeera Air from Kuwait also operate flights to/from Male'. There are also charter flights by airlines such as Air Italy, Belair, Condor, Edelweiss, Eurofly, First Choice, Hungarian, Livingston, LTU, Martinair Netherlands, Monarch, My Travel, Neos Spa, Star Airlines, Transareo and Volare Spa, but not all are non-stop.

The easiest option is to see your travel agent and buy a package holiday that includes flight and accommodation on an island resort. That will probably work out cheaper than doing it yourself. **From North and South America or Australasia**, flying via Singapore or Dubai is probably the best option. **From**

London and **other European cities**, the full-price airfares are higher than you would expect.

When planning to fly to a destination, a good way to check which airlines go there from your starting point is to find out which airlines leave the destination (see the list below). This gives a clearer picture of the air links and helps to plot a particularly interesting or convenient route. Unfortunately, travel agents tend to punch computer keys and quote what the screen shows them, ignoring the flight possibilities that a little timetable research and a world atlas could reveal.

Airline represented in Male' The following do not all fly to Male' but do have offices there.

Air Sahara Paradise Holidays, 1st Floor, Star Bldg, Fareedhee Magu; ✆ 3312090

Air Seychelles, Austrian Airlines, Cathay Pacific, Balkan Air, Condor, Lufthansa, LTU Charters Airline Division, Universal Enterprises, 38 Orchid Magu; ✆ 3334004

Aeroflot Intourist Maldives, 7th Floor, Fasmeeru Bldg, Boduthakurufaanu Magu; ✆ 3325273

Bangkok Airways Surf Travel, H Faalandhoshuge, Ameer Ahmed Magu; ✆ 3317117

British Airways Voyage Maldives, Narangis, Chandhanee Magu; ✆ 3327737

Edelweiss Voyages Maldives, Chandhanee Magu; ✆ 3322019

Emirates Ground Floor, ADK Tower, Ameer Ahmed Magu; ✆ 3315465

EuroFly Villa Travel, 1/12 Boduthakurufaanu Magu; ✆ 3330088

Indian Airlines Cyprea Travel Dep, Ground Floor, Gadhamoo Bldg, Boduthakurufaanu Magu; ✆ 3310111

KLM Royal Dutch Airlines 3rd Floor, STO Aifaanu Bldg; ✆ 3323069

Lauda Air Galaxy Enterprises, Boduthakurufaanu Magu; ✆ 3330311

Malaysia Air Systems Villa Travel, Shifa Boduthakurufaanu Magu; ✆ 3332555

Livingston Galaxy Enterprises, Boduthakurufaanu Magu; ✆ 3330311

Martinair Netherlands Speed Services, 3rd Floor, STO Aifaanu Bldg; ✆ 3323069

Mihin Air Mack Air Services, 4th Floor, STO Aifaanu Bldg, Boduthakurufaanu Magu; ✆ 3334708

Monarch Airways Voyages Maldives, Chandhanee Magu; ✆ 3322019

My Travel Airways Villa Travels, 1/12 Boduthakurufaanu Magu; ✆ 3330088

Royal Jordanian Jenin Agency, in Chandhanee Magu; ✆ 3327631

Qatar Airways 2nd Floor, STO Aifaanu Building, Boduthakurufaanu Magu; ✆ 3334777

Singapore Airlines Sunland Travel, 1st Floor, Gadhamoo Bldg, Boduthakurufaanu Magu; ✆ 3310031

Sri Lankan Airlines (PSA) Inner Maldives Holidays, H Faalandhoshuge Aage, Ameer Ahmed Magu; ✆ 3315499; f 3330884

Volare Airlines Voyages Maldives, Chandhanee Magu; ✆ 3327737

Viva Macau Inner Maldives Holidays, H Faalandhoshuge Aage, Ameeeru Ahmed Magu; ✆ 3315499

Finding a cheap flight There are alternatives to paying the full standard fare, but since Maldives is not served by lots of competing airlines, and because it is not on the way to anywhere else, finding cheaper fares is not as easy as for some destinations. Nevertheless, a good travel professional, even relying on the computer, should be able to come up with some offers. If none of these ways of obtaining a ticket to the Maldives is suitable, consider flying to Colombo first (whether from the USA, the Far East, Australia or Europe) and getting a second ticket there. You can buy tickets at the Sri Lankan Airlines counter outside Colombo Airport and Sri Lankan and Emirates operate more than 20 flights a week between Colombo and Male'.

Getting a flight that lets you feel as if you've got a good deal is difficult with such a popular destination as the Maldives. Getting the lowest price will require a lot of internet research and several phone calls and may result in some rather complicated routing for the journey.

From the UK

Airline Network ☎ 0800 747 000; www.airline-network.co.uk. Mostly holidays but some flights to Asia.

Brightsun Travel ☎ 0871 4242422; e info@ brightsunuk.co.uk; www.brightsunuk.com. Sells tickets for Emirates Airlines which serves the Maldives.

City Vacations Vacation Hse, 374 Cranbrook Rd, Gants Hill, Ilford, Essex IG2 6HW; ☎ 0870 242 0241; www.cityvacations.co.uk. Sell Qatar & Emirates air tickets, among others.

Ebookers ☎ 0871 223 5000; www.ebookers.com. Has flights worldwide with some Indian Ocean specials.

Dial a Flight ☎ 0870 333 3377; www.dialaflight.com. Offers air tickets for over 300 airlines & also books hotels.

Flight Centre ☎ 0870 499 0040; www.flightcentre.co.uk. An independent flight provider

with over 450 outlets worldwide. Also has offices in Australia, New Zealand, South Africa & Canada.

Quest Travel ☎ 0845 263 6963; www.questtravel.com. Has 4 offices.

Trailfinders ☎ 0845 058 5858; www.trailfinders.com. Has several offices around the UK. The main office is in London at 194 Kensington High St, London W8 7RG. Trailfinders now provides a one-stop travel service including visa & passport service, travel clinic & foreign exchange.

Travelbag ☎ 0800 804 8911; www.travelbag.co.uk. Provides tailor-made flight schedules & holidays for destinations throughout the world.

Wexas ☎ 020 7589 3315; e mship@wexas.com; www.wexas.com. More of a club than a travel agent. Membership is from £78 a year but for frequent fliers the benefits are many.

From the USA

Airtech e fly@airtech.com; www.airtech.com. Stand-by seat broker that also deals in consolidator fares, courier flights & a host of other travel-related services.

Around the World Travel ☎ +1 800 766 3601; e admin@netfare.net; www.netfare.net. Provides fares for destinations throughout the world.

Flight Centre ☎ +1 866 967 5351; www.flightcentre.com or www.flightcentre.us

STA Travel ☎ +1 800 781 4040; www.statravel.com (for worldwide offices & information). Has several branches around the country.

Worldtek Travel 111 Water St, New Haven, CT 06511; ☎ +1 800 243 1723 or ☎ +203 772 0470; e info@worldtek.com; www.worldtek.com. Operates a network of rapidly growing travel agencies. Contact details above for your nearest office.

From Canada

Flight Centre ☎ +1 877 967 5302; www.flightcentre.ca

Travel CUTS ☎ (toll free) +1 866 416 2887; www.travelcuts.com. A Canadian student travel

organisation with 60 offices throughout Canada. Call the telephone sales centre for your nearest branch.

From Australia

Flight Centre 157 Ann St, Brisbane, Queensland 4000; ☎ (toll free) +61 133 133; www.flightcentre.com.au. Over 200 stores in Australia.

From New Zealand

Flight Centre ☎ +64 0800 243544; www.flightcentre.co.nz

STA Travel ☎ +64 0800 474 400; www.statravel.co.nz

From South Africa

Flight Centre ☎ +27 0860 400 727; www.flightcentre.co.za. In Johannesburg & Cape Town.

STA Travel ☎ +27 0861 781 781; www.statravel.co.za

Airport formalities

Arrivals After a long-haul overnight flight, the warmth as you step out of the aircraft onto the tarmac of the Male' International Airport will envelop you like an affectionate embrace.

If you had a window seat, you would have wondered where the plane was going to land, since all you see from the air are tiny islands and the sea. The runway was built by flattening Hulhule island, ten minutes from Male', and extending it both ways into the sea. From Male' itself, it looks as if the jets are floating on the Indian Ocean as they taxi along the runway.

Airport Construction to expand passenger facilities at the Male' International Airport has been underway since before the third edition of this guide was published. While minor modifications were continuing at press time, there have been major improvements to make the flow of passengers and baggage swifter and more pleasant. The departure terminal has an extended smart 'duty-free' section and what are described as 'three gate launches' to reach the aircraft. A new control tower, air-traffic services building and a powerhouse have also been constructed. In addition, a separate domestic terminal for fixed-wing aircraft has been built adjoining the international terminal.

Passengers are bused or walk from the aircraft to the arrivals hall, where the informality of the Maldives is immediately apparent. Before the barrier of immigration counters, there are toilets. Since queues for passport checking will be long (unless you are lucky to be among the first off the plane) and you may have a long voyage on a vessel without facilities ahead of you, this could be a good chance to use the loo.

If you haven't been given an embarkation card on the plane, look for one on the ledge that runs along the length of the arrivals hall. The card itself is in three sections, of which the first is actually the Exit Card. Once stamped, this section is clipped to your passport to surrender on departure. Don't lose it.

The Entry Card requires more details, including name, date of birth, place of issue of passport, country of residence, etc. All independent visitors should give a hotel name in Male' for their address in Maldives. That is where you must be careful. If you are arriving without a reservation and you leave the space blank you may be told by the immigration officer to go out of the arrivals hall to the tourist reception area beyond customs and find a place to stay. The passport will be returned to you only when you have confirmed somewhere. You are recommended either to enter that choice in the appropriate place, then find somewhere you want to stay once in Male' (or a resort through a local agent) or to select an address from this guidebook, and reserve your first night in advance.

Immigration officers may ask to see your return ticket, and if you are an independent visitor they may even ask how much money you have, but they seldom check the amount. Passport details are scanned. Sometimes the health section of the card is scrutinised. There have been tales of passengers who seem to be health risks being marched off to be vaccinated, so carry proof of vaccinations if you are coming from dodgy parts.

Because of the wait for the immigration process, your luggage might be ready before you are. There are luggage trolleys that you can use from here right up to the boat jetty, but no porters. There are no red and green channels in customs; everyone is checked, but this is done by X-ray machine, for your luggage. You may be asked to open your luggage for hand inspection if the X-ray scan reveals something dubious, like a bottle in your bag. The importation of alcohol is not allowed and any alcohol will be detained by customs and put into bond for you to collect on departure. But you could have a problem (see page 60).

After leaving the customs hall there is a tourist information counter and bank before the exit doors. Make sure you bring some dollars in cash if you intend going to Male' independently, or to change some into local currency if the bank counter is open.

Representatives of the various tour operators and resorts will be waiting for you outside the doors with boards showing either your name or the name of the resort they represent. There is no shouting or hassles and it's all rather informal and cheerful. If you come out quickly after your arrival, the rep probably won't be there so look for the counters of the various resorts. There the reps will arrange transfer to your resort, or to Male'.

However, the resort rep may ask you to wait at a table in the café courtyard while he gathers other guests bound for the same resort. Then he will lead you to the jetty for the boat transfer. Guests flying to their resorts will be escorted to the domestic terminal or to the seaplane check-in desks for the bus ride to the seaplane jetty at the other side of the runway.

Even though the seaplane flight might take only 30 minutes, expect a wait of a couple of hours before boarding (see page 204).

Customs allowances Passengers, irrespective of age, are allowed to bring in 'a reasonable amount of cigarettes, tobacco or cigars' and a reasonable quantity of gifts. There is no restriction on the import or export of foreign currency or Maldivian rufiyaas.

A notice on the back of the immigration entry card states:

> Customs authorities remind you that following items should not be imported by passengers at all: alcoholic drinks of any quantity, dogs, pigs or pork, statues used for worship, nude or pornographic material, gun powder or explosive, weapons and fire arms, opium, ganja, cocaine, all other narcotic items that could be used as intoxicants.

See also *What not to take*, page 70.

Departures The resort where you are staying will arrange transfer to the airport, getting you there at least two hours before the flight's scheduled departure. When you arrive at Hulhule, the airport island, a resort rep will be on hand to give any assistance required and to tell you when, and to show you where, to join the line into the departure terminal.

Luggage trolleys are available by the landing piers, and can be wheeled into the terminal. On the left of the entrance is a post office counter and a souvenir shop. There is a snack-bar counter and plenty of places to sit in the roofed but open-sided area (not air conditioned) outside the entrance to the departure terminal. There is also a small play area for children. Passengers, once checked in for their flights, are sometimes allowed to return to this area to wait for departure but must undergo security screening to re-enter the departure terminal.

Your baggage will be X-rayed by security staff before you are allowed into the terminal. Sometimes there will be a customs search, too. It is unwise as well as irresponsible to try to export turtleshell or black-coral products.

After the security X-ray, you head for the check-in desks. There are separate desks for economy and business-class passengers, where you will receive baggage receipts and a boarding pass. You are not allowed to take luggage trolleys upstairs to immigration, so keep hand baggage manageable. Entrance to immigration and the departure lounge is up the escalators to the right.

Flight information For flight information at Male' International Airport, the local phone number is ✆ 3322211.

Immigration and bond storage The next stage is immigration, where the Exit Card will be removed and your passport stamped. After immigration, and before security at the departure-hall entrance, is a counter where you can claim anything removed from you by customs on arrival and held in bond for your departure. However, since you will not be allowed to take liquid on to the aircraft (unless it is purchased from and sealed by the airport duty-free shop) you will have to forgo any bottles of alcohol confiscated from you on arrival.

Departure hall After checking-in on the lower level, passengers proceed to the upper-level departure hall to await flights. This is a spacious and pleasant area with a snack bar (and a smoking room) with picture windows overlooking aircraft on the apron. There is a mall of duty-free shops including one selling liquor and another with perfumes, one with local confectionery, as well as souvenir and electronic shops.

There is a separate lounge for business-class passengers of subscribing airlines. Soft drinks, pot soups and snacks (but no alcohol) are available from a self-service counter. There are computer stations and a flat-screen television broadcasting world news.

Passengers file down to the lower level for a final security check of hand luggage and a brief body frisk before being allowed to the boarding gate lounge area. There is a separate smoking room and toilets, and a hall of seats in front of the funnels to departure gates where boarding cards are checked. Passengers walk across the tarmac to board planes, although buses are used for transfer if it is raining heavily.

Visitors Friends who come to the airport to see you off, or anyone not flying, must purchase a permit to visit Hulhule, from the security hut at the entrance to the airport complex after leaving the piers. This does not allow entrance to the terminal itself, but it is possible, in special circumstances, to buy a permit to enter the landside of the terminal building.

BY SEA Although most people will travel everywhere by sea when they are in the Maldives, getting there by sea from another country is no longer the way to do it. Up to the 1970s, access was only by sea, but now there is not enough demand, even for a passenger vessel to operate from Colombo. Of course, there are plenty of cargo vessels – you will see dozens anchored in the roads outside Male' – but they do not take paying passengers.

Cruise liners do visit occasionally (as *Silver Cloud* will in 2009), but none calls in on a regular basis. The prospect of some 2,000 cruise passengers descending on Male' is rather daunting and none of the resorts could cope with such an influx of visitors at once. However, organised cruising through the atolls and around the islands by small, chartered vessels for about ten passengers, or by the mini-cruise ship *Atoll Explorer*, has become very popular. (See *Cruising* in *Chapter 4*, page 115.)

Maldives is not on the usual yacht circuit, though visiting yachts do call occasionally on their way from Sri Lanka. (In Sri Lanka, look for them in Galle.) If you come on your own yacht, you must first check with the authorities in Male', both for customs clearance and for permission to visit anywhere other than tourist resorts. There is a yacht marina at the Island Hideaway Resort in the north of the archipelago.

HEALTH *with Dr Felicity Nicholson*

When you consider the number of jabs you need to go to India or Sri Lanka, which are not far from Maldives, it is a relief that a holiday here requires very little medical planning.

BEFORE YOU GO The Embarkation–Disembarkation card carries this warning, actually printed on the back of the Entry Card – which you don't keep, so the information won't be available if you need it:

Health Authorities Remind You You are requested to produce your vaccination certificate upon arrival. During your stay in Maldives if you experience symptoms of infectious disease (high fever, diarrhoea with vomiting or skin rashes) please contact Port Health and report immediately to the Government Hospital, Male', for treatment. Kindly share our concern to control the importation of diseases.

Attached to the Entry Card is a counterfoil, called a Health Card, which requires you to give details of the countries visited in the 14 days before your arrival in Male'.

It is vital that, if you are coming from a yellow fever area (eg: sub-Saharan Africa and South America), you should be able to prove you have had a yellow fever vaccination; hence the need for the certificate or an exemption certificate if the vaccine is contraindicated. Otherwise it is unlikely to be asked for unless you are coming from a high health-risk area.

It is also recommended that the following **vaccines** should be taken at least two weeks prior to travel: diphtheria, tetanus, polio, typhoid and hepatitis A. None of these are required for entry into the country but most health officials advise protection if there is sufficient time.

If you are planning to tour the atolls, where cleanliness and hygiene standards may be lower than in the resorts, and you are not accustomed to life in the tropics, then you may feel more comfortable having had a course of vaccinations as recommended by your local doctor at home.

Although it is claimed that malaria has been eradicated from the Maldives, it is still wise to use an insect repellent and cover-up clothing from dusk until dawn. Repellents should also be used if mosquitoes are seen in the day, to prevent other diseases such as dengue fever and Chikungunya. In any case repellents will help to protect you from uncomfortable bites. Since malaria is a very resistant bug, ask your GP for the latest advice before departure.

Bring whatever prescription drugs and contraceptives you need, as you may not see a shop, apart from resort boutiques, unless you visit Male'.

Holiday medical **insurance** is essential for a visit to the Maldives; not because it is a particularly hazardous country, but because any necessary medical treatment has to be paid for. You also have to consider that if you are taken sick on a resort then a transfer to Male' might be necessary, hence an unexpected expense.

TRAVEL CLINICS AND HEALTH INFORMATION
A full list of current travel clinic websites worldwide is available from the International Society of Travel Medicine on www.istm.org. For other journey preparation information, consult www.tripprep.com. Information about various medications may be found on www.emedicine.com.

UK

Berkeley Travel Clinic 32 Berkeley St, London W1J 8EL (near Green Park tube station); ✆ 020 7629 6233
Cambridge Travel Clinic 48a Mill Rd, Cambridge CB1 2AS; ✆ 01223 367362; e enquiries@cambridgetravelclinic.co.uk; www.cambridgetravelclinic.co.uk; ⊕ 12.00–19.00 Tue–Fri, 10.00–16.00 Sat
Edinburgh Travel Clinic Regional Infectious Diseases Unit, Ward 41 OPD, Western General Hospital, Crewe Rd South, Edinburgh EH4 2UX; ✆ 0131 537 2822; www.link.med.ed.ac.uk/ridu. Travel helpline (✆ 0906 589 0380) open: weekdays 09.00–12.00. Provides inoculations & anti-malarial prophylaxis & advises on travel-related health risks.
Fleet Street Travel Clinic 29 Fleet St, London EC4Y 1AA; ✆ 020 7353 5678; www.fleetstreetclinic.com. Vaccinations, travel products & latest advice.
Hospital for Tropical Diseases Travel Clinic Mortimer Market Bldg, Capper St (off Tottenham Ct Rd), London WC1E 6AU; ✆ 020 7388 9600; www.thehtd.org. Offers consultations & advice, & is able to provide all necessary drugs & vaccines for travellers. Runs a healthline (✆ 0906 133 7733) for country-specific information & health hazards. Also stocks nets, water

purification equipment & personal protection measures.

Interhealth Worldwide Partnership Hse, 157 Waterloo Rd, London SE1 8US; ✎ 020 7902 9000; www.interhealth.org.uk. Competitively priced, one-stop travel health service. All profits go to their affiliated company, InterHealth, which provides health care for overseas workers on Christian projects.

MASTA (Medical Advisory Service for Travellers Abroad) London School of Hygiene & Tropical Medicine, Keppel St, London WC1 7HT; ✎ 09065 501402; www.masta.org. Individually tailored health briefs available for a fee, with up-to-date information on how to stay healthy, inoculations & what to bring. There are currently 30 MASTA pre-travel clinics in Britain. Call ✎ 0870 241 6843 or check online for the nearest. Clinics also sell malaria prophylaxis memory cards, treatment kits, bednets & net treatment kits.

NHS travel website www.fitfortravel.scot.nhs.uk. Provides country-by-country advice on immunisation & malaria,

plus details of recent developments, & a list of relevant health organisations.

Nomad Travel Store/Clinic 3–4 Wellington Terrace, Turnpike Lane, London N8 0PX; ✎ 020 8889 7014; travel-health line (office hours only) ✎ 0906 863 3414; ✉ sales@nomadtravel.co.uk; www.nomadtravel.co.uk. Also at 40 Bernard St, London WC1N 1LJ; ✎ 020 7833 4114; 52 Grosvenor Gdns, London SW1W 0AG; ✎ 020 7823 5823; & 43 Queens Rd, Bristol BS8 1QH; ✎ 0117 922 6567. For health advice, equipment such as mosquito nets & other anti-bug devices, & an excellent range of adventure travel gear.

Trailfinders Travel Clinic 194 Kensington High St, London W8 7RG; ✎ 020 7938 3999; www.trailfinders.com/clinic.htm

Travelpharm The Travelpharm website, www.travelpharm.com, offers up-to-date guidance on travel-related health & has a range of medications available through their online mini-pharmacy.

Irish Republic

Tropical Medical Bureau Grafton St Medical Centre, Grafton Bldgs, 34 Grafton St, Dublin 2; ✎ 1 671 9200; www.tmb.ie. A useful website specific to tropical

destinations. Also check website for other bureaux locations throughout Ireland.

USA

Centers for Disease Control 1600 Clifton Rd, Atlanta, GA 30333; ✎ 800 311 3435; travellers' health hotline ✎ 888 232 3299; www.cdc.gov/travel. The central source of travel information in the USA. The invaluable Health Information for International Travel, published annually, is available from the Division of Quarantine at this address. Connaught Laboratories PO Box 187, Swiftwater, PA 18370; ✎ 800 822 2463. They will send a free list of specialist tropical-medicine physicians in your state.

IAMAT (International Association for Medical Assistance to Travelers) 1623 Military Rd, 279, Niagara Falls, NY 14304-1745; ✎ 716 754 4883; ✉ info@iamat.org; www.iamat.org. A non-profit organisation that provides lists of English-speaking doctors abroad.

International Medicine Center 920 Frostwood Dr, Suite 670, Houston, TX 77024; ✎ 713 550 2000; www.traveldoc.com

Canada

IAMAT Suite 1, 1287 St Clair Av W, Toronto, Ontario M6E 1B8; ✎ 416 652 0137; www.iamat.org

TMVC (Travel Doctors Group) Sulphur Springs Rd, Ancaster, Ontario; ✎ 905 648 1112; www.tmvc-group.com

Australia, New Zealand, Singapore

TMVC ✎ 1300 65 88 44; www.tmvc.com.au. 23 clinics in Australia, New Zealand & Singapore including:
Auckland Canterbury Arcade, 170 Queen St, Auckland; ✎ 9 373 3531
Brisbane 6th floor, 247 Adelaide St, Brisbane, QLD 4000; ✎ 7 3221 9066

Melbourne 393 Little Bourke St, 2nd floor, Melbourne, VIC 3000; ✎ 3 9602 5788
Sydney Dymocks Bldg, 7th Floor, 428 George St, Sydney, NSW 2000; ✎ 2 9221 7133
IAMAT PO Box 5049, Christchurch 5, New Zealand; www.iamat.org

South Africa

SAA-Netcare Travel Clinics Private Bag X34, Benmore 2010; www.travelclinic.co.za. Clinics throughout South Africa.

TMVC 113 D F Malan Drive, Roosevelt Park, Johannesburg; ✎ 011 888 7488; www.tmvc.com.au. Consult the website for details of 8 other clinics in South Africa.

Dr Jane Wilson-Howarth

Long-haul air travel increases the risk of deep vein thrombosis. Although recent research has suggested that many of us develop clots when immobilised, most resolve without us ever having been aware of them. In certain susceptible individuals, though, large clots form and these can break away and lodge in the lungs. This is dangerous but happens in a tiny minority of passengers.

Studies have shown that flights of over five-and-a-half-hours are significant, and that people who take lots of shorter flights over a short space of time form clots. People at highest risk are:

- Those who have had a clot before – unless they are now taking warfarin
- People over 80 years of age
- Anyone who has recently undergone a major operation or surgery for varicose veins
- Someone who has had a hip or knee replacement in the last three months
- Cancer sufferers
- Those who have ever had a stroke
- People with heart disease
- Those with a close blood relative who has had a clot

Those with a slightly increased risk:

- People over 40
- Women who are pregnant or have had a baby in the last couple of weeks
- People taking female hormones or other oestrogen therapy
- Heavy smokers
- Those who have very severe varicose veins
- The very obese
- People who are very tall (over 6ft/1.8m) or short (under 5ft/1.5m)

Switzerland

IAMAT 57 Chemin des Voirets, 1212 Grand Lancy, Geneva; www.iamat.org

IN MALDIVES

Health-care facilities Health service in the 19 atolls is provided through regional hospitals and primary health care centres, where physicians and paramedical personnel work. Family health workers look after the very basic essential preventive and promotive needs of the community at island level. There is a doctor available in each atoll.

The medical care in Male' has improved with the opening of the 200-bed **Indira Gandhi Memorial Hospital** (⤫ 3335335; f 3316640; e admindir@igmh.gov.mv; www.igmh.gov.mv), built on reclaimed land in the west of Male'. It is an impressive building, with a roof curving up like a *dhoni*'s sails when viewed from the sea.

Private medical care is available in Male' at the **ADK Hospital** (*Sosun Magu, Male';* ⤫ 3313553; f 3313554; e info@adkenterprises.com; www.adkenterprises.com). This is a delightful hospital (converted from the former government one) with a small garden at its entrance (and a café at its side). Doctors are available throughout the day for consultation or emergency treatment, and are on call 24 hours a day. There is also a dental surgery. In-patient care is available with private rooms.

A deep vein thrombosis (DVT) is a blood clot that forms in the deep leg veins. This is very different from irritating but harmless superficial phlebitis. DVT causes swelling and redness of one leg, usually with heat and pain in one calf and sometimes the thigh. A DVT is only dangerous if a clot breaks away and travels to the lungs (pulmonary embolus). Symptoms of a pulmonary embolus (PE) include chest pain that is worse on breathing in deeply, shortness of breath, and sometimes coughing up small amounts of blood. The symptoms commonly start three to ten days after a long flight. Anyone who thinks that they might have a DVT needs to see a doctor immediately who will arrange a scan. Warfarin tablets (to thin the blood) are then taken for at least six months.

PREVENTION OF DVT Several conditions make the problem more likely. Immobility is the key, and factors like reduced oxygen in cabin air and dehydration may also contribute. To reduce the risk of thrombosis on a long journey:

- Exercise before and after the flight
- Keep mobile before and during the flight; move around every couple of hours
- During the flight drink plenty of water or juices
- Avoid taking sleeping pills and excessive tea, coffee and alcohol
- Perform exercises that mimic walking and tense the calf muscles
- Consider wearing flight socks or support stockings (see www.legshealth.com)
- Taking a meal of oily fish (mackerel, trout, salmon, sardines, etc) in the 24 hours before departure reduces blood clottability and thus DVT risk
- The jury is still out on whether it is worth taking an aspirin before flying, but this can be discussed with your GP.

If you think you are at increased risk of a clot, ask your doctor if it is safe to travel.

There is a pharmacy open 24 hours a day at ADK and there are many other pharmacies throughout the capital. All have a good stock of medicines and qualified pharmacists, many of them Indian.

Every resort and guesthouse will have a contact telephone number in the event of a doctor, urgent medical attention, or even a dentist being needed. Some resorts have regular visits by doctors, or have resident doctors and nurses.

Emergency evacuation from resorts and inhabited islands is easier now that there are seaplanes available for charter. In the event of a diving accident there are decompression chambers on Kuramathi and Bandos, which also have a medical clinic and hyperbaric treatment centre for scuba divers.

The cost of drugs is, for example, Rf4 for one tablet of ciprofloxacin. A Seretide nasal spray costs Rf240. To obtain drugs such as these requires a doctor's prescription; to visit a doctor costs Rf50–75. There is a choice of 12 doctors at The Clinic; see below.

Contact details

ADK Hospital Sosun Magu, Male'; ✆ 3313553; f 3313554
Indira Gandhi Hospital ✆ 3335335, f 3316640

The Clinic 1st Floor, M. Nimsa Bldg, Fareedhee Magu, Male'; ✆ 3324207; f 3333753
Dr Didi (dentist) & **Dr F M Didi** (eye clinic) are marked on the city map.

Natural hazards There are no dangerous animals or reptiles in the Maldives. Biting insects may be a minor nuisance in resorts but do not present a significant danger to health. See *Fauna* on page 11 for further information.

Sun protection Give some thought to packing suncream. The incidence of skin cancer is rocketing as Caucasians are travelling more and spending more time exposing themselves to the sun. Keep out of the sun during the middle of the day and, if you must expose yourself to the sun, build up gradually from 20 minutes per day. Be especially careful of exposure in the middle of the day and of sun reflected off water, and wear a T-shirt and lots of waterproof suncream (at least SPF15) when swimming. Sun exposure ages the skin, making people prematurely wrinkly, and increases the risk of skin cancer. Cover up with long, loose clothes and wear a hat when you can.

Water safety Personal safety when you are swimming in the sea is your own responsibility. Always wear a lifejacket when doing serious snorkelling out of your depth, or far from the island. Although the lagoon may seem idyllic, look out for currents when swimming and snorkelling, especially the outward current when your fascination with what you are watching may result in it taking you further from shore than is safe.

When diving, always observe the proper safety procedures that you have been taught and do exactly what the instructor says.

Drinking water Visitors are recommended to stick to bottled drinking water. Tap water in Male' is best avoided. This applies on the resort islands as well.

SERVICES

WATER The main sources of drinking water have traditionally been the aquifers that float on saline water a few feet below ground level in most islands, from which water is accessed by well. The soil being generally porous and most of the islands being small, the available groundwater supply is susceptible to pollution. Consequently, water-borne diseases used to reach epidemic proportions in overcrowded islands, particularly in Male'.

A project to upgrade Male's water supply has been in existence since 1992, with assistance from the Danish government. The Male' Water and Sewerage Company Limited held its first board meeting in April 1995, with Maldivian and Danish directors. Its main objectives are the supply of piped water to all households in Male' and the provision of sewerage services. The service developed rapidly and now piped water is available to private houses and at public standpipes throughout Male'. It is produced by desalinating seawater, an expensive but necessary process since the layer of water in Male' could not support the population. The service is provided by what is now known as the Maldives Water & Sanitation Authority (*Majeedhee Magu, Male'*; ✆ *3321523*; f *3317569*).

Under programmes improving the sanitation in the atolls, nearly 60% of the population in the outer atolls have access to safe drinking water. Lines of circular cement or fibreglass government rainwater storage tanks are a common sight on many inhabited islands, supplementing the private well supply of water.

Resort islands now have their own desalination plants providing water for the bathrooms and, after treatment, for drinking. (Even Coca-Cola is produced in Maldives from desalinated water.) Flasks of drinking water are normally provided in all hotel bedrooms – whether you drink it or not depends on your constitution; the fastidious prefer bottled mineral water which can cost as much as US$5, more than a beer in some resorts, or about US$0.75 in Male' grocery stores.

Bathrooms with Western-style showers and toilets do exist in inhabited islands, although these often show a Maldivian fondness for nature and the open air. They may have no roof even if the walls are plastered instead of being made of palm leaf thatch. By tradition, someone climbing a coconut tree near village houses is supposed to shout to announce his presence to those using the toilets below. Building houses of two storeys – as is now happening in some islands – has led to social complications where those overlook the bathrooms.

The local-style bathing area, called *gifili*, consists of a small garden and a well, sometimes divided by a wall so someone else can use the well from the other side of the wall at the same time. Water is drawn from the well using a *dhaani*, a small can attached to a long stick. It is not as easy to use as it sounds, because the other end of the stick inevitably bangs against something, like the bushes growing in the *gifili*, washing lines or a roof overhang. You use the *dhaani* to pour water into a bucket with which you douse yourself. It is also used to supply water to flush the toilet, which may be the hole-in-the-ground type common to Asia.

Some resorts have copied the style of village toilets, by providing bathrooms which are only partially roofed and have a garden in them, but with a wall around for privacy.

SANITATION There has been a nationwide project to provide safe and environmentally sound sewerage systems to the atolls, with over 40 islands selected on the basis of size and density of population. With UNICEF assistance, sewerage pipes from houses to septic tanks have been laid. In smaller islands you may find the 'four-gear toilet', so called because it consists of a stick to dig a hole in the sand with four deft strokes.

ELECTRICITY All electricity generation is by fuel-powered generators and output is in the range 220–240V. Power points are of various types but, subject to voltage requirements, a standard traveller's adaptor set will usually fit one way or another. Electricity in Male', the resorts and a few inhabited islands is supplied throughout the day; on smaller inhabited islands it may only be available 18.00–23.00. Electricity in Male' is supplied by the State Electric Company Ltd. There are government and private generators supplying islanders in the atolls.

The resort islands have huge generating plants, usually concealed in the interior or at the least attractive end of the island, where they will not be visible to guests. The standard of maintenance is very good but there will still be moments when electricity fails, so it is always advisable to have a torch handy at night.

RUBBISH DISPOSAL The disposal of rubbish or garbage (trash) is of great concern to both government and resort operators, since everyone is aware that just chucking it in the sea has grave consequences. On islands with a reclamation project, garbage is used as landfill. In Male' Atoll, a new island, Thilafushi, has been created out of a sandbank by garbage, which is towed to it on rubbish rafts and dumped. The first building on this new island created out of garbage was a mosque. The island is being developed for industrial use.

German visitors are strict about correct garbage disposal, and will take their non-disposable trash back to Germany with them in garbage bags provided by their tour operator. Many island resorts use other innovative methods to dispose of their waste. On Madoogali, a pretty island like a miniature botanical garden, there is a suprising flowerbed border of up-ended wine bottles stuck in the soil. This is a novel way of disposing of glass bottles. They were to be cemented over, forming the base of a low garden wall.

2

Also in Madoogali, fish waste is buried to enrich the soil. The manager of another resort, though, has said that he throws the discarded fish parts into the sea by the reef so that these will attract more fish to the reef, to the delight of divers and snorkellers.

At Madoogali, the water that drips from the air-conditioning boxes sticking out of the back of each accommodation unit is collected in a tray, instead of being allowed to seep into the sand and be wasted. It is then used to water the plants around each room, helping to keep the island lush.

The Maldives Association of Tourism Industry (MATI) has been active in finding solutions to the problems of waste disposal. With the co-operation of the Ministry of Tourism, a Norwegian-assisted project to install incinerators at the resorts is under way.

The disposal of waste has become an art in the resorts. Ingenious methods are used to recycle waste material, while what can be burned is incinerated. Some islands have developed mini sewage-treatment plants as an alternative to septic tanks.

In his book, *A Man for All Islands*, Royston Ellis wrote:

> A brainwave that caught the imagination of all Maldivians was the national programme announced by President Gayoom on Independence Day in 1996, with the slogan: 'Independent Maldives – Clean Maldives'. The slogan played on Maldivians' pride at their independence, subtly implying that to disregard cleanliness was national disrespect. The programme, which continues with different campaigns based on various themes, is co-ordinated by the President's office.

> The President participated energetically in the campaign, joining in cleaning up exercises in Male' and other islands. When he helped in a reef cleaning programme, tourists were astonished to meet the head of state actually taking part by loading rubbish gathered by them at the reef onto a *dhoni*, instead of just inspecting the work being done.

SAFETY

CRIME The overall feeling of life in Maldives for a visitor used to be of a mainly crime-free society. Visitors could walk the streets of Male' without fear and without seeing a beggar, and without feeling any threat from mugging, pimps or hustlers. However, a bomb explosion in Sultan's Park in Male' in September 2007, which injured some tourists, changed that carefree atmosphere. It was seen as a one-off expression by malcontents (not terrorists), who were swiftly rounded up and sentenced to long jail terms. While street crime is not visible, there can be disruptions to daily life and even demonstrations as embryo-politicians test their strength. There is also a rabid undercurrent drug culture among the disaffected youth. Away from the capital island, the respect for the law remains inbuilt in the Maldivian psyche. Where there are no police stationed on the inhabited islands, the island chief's rule is paramount. The most common form of punishment for offenders is banishment to a distant island, sometimes for a period as long as 12 years, although there can be a reprieve after two years. It means enforced transportation from one's home island to another where one suffers the opprobrium of one's peers. The quality of life during banishment depends entirely on the convict's own behaviour and personality. However idyllic it may sound to a stress-weary Westerner to be banished to a tropical island, it can cause psychological anguish for Maldivians.

When a crime is committed on an inhabited island, an investigation is carried out by the island chief who can request help from the atoll chief and from the authorities in Male' if necessary. To secure a conviction for alcohol consumption, two witnesses are necessary.

SECURITY By law, all resorts and hotels must provide safe deposit facilities for guests to store money, jewellery and other valuables. Filing cabinets, cupboards and drawers, even if lockable, are not acceptable; a real safe must be available. Some resorts have individual safes in their guestrooms; in others you make the necessary arrangements via reception.

If something goes astray, you should report it immediately to the resort manager and, for insurance purposes, ask him to sign a record of your report. The management will contact the police if the seriousness warrants it, after conducting their own investigation. You may not notice (better if you don't) that resorts have their own security guards, and the arrival of any strangers (such as visitors on island-hopping excursions) is discreetly monitored.

Every resort has a plan in case of disaster and rooms show exit points in the event of a fire. There is also a life jacket in every room for every guest, a lesson learned from the 2004 tsunami.

POLICE Formerly part of the National Security Service (NSS), the police force is now a separate entity with headquarters in Male'. On inhabited islands without a resident police presence, HQ can be contacted through the nearest atoll office, or via the nearest island chief's office. The emergency police telephone number from anywhere in Maldives is ✆ 119.

WHAT TO TAKE

The absolute minimum; whatever you need could be packed into a bag small enough to carry on to the aircraft. Above all, the Maldives is hot, so beach wear is normal and anything reaching your ankles (for men as well as women) is positively formal.

The only dress rules in the Maldives are: don't take everything off on the beach (nudism is punishable by a fine of US$1,000); and do wear at least a T-shirt and shorts (non-diaphanous material) covering your thighs when visiting inhabited islands. When visiting Male', dress modestly. Local Muslim dress is conservative, and visitors should remember and respect this. Holidaymakers and even honeymooners should leave their Western liberated dress sense back in the privacy of their beach villas, and not strut about town dressed for a romantic encounter.

Make sure that what little clothing you do take for daytime wear is light cotton. Except on special occasions or for business meetings (when a man might need a tie but no jacket, or a safari suit, and a woman a sensible outfit), casual clothing is customary. Resort dining is a wonderful opportunity to show off fashionable leisure wear, but T-shirts and shorts may do just as well, except where the restaurant's dress code specifically requests otherwise. A lot depends on the resort. More resorts have cast themselves in the upmarket mould, and both men and women would want to dress accordingly for dinner. Some resorts, like Kurumba Maldives and Full Moon, have fine dining restaurants where anything less than elegant clothes would be an insult to the talents of the chef, the staff, fellow diners and the ambience.

While T-shirts are great for men and women visiting Male' and inhabited islands, check the slogan, since risqué ones could cause offence. Sandals are the best footwear, especially as they can easily be removed for entering a Maldivian's home or a mosque.

Take the prescription medicines you need and enough of your favourite shampoo and hair care and beauty items, cosmetics, feminine hygiene products, contraceptives, etc, since you might not see a shop, other than the resort gift shop, if you don't visit Male'. Resort-island shops do stock basic supplies as well as souvenirs. If you wear spectacles and have a spare pair, take them, since replacing lost ones would be difficult. Sunglasses are essential.

Good-quality sun-protection cream or lotion is also essential for everyone, as the power of the sun is deceptive. Bring plenty, as buying locally could be expensive, especially if you have to make a special trip to Male' from your resort island to find the brand you want.

Mariyam Zulfa has suggested I add a woman's perspective on what to bring, particularly concerning hair care. Hairdressing salons are available at only a handful of resorts. Options are to come prepared to do it yourself, to have your hair done during a trip to Male', or to abandon elaborate hair care as part of the holiday mood. Bring sufficient hair conditioner, as your hair will be ill-treated by the sand and salt water. For information on adaptors for electrical equipment such as hairdryers, see *Electricity* on page 67.

Spas have sprung up on all but the most modest of resorts and some feature exotic beauty treatments as well as a thrilling range of massages, whose price alone can send shivers down your spine. They are nevertheless very popular, and spa treatment can be a highlight of the holiday, so make appointments well in advance.

There will be plenty of time to read those books you have always been meaning to read, so take them, too. A notebook or diary is useful for writing memos to yourself; don't forget a pen. A torch (flashlight) might be useful, particularly for walking back to your room at night. Smokers should take enough of their favourite brand, or use the holiday as a chance to give up.

Take photocopies of your personal travel insurance policy, air tickets and passport details and keep them separate from the real ones (put those in the room safe). Jewellery is superfluous, so leave it at home. Better to take a cheap watch than an expensive one, which you might worry about leaving on the beach when you suddenly want a swim.

If you have flippers, snorkel and mask, take them, although you can buy them in Male' or hire them on resort islands. Divers could take their own wetsuits, but they are not essential as the water is not cold; other equipment can be hired. If you plan to do any scuba diving, make sure your insurance policy covers that. Take a small camera for memento shots, and more film than you think you'll need.

This is not a hardship destination, so water-purifying tablets, snakebite kits, etc, are unnecessary. Do take tummy-upset tablets, as although food preparation is hygienic, change of diet and the long flight can affect newcomers. Seasickness pills, if you are likely to suffer and the voyage to and from your resort is long, could be useful.

If you do forget anything, the shops in Male' are remarkably well stocked. Remember that shopping locally is a way of helping the Maldives' economy. Beach wear, sunhats and T-shirts will be available in the resort shops. You are unlikely to need an extra bag to carry souvenirs home. Some visitors, however, do take garbage bags to carry all their personal litter back home with them.

For local expenses not pre-paid, bring US dollars or US dollar travellers' cheques as well as credit cards.

WHAT NOT TO TAKE Alcohol! If you have been tempted to buy duty-free liquor at the departure airport or on the plane, it will be politely removed from you by customs on arrival. If you do happen to enter the country with alcohol, on no account offer it to Maldivians. You can fly away, but a Maldivian caught with liquor can be banished for years. 'Statues used for worship' will also be held in bond for your departure. Pork is a forbidden import, so don't take your favourite salami (you'll get plenty in your resort). Dogs are definitely out. Pornography is prohibited and this could include magazines on general sale elsewhere, even if they contain only partial, innocuous (to you) nudity such as underwear advertisements.

Also banned is the import of gunpowder or explosives, weapons and firearms, opium, ganja (marijuana), cocaine and all other narcotic items that could be used as intoxicants. See also *Customs allowances* on page 60.

Do not take lots of luggage; you won't need half the things you normally carry.

$ MONEY MATTERS

CURRENCY The first currency was cowrie shells (those small gastropods with a highly polished shell of the *Cypraeidae* family) and Maldives was a source of supply for both Africa and south Asia. The word itself comes from the Urdu and Hindi *kauri*, which reveals the long-established Indian connection. You can still buy cowrie shells (packed in pretty boxes by Novelty) or pick them up on the beach or the sandy streets of village islands.

Early in the 14th century, Ibn Battuta observed:

> The inhabitants of these islands use cowrie shells as money. This is an animal which they gather in the sea and place in pits, where its flesh disappears, leaving its white shell. They are used for buying and selling at the rate of four hundred thousand shells for a gold dinar.

Coins were first minted in Maldives in the late 16th century; they were hairpin shape, not round.

The present-day unit of currency is the rufiyaa (Rf), which is divided into 100 laari (L). You will hear Maldivians use the word *laari* for money. Coins in circulation are one, two, five and ten laari, both copper and alloy types, with dimpled edges; 25 laari; 50 laari; and one rufiyaa. Gold and silver coins were issued to commemorate the silver jubilee of independence on 26 July 1990. Notes in circulation are: Rf2, Rf5, Rf10, Rf20, Rf50, Rf100 and Rf500.

The design of the notes makes them interesting for collectors, or as an unusual souvenir. The first Rf500 note was issued on 26 July 1990. Its main colour is red, size 150mm by 70mm. The bow view of a typical *odi* in full sail appears on the right of the main side. This lateen-rigged boat was the common mode of long-distance cargo and passenger transport in Maldives until the 1960s. The centre of the note shows a cluster of coconuts. The state emblem is reflected in the watermark. On the reverse the central feature is a façade of the Islamic Centre. The ornate latticework in the foreground is representative of the carvings decorating the old Friday congregational mosque in Male'. A bouquet of roses, the national flower, appears in the top left-hand corner.

Bank notes printed in 1983 are still in use, together with those printed in 1990. Each note contains a security thread and a watermark. All notes are the same size (150mm by 70mm), but each denomination is a different colour.

On the front of all notes is a bunch of coconuts in the centre and the *odi* in full sail on the right. The date of issue appears in Dhivehi, and the amount is in the top left and lower right corners. The back of each note shows a different scene or monument with the value given in English and the words Maldives Monetary Authority. The 1990 issue was printed by Thomas de la Rue & Company Limited; the 1983 issue by Bradbury Wilkinson.

The Rf100 note is green in colour and shows the tomb of Abu Barakaath Yoosuf Al-Barbari. The Rf50 note is blue, with a Male' market scene. The Rf20 note (a new introduction in 1983) is purple with a design of waterfront and boats depicting the inner harbour, Male'. The Rf10 note is brown and shows life in a village island, with handicrafts and chickens. The Rf5 note is mauve (darker than the Rf20 purple) with sailing *dhonis* successfully fishing with rod and line.

CHANGING MONEY The exchange rate between the rufiyaa and the US dollar at press time was fixed at Rf12.75. Rates for other currencies fluctuate according to the cross rate. In July 2008 the rate of exchange was Rf25.23 for UK£1 and Rf20.06 for €1 (euro). The day's rates are set by the Maldives Money Authority. (See *Banking*, below.) The US dollar is legal tender and the currency of the island resorts.

If you have US dollars in cash, and are bound for a resort island, it is better not to change them into Maldivian rufiyaas since dollars are appreciated as tips by the non-Maldivian staff. The rates of exchange for cash or travellers' cheques are similar, but a commission is levied on the encashment of the latter. At hotel resorts, travellers' cheques are accepted only for the payment of bills, not to exchange into cash.

Dollars (but not travellers' cheques) can be used or exchanged in many shops in Male', particularly souvenir shops along Chandhanee Magu, the main street leading inland from the waterfront. For tourist shoppers it is easier to use dollars, but the change may be given in the rufiyaa equivalent. It is usually quicker to change currency in a shop than in a bank, which may be crowded. However, changing other currencies (even euros and pounds) and travellers' cheques can only be done through a bank, or your resort's cashier.

BANKING New banks are joining the five in Male', but only one of them, the Bank of Maldives, is permitted to open branches in the islands. The State Bank of India was the first bank; it opened in 1974. Bank activities are regulated by the Maldives Monetary Authority, established in 1980. Bank accounts can be maintained in rufiyaas or US dollars. There is no offshore banking system. Banks are normally open 08.00–13.30 Sunday to Thursday.

To have emergency funds sent from overseas, check with the bank of your choice for what they advise is their swiftest method. There is an American Express office (❧ *3317925*) in the Universal Enterprises building in Orchid Magu. Two other options are Money Gram/Xpress Money, a service operated by Maldives Post at the Atoll Post Building, Boduthakurufaanu Magu (❧ *3321558, ext* 112), and Western Union at Villa Travel & Tours, Boduthakurufaanu Magu (❧ *3330088*).

Male' banks

Bank of Ceylon 12 Boduthakurufaanu; ❧ 3323045; f 3320575; e bcmale@dhivehinet.net.mv
Bank of Maldives 11 Boduthakurufaanu Magu; ❧ 3322948; f 3328233; e info@bml.com.mv; www.bankofmaldives.com.mv
Habib Bank Ltd Orchid Magu; ❧ 3322051; f 3326791; e hblmale@dhivehinet.net.mv

HSBC Boduthakurufaanu Magu; ❧ 3330770; f 3312072; e maldivesbranch@hsbc.com.lk
State Bank of India Boduthakurufaanu Magu; ❧ 3323052; f 3323053; e sbimale@dhivehinet.net.mv

ATMs There are a few ATM machines in Male' that accept overseas visitors' cards, but none in the resorts. Some of the main ones are:

Bank of Ceylon (Visa/Mastercard) Ground Floor, Bank of Ceylon, Boduthakurufaanu Magu
Bank of Maldives (Visa/Mastercard/Amex) Main Branch, Boduthakurufaanu Magu; Majeedhee Magu branch; IGMH Hospital branch; Maldives Ports Authority

branch; Ministry of Finance & Treasury branch; Male' International Airport branch (arrival lobby)
HSBC (Visa/Mastercard) MTCC Tower, Boduthakurufaanu Magu

Credit cards Local offices of international credit cards are provided by three banks:

Bank of Ceylon (Visa & Mastercard) Ground Floor, Aage, Boduthakurufaanu Magu; ❧ 3323046; f 3310575

Bank of Maldives Card Centre (Visa/American Express/Mastercard), Boduthakurufaanu Magu; ☎ 3330200; f 3335999

HSBC (Visa/Mastercard), Cyprea Card Centre, 25 Boduthakurufaanu Magu; ☎ 3312211; f 3315177

BUDGETING

How much money to take Total expenses will depend on whether you are an independent visitor or on a pre-paid package holiday. The complaints usually made in resort comments' books are about the cost of extras, which the holidaymaker had not anticipated. Guests who think they have found a cheap package, when they pay for it in their home country, overlook the isolation of the Maldives, which means that everything is more expensive since it has to be imported. So unless you are on a package that really does include everything from cigarettes to afternoon tea, you will need to budget a significant amount for extras.

Some resorts are all-inclusive (including drinks), others offer a bed-and-breakfast rate and some include dinner as well, so it is impossible to recommend a daily figure for extras. Allowing US$100 a day per couple should take care of resort drinking and dining and an excursion, but a lot more would be required if your resort is upmarket or you plan to go diving.

The independent traveller, either alone or with a partner, without pre-paid accommodation, should allow at least US$65 a night for accommodation in Male', but will save on meals. What a sandwich costs in a resort (say US$10) could cover all meals, tea and soft drinks for a day in one of the many cafés in Male'. Since anyone staying in Male' will need to travel by *dhoni* to visit beach islands, that cost must be taken into account, too.

There are a score of low-priced resorts where accommodation (if available), if booked on the spot through a Male' travel agent, could be had for around US$250 a night for two, with breakfast. So independent travellers, without pre-booked accommodation, really would need a minimum budget of around US$350 a day for two if staying in a resort, not in the capital. Expensive? That's why most visitors come on a pre-paid package.

The best way to see resort islands and also visit fishing villages and uninhabited islands on a defined budget is to take a cruise, on the *Atoll Explorer* for example (see pages 116), where everything (except voluntary tips and champagne) is included in the per-person per-day fare starting at US$250. Or charter your own safari boat from US$700 per day with drinks (and sometimes fuel) extra.

The minimum required by law (to be shown as proof of funds for extending the visa-stay period) is US$25 a day. If you are staying on a full- or half-board basis (that is, with all or some meals included) on a resort island, keep out of the bar, don't go on excursions or diving, do your own laundry, enjoy your time snorkelling (with your own mask and flippers) and lazing on the beach, then go to bed early, you could – perhaps! – get by on only US$10 a day each.

Since the resort islands take credit cards (as long as you inform them in advance of departure to allow time for processing) you will actually only need a lot of cash (or travellers' cheques) if you don't have a credit card. Bills are either calculated in, or converted to, US dollars, so any travellers' cheques or cash you bring should ideally be in that currency. For cash payments, bills are rounded up to the nearest dollar.

Small amounts of US dollars would be useful for shopping in Male' and inside the duty-free area of the airport departure terminal.

Budgeting for extras To enjoy a Maldives holiday to the fullest, it is prudent to budget for unexpected extras. Even if all meals are included in the price you have paid in advance, there are cocktails to try, and what about having a mid-morning fruit juice by the pool, or afternoon tea?

Some islands have superb restaurants and it is better to be on a bed-and-breakfast basis rather than half or full board. That way you can try everything that is available. However, since a meal in a top resort could cost from US$50 per person, you must allow for it. Cocktails are from US$10. At most resorts a large bottle of locally produced mineralised water will cost as much as a beer (US$4 or $5) so include a water allowance in your holiday budget. On top of that is the service charge of 10%.

Since you are not allowed to bring duty-free liquor into the country, you could find you spend more money at the bar than if you usually drink from your own supplies in your own room on holiday. The resort's bars, being the only place to go at night, can become very jolly and you may find you spend a lot of time, as well as money, in them.

If you want to get off the island, perhaps to visit another resort for lunch, there are excursions (allow from US$50 a head). And what about watersports or scuba diving? These costs are mentioned under the relevant sections.

Little things add up, too. Laundry can be expensive, but it is easy to do your own washing since clothes can dry quickly. The cost of overseas telephone calls can surprise some guests who use the international direct-dial telephone in their rooms as though they are at home. Pre-paid calling cards for international calls are available from the telephone company, Dhiraagu, in Male' to use at public phone booths, but you won't find those on resort islands. Call-back facilities are not available at the resorts. Roaming mobile phones can be used where compatible with the local services, which could save on IDD calls. The islands which allow guests access to the internet charge heavily for the privilege.

TIPPING Tipping is actually an inexpensive extra. The government policy is not to encourage tipping, but if you tell your waiter that, it won't endear you to him. In Male' if you take a taxi or eat in a tea shop, you don't tip. However, hotel employees (waiter, room boy, porter) have learned that tourists are in the habit of tipping and you won't be expected to be the one who breaks the habit.

Unlike hotels in other countries in the region, there is usually no service charge added to the room rate, so tipping is something that should be budgeted for. One tour operator, in notes for its clients, suggests US$1 per guest per night of stay to the table waiter and the same amount to the room boy. This amounts to US$4 a day for a couple but this seems rather mean if your room rate is over US$250 a day. You might be happier allowing an average minimum of US$20 a day per couple to distribute to restaurant and housekeeping staff. The porters who carry your bags from the island's jetty are sometimes also the beach cleaners. Some come from Bangladesh, as I discovered when I offered one porter a tip and he refused local currency saying he wanted dollars.

By realising in advance that there are going to be extras and allowing for them, since there is no opportunity to pop out and look for somewhere cheaper, the Maldives are actually good value, especially when compared with Europe or even upmarket hotels in India.

COST OF LIVING The cost of living for expatriates depends a lot on the cost of accommodation since rent can be high, from US$1,000 a month for a small apartment, and shopping or anything more than basics can be expensive due to the extra cost for frieght, wharfage and so on for imported items.

GETTING TO YOUR RESORT

If you already have a resort booked, either independently or as part of an organised holiday, you first need to find the resort representative. With hotel name signs and agency clipboards in their hands, or standing by soapbox-like counters under travel agency banners, the tour operators' representatives wonder if you are their client, while you look to see which one is waiting for you.

If you have organised your holiday through a major tour operator, like Kuoni or TUI, their reps will be easily identifiable. Most tour operators are represented by their Maldivian agents, and you will locate them by their clipboards or briefcases with huge agency stickers.

If you do not have pre-booked accommodation, the adventure starts here. There is an information counter on the right of the arrivals hall exit where you can pick up brochures and request hotel-rate details. Go to one of the local agents' counters to check which resort has vacancies, and the day's rate. You need to have a good idea of your budget, activities and interests before deciding on a resort. Out of high season the agent should have an allocation of rooms in different resorts, but if his selection does not suit you, one of his colleagues will offer something. These agents set their own prices, based on the net room rate quoted to them by the resorts. If you decide to telephone a resort and check the room rate yourself, the price the resort will quote will be higher than the agent is offering. There is no catch; it's business. As one of them explained, these freelance travel agents keep the tourist dollar, and the commission, in the Maldives, instead of the profit going to enrich overseas agents. Find a good agent at the airport and you will have someone who will take care of all your problems in Maldives, even extending your visa or helping you to get a permit to visit the fishing atolls.

Mohamed Firaq, the affable genius behind Inner Maldives Holidays, tells the story of a new arrival who had been informed by his overseas travel agent that he would be met at the airport by *dhoni*. The man brushed aside all offers of help on arrival, insisting he was to be met by someone called Mr Dhoni, believing *dhoni* to be a person instead of the vessel which would take him to his resort.

Having located someone to help you, transfer to the resort will be arranged. If you are going by *dhoni* or speedboat, you will have to go along the waterfront to the pier indicated by the rep. There could be a wait of an hour while all the passengers for the same resort are cleared through immigration and customs. Each resort has its own boat; there is no 'bus service' with boats dropping off passengers at different islands. Transfers are also possible by seaplane and high-speed passenger speedboats, if arranged in advance. The cost of transfers is usually included in pre-paid holidays, but will be billed as an extra if you are travelling independently.

There is a hotel on Hulhule, the airport island, which tourists use when they arrive late or depart early, and have to take domestic flights or long speedboat connections.

TO MALE' FROM THE AIRPORT There are ferries from the airport to Male'; they can be found at the main jetty. The other jetties are where the resort boats collect their passengers.

The price per passenger for a ride on the *dhoni* to Male' is Rf20 (you can pay US$2 if you haven't got local currency, but don't expect any change). A *dhoni* is supposed to leave every 15 minutes, or as soon as it has ten passengers. For those feeling exclusive or merely in a hurry, a *dhoni* can be chartered for the ten-minute run.

TO THE AIRPORT FROM MALE' The *dhonis* carrying staff to the airport leave from alongside the Presidential Jetty, which is opposite the park known as Jumhooree Maidan. These are intended for airport staff, including customs officials, so you will need either to be invited aboard or to ask the skipper's permission. Other *dhonis* bound for the airport leave from the eastern end of the waterfront, in the area opposite where the former Nasandhura Palace Hotel used to be. The usual fee is Rf10 per person.

Dhonis for charter are tied up in the same area along the waterfront. Their willingness to take you somewhere will depend on how brisk business is. On a quiet day, rates will be more reasonable. As always, it is better to let a local rep negotiate; he will not necessarily build in a commission before quoting you the price, if you have already become his regular client.

GETTING AROUND

Any independent visitor to Maldives – and those on a pre-paid holiday who decide to do things for themselves – will benefit from dealing with a local travel agent to get around. For details of maps, see pages 89.

ON LAND Taxis are available in Male' and on Gan. There are no self-drive hire cars available in the Maldives at all. Motorcycles and bicycles may be hired in Male' and some other resort islands. If you use these, make sure that your travel insurance policy covers travel on two-wheeled transport, as not all do.

BY BOAT

Island hopping Most resort islands organise island-hopping excursions from US$50 per person. These usually include a visit to a neighbouring resort and also to a village island, and, perhaps, to a genuine uninhabited island for picnic lunch.

Island hopping can easily be arranged independently by chartering a *dhoni* or speedboat with crew from your resort and arranging to visit islands of your own choosing. This can cost from US$1,000 a day for a speedboat hired at a resort.

Chartering a *dhoni* or speedboat in Male' might be cheaper, especially if done through a local rep who could also accompany you to act as interpreter and make sure the crew takes you where you want to go. A brief island-hopping trip from Male' could cost from US$150 for a day, depending on your bargaining skills or, more likely, how busy the *dhoni* captain is. When Siân and Bob enquired, the captain said, 'So you want to hijack a boat for the day...'

A popular uninhabited island to visit near Male' is Kudabandos. Permission has to be obtained in advance from the resort island of Bandos, which uses it for its guests, except on Fridays and public holidays when it is exclusively for Maldivians. A small fee is payable.

In days gone by it was possible to island hop from Male', at minimal expense. Since even the most distant resort must have a boat calling at Male' sometimes, to pick up mail, collect supplies, or give staff leave, hitching a free ride when it returned to the resort was a possibility. With most resorts heavily booked now, it is not so easy to just drop in for a night or two. In any case, resort boats don't have fixed schedules. Also the boat crew will not have the authority to take strangers on the staff boat.

The other option, for which you will probably have to pay the standard passenger transfer charge of anything from US$20 to US$200, is to island hop via the airport. Every resort sends a transfer boat of some kind to pick up arriving guests or to deliver them to the airport for the flight home. You could arrange a ride on that, stay until the next airport transfer, and then repeat the procedure to another island. This might be easier in low season, but in any case you are unlikely to be allowed to just hop on a boat without a prearranged reservation at the resort.

Inter-atoll vessels *Dhonis* from inhabited islands as well as larger cargo/passenger vessels tie up at the waterfront opposite the fish market, to the west of the

What is a *dhoni*? It is a Maldivian-designed boat used for fishing and transport, and was traditionally a sailing craft with a splendid, curved prow. Now most *dhonis* are motorised and the prow is removed except on occasions when the skipper wants to create an impression, or for photographs.

The *dhoni* is made of wood, with a broad beam and a remarkable amount of space. Usually it has no deck but *dhonis* converted for passengers have a deck and awning added. When a more efficient design was introduced by the government boat-building yard at Alifushi, there was considerable resistance among local fishermen and boats had to be sold at a discount. Now the modified design is so popular, the yard is always busy.

You will see the word also spelt as *dhoani*. A *masdhoni* is a fishing *dhoni*. A sailing boat in Dhivehi is called *riyalu dhoni*, and a mechanised one is *ingeenu dhoni*. A *batteli* is a larger, modified *dhoni* primarily used for inter-atoll transport of cargo.

Passenger *dhonis* have some form of radio communication and life jackets. A fishing *dhoni* will have a pair of logs per crew member instead of life jackets. If you are chartering a *dhoni*, you can tell if the crew are good by the condition of its anchor, propped up in the bow. If it is oiled and not caked with rust, and the *dhoni's* deck is well scrubbed, then its crew are likely to be good seamen with pride in their expertise. A typical *dhoni's* speed is about 13km per hour.

Presidential Jetty. An even better place for boat spotting is the Southern Harbour at Male's southwest corner. With wide boulevards and vessels tied up beside the pavement, it is a fascinating place to roam around. At nights it is also a favourite area for promenading, and features many waterfront cafés and snack bars. You will see curious, tall craft with a protruding square stern and covered decks, which voyage between Male' and the far-flung atolls of the south. The stern has the galley on one side and the toilet (a hole in the deck in a cubicle overhanging the sea) on the other. These carry passengers as well as cargo, with passengers sleeping as best they can on top of the cargo.

Getting a chance to travel on one of these vessels is, like the voyage itself, a little tiresome. The friends you make in the waterfront cafés may be perfectly willing to take you with them to their distant atoll, but there is the matter of a permit. If you have an influential sponsor, like the island chief himself or someone well respected in Male', it can be arranged.

The problem might be who will collect the government head tax of US$8 a night for you, since the inter-island cargo boat, on which you will have to spend a night or two at sea, is not licensed to carry foreign passengers and therefore cannot collect the tax. But the tax must be collected for every night a foreigner (without a residence permit) spends in the Maldives. Let your Male' man sort it out as, officially, inter-atoll ferries are available only to locals, not to visitors. However, visitors can take the ferries to the Male' satellite residential islands of Vilingili and Hulhumale' in the same atoll (see page 149).

Smaller *dhonis* also tie up alongside the fishing *dhonis*, some with canvas awnings hung like tents over their open decks. There is neither galley nor toilet on them; the stern of the boat, behind where the skipper stands at the tiller, serves the purpose for both. Food is cooked over a kerosene stove, dough rolled on a piece of board to make *roshi*, fish gutted and popped into a pot with seasoning for lunch. For the toilet, crouch low over the stern platform, hanging on carefully while you and the *dhoni* are in motion, and the captain stares ahead.

If there is a particular atoll or island you are determined to visit (or perhaps have something to send for a friend who is resident there), it is quite easy to locate a boat going there.

On its bow, every vessel has a registration number written in Roman letters and Arabic figures. The letter indicates which atoll the vessel comes from, and the number shows the island. Even if you have no wish to go anywhere, *dhoni*-spotting and identifying which boat comes from where is fun. For a listing see *Appendix 2*.

Speedboat charter The equivalent of a chauffeur-driven limousine in the Maldives is a privately chartered speedboat, which comes complete with uniformed skipper and at least a couple of boat boys who throw ropes about and help passengers on and off. (Every speedboat has to have a minimum of three crew, plus lifejackets for all passengers and crew.) There are a few companies that operate speedboats under contract for tour companies and resorts but because of demand they might not have boats available for private hire. One company that does specialise in independent charters by the day or for a quick trip to a resort and back is Inner Maldives Holidays (see page 50). The company operates a fleet of six fast launches available at any time. They are suitable for non-stop journeys of up to three hours. Charter costs are from US$400 per day (for 12 hours from 06.00 to 18.00) with fuel extra. Point-to-point and short hires are based on time and fuel cost. Each speedboat has two 200hp engines and can carry 20 passengers. There are toilet facilities on board. The crew of all the launches are young Maldivians, experienced in local waters, and always eager to please. As a service to the industry, the company provides free transportation to accident victims if they have a launch in the area, and also to Maldivians when a launch is returning empty to Male' at the end of a charter.

Cruise and safari vessels For information on these, see *Chapter 4*, pages 113–16.

✈ BY AIR
Internal flights With tourism spreading throughout the atolls, flying from one end of the archipelago, via Male', to the other by conventional aircraft or seaplane is becoming commonplace. Seats are booked in conjunction with resort accommodation, since foreigners can only stay in hotels or guesthouses licensed to accept them. Fares can be built into the holiday package but where they are paid for separately they can add up to U$500 or more to the cost of a holiday. Maldivians fly at concessionary rates.

There are five domestic (regional) airports in operation served by flights from Male' where there is a new domestic airlines terminal with planes using the same runway as international flights. New airports are being planned in atolls to serve passengers holidaying in resorts under construction. From north to south, the regional airports are:

- **Haa Dhaal Atoll**, Hanimadhoo, 155 miles, 48 minutes from Male'
- **Shaviyani Atoll**, Farukolhu. Planned
- **Lhaviyani Atoll**, Madivaru, 77 miles, 25 minutes from Male'
- **Dhaal Atoll**, Maafushi. Planned
- **Thaa Atoll**, Olhugiri. Planned
- **Laamu Atoll**, Kadhdhoo, 138 miles, 38 minutes from Male'
- **Gaaf Dhaal**, Kaadehdhoo, 225 miles, 55 minutes from Male'
- **Gaaf Dhaal**, Raalheodegella. Planned
- **Addu Atoll**, Gan 293 miles, 1 hour 10 minutes from Male'

Domestic carriers

Island Aviation Services Ltd 26 Ameer Ahmed Magu, Male'; ☎ 3335566; f 3314806, e info@island.com.mv; www.island.com.mv. Reservations & ticketing 1st floor, Aifaanu Bldg, Boduthakurufaanu Magu; ☎ 3335544; f 3328456; e sales@island.com.mv; ⏰ office hours 08.00–17.00 Sun–Thu, 09.00–12.00 Sat. Regional offices: Hanimadhoo ☎ 6520095; f 6520067; e iashaq@island.com.mv; Kadhdhoo ☎ 6800706; f 6800706; e iaskdo@island.com.mv; Kaadedhdhoo ☎ 6840024; f 6840024; e iaskdm@island.com.mv; Gan ☎ 6898035; f 6898031; e iasgan@island.com.mv. Island Aviation, a government-owned airline formed in 2000, operates a fleet of turbo-prop aircraft with 16-seater Dornier 228s & 37 & 50-seater Dash-8 planes on its domestic services. (International services began in Jan 2008 with flights linking Male' with Trivandrum in India.) Regional flights (even the small 16-seater aircraft) have inflight crew who give a safety demonstration & serve soft drink & crackers. In the seat pocket is a laminated map identifying the inhabited & resort islands & historical sites being flown over. Several flights a day link Male' with the regional airports, & flights can also be chartered, with the Dornier 228 equipped with sliding door & harness seats for photo flights. Island Aviation also provides passengers & baggage handling for international airlines at Male' & Gan airports, VIP passenger lounges, cargo & engineering as well as General Sales & Passenger Agency services for airlines.

Trans Maldivian Airways ☎ 3348400; f 3348409; e mail@tma.com.mv; www.tma.com.mv. TMA, which operates 16 sea planes (see below), introduced scheduled flights to domestic airports by 50-passenger ATR 42-300 aircraft in 2007, commencing with twice daily flights between Gan & Male' & later adding a service to Hanimadhoo, the northernmost airport. Fares for foreigners between Male' & Gan at press time were US$135, economy, & US$195 business class, one way. There was a free luggage allowance of 20kg (25kg in business class) with a 5kg carry-on allowance. Excess luggage US$1.50 per kg. Check-in at the airline's terminal is 2hrs before scheduled departure.

Seaplane services There are two companies providing seaplane transfer services between Male' and the far-flung resorts. Both operate from terminals and jetties on the east side of the main Hulhule runway. Together they operate over 35 seaplanes, which makes Maldives the largest base of Twin Otter seaplanes in the world.

Trans Maldivian Airlines (TMA) Airport; ☎ 3348400; f 3348409; e mail@tma.com; www.tma.com.mv. TMA grew out of the Hummingbird helicopter operation begun in 1989, with seaplanes added in 1997 before it became exclusively seaplane from 1999, adding 2 turbojets in 2007. Its 16 Twin Otter seaplanes are painted blue & yellow & serve a score of resorts.

Maldivian Air Taxi Pte Ltd Airport; ☎ 3315201; f 3315203; e mat@mat.com.mv; www.maldivianairtaxi.com. Is the largest & oldest (it began operations in 1993) seaplane company in the islands. Its aircraft are painted a distinctive red & white.

Both companies operate a fleet of 16-seater De Havilland Twin Otters, a Canadian-manufactured aircraft fitted with floats instead of wheels. They can only land on the sea and so are popular for chartering to designated desert islands for a picnic, since they can manoeuvre right up to the beach after landing in the calm waters of a lagoon. At resorts, they either tie up to the resort's jetty for passengers to disembark, or at an offshore pontoon secured in the lagoon from where passengers transfer by a *dhoni* or speedboat to their resort. Pilots are dressed appropriately for the tropics in shorts and pilot shirt with epaulettes and they fly barefooted. While the cabin crew are Maldivian, the captains are international with Maldivian co-pilots.

The seaplane departure terminals are located on the east side of the runway, the opposite side to the international departures terminal. Seaplane company coaches ferry passengers and luggage from the coach park near the passenger jetties on a journey around the island. This begins with a run southwards along the west coast the full length of the runway, then across the island at the end of the runway, and back northwards to the other end. The departure hall of MAT is attractively furnished with granite-tiled floors, chunky wooden chairs and plaited screwpine weave ceilings, giving a foretaste of tropical décor at the resort. There are also special lounges dedicated to the top upmarket resorts with complimentary refreshments. The TMA departure terminal has a VIP lounge as well as four dedicated resort lounges and a public area with a café.

At check-in, passengers are weighed along with their luggage, and the luggage is piled up by a sign indicating the flight. The hall is open-sided with a view of dozens of seaplanes tied up at the wooden jetties on one side, and of huge jets taking off from the runway on the other side.

Seaplanes serve the resort islands and, if there is space, take Maldivian passengers, too, bound for their home islands near the resort. The cost of seaplane transfer to and from a resort is usually built into the holiday price if you have bought a package. If not, the flight must be arranged through a local travel agent. Neither airline quotes a fixed price for transfer costs to any of the resorts they fly to, due to contractual agreements with the resorts, Male' travel agents and their overseas tour operators. All flights are booked on behalf of the foreign tour operators by their local Male'-based travel agents. Seaplanes can be chartered from both companies for photo flights, independent picnic excursions, etc. It is also possible to buy a round-trip ticket at a special price at the last moment, if seats are available, on a flight to and from a resort, but this would just be for the scenic flight experience since passengers are only allowed to disembark if they are guests of a resort.

There is no regular schedule for seaplane flights because they fly according to demand. In an edition of the inflight magazine of Maldivian Air Taxi this is explained thus:

> We do not have fixed timings; we adjust to the needs of our passengers, not the other way round. When we receive a booking request from one of our contract partners, either a tour operator or a resort, we register the name, arrival date and time and flight number. When all bookings have been received, usually not more than a day or two before the actual flight, the final schedule is laid. This is a bit of a puzzle as we do not want to keep passengers waiting, but our skilled and experienced reservations staff make it possible, aided by tailor-made computer software. No two schedules are alike, every day a new timetable is created.

That's why, when guests on a resort enquire from reception about the time of their departure by seaplane from the resort to catch their flight from the International Airport, they are told to wait until the evening before departure for the information. Some guests worry they will miss their flight, but the schedules always allow plenty of time to check in and make the connection.

🏠 ACCOMMODATION

All accommodation is listed and described either in *Chapter 5* (Male') or in the resort listings in *Chapters 6, 7, 8* and *9*. For an alphabetical list of all resorts and the atolls in which they are located, and for the page number on which they are reviewed, see *Appendix 3* (page 204). A general guide to resort facilities appears in *Chapter 3*.

✖ EATING AND DRINKING

FOOD One of the greatest pleasures in Maldives, after all that sunbathing and fish watching, is eating. There are three kinds of cuisine: Maldivian, international and island resort. Fortunately, the first doesn't cost much and is easy to sample if you happen to be in Male', since it is available throughout the day in cafés. The second, at some restaurants in resorts close to Male', will be comparable in cost to a good restaurant at home. The third tries hard to satisfy full-board guests from different countries three times a day, and tests (and often proves) the ingenuity of a chef working on an island miles away from the nearest meat and vegetable markets, but with fish on the doorstep.

Maldivian cuisine is much more than that usually offered on the Maldivian Night buffets once a week at the resorts. Since that is often prepared by chefs from Sri Lanka, it will have more in common with that country's national dish, rice and curry, than with the subtleties of Maldivian preparations.

The best way to sample Maldivian cuisine is to drop in to one of the many cafés in Male'. It is usually impossible to see from the outside what a place is like inside. Doors are kept closed to keep out flies and dust and, since the best cafés are known by their reputation, they don't find it necessary to advertise.

Inside will be an array of short eats (little snacks) set out on a counter under glass or plastic covers. You help yourself to, or are served with, what you want; it's best to point to the items that look interesting since some of the names are a bit difficult to remember. Or a selection of the café's specialities will be brought without you asking as soon as you sit at a table. A glass of water will also be presented without being requested.

Many of the short eats are on the samosa principle of fried pastry of different textures wrapped in various shapes around a filling, usually spicy, and, this being Maldives, fishy. There are some surprises. One is a delicious tiny edible parcel containing cabbage, others are the different flavoured and textured balls. The sweet items are wobbly cubes of goo and a variety of coconut-based delicacies. Longer eats such as fried fish and curries, eaten with *roshi*, a pancake-style bread, torn up in it, are also available.

The café life is not restricted to Male'. Many of the inhabited village islands have tiny cafés with a limited, home-cooked range of short eats washed down with a canned soft drink. A popular, and tasty, meal prepared at short notice in such places is instant noodles with canned tuna mixed in it.

Eating out Most opportunities to eat out are in Male': see *Chapter 5*, pages 139–40, for some recommendations.

Breakfast Most resorts serve breakfast as a buffet, a boon for those on half board whose next meal might not be until dinner, so they can stock up. Taking food out of the restaurant, even bread to feed the fish waiting by the jetty, is frowned upon, however. The better resorts include a curry and *roshi* on the buffet counter and this really is a good start to an energetic day. If no curry is available, you could request it, since every resort makes curry in the morning for their staff. Maldivian curry is not as fierce as Indian or Sri Lankan.

Home cooking Whenever you are invited to a Maldivian home, short eats of some kind will be served. Although fish is the main ingredient of a Maldivian meal, the preparation of it does not vary much. One wit said there are two kinds of meal cooked at home: fish and rice and rice and fish.

Vegetables do not feature much in home cooking, and even eggs and chicken are rare unless an island fowl is popped into the pot on a special occasion. The main meal is eaten at around midday, with a lighter version in the evening.

Eating is usually done with the fingers of the right hand, rolling the food up in a ball and sliding it into the mouth with the thumb. Spoons will be found if required. Do not use your left hand, that's for washing in the toilet.

Typical Maldivian food Maldivians serve fish, usually tuna, for virtually every meal of the day. Combined with onions, chillies, coconut, lime juice and rice, fish

Jean Petty

In Male', throughout the day and well into the night, Maldivian men will go to the local tea shops which serve curries, sweet tea, soft drinks and snacks which are called short eats or *hedhikaa*.

A number of the more popular short eats are listed below:

GULHA These are fish balls made by mixing the *valhoamas* with coconut, onions, chilli, ginger and lime juice. The hand is used to form this into small balls. A pastry-like dough is made with grated coconut, flour and water. This is formed into a small cup-like shape and a fish ball is encased in the pastry. These are then shallow fried.

BAJIYAA These are made with thinly rolled, half circles of dough formed into a cone shape. A filling of tinned tuna, onions, chilli, ginger and lemongrass is put into the centre and the pastry is folded down over the filling and sealed with a flour and water paste. The resulting little triangles are then shallow fried.

KULHI BOAKIBAA Rice is soaked in water overnight and mixed with *valhoamas*, onions, chilli, ginger and coconut. This mixture is kneaded and placed in a greased baking dish. It is baked and cut into squares.

HUNI FOLHI This is a sweet short eat of coconut, honey and water cooked to a paste and then used to fill a *roshi*. It is rolled up like a spring roll and then shallow fried.

FONI BOAKIBAA This is a sweet made with coconut, rice flour, water, sugar and rose water. It is baked and cut into squares.

DHIYAA HAKURU Another sweet favoured by Maldivians, especially during Ramazan, it is made from the sap of the palm trunk, called *raa*. This sap is cooked until it is like honey. It is then mixed with pre-cooked rice and banana.

Jean Petty and her husband, who worked for Dhiraagu, lived in Male' for several years.

forms the basic diet. The tuna can be freshly caught or it could be boiled, smoked and sun-dried (which is called *hikimas*) or just smoked (called *valhoamas*). Sometimes they use locally canned tuna.

In a large percentage of Maldivian homes, the women still cook on wood-burning stoves. The kitchen is in a separate building or area, away from the living and sleeping parts of the house. This is to avoid the smoke from the burning firewood. Wood-burning stoves are slowly being replaced by electric and gas ranges in more modern homes, but the layout is still the traditional one, with the kitchen separated from the rest of the home.

The coconut used in cooking is always freshly grated. This is done on a low stool with a sharp serrated blade fixed on the end. The coconut is split in half and the meat of the coconut is grated on the serrated blade and caught on a tray placed underneath. The stool is called a *huni-gon'di*.

For breakfast, you might have *valhoamas* mixed with coconut, onions, chilli and lime juice. This is called *mas huni* and is served with the local bread called *roshi*. *Roshi* is made of flour, water, oil and salt. It is formed into a dough, which is rolled out into a thin round and then cooked on a hot griddle.

Another version is *mas roshi*, made from flour, water, coconut and salt. Pieces of this dough are formed into thick rounds with the hands. A mixture of coconut, fish, onions, chilli and lime juice is placed in the centre and the dough is formed around the filling, patted with the hands to form a flat cake. This is then fried on a hot griddle.

Garudhiya could be called the food of Maldivians, especially so in the outer islands. It is a clear soup containing chunks of tuna. While guests in resorts would drink it like a soup, islanders use it to smother rice which has been cooked with coconut milk and served with lime, chilli and onions.

Also favoured by Maldivians is a concentrated tuna paste called *rihaakuru*. This can be mixed with cooked rice, chilli and onions, or it can be spread on warm *roshi*. Many Maldivians like *rihaakuru* with grated green mango and chilli. *Rihaakuru* can also be bought in small packets to try at home, perhaps spread on toast.

Hanaakurimas is a dry fish curry. It is prepared by frying small pieces of fresh fish with many spices until the fish is dry.

The main source of carbohydrates in the Maldivian diet is almost invariably rice. In some islands, however, breadfruit plays an important part in the diet. When eaten as a curry, this is called *babukeylu hithi*. Breadfruit can also be thinly sliced, fried and served as a snack.

Other vegetables grown locally and eaten by Maldivians are taro and sweet potato.

For a special family occasion or religious celebration such as a wedding or a son's circumcision, or the Eid al-Fitr which follows Ramazan, the month of fasting, a dish like chicken curry or biryani would be served.

A Maldivian meal is usually finished by serving a tray of thinly sliced betel (areca) nut, betel leaves and lime paste which is for chewing as a *digestif*.

DRINK There are several kinds of soft drink, both imported and of local manufacture. The Male' Aerated Water Company produces a range of soft drinks of international standard, including Coca-Cola, on the island of Thulusdhoo. There, a modern plant in landscaped gardens transforms seawater (that is what desalinated water comes from) into Coke, which passes the most stringent quality tests. Also produced there is a mineralised bottled drinking water called Aquarius.

For anything stronger, visitors to the Maldives have to go to the bars in the resort islands, since no alcohol is sold anywhere else, apart from the hotel and the duty-free shop at the airport. Expatriate residents with special permits can keep liquor at their homes, but it is strictly for their own consumption.

FESTIVALS AND HOLIDAYS

The most important occasion in the religious calendar is Ramazan (or Ramadan, known in Dhivehi as Roadhamas), the ninth month of the Muslim year, a moveable fast on the Gregorian calendar. It is rigidly observed in Maldives, with fasting for 30 days from near dawn until sunset each day. All restaurants are closed during this period. As well as renouncing food, Muslims are also supposed to abstain from all worldly pleasures. For guests on the resort islands, however, life goes on as usual. Fasting during Ramazan is one of the principles of Islam, based on the words of the Holy Prophet who said 'whoever fasts during Ramazan, out of faith seeking no rewards, will have all past sins forgiven'.

The following is the list of holidays for 2008 and 2009. The days on which religious and some other holidays fall each year are decided by the lunar calendar, and some depend on the sighting of the moon. Islamic holidays begin at sunset the previous evening. In addition there are holidays fixed according to the Western calendar (indicated in **bold** below).

2008

3 November	**Victory Day**
11 & 12 November	**2nd Republic Day**
December	Hajj Day
9 December	Eid al-Adha (Feast of Sacrifice; 4 days)
9 December	on the occasion of Eid al-Adha Day
10 December	on the occasion of Eid al-Adha Day
10 December	**Fishermen's Day**
11 December	on the occasion of Eid al-Adha Day
29 December	Islamic New year

2009 At the time of going to press dates were still to be confirmed for some of the following holidays. Consult www.worldtravelguide.net for the latest information.

1 January	**New Year's Day**
9 March	Prophet Mohamed's birthday
April	National Day (to be confirmed)
April	The day Maldives embraced Islam (to be confirmed)
28 June	Huravee
26 & 27 July	**Independence Day**
22 August	Beginning of Ramazan
21 September	Eid al-Fitr Day (end of Ramazan, 3 days)
22 September	on the occasion of Eid al-Fitr Day
23 September	on the occasion of Eid al-Fitr Day
September	Martyr's Day
3 November	**Victory Day**
11 & 12 November	**2nd Republic Days**
28 November	Eid al-Adha (Feast of Sacrifice; 4 days)
29 November	on the occasion of Eid al-Adha
30 November	on the occasion of Eid al-Adha
1 December	on the occasion of Eid al-Adha
10 December	**Fishermen's Day**
December	Hajj Day (to be confirmed)

Martyr's Day recalls the death of Sultan Ali VI in 1558 while defending the nation against Portuguese attack. The ousting of the Portuguese in 1573 is commemorated by National Day. Huravee celebrates the victory over the Indian occupation in 1752. The Independence holiday commemorates the end of the British protection period and Victory Day celebrates the defeat of the Tamil mercenaries in 1988. The November holiday commemorates the founding of the Second Republic in 1968. For fuller explanations of all these, see *History*, pages 17–23.

Where a fixed or Islamic calendar holiday falls on a Friday, an extra day is added. Friday, being the weekend, is always a holiday; Christmas never is.

Maldivians generally tend to spend Fridays quietly at home, after going to Friday prayers, although some Male' residents enjoy outings to neighbouring islands. Shops and other businesses in Male' are invariably closed on Friday mornings, though shops and restaurants often open in the late afternoon and evening. The airport normally shuts down for a few hours for part of the day also. At resorts it is business as usual, though staff will attend the Friday prayers.

VISITORS WITH SPECIAL REQUIREMENTS

DISABLED TRAVELLERS The Maldives appear ideal for the disabled traveller who might occasionally need some help. There are none of the hazards of most major cities, like having to cross a road in heavy traffic, and few stressful situations. At the airport on arrival and departure, there are plenty of people willing to help, and boat crews are used to assisting passengers in and out of their vessels.

In the resorts, most guestrooms are at ground level. Management will make ramps available for wheelchairs at restaurant or guestroom entrances, if requested in advance. Disabled guests who like swimming need have no fear of currents or getting out of depth in the shallow lagoons of most resorts.

Any special accommodation requirements for disabled travellers (such as a room close to the restaurant or swimming pool) should be communicated in advance direct to the resort. In the resorts, staff are always willing to lend a hand. There are no hills or steep slopes anywhere in the Maldives, but it may be worth checking with resorts whether paths and walkways have appropriate surfaces for a particular traveller's needs.

CHILDREN The Maldives is particularly safe for young children, especially since there are no cars (nor roads) on the resorts. Kids can roam around quite happily, though obviously they will need to be supervised when in or near the sea or a swimming pool. Some resorts have special facilities and play areas and even clubs for children, and babysitting can usually be arranged. Maldivians are fond of children and like spoiling visitors' kids.

Older children will find amusement in the regular outdoor activities available, and could even learn scuba diving. Most resorts feature discos, or even live bands, on a few evenings each week.

SOLO OPTIONS Lots of single travellers go to Maldives, but there is no 'singles' culture or any resort or island dedicated to those who want to party with other singles. Most visitors who travel to the Maldives alone are enthusiasts of some kind, such as divers or surfers, and soon link up with fellow enthusiasts. Some hotels available through package holidays have a single supplement, since each hotel room is designed for two. When you book direct, there is a different price for single occupancy, ranging from 20% to 50% less than for double occupancy.

In the island atmosphere, it is very easy for a single guest to make friends and be involved in activities. In most islands, the expatriate staff, both male and female, at the watersports centres are single, so the young might find companionship there. The resident guides, usually female, are single, too, but they are usually so busy you will rarely see them except during tour group briefings.

There is no threat to single travellers in the Maldives; it is not in the Maldivian nature. Women will feel particularly relaxed that their enjoyment of the sun, the fresh air and the music of a tropic night is unlikely to be misunderstood by resort staff. Guests, on the other hand, are something else.

If, as a single, you decide to come with a friend, make sure you know that person well since, if something goes wrong, there is not much chance to escape from your companion on such small islands.

RETIREMENT This is not a practical place for retirement, nor is the lifestyle suited for either retirees or dropouts, however much the idea of being an island beachcomber living off one's savings might appeal. The accommodation available in Male' for renting is priced for professionals, not unemployed retirees, and the capital is hardly the place where anyone would want to spend retirement. The only other places where foreigners are allowed to stay are those uninhabited islands which have tourist resorts, so the alternative is to live as a tourist. That is what many people who have retired in their home countries actually do. They stay in a resort as long-term guests during the European winter, with everything (including

2

visa extensions) arranged by the resort, and the additional advantage of having ever-changing fellow guests for company.

🛍 SHOPPING

WHERE TO SHOP Almost all shopping opportunities in the Maldives, apart from some handicrafts, are to be found in Male'. For further ideas on where to go, in addition to those discussed below, see *Chapter 5*.

DUTY-FREE SHOPPING The duty-free shopping mall at Male' International Airport is one of the best in the region. Not only is it well designed, making shopping a pleasure, but the goods are also generally reasonably priced. For goods like cheap watches and electronic equipment, however, shopping in Male' itself offers more variety and low prices, but for those who have been marooned on their holiday resort island for a few days and have been deprived of shopping, the airport is like an oasis to the thirsty.

Prices compare favourably with Dubai and Colombo, the likeliest stopovers on your way home, and there is a large variety. Expensive spirits in smart bottles are favoured by Japanese shoppers; cold beer is available from the self-service fridge. Sharing the centre of the mall is the perfume shop with a wide selection, and helpful staff (many from the Philippines) to persuade customers to choose a new fragrance.

The mall also includes a fancy-goods shop with luxurious brand-name clothing accessories, an electronics store, a watch and camera store, and a toy shop. There is also a bookshop with a wide range of books on the Maldives. Next to it is a curious souvenir store where, if you spend a certain sum of money, you participate in an everlasting lottery. A confectionery and fine-food supermarket adds to the range of goods available.

All the shops quote prices in US dollars. Payment may be made by credit card or travellers' cheques.

It is possible to bargain, unusual in duty-free shops. Staff speak Japanese and Italian, as well as some German, French and other languages. 'Prices marked on goods,' said a salesman, 'are the highest indicative prices.'

WHAT TO BUY 'Leave only footprints, take home only memories' is the theme some resorts like to foster. Since most souvenirs available in the gift shops are T-shirts with slogans stencilled on them locally, or are wholly from Indonesia or Sri Lanka, it is not easy to find something authentic or unusual. Yet genuine souvenirs of a place keep memories alive.

So if you want to take home something to remind you of the Maldives, what can you buy?

Conventional souvenirs You will find lots of T-shirts proclaiming 'Maldives' across the chest. As well as white T-shirts sponge-stencilled in front of you in the resort gift shop, there are T-shirts which have almost become an indigenous art form because of the ingenious techniques used. The backrooms of a few Male' souvenir shops have been turned into workshops where colours are blended, stencils shaped and slogans devised to make attractive and unusual designs. The shirt itself is imported, but the design and work is Maldivian.

Chandhanee Magu, from the waterfront to Fareedhee Magu, is where to find the conventional souvenir shops in Male', as well as along Fareedhee Magu itself. You will be thrilled or appalled by the kitsch that's offered; it ranges from wooden masks from Sri Lanka to wooden fruit from Indonesia. Something 'Made in Maldives' is difficult to find, unless you go for garments.

On village islands visited during island-hopping tours from a nearby resort, the selection can be disappointing if you are keen to buy something produced in the village to help keep a local craft alive. The stalls set out in the village street as soon as tourists turn up testify to the skill of overseas craftsmen, not to the village wood turner or mat weaver. But there is currently an attempt to revive local crafts on the islands, so keep a look out for truly local souvenirs.

Local handicrafts The making and marketing of local handicrafts is officially much encouraged. Overseas experts have surveyed and advised, exhibitions are held, and craftsmen are exhorted to use the skills handed down to them by their forefathers.

On Bandos island, visitors can see two traditional crafts being kept alive: lacquerwork and mat weaving. These are demonstrated by craftspeople, who offer the results for sale. In villages, if you can stay longer than is usually allowed on an island-hopping trip, you may discover villagers making items for themselves, but not normally to sell.

Cadjan weaving is common. *Cadjan* is a mat made from coconut leaves sewn together with coir rope. It is used for thatching houses and for fences. In some villages, the bundles of reeds that provide the thatch for rustic resort cabana roofs are stitched together by patient women, using long wooden needles and coconut-fibre thread. Since a roof made of that thatch needs renewing very often, it is more expensive to use the local product than imported roofing material. *Sataa*, a soft lattice mat woven from thin strips of dried screwpine leaf, is popular for ceilings in many resort cabanas.

Coir rope is spun from the fibre salvaged from a coconut husk after it has been soaked in the sea for a few weeks. The fibre is pounded with wooden mallets to separate the fibre strands, and then dried. The strands are twisted and combined by hand to produce a strong rope of a required thickness. The string is a bit coarse but, if you could find some to buy, it would make an ecologically correct gift.

Since nothing of the coconut tree is ever wasted, you may come across other items being used, but not for sale. The double-shell vessel of the toddy tapper is attractive for its egg-timer shape. Toddy, known as *raa*, is the nectar tapped from the coconut flower, and is a sweet, natural drink. Like many of the traditional handicrafts, even toddy is becoming scarce since young men prefer to fish (or work in a resort) rather than climb trees to tap for it.

Lacquerwork is a highly skilled decorative art in which the craftsman first shapes the wood, whether he is making a vase or a chess set, usually using a hand-powered lathe. The lacquer is burnished on and etched in designs that owe a lot to tradition, but may also have the artist's original touch. Lacquer vases and boxes, pots and sticks are popular; so popular that they are rarely to be found even in the souvenir shops.

On Thulhaadhoo island, the *holhu-ashi*, the open-sided community shelter where villagers relax together, has posts of lacquerwork. It is possible to see the work being done, but difficult to buy any examples, since the few craftsmen produce only for order.

The weaving of mats of various sizes and shapes from reeds or strips of dried stems of coconut palm leaves, and the making of containers and food covers (used as lamp shades in some resorts), is practised on many islands. On Kihaadhoo, in Baa Atoll, I found women and older people at work in their cottages fashioning *sataa* covers and containers for a resort's décor but not as souvenirs for sale. I was delighted to find this proof that tourism is helping to keep an otherwise dying craft, and the village elders, alive.

Although there is a flourishing boat-building industry with many skilled carpenters throughout the islands, there is not much tradition of building model boats. On Alifushi, an island dedicated to boat building, I met a retired carpenter who carves an occasional model *dhoni*. He said he knew of no-one else making wooden boats for sale.

On Kadholhudhoo, in Raa Atoll, I watched a silversmith at work on the porch of his home. He plaited silver wire bought in Male' to make chains and bracelets, a skill he had learned 25 years before in his home island of Hulhudheli in Dhaal Atoll, renowned as the atoll of silver and goldsmiths. His companion operated the bellows to keep the tiny charcoal fire alight while he fashioned a dainty silver chain. He said islanders buy all he could produce; none was left over for souvenirs.

Unusual souvenirs Do not despair if the conventional souvenirs are disappointing and local handicrafts are unobtainable. While you might not find much that is unusual in your resort gift shop, Male' has a wealth of items not normally thought of as souvenirs. The place to look for what Maldivians use is where they shop, in the dimly lit, dusty grocery and hardware shops close to the fish market. These are the shops along the lanes leading inland from the waterfront to Orchid Magu.

I bought a *gudu-guda* from one of them. This is the water-pipe beloved by older Maldivian women, and for the tourist it makes a conversation-piece ornament. It was sold in parts, beginning with the bulbous bottle that forms its base. Metal tubes and a thin, rubber hosepipe came from another part of the shop. A funnel with a cone-shaped top and a lid to trap the charcoal were also produced by the shopkeeper. To complete the purchase, he sold me an onion of sweet-smelling, moist tobacco. The whole hookah cost less than US$25. It reminds me more of the Maldives than any T-shirt.

Household items like coconut graters, granite stone spice crushers with a stone rolling pin, wooden mortars and pestles and coconut shell spoons can all be unearthed in the hardware stores.

Marine implements (perhaps an anchor is too big a souvenir!) are on sale at Shabim Emporium on the waterfront, as are forgotten lacquer boxes.

On the waterfront, at the commercial (ie: west) side of the Presidential Jetty, are the markets. There is a dried-fish market fenced in with netting to keep out the flies. Sri Lankan visitors patronise it, since the wood-like pieces of dried fish, known in Sri Lanka as 'Maldive fish', sold there are the best souvenirs for them, highly prized for Sri Lankan cuisine. However, it might not be the best present to take back to Europe.

The vegetable market yields unusual items to eat: breadfruit chips in packets and various rolled sweet concoctions, some of which taste, rather disconcertingly, of chilli. This is the place to buy areca nut and betel leaf chew, but would customs officers at home understand? The STO supermarket in Orchid Magu is a good source of locally used items, such as a large rice-serving spoon, which you won't usually find at home.

They might seem tame, but Dhiraagu's phonecards are unique to keep as they have a good photograph on one side and state that they are valid only in the Maldives on the other.

Philately Stamps are one of the best souvenirs, since they are inexpensive, easy to carry, depict local scenes and are colourful. Stamps set in plastic as key fobs make a good souvenir.

Stamps were first used in the Maldives in 1906, when a postal service was introduced. They were actually Ceylon stamps, which were overprinted with the word *Maldives*. The design was a profile of King Edward VII and they are now highly valued by collectors.

The first stamps dedicated to the Maldives were introduced in 1909: a set of 12 differently coloured and valued stamps all with the same design, featuring the minaret of the Friday (Hukuru) mosque in Male'. They were replaced in 1933 with a new set of ten stamps, and this set remained in circulation until 1950. The replacement set of nine values reflected the new currency, with stamps for two laari up to one rufiyaa, showing a palm tree and a sailing boat.

A new pictorial definitive issue was released in 1956. Lower values showed Male' harbour, and the high denominations depicted the fort and government buildings. In 1960 came a new definitive issue, showing local landmarks and scenery. Local events commemorated in special issues included the 55th anniversary of the first Maldivian postage stamp in 1961, and in 1964 the anniversary of the islands' conversion to Islam.

By the end of 1994, there had been almost 300 different issues of stamps, 90 of them during the period June 1987 to October 1994. This frequent issue of stamps was to cater to the demand by collectors for thematic issues, stamps designed to a particular theme. Frequently the theme had no local relevance, as in the splendid Trains of Asia series in August 1994. Wonderful for train fans and stamp collectors, but odd for this nation of islands where most of the population have never seen a train.

Maldives Post (see box on page 94) now employs its own stamp designer. Their first issue of stamps was to commemorate UNDP Sustainable Human Development and was released, together with a decorative first-day cover on 24 October 1994.

Recent issues of stamps include art, dinosaurs, butterflies, a special issue to celebrate the 25th anniversary of the Republic, birds, shells and fish, flowers, mushrooms and 100 years of the National Security Service.

Most stamps at face value in mint condition or cancelled to order can be obtained from the new GPO in Boduthakurufaanu Magu in Male', Maldives Post Shop, as can pictorial first-day covers. The stamps are printed in the UK on non-phosphor unwatermarked paper sheets, and are produced in association with the philatelic agent appointed by the government. Maldives' stamps can also be obtained from the agent: Inter-Governmental Philatelic Corporation, 460 West 34th Street, New York, NY 10001, USA.

Maps and books For the Maldives, you need a chart rather than a map. In England, Admiralty Charts for the area are available from Kelvin Hughes Limited (*New North Rd, Hainault, Ilford, Essex IG6 2UR, UK; ⤷ 020 8502 6887; f 020 8500 0837; e marketing@kelvinhughes.co.uk; www.kelvinhughes.co.uk*).

Maps showing the Maldives as part of the Indian Ocean or Indian subcontinent are available from Stanfords (*12/14 Long Acre, London WC2E 9LP; ⤷ 020 7836 1321; f 020 7836 0189; www.stanfords.co.uk*).

There are plenty of pretty pictorial maps on sale in the resort gift shops and in Male' which are useful for working out which island you are on and its relation to other islands and atolls. The Atoll Editions Maldives Map is a particularly good one.

For the enthusiast, it's worth trying to get hold of a 24-page booklet called *Map of Maldives* published in 1979 by Novelty Press, Male'. It contains a directory of the islands with locator key (over 1,000 in all). Atolls and their islands are shown on separate pages as sketches, not to scale but with a longitude and latitude grid. Place names are typewritten in English and in Dhivehi script. It's a bit confusing, more for reference than for finding your way around the ocean.

More recent, and much prettier, is *Malways: Maldives Island Directory* (see *Appendix 4*, page 208) with maps of each atoll on separate pages and an index in English of all the islands. This can be bought at gift shops in Male'. It's expensive but a fine and useful souvenir.

2

The Ministry of Tourism has produced a colourful brochure, which includes a map of the atolls showing the location of resort islands, and also a separate street map of Male'. Unfortunately, this is too small to show the names of streets and Male' is such a maze (and street signs are usually in Dhivehi) that the map is best used for finding the main landmarks, not for locating a friend's house. See also the various magazines discussed under *Media and communications* (page 92).

For a colourful taste of the Maldives read *Toni The Maldive Lady My Story* by Toni de Laroque and Royston Ellis (published by Times Editions, Singapore). This can be ordered from **Maldive Travel** (*3 Esher Hse, 11 Edith Terrace, London SW10 0TH;* ℘ *020 7352 2246 or 7351 9351;* f *020 7351 3382;* e *maldives@dircon.co.uk; www.maldivetravel.com*).

HAIRDRESSING

Only a few of the resorts have hairdressing salons; the most notable is Bandos which can easily be reached by boat from Male'. Its hours are 10.00–12.30, 13.00–17.30 and 20.30–22.00 daily, except Sunday when it is open 10.00–14.00.

There are salons in Male', too, many of them with Sri Lankan hair stylists. A favourite barber is in Male': an Indian who works from a 'hole in the wall', a place without a name in a street linking Orchid Magu and Chandhanee Magu. There are more fashionable places for men (Jingles in Chandhanee Magu has been recommended) but the cost is higher.

☺ ARTS AND ENTERTAINMENT

EVENING ENTERTAINMENT AND NIGHTLIFE Nightlife in Maldives is like scuba diving in Bangkok: you are in the wrong place if that's what you want. Not everywhere is moribund after dinner, though. Male' itself throbs with activity until 23.00, when the last of the shops put up their shutters. People promenade, chat in cafés, call on friends and do all the things it was too hot to do during the day. But there are no discos, bars, nightclubs or bingo halls.

The resorts make an effort to keep guests entertained, starting with night fishing before dinner and a band, disco, karaoke or folk dancing after it. Bandos, when flight crews are on a long stopover, can get boisterous in its Sand Bar if there is a band playing. Kurumba and Full Moon share a Filipino band, which belts out pop tunes. Then there is moon-watching on the beach…

MUSIC Of the various forms of local music (see *The arts*, below), *Bodu Beru* is performed for hotel guests to experience, and it is still part of the island culture. *Bodu Beru* is similar to some of the songs and dances found in East Africa, although it lacks the raunchy verve of the *sega* of Mauritius. It is also known as *Baburu Lava*, 'negroid song', and was introduced into the Maldives by seafarers and settlers from Africa.

Bodu Beru is performed by a group of 15 people, which includes three drummers and a lead singer. The other members of the group dance to the music, expressing themselves in at times grotesque and satirical postures. 'As the song reaches a crescendo,' states a Department of Information leaflet, 'one or two dancers maintain the wild beat with their frantic movements ending in some cases in a trance.'

Women do not usually perform *Bodu Beru*, although, from an impromptu performance I witnessed in one village island, they certainly enjoy it. According to the published leaflet:

In the early days the people gathered together to perform *Bodu Beru* and it became widely accepted as the music of the common people. The performing of the music is often referred to as 'vibrating the island'. A notable point about *Bodu Beru* is its noise and sometimes meaningless lyrics sung. The lyrics do not have a meaning because it consists of a mixture of local, neighbouring and some African words.

Today's disco dancers might find the dancing of *Bodu Beru* a little turgid and the music monotonic. Performances in hotels are livened up so that guests can join in. The performers are sometimes hotel staff letting their hair down, while resorts near islands bring the village *Bodu Beru* players over for an evening. The costume of the performers is a sarong (an ankle-length cloth wrapped around the waist) and sometimes a T-shirt which sports the name of the group, often the village sports club.

More modern and rhythmic music is played by some local dance bands, who do good versions of popular hits. They have the latest equipment and like to demonstrate its power, which could be annoying on a small island if you want to go to sleep early, but usually they finish by midnight.

ROMANCE The islands are undeniably romantic and perfect for a honeymoon. For the solo traveller in search of holiday romance, the possibilities are not great, since every island has only a limited number of guests and they are mostly couples. Becoming involved with a Maldivian will depend on circumstances and opportunity. As a resort manager reminded us, 'In Maldives, you can't do anything without being seen.'

There is no **gay scene**. Same sex relations are illegal and visitors should remember that while they can fly away, their Maldivian partner, if caught or suspected, cannot. Holidaying gay and lesbian non-Maldivian couples who confine their defining activities to the privacy of their resort guest rooms can enjoy the romantic ambience to their hearts' content, but should be discreet in the resort's public areas and everywhere else in the country.

GAMBLING Gamblers are out of luck! There are no casinos.

THE ARTS Displays of local handicrafts can be seen in the museum (see pages 143–5). People talk enthusiastically about local lacquerwork, and, although it had been a dying art, attempts are now being made to revive it. I went to Thulhaadhoo in Baa Atoll, which is the centre for lacquer, and found a few people still involved.

One, an old man who could barely see, was working a lathe built out of an old pedal sewing machine to create the wooden pieces for a chess set he was to lacquer. He was using calipers passed down over the centuries, together with the secret of his craft. I also met a young craftsman preparing wooden vases with the distinctive colours of black, yellow and red lacquer in chinoiserie designs for an exhibition.

The performing arts are represented by folk music, kept alive by schoolchildren performing folk dances on state occasions. One dance which sounds fun to watch is *Bandiyaa Jehun*, a pot dance. It is performed only by young women, who mark time by beating the metal pots they are carrying. I was told of islands where it was still performed but I was too late; in every island where I went to see it, we discovered it was no longer performed there. However, passengers on *Atoll Explorer* cruise are sometimes treated to enthusiastic (if over-long) performances of the pot dance and other folklore dances by women from village islands during its stopover at an uninhabited island for a barbecue dinner.

A leaflet issued by the Department of Information and Broadcasting lists examples of traditional folk music and dances. The *thaara* is a performance of tambourine music introduced by Gulf Arabs in the 17th century. The songs of the workers' dance, *Gaa odi lava*, were also in Arabic but were adapted for local use, to express satisfaction at the completion of a job. There are stick dances of various kinds and a special dance performed by women who sing while offering gifts. These, and other dances, are only seen now at special stage performances and not in a natural village setting, as is *Bodu Beru*.

The Maldives Association of Film Industries was inaugurated in 1995, and its members include actors, actresses, directors and film producers of the Maldivian film industry.

Local artists have matured from the days when their only form of expression was painting on T-shirts. Some are painting on canvas and local work can be bought, although artists are few and exhibitions of work rare.

PHOTOGRAPHY

The rules about taking photographs in Maldives are very simple. No photography is allowed in the museum in Male', nor in any mosque, and no photographs should be taken where you can see a road sign with a red slash across an image of a camera. The main place to avoid is the National Security Building in Male', which is the white, fortress-style edifice at the back of the waterfront park. You walk alongside it to the Islamic Centre.

When taking portraits of people, especially in the village islands, ask permission first. Don't be offended if someone's shyness leads to a refusal. In the islands it is better to have a Maldivian explain why you want a picture and arrange it for you. No payment is expected.

Commercial filming requires permission from the Ministry of Information, Arts and Culture. A lot of filming is done by film teams from different countries, and a list of the relevant rules and regulations is available from the Ministry. There is no fee.

On Friday afternoons in Sultan's Park in Male', you will see Maldivian photographers waiting with their cameras to snap souvenir pictures of people enjoying an afternoon stroll. There is a charge and the picture is delivered to the park the following Friday, or to a Male' address.

Standard films are sold in Male', but if you use special film, bring your own. There are a few photographic labs for processing colour prints, but the cost will be higher than at home.

MEDIA AND COMMUNICATIONS

NEWSPAPERS There are three daily newspapers: *Aafathis* and *Miadhu* published in the morning, and *Haveeru* in the evening with *Evening Weekly* also produced by *Haveeru*. They are all available at various bookshops in Male', but not in the islands. All are tabloid format with pages opening from left to right, starting at what, for Westerners, is the back. As well as their material in Dhivehi, they usually have four pages in English containing a useful summary of the main news from agencies, as well as the day's currency exchange rates.

Aafathis Dhunbugas Mahu, Male'; ☏ 3318609; www.aafathisnews.com.mv
Haveeru Ameeni Magu (PO Box 20103), Male'; ☏ 3313825; f 3323103; e haveeru@

dhivehinet.net.mv; www.haveeru.com; www.eveningweekly.com.mv
Miadhu Handhuvari Higun, Male'; ☏ 3320500; www.miadhu.com

Television Maldives (*Buruzu Magu, Galolhu, Male'*; ☏ *3325081;* f *3325083*) and the *Voice of Maldives* radio station (*Moonlight Higun, Henveiru;* ☏ *3315529;* f *3328357;*

www.vom.gov.mv) are government-run. They broadcast news in English every day and, on television, English-language films and cartoons, although these are rarely shown in full because of breaks in transmission for prayers or for a news bulletin. After the break a new programme usually begins, instead of resuming the movie. There are two national television channels and some CNN programmes are rebroadcast every day on these. Maldives Television can also be viewed in the islands that have satellite dishes to receive it. CNN and other satellite channels, including Indian-sourced ones, are viewable at most resorts and at hotels in Male', and private homes also receive satellite broadcasts.

The *Maldives News Bulletin* of several A4-size pages in English is issued weekly by the Maldives News Bureau of the Ministry of Information, Arts & Culture, Buruzu Magu, Male' (in the television station building).

BBC World Service Radio broadcasts on various frequencies in the Maldives. Frequencies change frequently! Check on the BBC website for the latest.

International news magazines are sold in Male'; they and the *International Herald Tribune* are available for guests at major resorts such as Kurumba and Full Moon. Magazines are occasionally produced in (or about) the Maldives.

A freebie that is of interest to visitors is called *Hello Maldives*. This describes itself as 'a user-friendly handbook for tourists, tour operators and everyone else'. It is published in India by QR Publications Pvt Ltd and distributed in the Maldives through a local office (*GPO Box 2165, Chandhanee Magu, Male'; ☎ 3313706; f 313764; e hminfo@hello-maldives.com; www.hello-maldives.com*). It contains varied and very detailed information of interest to visitors.

✉ **POST** Delivery time by international airmail is from three to eight days; by seamail it takes the same number of weeks. There is an Express Mail Service (EMS), which takes 30–72 hours to Colombo, Kuala Lumpur and Singapore.

As well as the new post office (on the western wing of Boduthakurufaanu Magu, opposite the harbour customs), there is a post office at the airport (on the left of the departure hall entrance). In the village islands, postal agencies have recently been set up. Mail posted in the resorts will be brought to the post office by staff for mailing in Male'. Mail for resorts is delivered to their Male' offices, while mail for the village islands is despatched by island *dhonis*. Male' residents have their mail delivered by that cheerful chap, the postman on a bike.

COURIER For sending or receiving urgent mail, the courier system in Male' works well. Delivery to resorts, however, is via the resort's Male' office. Services are provided by:

DHL International Ltd Cyprea Travels & Tours Pvt Ltd, Soasun Magu; ☎ 3326688
EMS International Courier Maldives Post Ltd, Boduthakurufaanu Magu; ☎ 3322255

FedEx Universal Travel Dept, 39 Orchid Magu; ☎ 3332244
TNT International Express, G Lagana, Hadheebee Magu; ☎ 3340004

DHIRAAGU Dhiraagu is not another inhabited island, but access to the world. It is actually an acronym for Dhivehi Raajjeyge Gulhun Pte Ltd, which means Maldives Telecommunication Company. It began as a joint venture between the government and Cable & Wireless, the UK telecommunications giant. Its main office for telephone calls, sending faxes and telegrams, and buying phonecards, is on Meduziyaarai Magu, close to the entrance to Sultan's Park, on the corner with Chandhanee Magu. The counter is open 07.30–20.00 on weekdays, and 08.00–18.00 on Fridays and public holidays. (☎ 3322802; f 3322800; e info@dhiraagu.com.mv; www.dhiraagu.com.mv.)

MALDIVES POST LTD

The handling of mail in Maldives is now done by a limited company set up by the government under a managing director, not a postmaster. The aim is to be customer-oriented rather than service-oriented, since civil service organisations are not known for the dynamism a private company needs.

'The postal service has to compete with commercial operations which perform parallel services,' said the managing director in an interview. 'If we are to compete, we must follow the same line.'

One reason the postal service in Maldives did not develop, despite being nearly 90 years old, is because of the closed nature of island society, with people preferring to hand over a letter to the recipient themselves, if they ever wrote one, or by trusted messenger. Now people do not have the time to be mail carriers. Since July 1994 postal agencies have been set up in the inhabited islands, to make it easier for villagers to send a message by mail, instead of giving it to a *dhoni* captain to deliver.

It is reassuring to see the bright-red postal agency sign outside a shop in an otherwise somnolent island. I posted many letters from such agencies and I was the first customer sending overseas mail in some of them. All had stamps and a rate list but I had to explain the details of overseas mail. The stamps on the envelopes were franked in front of me, except at one shop where the franking stamp was locked up in the island chief's office. Letters posted at an agency are kept until a *dhoni* is going to Male' and its captain is charged with the duty of taking the mail to the post shop. The postal agents are paid a monthly commission, initially fixed, as commission based on so little business would not be very attractive, until the service is accepted and becomes more widely used.

Mail destined for other islands goes via Male'. Since all boats have to report to the port authorities on arrival and departure, and need clearance to depart, the Post Shop gets information from the port authority about which boats are bound for which atolls, and sends the mail with them. Without an organised, central government-controlled transport system, there could be no official mail carriers or regular service to the atolls. Even so, this relies on private *dhonis* sailing when it suits them. Mail also goes by air via the regional airports. The mail system is developing, especially as the tourism industry requires people to work away from their home islands. More mail flows from Male' to the atolls than vice versa.

Maldives Post Ltd also runs a thriving philatelic service (see *Philately* on page 88) and has a line in postal souvenirs.

C **TELEPHONE** A fully automatic telephone service is provided to all inhabited islands. It seems remarkable to be able to make an IDD call from a beach cabana bedroom on a resort several hours by *dhoni* from the capital, especially when the only communication 40 years ago was by Morse Code. Even more remarkable is the linking of every inhabited island by IDD and payphone telephones with the outside world, and the archipelago-wide coverage by mobile cell phones.

The lack of a telecom infrastructure of any kind enabled the latest systems to be introduced during the 1980s, instead of having to build on antiquated systems already installed. While some resorts may still require guests to go to reception to make or receive an overseas call, that is through policy (the resort style) and not through lack of technology.

Numbering There are no area codes in Maldives. Telephone numbers were changed in 2005 and all now consist of seven digits with the first three digits giving the clue as to which atoll or island the subscriber is in. These prefixes are:

↘ 650	Haa Alif	↘ 335	Hulhule	↘ 678	Thaa
↘ 652	Haa Dhaal	↘ 339	Vilingili	↘ 680	Laamu
↘ 654	Shaviyani	↘ 664	Kaaf	↘ 682	Gaaf Alif
↘ 656	Noonu	↘ 666	Alif	↘ 684	Gaaf Dhaal
↘ 658	Raa	↘ 670	Vaavu	↘ 686	Gnaviyani
↘ 660	Baa	↘ 672	Meemu	↘ 688, ↘ 689	Seenu
↘ 662	Lhaviyani	↘ 674	Faafu	↘ 770–776	Pre-paid mobile
↘ 331, ↘ 332, Male'		↘ 676	Dhaal	↘ 777–779	Post-paid mobile
↘ 333, ↘ 334 Male'					

International dialling For dialling overseas, the international access code is 00 followed by country code, area code and number. To call Maldives from abroad, the access code is ↘ 960, followed by the seven-digit number.

Costs The prices for **national** calls depend on where you are calling from and to. The lowest is 25 laari for a one-minute call within Male'. Calls to the atolls from Male' are between Rf0.65 and Rf1.70 per minute. The highest rate is for mobiles at a fixed rate of Rf2 for one minute to any atoll from Male' or any other atoll. Directory enquiries (↘ 110) cost Rf1 from anywhere on normal phones.

The standard **international** rates fall into four price bands: the six SAARC countries (subcontinent countries): Rf16 or Rf12 IDD cheap rate per minute; Southeast Asia, China and UK: Rf22 or Rf17; Japan, Australasia, both Koreas, Fiji: Rf22 or Rf17; all other countries, the Americas, Europe, Middle East and Africa: Rf28 or Rf20.

Telephone calls from hotels in Male' and the resorts are charged according to the resort's pricing policy and will be more expensive than the rates given above.

Operator services A 24-hour operator and directory service (for which a charge is made) is provided. Service numbers are:

International Telephone Operator	↘ 190	Wataniyaa Directory Enquiries	↘ 120
International Directory Enquiries	↘ 190	Internet & Mobile Help Desk	↘ 170
National Directory Enquiries	↘ 110		

Emergency and other numbers

Ambulance	↘ 102	Maritime Radio Operator	↘ 188
Electricity	↘ 104	ADK Hospital	↘ 3313553
Water	↘ 105	Indira Gandhi Memorial Hospital	↘ 3316647
Fire	↘ 118	Ministry of Tourism	↘ 3323224
Police	↘ 119	Maldives Tourism Promotion Board	↘ 3323228
Coastal Radio Operator	↘ 182	Flight Enquiries	↘ 3322211
Atoll Communications Operator	↘ 188		

Mobile phones When mobile phones were introduced in the Maldives in 1997, they were an instant success, making nonsense of the predictions that there would not be much demand. Ten years later, there were over 200,000 mobile phones in the country, where the adult population is under 300,000. The service covers the whole country, although some sea areas may not have complete reception. The pioneering service is operated by Dhiraagu, who supply portable and transportable mobile phones from their Teleshop (*Medhuziuyaari Magu 19;* ↘ *123;* e *info@dhiraagu.com.mv; www.dhiraagu.com.mv*). A second service is provided by Wataniya Telecom Maldives Pvt Ltd (*Shabnam, Majeedhi Magu;* ↘ *9613929 or* ↘ *929;* e *929@wataniya-maldives.com; www.wataniya.mv*).

Pagers The national paging service covers Male' and its neighbouring islands. Small portable pagers (numeric, alphanumeric, and voice) are available for purchase from Dhiraagu's Teleshop. Messages can be sent from any touch-tone telephone to pager numbers.

Phonecards Public Phone booths are card-operated. The booths are in blue and grey with glass sides and a door, and are to be found in popular places throughout Male' and in the inhabited islands and resorts (where they are usually for staff-only use).

Perhaps with an eye to their souvenir value, the phonecards bear attractive underwater scenes and views of the Maldives. They are available at Rf50, Rf100, and Rf200, and can be bought at the Dhiraagu head office as well as at more than 530 agents throughout the country. The higher values can be used for calling overseas.

Telephone directory The Maldives telephone directory is in English and Dhivehi. It is even more unusual because it includes subscribers' listings by name in one section and subscribers' listings by address in a second section. This is a leftover from the old system, which was for a telephone to be provided to an address, in the name of the landlord. There would be many people using it, so the house name was used for identification, not the landlord's; not much help if you did not know someone's address but only their name. Now telephone numbers are assigned to an individual or a business, not to locations. A Male' subscriber can keep the same number when changing address.

Although there is an alphabetical listing, finding numbers in the directory is like finding someone's house in Male': not very easy. Since Maldivians do not have surnames in the Western sense, entries are listed by first-name order, and nicknames may be placed before the first name. Entries containing initials appear at the beginning of each letter's section; thus G T Manik is found under 'G', not under 'M' for Manik. House names which incorporate numbers have the numbers written in words, thus *2 Flowers* is found under 'T' for *Two*. And for *The Reef*, you look under 'T' for *The* instead of under 'R' for *Reef*. If you still cannot find the name you are looking for, check an alternative spelling. For instance, Gasim could be listed as Qasim.

The directory contains several other sections: a listing of government departments including atoll offices, a diplomatic listing, and a fax directory. There is a separate *Yellow Pages* edition.

FAX Bureaufax (in the Dhiraagu Telecom office) is a public fax service for sending and receiving documents; fax number f 3322450.

e INTERNET CAFÉS There are several cyber cafés in Male'. For visitors to Male', as well as for locals who do not have private access to a computer, cyber cafés are a boon for surfing the internet or sending emails. They offer instant internet access to walk-in customers. There is a dial-up service for local telephone subscribers.

Prices vary slightly, but as a general rule, 15 minutes costs around Rf10, 30 minutes Rf15 and one hour Rf25.

BUSINESS

BUSINESS HOURS Work starts early and may end late. Government offices open at 07.30 and close at 13.30. It is not unusual, though, to find senior people working in their offices in the evening.

Private sector offices begin their day at 08.30 or 09.00 and while senior executives may be absent in the afternoon, they are likely to be at their desks in the evening. It is not unusual for people to work until midnight, especially in businesses which maintain fax or email contact with the rest of the world.

Shops open from 06.00, or 08.00–09.00, and close at 20.00 or 23.00, with breaks at prayer times. Banks open 09.00–13.00 but are staffed until 17.00, except on Thursday which is a half day.

Government and private offices and banks close on Friday, which is the weekend, but some shops open on Friday evening. Restaurants are open only at meal times, while cafés are open all day, some until after midnight.

FOREIGN INVESTMENT Investment by foreigners in new enterprises that are economically and socially viable is possible, provided the project has been vetted and preliminary approval granted by the Foreign Investment Committee of the Ministry of Trade and Industries. A thorough investigation of all aspects of the proposed investment is conducted before final approval is given.

Preference is likely to be given to industries located in outer atolls, which cannot be started by local investors because of the size of investment required and/or lack of technical expertise. An industry that leads to a reduction in imports or utilises locally produced materials, and would lead to training and employment at technical, skilled and management levels, is most likely to be considered. An agreement is drawn up to suit each individual project setting out terms, including repatriation of profits, conditions and means of implementation, and this has to be signed with the Ministry of Trade and Industries.

The Foreign Investment Services Bureau is in the Ghazee Building, Ameer Ahmed Magu (↘ 3328754; f 3323756).

BUSINESS SERVICES Visitors on business staying in a resort close to Male', such as Kurumba or Bandos, have the back-up of staff who can provide necessary business assistance with dedicated business centres. Kurumba, Bandos and Paradise Island have convention centres with full business support.

Since all resorts have faxes and IDD telephones available (although not all have the IDD facility in guestrooms), it is possible to remain in touch for business even in a remote resort.

SETTLING IN

CULTURE SHOCK Since visitors are usually confined to a resort island with other guests from overseas whose behaviour is similar, culture shock should be minimal; it might even be a simple case of jet lag.

Advance knowledge of the Maldives will prevent the misconceptions that could spoil your visit. Before you go, you must realise it is not easy to move about between islands. You are going to be on one small island for the whole of your holiday, unless you go on excursions. That is what the Maldives is like, so don't expect to be able to wander about by yourself when you want something different to do. Except on Kuramathi which has three hotels, or at Equator Village on Gan, which has a causeway link to village islands, there is nowhere else to go on an island resort.

Do not expect to meet the locals in cheap tapas bars, find charming little inns off the beaten track, or see somewhere you alone can discover where tourists never go. Whatever and whoever is in a Maldives resort is, like you, coming from somewhere else. Be aware, too, that your holiday is not going to be cheap; although, considering the excellence of food, service and accommodation, it will be good value.

If you are lucky enough to mix with Maldivians in their own islands, their lack of urgency may cause a slight short circuit, but nothing will give you the serious culture shock of being set adrift in, say, India.

Maldivians in their islands are very hospitable people because every visitor, whether local or foreign, comes from over the seas and consequently will need board and lodging. Thus strangers are made welcome without fuss. Villagers are likely to be startled by boorish behaviour and may find you rather strange. When you leave, even though you are convinced you have made a friend for life (and probably have), the parting will be casual. Saying goodbye is nothing new to islanders.

An old leaflet issued by the Ministry of Tourism states: 'Your holiday in the Maldives will be both happy and memorable if you are in harmony with our customs and traditions.'

PALM FEVER Stay too long in the Maldives, say some expatriate tour guides, and you will begin to suffer from palm fever. The symptoms are a yearning for the noise and bustle of city life, a longing to do something not even outrageous without everyone knowing, and a tendency to be cynical instead of having a sunny disposition. Foreign tour guides are overwhelmed by the impulse to be rude to their guests. Physically, a real feeling of nausea and headaches could develop, not just from too many cocktails during the bar's happy hour, but perhaps from the pressure of being nice all the time.

It must be difficult for any foreigner living in the Maldives to have a complete change. The cure for palm fever is to recognise it in advance and to lead a varied life. One tour guide I know took advantage of being based in the Maldives to learn windsurfing. A British expatriate developed an interest in photography in a big way; another is writing a book. Even with palm fever, anyone lucky enough to be based in the Maldives soon wants to return whenever they have a few days out of the islands.

The yearn to return is a feeling shared by most visitors; they finish their holiday surprised how fast it went, and wishing they could stay longer.

SMOKING There is a vigorous campaign against smoking, although many men are heavy smokers. In 1994, the government banned smoking in public offices and prohibited cigarette and tobacco advertising from the beginning of 1995. Some inhabited islands have been declared no-smoking zones by the inhabitants.

Cigarettes are, however, freely available, as is the local version, a slim, hand-rolled piece of paper with coarse tobacco in it, called a *bidi*. Fifty of them sell for half the price of 20 cigarettes.

Women especially delight in smoking a *gudu-guda*, the onomatopoeically named gurgling water-pipe of the Maldives. Tobacco is also chewed, as is the areca nut slice and green leaf known as betel. Together with lime paste and cloves, it is a popular after-lunch munch and the favourite chew of fishermen.

THE NON-SMOKERS OF GURAIDHOO

On Non-Smoking Day in 2000, the women of Guraidhoo Island in Thaa Atoll all finally kicked the habit, thanks to a determined awareness campaign carried out by the island's Women's Committee. The chairwoman at the time is quoted as saying that it had taken around two years to achieve this result, and that the toughest convert was a 50-year-old woman who was very attached to her *gudu-guda*. The women then planned to use their persuasive powers to convert the men of Guraidhoo too, so that the whole island (population over 1,700) would be non-smoking. I have no information about the success or failure of their efforts...

SOCIAL ORGANISATIONS There are no social organisations like Lions or Rotary, although there are some professional associations and sports clubs.

Social interaction in Male' is informal. Some expatriates, like the Sri Lankans, organise cricket tournaments or concerts as get-togethers. On Friday afternoons, Sri Lankans and Maldivians gather to stroll around the Sultan's Park garden in Male'.

Other expats use Friday as a day to form a group and visit one of the resorts. Diplomatic representatives are the best people to contact if you want to meet others from your home country.

CULTURAL ETIQUETTE For information on meeting Maldivians, see page 37. You can find advice for gay travellers on page 91 and tips on taking photos in the Maldives on page 92.

GIVING SOMETHING BACK with Janice Booth

The Maldives is potentially a country that should have sustainable development through tourism and, as such, does not really fit into any category like 'third world' or 'poor developing nation'. Visitors are effectively giving something back throughout their holiday in the form of head taxes and the money they contribute. The problems in the Maldives are more to do with finding ways to sustain the environment and the growth of tourism.

Tourists are likely to see very little obvious poverty, particularly if they spend all their time in the resorts and Male'. However, there is inevitably a big gap between the incomes of Maldivians who are involved with tourism (or the service industries) and those who are not. For some of the latter, the cost of living may well be higher than their wages; the UN estimates that those at the lower level – for example on the more remote inhabited islands – subsist on less than US$2 a day.

Following the tsunami of December 2004, some of these non-resort islands did experience the benefits of tourism at first hand, as the staff of the resort islands joined in the relief effort and provided manpower, equipment and expertise. In several cases, former and current guests at the resorts also made financial and material donations.

INDIVIDUAL CONTRIBUTIONS Although some overseas-based activists suggested a boycott of certain resorts for political reasons, the most valuable contribution that travellers can make to the Maldives is to continue visiting the islands. A drop in the level of tourism would be a serious loss to the economy – and thus to the country's ability to repair the infrastructures and livelihoods affected by the tsunami. It would also harm those Maldivians who – directly or indirectly – earn their living from tourism.

Most visitors find themselves enchanted by the Maldivians they meet and may feel like making some contribution to the on-going relief and reconstruction activities. A contribution of money is by far the best way, either directly to Maldivians in need, although they might be too embarrassed to accept it, or – to save upsetting people – via established agencies helping the Maldives, some of which are listed below.

CHARITIES AND NGOS

International Because of the specific nature of the country and its regime, there are fewer international charities working regularly in Maldives than would be found in, for example, one of the sub-Saharan African nations.

Save the Children www.savethechildren.org
Voluntary Service Overseas www.vso.org.uk; in Male'
↘ 3318748, 3315380; f 3320652. Phasing out its
involvement as the need for it lessens.
UNDP or **United Nations Development Programme** UN
Bldg, Buruzu Magu, Male'; ↘ 3324501; f 3324504;
e registry.mv@undp.org. UNDP has developed an
initiative – the *Adopt an Island* scheme – to
support the Maldives government in its tsunami
recovery work in 3 key sectors: shelter
reconstruction, infrastructure rehabilitation &
restoration of livelihoods. Supporters so far include
businesses, civil society organisations, foundations,
governments & individuals. Via emailed annual &
semi-annual progress reports, UNDP Maldives keeps
donors informed about the activities supported, lists
the ones to which their funds have been applied &

gives details of the benefiting communities. For
Adopt an Island details: e adoptanisland@undp.org;
www.mv.undp.org/adopt/adopt.htm.
**UN Educational, Scientific and Cultural Organization
(UNESCO)** www.unesco.org/csi/smis/siv. Among other
activities, UNESCO operates the *Small Islands Voice*
(SIV) scheme in Maldives; see the *Eydhafushi* box on
page 179. Launched in 2002, SIV's longterm vision is
that the voice of the general public in small islands
should be heard loud & clear, & that this voice
should become a driving force for island
development.
World Health Organization (WHO) In the HSBC Bldg,
Male'.
United Nations In Buruzu Magu near the Relax Inn,
Male'.

National   There are national welfare organisations covering the various areas of
need.

Society for Health Education (SHE) Kulunvehi Buruzu
Magu, Male'; ↘ 3316231. SHE is very active
throughout the country, especially in screening for
thalassaemia, a chronic hereditary blood disorder
that affects many Maldivians, & in family planning.
**Volunteers of Environment, Social Harmony &
Improvement (VESHI)** Contact is via the Ministry of
Fisheries, Agriculture & Marine Resources in Male';

↘ 3322625; f 3326558. VESHI is involved with
UNESCO in the *Small Islands Voice* schemes. *Veshi*
means 'environment' in Dhivehi.
Human Rights Commission New commission, set up in
2004 & supported by the UNDP, in the ADK
Building.

In Maldives, the ethos of voluntary community work and participation in
development is well established. There are numerous small – in some cases very
small – NGOs and local groups in Male' and around the islands, covering issues
such as health, education, sport, conservation, the environment, infrastructural
improvement, etc. All must be registered with the Ministry of Home Affairs,
Housing and Environment in Male' (*Huravee Building; www.homeaffairs.gov.mv*), so
this is where to locate the relevant ones if you're interested in helping with a
specific developmental issue. A 2001 listing gives a total of 490, 206 of them in
Male' and 284 out in the atolls, so there is no shortage of choice.

3

Resorts: What to Expect

Any voyage through the Dhivehi alphabet of atolls is necessarily imaginary. Apart from President Gayoom, not many Maldivians have visited all the inhabited islands. The atolls each have a traditional Dhivehi name (which is often long, and difficult for non-Maldivians) and also an alphabetical code name by which they are most often known. These range from the first letter of the Dhivehi alphabet – Haa Alif – to Seenu, the 19th.

The standard definition of an atoll is a ring-shaped coral reef enclosing a lagoon, or a group of islands surrounded by deep sea. For Maldivians, the definition becomes 'a group of islands surrounded by deep sea from which we can catch tuna'. For administrative purposes, an atoll is a district. Some atolls have been grouped into one atoll-district while large atolls have been administratively split.

Geographically, there are 26 atolls. The description (in *Chapters 5–9*) starts from Male', describing first the North and South Male' atolls, then Ari Atoll, then the northern and finally the southern atolls. The name in brackets after the traditional name is the Dhivehi code name, based on the Dhivehi alphabet. The numbering (or lettering) system starts from north to south; each atoll is identified by an alphabet letter. The letter and number after each island indicate its boat registration code. See also *Appendix 2*, pages 200–3.

This chapter covers resort facilities and standards, costs and choices.

RESORT FACILITIES AND STANDARDS

When the first edition of this book was compiled in 1995, there were 72 island resorts, making a total of 74 places to stay (since Kuramathi is actually three separate establishments). Ten years later, in 2005, 87 resorts were listed in the MTPB list, including the Equator Village in Gan, plus six hotels in Male'.

The expansion followed the government's decision to invite tenders for the development of uninhabited islands in atolls previously unexposed (or with very limited exposure) to tourism. These included new resorts in the far northern atolls and the southern atolls south of Meemu Atoll.

A document issued by the Ministry of Tourism, when the plan for the development of 14 uninhabited islands for tourism was announced, stated that islands would be leased to private-sector investors on the basis of open tender.

'All proposals submitted for development of the island are then evaluated by a committee from the government, and the island is leased to the party submitting the winning proposal. If any new island is open for public tender, it will be advertised in our website: www.visitmaldives.com.'

Watch that space! The word in Male' at the time tenders were being submitted was that the creation and construction of a resort would cost at least US$10 million. What has amazed observers since the tenders were awarded is the time (less than a year) in which uninhabited and remote desert islands have been

Royston Ellis

With 44 uninhabited islands being transformed into luxury beach resorts to join the 90 in existence at the beginning of 2008, the need for innovative tropical architects was high. There are very few Maldivian architects but one, Mohamed Shafeeq – universally known as Sappé – is popular because he has revolutionised the concept of holiday island architecture and his influence is even seen beyond the Maldives.

Sappé is the architect of a dozen successful new resorts in the Maldives, relying on light and space to create a stylish identity that nurtures the relaxed, holiday mood. As a Maldivian he is exceptional because he has also planned resorts for Dubai, Seychelles, Mauritius, India and the Philippines.

Of the six new resorts being built in the Maldives at press time, five were to Sappé's plans. He is in demand because he understands what visitors to the Maldives want on holiday, and how to turn a remote, desert island wilderness into a dream destination. His clients, who are Maldivian and international entrepreneurs, trust his instinct and inspiration.

Although he claims not to have a signature that characterises a Sappé-conceived resort, he has incorporated traditional Maldivian building styles into his work. This is especially noticeable in his re-fashioning of the standard hotel bathroom into an open-roofed, garden courtyard for indulgent bathing.

Sappé doesn't create a typical tourist bedroom for a resort. 'When you stay at a tropical island resort,' he says, 'all you want to do is relax, enjoy, and make love. I create a lifestyle more than simply containing interior space under a canopy.'

Lily Beach was in the style of the second generation of resort architecture in the Maldives. The first, after the ramshackle rooms at the beginning of tourism, was a kind of tropical suburbia with beachfront blocks of chalets with small bathrooms and no bathtub, clustered close together. The second generation brought about detached rooms with verandas, but still no privacy from neighbouring guests. It was at the beginning of this century, with more uninhabited islands being licensed by the government for converting into resorts, that the third generation of spacious accommodation – with a pool, jacuzzi, privacy, stunning layout and breathtaking settings – was introduced.

To meet the demand for different room designs, Sappé returned to his roots of traditional local architecture, which always included an outdoor element: a place to sit and an open-air bathing place, the *gifili*.

The *gifili* was Sappé's inspiration for the sumptuous bathing courtyards associated with his designs. He draws on the relationship between the components of the traditional island homestead with open-sided living spaces, sheltered sleeping spaces and the intermingling and free flow of one space to the other. 'The importance,' he

transformed into upmarket, luxury resorts with remoteness conquered by seaplane and IDD telephone.

These new resorts add a greater variety to choose from, and provide an opportunity for more holidaymakers to enjoy themselves in the Maldives.

The prosperity that tourism brings enables development to spread throughout the Maldives far from the tourist belt. The policy of accommodating tourists on designated, uninhabited islands away from village communities tempers the impact of so many foreigners descending on the country.

RESORT FACILITIES Although all resorts have the usual guest facilities in common, every one has a different ambience, even those run by the same company. In some you will never know who the manager is, because he runs says, 'is on the covered and sheltered spaces within the building rather than on the form.'

Borrowing from village houses of bygone days, he creates a sense of arrival and importance through elaborate entry gates into a walled compound, which itself provides an atmosphere of personal property and security. The guest has a feeling of individuality and of being cocooned and, as Sappé puts it, of 'being in a place to make love and to dream'.

The influence of the traditional can be seen in Sappé's work in Kurumba with pools based on ancient ponds and in the *salas* for outdoor relaxing developed from the *holhuashi* resting pavilion of village islands. At Huvafenfushi he designed a restaurant whose thatched roof resembles the upturned hull of a *dhoni*, a local fishing boat, while in Baros he has entrances and public areas with elaborate cross-beamed roofs like ancient thatched buildings. He transformed Full Moon with thatched overwater bungalows.

Thatch has replaced the harsh composition roofs of the second generation and Sappé likes it because of its colour and warmth as well as being a natural material, part of the tropical island experience. He used thatch at Anantara, a blend of tropical fantasy and contemporary technology with spacious suites and roomy beach front villas.

The development of his style has reached a new zenith at the resort of Naladhu, a sister island of Anantara. Each of its six beach and 13 ocean houses has a colossal 300m^2 of gorgeously stylish and bright living space. Completely self-contained, the accommodation is perfect for a rainy day as well as for a sunny one.

Sappé wants his buildings to be a delightful surprise and a pleasure for guests. He focuses on convenience and on the importance of light and lighting to make sure his buildings are comfortable, not intimidating.

Ask Sappé what will be the fourth generation – the Maldives resorts of the future – and he suggests it could be a resort with only one or just a few accommodation units. Each unit would consist of several inter-connecting pavilions with dining area and pantry and kitchen, a pool, garden, spa and gym, as well as sleeping areas. Guests need never leave the privacy of their holiday dwelling. Meals could be prepared in-house by a personal chef or by the guests themselves.

'I have noticed,' says Sappé 'that 70% of the millionaire guests staying in the Maldives occasionally like to prepare their own meals. Sometimes they raid the hotel kitchen or fly in their own provisions.'

Sappé's eyes light up at the challenge of designing something different yet again, keeping the Maldives at the forefront of tropical hospitality.

Extracted from Open Skies, *the inflight magazine of Emirates Airlines, February 2008*

3

things smoothly behind the scenes, leaving the frontline professionals such as restaurant manager and front office manager to do their jobs. On others, usually those with European management, the manager is like a host, making guests feel at home.

All resorts offer the same basic facilities and arrangements. However, since resorts are always upgrading their product, it's advisable to check directly with a resort on what it actually has. All provide some kind of assistance at the airport to help the guest get to the resort. Even if you go by seaplane, you will probably have to use a boat to take you from where you land. The island jetty will probably be short, but, if the lagoon is very shallow or broad, the jetty has to be long enough to reach deep water. That will mean a long walk. Some islands have approaches that are difficult, especially if the sea is a little choppy.

From jetty to the reception area is usually a short distance, since the island itself is small. Your baggage will be unloaded from the transfer boat and eventually delivered to your room. At the reception area, a welcome drink (non-alcoholic) is usually offered; the more glamorous the island, the more exotic-looking the drink.

You will have to register at reception, which might be a counter in an open-fronted hut with sand on the floor, or an elegant, marble-floored lounge where you can sit while you do the paperwork. This is the time to re-confirm what is included in the rate (some islands charge 10% on all extras as service charge, some don't) and what is the island time, meal times, etc.

Usually the restaurant and bar will be close to reception, either in separate pavilions or as part of the main complex. Public toilets and a gift shop will be in the same area, too. While some islands favour a laid-back approach with sand on the floor and staff in casual wear, others have tiled and covered walkways and staff you can't mistake for guests.

Everywhere, of course, is sand and you will have to trek across it to your room. Although the room won't be very far from reception, it can seem a long way if you have just had ten hours cooped up on a plane and an hour on a *dhoni*. Hotels in the islands spread out horizontally, not vertically. The vegetation is tropical, with some resorts carefully landscaped while others are luxuriant and jungly.

Your room will have a veranda or balcony and, through the vegetation, a sea view. You will hardly be able to hear the sea, though, as it is just a gentle ripple on sand, no waves crashing against rocks. The bed will usually be a double, since many guests are honeymooners. Sometimes the double is, in fact, two twin beds pushed together. If you need two separate beds (as preferred by Japanese visitors to Maldives), specify this when making the booking.

The bathroom will have a shower, and some resorts have baths too. While all have hot water on tap, you may have a surprise if the hotel architect has copied the local style and the bathroom is open to the sky and has a garden in it. Real rustic resorts (and those pretending to be) may not have air conditioning but there will be an effective fan system. Most resort rooms have both. Do not assume that the room will have a television set as some resorts deliberately don't. The cynic might say this is to encourage guests to patronise the bar in the evenings but it's because not every guest wants television on a 'get-away-from-it-all' island holiday. Many resorts have overwater villas and these are usually elaborately designed cabanas or deluxe cottages built on pillars in the lagoon, reached by boardwalk jetties.

Most of the resorts have a laundry service although clothes might take a few days to be washed in the smaller resorts. If you wash your own smalls – or wish to dry swimwear – you will probably find a line on which to hang clothes in the bathroom, or by the outside shower or across the veranda. Hotel laundry can cost as much as US$3 for a shirt, trousers or skirt, plus 10% service charge.

At the last count every resort had a dive centre/school, usually located on or near the landing stage. Most have other beach activities, windsurfing, canoeing and catamaran sailing; others have waterskiing, banana boats, ringo riding, wake boards and parasailing. If you are interested in a particular watersport, it is best to check the resort websites to be certain they can offer it, as the facilities do vary from one to another. Surfers in particular should research carefully, as only certain resorts are suitable. Snorkelling is good at the majority of resorts and takes place on the house reefs, the reefs that encircle the resort islands.

Entertainment varies a lot; some resorts (particularly those with a majority of Italian guests) have animators, others leave you alone. If you are a party animal, the larger resorts aim to please the gregarious. If you want quiet, romance and intimacy, the smaller resorts are more likely to provide the right ambience. If you are feeling energetic and would like to spend action-packed days in and under the sea, resorts with active diving centres would be best. Most resorts have swimming pools; those that don't, claim to have the biggest pool in the world: their vast lagoons and the sea. The top resorts have swimming pools attached to some of their villas. Even the more modest resort will have some kind of spa facility while the modern, upmarket resorts feature divinely decadent spas in designer sanctuaries. On all resorts there are chairs (plastic in the low cost, teak loungers in the upper bracket) for lounging on the beach, and the beach is swept clean every morning.

Meals will generally be taken in the main restaurant with a set menu. Breakfast and many meals are served as buffets. Where à-la-carte service is available, it will be in the coffee shop (sometimes part of the bar or reception lobby) or in a speciality restaurant such as a beach grill.

Fans of 'eat as much as you can' meals will enjoy the buffets. As a rule but not always, the best buffets are to be had in the larger islands, because they have more guests to cater for and so can more easily put on buffets with a greater choice of dishes. Most resorts will have a happy hour in the bar, when drinks are sold at a discount; some resorts open the bar as early as 08.00, closing only when the last guest has left.

You can request a flask of drinking water in your room. Bottled mineralised (produced locally with minerals added) water is sometimes provided free of charge, according to the resort's policy/standard. Not all resorts have room service, or even a minibar refrigerator, in which case you will need to take your water supply with you from the bar. While all resorts have room boys to clean and make the beds, you may only see them in the morning as not all provide an evening turn-down service as well.

When choosing a resort, consider its location carefully. While some travellers don't mind a long journey from the airport, others do. Resorts in Male' Atoll are closest to the airport. Those in Ari, Raa, Baa, Lhaviyani, Faafu, Dhaal, Meemu and Seenu atolls are a long way off and best reached by air. With the waiting time to board, and the flight itself, transfer by air adds considerably to the journey time after the long-haul flight, as well as to the cost of the holiday. Most visitors on packages will not have to consider transfer costs, but check in case it's not included in the holiday price you are quoted. Speedboats are modern vessels with enclosed seating areas, often air-conditioned. Long speedboat rides could make some feel queasy. *Dhonis* are used only for transfer to resorts close to Male' these days.

In the event of an emergency, help is closer at hand the nearer you are to Male', especially if the island is large and efficient enough to have a fleet of speedboats and *dhonis* available at any time.

If you want to visit Male' often, stay close to the capital. On the other hand, if you want to visit village islands, there are plenty in Ari Atoll and you don't need a permit to drop in on them for a day, if your resort is in that atoll. In theory, the newest resorts could offer a better (less spoiled) diving environment. In theory, too, people on the village islands in the atolls recently opened up to tourism should also be less 'spoiled'. However, Maldivians unused to foreigners are likely to be very shy and a foreigner would learn more about the Maldives from a walk through Male' than by strolling through an apparently deserted village island.

Reality returns on the last night of your stay when the bills are presented. Since you will have been signing for everything, spending will have been painless. You can, of course, check the bill from time to time and settle it periodically. Inform the cashier at least three days before paying if you intend to pay by credit card, in case your bill exceeds the hotel's credit allowance per card and authorisation has to be obtained.

Check-out is usually noon. If you have an evening flight, arrangements can be made to have a day room, for a fee. Far-flung resorts may put you up in Male' or

Most tourists visiting Maldives purchase a package holiday that includes the air fare, resort accommodation and meals on either a bed & breakfast, half board (usually breakfast and dinner) or full board (breakfast, lunch and dinner) basis.

Since there are many international travel agents using the same resort for their guests, if you are the only one who books with, say, Kuoni, and all the other guests have booked their holiday through, say, Thomas Cook, you could feel neglected, especially when you see in the travel agent's compendium at the resort that the local representative of Kuoni might not be able to visit your resort during your stay because she stays at a resort on another atoll.

So when booking a package holiday it is important to understand exactly what you are buying, to avoid disappointment. Obviously, if the cost of the holiday seems ridiculously low for such an exotic destination as the Maldives, don't expect frills.

On arrival at Male' International Airport, you will usually be met as you emerge from the customs hall by your tour company's rep bearing a board with the company's name and logo. If not, there are some 40 counters lining the open-sided concourse leading to the transfer boats where resort and tour operators' names are displayed. Go there for help.

There will probably be a queue at the counter so make sure you join the right line as it will take about 30 minutes to process everyone. Once you've been identified as being on the counter clerk's checklist, you will be directed to the open-sided café to sit and wait. With trolleys stacked with oversized luggage packed around the tables, and anxious and confused passengers milling around, it is more chaotic than the brochures suggest. Use this moment to head for the loos.

Eventually a representative for the resort to which you are longing to go, will pass around holding a sign with the resort's name, accompanied by one of the café's stewards shouting out the name of the resort, not yours. Keep alert to read the signs since the way

at the airport hotel overnight if transfer is too difficult on the day of your departure.

MINIMUM STANDARDS The development of any uninhabited island into a resort is now done to minimum standards stipulated by the Ministry of Tourism. This guarantees that an island's environment is preserved.

The specification states:

> The fact that Maldivian beach resorts are beach-oriented is well known among our visitors. Hence it is important to provide enough beach area that will satisfy the tourists. Therefore all guest rooms should be facing the beach and a minimum of five metres shall be available for every room. 68% of the total length of beach shall be utilised for guest rooms. Of the remaining 32%, 20% shall be left for general facilities like jetty, the reception, restaurant, etc and 12% shall be utilised as empty space in between the guest rooms. However, at least two metres should be allowed in between any two buildings.

The preservation of the natural beauty and environment of an island was realised to be important when the Ministry did a survey of resorts that developed before regulations were introduced, and found that only about 14% of the land area of an island was used for buildings. For new developments, it stipulated that 'the maximum area to be used on buildings shall be 20% of the total land area'.

Because it is seen as very important to leave enough empty space on an island, the regulations state that for every room built out over the lagoon, equal space should be left free on the island. It is also stated that 'No building should appear the Maldivian steward pronounces, say, Kuramathi, is not the way it looks to you. It sounds like somewhere else, and you don't want to miss the boat, literally.

Next, with baggage trolleys, luggage on wheels, and eager kids, you will be invited to form a crocodile of guests to the jetty for the boat transfer, or to the coach for transfer to the seaplane dock. You will be told to abandon your luggage on the quayside and board the launch. Don't worry, the baggage is loaded afterwards on the boat. You will be asked to identify it on landing at the resort so it can be delivered to your room. Allow at least an hour after you've found the room for the luggage to find you.

If there is a rep from your tour company on hand, she will board the boat and give a rapid account of what's supposed to be happening – and then leave. On arrival at the resort, you'll be directed to the reception lobby – sometimes a long walk up a jetty from landing – to be allocated your room. Some resorts have room registration cards for you to fill in during the boat journey; others present them at reception.

If you have paid for an upgrade on the flight to the Maldives, do not expect to be treated any differently at the resort. Whatever you pay to get there, you will be treated the same as everyone else once you get there. However, guests staying in the more expensive rooms may be assigned to a dedicated restaurant for meals, have better in-room amenities, sometimes including a fruit bowl and a welcome bottle of wine. Usually someone will escort you to the room and explain how the various gadgets work.

If your tour company has several guests staying at the resort, the rep, usually an expat, will meet all the company's guests for a briefing on the evening of arrival. However, only if the rep is staying on the resort will you see much of her or him. If you want a resort with a tour company rep on the spot, then choose one that guarantees a resident rep.

Of course, on a smaller, more exclusive – and consequently more expensive – resort, you will feel less like a packaged holidaymaker and more like an honoured guest.

above the tree tops. While clearing land for construction, enough trees or vegetation should be left untouched in the area to block views of the buildings that are constructed.'

Even a budget resort will have rooms with the required minimum floor area. Not only are the minimum dimensions and building standards of the guest public areas like the restaurant and bar carefully defined, the staff areas are given equal consideration. Even the floor area of the mosque, which every resort island has, is set out for every Muslim employee; three Korans are available, as well as running or well water for ablution and sufficient lighting for praying or reading at night.

Complaints The Ministry of Tourism rarely receives complaints from vacationers. There is no standard procedure for complaining, or for dealing with complaints. The response by a member of staff will be helpful and understanding, but there are limits as to what can be done. The Ministry is unable to be involved in 'financial maltreatment'.

The best method, if you have a complaint in a resort, is to discuss it calmly with the manager or department supervisor. That is the only way to get the matter resolved. If you keep quiet until you get home, no remedial action can be taken on the spot. If you are gathering evidence to make a claim for a free holiday from your travel agent, be warned. Tour operators and holiday wholesalers in the UK and other source countries keep lists of regular complainers which they share, so will be monitoring what you are up to.

Complaints work both ways. The police used to receive complaints and requests to detain tourists as they waited at the airport to depart. A procedure has been set up so that any resort with a complaint about a guest must report it immediately to the Ministry of Tourism. If the Ministry is convinced the matter cannot be settled in the absence of the tourist concerned, then a request will be issued to the police to detain the tourist.

COSTS

ROOM RATES Prices vary so much, even within one resort and according to the time of the year, the price indications shown in this book should be taken as a general guide, not necessarily the actual room rate. This is because the hotel's rack rate is often fictitious, reflecting the maximum the property would like to charge, not the price at which rooms are contracted to travel agents and tour companies who add their own mark-up.

Even independent travellers are expected to book and buy accommodation through a Maldives agent, who will quote a price according to demand and availability, based on what the agent actually has to remit to the resort. Some agents will build in a handling fee, from US$10 per person per booking. Bookings made through the internet will be handled through one of the resort's agents and prices will be less than the hotel's published rates. Some resorts that are part of a group will accept room reservations directly from a prospective guest but these will not be lower than a rate that can be secured through an agent, and may even be more.

Most visitors who come to Maldives on holiday purchase packages that include international flights as well as accommodation, so the room rate will be less than that quoted here. Most resorts also include the US$8 head tax payable per person per day, although some of the most expensive ones add that as an unexpected extra.

The price ranges quoted here are based on the high season (January to April) rates. Prices drop out of season (May to July, September to October) and fluctuate according to demand. They can also rise, especially over Christmas when a premium and a minimum-stay requirement are imposed.

To all room rates must be added the cost of return transfer between the airport and the resort. Transfer by seaplane to far flung resorts could cost as much as an extra night's stay.

Since some 50 new resorts are scheduled to be opened by 2010, there might be some price adjustment at existing resorts, and special deals in the newly opened ones. (As an example, for its opening in 2008 Kandooma was offering a discount of 60% on its rack rate.) Some resorts, classified in the lower price range, may undergo refurbishment during the life of this edition and re-emerge in a higher category. So these rates, while being a guide as to how the resort sees itself, may not be what you are actually asked to pay.

My category of 'Celebrity' rooms is dubbed that way because the accommodation is designed to appeal to those to whom the price is of no

RESORT ACCOMMODATION PRICE CODING

Double room per night with breakfast (see page 138 for details of prices in Male')

Economy	$	under US$250
Comfortable	$$	from US$250
Luxury	$$$	from US$500
Super Luxury	$$$$	from US$750
Celebrity	$$$$$	skywards from US$1,000

Many resorts offer 'all inclusive' rates. To be sure about your holiday budget, it is worth asking just what 'all inclusive' means. Alas, one thing it does not mean is: all inclusive! Included is only the food and a small part of the beverage element of a holiday.

'Full board' (FB) means breakfast, lunch and dinner, either self-service from buffet counters, or according to a table d'hôte (set meal) menu. This is taken in the main restaurant. While FB meals are included in the term 'all inclusive', not all drinks are. At meals, drinks are limited to red or white house wine served by the glass, with some cocktails and spirits served from the bar before meals.

Royal Island sets out very clearly what 'all inclusive' means on that resort and this extract is typical of how it works.

> All the beverages (alcoholic or non-alcoholic) are strictly for the guest's personal consumption served by glass one at a time, ordered while at the resort's main restaurant (during buffet lunch and dinner), the main bar, pool terrace and Fun Pub. Beverages (alcoholic and non-alcoholic) can be ordered one at a time and not in advance.

All guests staying in the same room should be on the same 'all inclusive' package. Alcoholic drinks will not be served to persons below 18 years of age. There are no refunds for missed meals, and benefits of the package cannot be transferred to another person. The 'all inclusive' package is charged for the guest's entire stay and guests who cut short their stay will not be refunded. That's because resorts have a minimum-stay requirement for 'all inclusive' packages.

Drinks from the room's minibar and any drinks not on the all-inclusive menu are charged extra. All drinks requested outside the designated bar's opening hours are also charged extra. It is not permitted to take all-inclusive drinks from the bar to the room.

So what is included? Usually there is self-service tea or coffee at defined times in the morning and afternoon. As an example, Chaaya Lagoon Hakuraa Huraa offers 'afternoon snacks, 16.00–17.00, and night snacks at 23.00'. Included beverages at that resort are listed as: 'All regular brands of liquor (whisky, brandy, gin, vodka, aperitifs, liquor, sherry, etc), house red and white wine served by the glass, draft beer, carbonated soft drinks and cordials and bottled water, not fruit juices.' Some resorts include a 'cocktail of the day' while others offer a special list of cocktails for the all-inclusive guest.

In addition, some resorts include activities such as windsurfing, canoeing, tennis and even snorkelling equipment at no extra charge for their all-inclusive guests, although this depends on availability.

Some resorts identify guests on their all-inclusive plan by giving them a plastic bracelet to wear. Others rely on the barmen or stewards to identify a guest's billing status from the occupancy and room number list, or computer.

How much extra does 'all inclusive' cost? At resorts where it is available, the price is calculated as an add-on to the full-board room rate. It starts from US$35 per night, per person. Since it includes afternoon tea, unlimited bottled drinking water, which could cost as much as a beer (US$5), as well as house wine normally selling at US$6 a glass, and a cocktail (think from US$10 for one), it seems to be a bargain.

consequence. If guests are not celebrities they are likely to be the incognito (or newly) wealthy or on vast expense accounts. 'Super Luxury' is equivalent to a 5-star hotel in style and service, while 'Luxury' represents the 4-star level. 'Comfortable' is mid-range, good value accommodation, while 'Economy' means that perhaps the infrastructure is not so fancy, meals are buffets, and the place is very relaxed.

Where a resort review ends with a pair of symbols, such as $$$–$$$$$ it signifies that the resort has rooms in several price categories. Prices of all resorts and hotels in the Maldives are quoted in, and charged in, US dollars. The price is for a double room per night, with breakfast for two, unless stated.

FOOD COSTS AT RESORTS The cost of meals and drinks in the resorts is far higher than in Male', because all food has to be imported to the island and the standard is high. This guide to restaurant prices, in US dollars since that is the currency used in all resorts, is based on the minimum you should expect to pay. Of course, the more upmarket the resort, the more the extras will cost.

1½ litres mineral water	US$5	1 glass of Coca-Cola	US$3
1 cup of tea	US$3	1 steak in snack bar	US$20
1 cup of coffee	US$4	1 buffet dinner	US$35–40
1 glass of wine	US$6	1 à-la-carte dinner	US$60
1 bottle of wine	US$30	1 pizza	US$16
1 glass of gin/port/sherry	US$6	1 Chinese main dish	US$10
1 glass of liqueur	US$6	1 barbecue grill	US$30
1 cocktail	US$10	1 dessert	US$7.50
1 glass of fruit juice	US$3		

It is impossible to quote a price code for à-la-carte dining at resorts. The cost of a meal will be based on the standard of the resort. Where meals are not included in the package price, there will be at least a coffee shop for independent dining (say US$50 for two without wine) while the grander resorts have several theme restaurants at which a meal for two without wine would cost at least US$100.

DAY TRIPS Excursions to Male' are really only possible from the closer resorts and are likely to cost from US$50 per person. A full-day island-hopping trip will probably cost from US$50 per person. Half-day snorkelling trips, where necessary because the house reef is too far away, or simply for interest, cost from US$20; and night fishing, with a chance to enjoy the catch at dinner afterwards, from US$40. All these prices will depend on the grade of the resort, and may attract a 10% service charge.

MAKING YOUR CHOICE

WHICH RESORT SHOULD YOU CHOOSE? The resorts' listings are intended as a guide only, not as a definitive rulebook, with each island and resort being described very briefly. If you have any queries, check directly with the resort, or its Male' office, by fax or email, or by looking at its website. Rooms, restaurants and facilities change quite frequently, but the overall ambience of a resort, its main features and the attractions do not vary significantly. As a rule, the ambience of a resort remains constant, in an endeavour to carve out a particular niche for itself. Assessing the worth of a holiday or a resort depends on personal expectations. People value different things – room décor, food, service, value for money, and comfort – differently.

With all resorts providing websites and information, the intending tourist has a new tool to make judgements, even though some of the websites appear to be written by someone wearing rose-tinted spectacles. The popular website www.tripadvisor.com gives reviews by people purporting to have stayed at the resorts. The comments that follow in the next chapters are general impressions, not the resort's publicity information. It is, however, true to say that when selecting a hotel in the Maldives, price alone is not necessarily the best criterion to use. If price is the main concern, a cruise on the all-inclusive *Atoll Explorer* is probably the best bet for a comfortable holiday that lets you see the Maldives at reasonable cost.

What's the best resort? Where you have fun and don't feel overcharged for it; where you emerge from the holiday and feel you would like to go back; where you have discovered somewhere to recommend to friends. What the best resorts have in common is that they succeed in making guests feel they would like to return.

RESORT DESCRIPTIONS In *Chapters 5–9*, the guide reports on all the resorts open to tourism. As you will realise, for one person to visit every resort needs a limitless budget and an endless holiday. Some resorts declined to reveal their attractions as they are pre-sold to guests on long-term 'exclusive' contracts with tour operators. As explained elsewhere, independent travel within the islands of the Maldives is difficult and expensive.

So this latest updating of the resorts has been achieved by a combination of visits to resorts by myself in 2006, 2007 and 2008 and in 2004 by Siân Pritchard-Jones and Bob Gibbons, together with scrutiny and reading between the lines of Maldives Tourism Promotion Board literature, brochures and information from resorts and travel companies (local and overseas), photographs, and the comments of tourists interviewed at Male' Airport. In addition Siân and Bob have looked at some of the resorts' websites, which is what I advise readers to do for a view of what a resort thinks of itself.

The report gives contact telephone and fax numbers of the resort itself together with email address and website address, the number of rooms, the price range, and the types, and journey time, of transfer to the resort. We have not given prices for transfers, as these are subject to fluctuation in line with fuel costs and are usually an item included in the holiday cost. The brief descriptions cover the basic geography, rooms, restaurants, entertainment and any specific activities available, in an effort to give the 'feel' of the place. More detailed information about what the resort actually provides in terms of in-room amenities and activities can be found on the resort's website or on the website of MTPB (*www.visitmaldives.com*).

You will also find in the atoll descriptions the names of resorts that are currently under construction or planned. Most of the new projects are on islands and atolls that have not previously been touched by tourism. Since they have not been completed yet, no details have been included other than their names. If you stay in one of them, please let me know for the next edition.

English spellings of resort names can vary, even in official sources. I try to be consistent in this book and use the most common spellings but you should be aware, for example, that Kuredhu, Kuredoo, Kuredhdhoo and Kuredu are all the same place.

FURTHER INFORMATION For an alphabetical listing of resorts and to check which resorts are in each atoll, refer to *Appendix 3*, pages 204–7.

The Maldives Tourism Promotion Board (MTPB) publishes an annual directory of resorts and their facilities, called *Destination Maldives*, as well as an annual booklet, *Maldives Visitor's Guide*. The latter can be downloaded from www.visitmaldives.com.

Green sea turtles

4

Safaris, Diving and Other Activities

HOLIDAYS AFLOAT

SAFARI BOATS The way to travel around the Maldives archipelago in style is by cruise ship or, more basic, on a safari in a chartered vessel. These boats are based on the traditional *dhoni* form, but with engines, cabins, toilets and showers. They vary from 15–25m in length and come with a crew that includes a cook and, on diving safaris, a qualified diving instructor.

Safari cruising, whether for diving, snorkelling, adventure sailing or leisurely island hopping, is growing in popularity. It is a good way to visit several islands, or unspoiled dive locations, far from the resorts. For long trips requiring tourists to spend a night or more on board, only vessels registered with the Ministry of Tourism to accommodate visitors may be used. Such a vessel has to have a Certificate of Safety at Sea and permission to transport passengers as well as to collect the head tax payable per person per night.

The Maldives Tourism Promotion Board lists over 80 safari vessels on its website (*www.visitmaldives.com*). The MTPB also has a brochure giving the street and email addresses, telephone and fax numbers of each vessel's operator. The brochure includes details under the following headings: language spoken, length, soundproof generator, cruising speed, passenger capacity, number of cabins, cabins with attached toilet, hot water, separate diving *dhoni*, night diving, unlimited diving, oxygen, rental equipment, radio telephone, mobile telephone, VHF, CB radio, air conditioning, desalination, 220 volts, 110 volts, DC-volts, sun deck, big-game fishing, surfing, bar facility, video facility.

Typical accommodation will include individual cabins for two with bunks or, in some cases, a large common cabin with pairs of bunks separated by curtains. They will have toilets (flushed with seawater) and at least one freshwater shower. There will be a galley and a saloon (usually doubling as the wheelhouse), a refrigerator, generator and CB radio. A dinghy with an outboard motor is standard, and other extras such as diving equipment and even a bicycle may be carried. Some safari vessels are air conditioned.

The law on tourism stipulates that cruises for tourists should be conducted only in atolls where tourist facilities are available. Areas approved are Baa, Lhaviyani, Kaaf (Male'), Alif (Ari) and Vaavu atolls. With the opening of new resorts, tourist facilities have also become available in Raa, Faafu, Dhaal and Meemu atolls.

This actually gives a wonderful opportunity to see inhabited islands unaffected by tourism, as well as to discover some idyllic, uninhabited islands. Nights are spent on board, although sometimes the safari boat will anchor near a resort island (if permitted to do so; some resort guests regard safari boat passengers as intruders) as passengers sometimes like the chance to visit a resort bar in the evenings. At least one day would normally be at leisure on a deserted island or an interesting inhabited spot where some cultural entertainment might

> As soon as our boat was in sight, the dull main street of sand took on the genteel excitement of a village fête.
>
> Women in the colourful Maldives version of a wimple stood at trestle tables offering an odd assortment of wares such as imported shell necklaces and wooden fish from Indonesia. A woman sucking a *gudu-guda*, the gurgling water-pipe of the Maldives, watched impassively. As we sailed away, taking none of the junk with us, the stalls were dismantled.
>
> *Business Traveller magazine*

be arranged, such as the famous *bodu beru* drummers. Barbecues and picnics on other islands may feature, and there is generally some time in Male' at the end of the cruise.

Meals are prepared on board and usually consist of fish caught by crew or passengers, with the addition of canned items and pasta or rice. Passengers are welcome to assist in on-board chores, and may be obliged to if the crew don't.

One company (Voyages Maldives, which has eight boats) quotes the average cruise holiday as lasting ten nights; it's a fine way to get to know the Maldivian crew as well as the islands.

Rates quoted for safari cruises – without the extras necessary for a diving safari – start at around US$150 per person per day, according to the boat's total passenger complement, probably ten. Rates include the government head tax of US$8 per person per night, and food is generally included, although some boats charge separately for meals. Extras such as soft drinks and mineral water may have to be paid for by the passengers. Diving is also extra, from US$25–35 per dive.

Some safari (live aboard) boat operators and some of their vessels

AAA Travel & Tours Pvt Ltd STO Trade Centre, Male' 03–02; ✎ 3324933, 3322417; f 3331726; e trvlntrs@aaa.com.mv; www.aaatravel-maldives.com

Ahmed Waheed Ma Silverdaze, Male'; ✎ 3324213, 7771177; f 3318354; vessels: *Hammer Head, Hammer Head II*

Aquasun Maldives 3rd Floor, Beach Tower, Boduthakurufaanu Magu, Male'; ✎ 3312256; f 3332870; e aqua@dhivehinet.net.mv; www.aquasunmaldives.com; vessel: *SY Dream Voyager*

Atoll Vacations Hithahfinivaa Magu, Male'; ✎ 3315450; f 3314783; e atvac@ dhivehinet.net.mv; www.atollvacations.com; vessel: *Cyrus*

Blue Horizon Feeroaz Magu, Male'; ✎ 3321169; f 3328797; e bluehrzn@dhivehinet.net.mv; www.blue-horizon.com.mv; vessels: MV *Horizon, Horizon II*

Desire Maldives Travels & Tours Orchid Magu, Male'; ✎ 3331811; f 3318815; e info@desire-maldives.com; www.gaavia.com; vessel: *Gaavia*

Diving Adventure Maldives Ithaa Goalhi, Male'; ✎ 3326734; f 3326734; e divemald@ dhivehinet.net.mv; www.maldivesdiving.com; vessel: *Adventurer I*

Eslire Maldives Alikelegefaanu Magu, Male'; ✎ 3312743; f 3326542; e eslire@dhivehinet.net.mv; vessels: *Rani I, Rani II*

Grey Dolphin Travel Fasmandhu, Male'; ✎ 3315439; f 3321549; e info@bluedolphin.com.mv; www.bluedolphin.com.mv; vessel: *Blue Dolphin*

IAL Yacht Tours Finihiyaa Goalhi; ✎ 3322265; f 3318521; e i.a.yacht@dhivehinet.net.mv; www.maleesha.com.mv; vessel: *Maleesha Royal Cruiser*

Inner Maldives Holidays Pvt Ltd H Faalandhoshuge Aage, Ameer Ahmed Magu, Male'; ✎ 3327225; f 3327256; e opsaviation@innermaldives.com; www.innermaldives.com; vessel: *Dorado*

Interlink Maldives H Ashan Lodge, Vaijbey Magu, Male'; ✎ 3313537; f 3313538; e info@ interlinkmaldives.com; www.interlinkmaldives.com; vessels: MV *Keema*, MY *Jaariya*, SY *Marana 22*

Maldives Boat Club Kudhiraymaa Goalhi, Male'; ✎ 3314841; f 3314811; e info@ maldivesboatclub.com.mv;

www.maldivesboatclub.com.mv; vessels: *Eagle Ray, Sting Ray*

M Stella Male'; ☎ 3327826; f 3326382; e info@blueshark.com.mv; www.blueshark.com; vessels: *Blue Shark, Blue Shark 2*

Muni Travels Shaheedali Higun, Male'; ☎ 3331512; f 3331513; e munitrv@dhivehinet.net.mv; www.muni.com.mv; vessels: MY *Moodhumaa*, MY *Moonimaa*

Panorama Maldives Sabudheyli Magu, Male'; ☎ 3327066; f 3326542; e panorama@dhivehinet.net.mv; www.panoramamaldives.com; vessels: *Nasru, Panorama, Haveyli, Flying Fish*

Phoenix Hotels & Resorts Pvt Ltd Medhuziyaarai Magu, Male'; ☎ 3323181; f 3325499; e phoenix@dhivehinet.net.mv; vessels: *Dhandahelu II, Suwasa II, Kureli, Mandhu*

Platinum Capital Holdings M Mahi, Boduthakurufaanu Magu; ☎ 3343840; f 3343841; e sales@pch.com.mv; www.pch.com.mv; vessel: *Catfish*

Seafari Adventures ☎ 3329338; f 3328946; e seafari_maldives@iol.it; www.maldivesliveaboard.us; vessels: *Madivaru 7, Madivaru III*

Radiantheat Travels Ameenee Magu; ☎ 3312985; f 3324948; e info@radheattravel.com; www.radheattravel.com; vessels: *Handhu, Handu Falhi*

Sea Explorers Association Bodufungandu Magu, Male'; ☎ 3316172; f 3316783; e seaexplo@dhivehinet.net.mv; www.seafariadventures.com; vessels: *Baraabaru, Baratheela*

Sultans Travel Ground Floor, Fasmeeru Bldg, 25 Boduthakurufaanu Magu, Male'; ☎ 3320330; f 3320440; e travel@sultansoftheseas.com; www.sultansoftheseastravel.com

Sunland Travel Pvt Ltd Male'; ☎ 3324658; f 3325543; e sunland@dhivehinet.net.mv; vessels: *Maldivian Romance, Maldivian Romance II*

Sun Travel & Tours Pvt Ltd Meheli Goalhi, off Boduthakurufaanu Magu, Male'; ☎ 3325977; f 3320419; e info@sunholidays.com; www.sunholidays.com; vessels: *Sunset Cruiser, Fathhul Bari*

Tropical Excursions H Hithigasdhoshuge Aage, Male'; ☎ 3321447; f 3317850; e tropical@tropicalexcursions.com.mv; www.tropicalexcursions.com.mv; vessels: *Cozy, Hariyana*

Universal Enterprises Pvt Ltd 39 Orchid Magu, Male'; ☎ 3322971; f 3322678; e sales@unient.com.mv, explorer@dhivehinet.net.mv; www.atollexplorer.com; vessels: MV *Atoll Explorer*

Vista Company Pvt Ltd 3/4 Faamudheyrige, Faamudheri Magu, Male'; ☎ 3320952; f 3318035; e vista@dhivehinet.net.mv; www.vistamaldives.com; vessels: *Island Safari, Island Safari I*

Voyages Maldives Pvt Ltd Narugis Bldg, Chandhanee Magu, Male'; ☎ 3323617; f 3325336; e info@voyagesmaldives.com; www.voyagesmaldives.com; vessels: *Gahaa, Gulfaam, Koimala, Sea Coral, Sea Farer, Kethi*

Yacht Tours Maldives H Vilares, Finihiyaa Goalhi, Male'; ☎ 3316454; f 3310206; e yachtour@dhivehinet.net.mv; vessels: *Silverster, Kirudooni, Alpashah, Dhondhooni*

CRUISING If cruising around the islands sounds the perfect idea for a holiday but you seek more than basic comfort, a guarantee of reasonable food and tolerable companions, and aren't that interested in spending the whole holiday diving, then a scheduled cruise is the answer. While there have been a few vessels doing this within Maldivian waters, only one has been successful: the *Atoll Explorer* (*Universal Enterprises Pvt Ltd, 39 Orchid Magu, Male'; ☎ 3322971; f 3322678; e explorer@dhivehinet.net.mv; www.atollexplorer.com*). For details, see box overleaf.

Some safari boat companies also operate vessels that cruise through the islands for those who want a leisurely, scenic experience without diving. With over 25 years' experience Voyages Maldives is the leading live-aboard operator, with a website (*www.voyagesmaldives.com*) that clearly sets out the various options (cruising, diving, sailing and surfing safaris) and includes deck plans of its vessels. The smallest (*Sea Farer*) has two cabins with double beds and two cabins with couchettes and can be chartered for a minimum of four people from US$330 per day, low season. The largest vessel (*Koimala*) sleeps 14 at a squeeze and costs in high season from US$770 per day for four guests, with each additional guest at US$135 per person per day. Included in the price is boat charter with crew and fuel (but there is a US$20 per day fuel surcharge), full board, head tax, snorkelling and fishing gear, soft drinks and a T-shirt.

It may not look pretty, but the *Atoll Explorer* provides a way of seeing all parts of the Maldives that is pretty hard to beat. Formerly an oil rig supply ship and converted for passenger cruising in the Maldives in 1997, it sets off from its anchorage at Kurumba Maldives every Monday morning for a seven-night cruise around the atolls. There are two itineraries, making a back-to-back cruise doubly interesting, with one including visits to islands in Vaavu Atoll and the other to Ari Atoll.

The ship has 20 cabins: eight with double beds and balconies and 12 with twin beds and picture windows. They are compact and lack drawer space but each boasts a clothes cabinet, lots of hooks and mirrors, individually controlled air conditioning, plenty of square three-pin plug sockets, and bathroom with hot-water shower. There are fore and aft sun decks (two jacuzzis aft) linked by an open-sided deck converted with transparent screens into a light and airy restaurant.

At the stern on the lower deck is the dive centre (a five-dive package is from US$185; PADI Open Water course from US$356), reception office, a shop for sundries, and – the heart of camaraderie on this cruise – an air-conditioned bar, which doubles as a smoking lounge. A glass panel behind the bar counter gives a view of the diving centre and the sea. The bar functions from 09.00 until 01.30, with cocktails, tea/coffee, soft drinks, spirits and house wine (but not champagne) included in the fare.

Passengers are usually British and a good mix of young and old, divers and non-divers, so a house-party atmosphere quickly develops. This is helped by the lack of formality: dress code is shorts by day and casual at night. There are no annoying animators and Captain Fulhu has a loyal, caring and long-serving crew who anticipate passengers' needs. The captain himself helps passengers on and off the ship when they transfer to a *dhoni* to visit beaches *en route*.

The ship anchors at night and cruises only for a few hours each morning, but that is enough to discover real castaway desert islands, little-visited inhabited islands and remarkable dive spots. Halfway through the cruise there is a barbecue on a desert island; other evenings include a Maldivian dinner and *bodu beru* dancing display, and a dinner dance with live band on the last night.

Meals are buffets with breakfast cooked to order, lunch and dinner with soup, salad, a choice of main courses (with fish always an option) and dessert. Vegetables are fresh (flown in weekly from Sri Lanka) and special dishes are arranged on request.

One evening is spent night fishing, sitting in a *dhoni* with baited line dangling over the side, waiting for a bite. The Captain's Dinner menu reflects the fishy aspect of the onboard diet: bouillabaisse, tuna pie, grilled fish with lemon and parsley butter, beef bourguignon, seafood thermidor, peppered chicken, boquetière of vegetables, geera rice, pineapple and sausage salad, chef's salad with fried fish, tomato salad, desserts, then tea or coffee.

As a way of seeing different aspects of the Maldives as well as getting to know polite Maldivians who form the crew, a cruise on *Atoll Explorer* is amazing value, and very different from being isolated on a resort island for a week, although many passengers plan their holiday to include both. Cruises are usually booked as part of a package through travel agents – like Kuoni (see page 48) – but can be arranged independently through local operators from US$250 per day per person, full board, all inclusive (but diving extra) for a cabin with balcony.

At the beginning of 2008 a one-week holiday on *Atoll Explorer* including flights from London was being offered by www.globalholidays.co.uk/holidays-the-maldives-cruising.htm from US$2,000.

WATER-BASED ACTIVITIES

DIVING

Seasons Any time of year is a good time to dive, but, for the very enthusiastic wishing to get the maximum from their holiday, there are some better periods. As a rule the best time is from January to April, when skies and the sea tend to be clearer. Plankton is more abundant in October to November, and it makes the sea murkier. The compensation is that the bigger fish may be more active and more easily seen.

Where to dive The best areas for divers are the reef edges, the *kandus* where currents attract big fish, the *thilas* where wave actions and currents attract a multitude of fish, and the wrecks dotted around where seafarers suffered misfortune. Some of the better-known dive sites are indicated on the atoll maps in the later chapters, as are the main protected marine reserves.

Diving maps For details of the best diving sites in the Maldives, enthusiasts should get a copy of the *Maldives Map for Divers and Travellers*, which is produced by Atoll Editions in Australia (f +61 3 5237 6332). It lists all the protected marine areas, as well as other dive sites, wrecks, *thilas*, caves and *kandus*, etc.

Regulations Regulations are in force to support the development of the underwater appeal of the Maldives, as well as to protect the marine environment from pillage and pollution. The maximum depth allowed for dives is 30m/100ft.

Diving instructors, base leaders, assistant diving instructors and diving guides must have up-to-date certification of their ability from PADI, NAUI, CMAS, BARACUDA, VIT, POSEIDON or equivalent. All diving centres and schools must be registered with the Ministry of Home Affairs, Housing and Environment. They must be equipped with adequate facilities and have workable arrangements for obtaining quick professional medical attention.

The use of harpoons or spears is prohibited and it is forbidden to remove corals, dead or alive, or any other sea animals, including fish, even if you find you can actually pick them up out of the sea. Fishing by net or rod and line in resort lagoons is prohibited too, with resorts fining guests up to US$1,000 for doing so.

Learning and courses Beginners wanting to learn to dive can find unlimited opportunities in the Maldives. It is estimated that between 25% and 40% of visitors to the Maldives go there either specifically to dive or decide to take an introductory diving course while they are on holiday. Many others try snorkelling, since the waters are not only as clear as gin but are also full of cocktail-coloured fish. In response to this, all the resorts have dive centres, usually with expatriate diving

UNDERWATER ACRONYMS	
PADI	Professional Association of Diving Instructors
NAUI	National Association of Underwater Instructors
CMAS	Confédération Mondiale des Activités Subaquatiques
SCUBA	Self Contained Underwater Breathing Apparatus
BARACUDA	Baracuda International Aquanautic Club
VIT	Verband Internationaler Tauchschulen (Association of International Diving Schools)
POSEIDON	Poseidon Nimrod International Diving Club

Gemunu Amarasinghe

Like many visitors to the Maldives, I had no thoughts of learning to dive when I first went there. My interest began one afternoon when I hired snorkel, mask and fins, and floated around the lagoon at Full Moon. I was completely captivated by the underwater world and was tempted to go out of my depth as I explored, nose down, even though I was a poor swimmer.

I wondered then if I would be able to learn to scuba dive; it sounded a very adventurous thing to do. Actually, as I discovered when I met Peter and Eva Christoffersson of the Euro Divers school at Kurumba Maldives Resort, it was not so difficult.

First, they took me on an introductory dive. There were three of us in the group and in the dive school we were fitted with equipment and then led, with air tank and weights buckled on, to the lagoon. In the water, we were shown some basic skills and when Peter was satisfied that each of us understood, we swam gently to the nearby house reef … and dived.

I was determined from that moment to learn to dive properly. I signed up for the PADI Open Water Course and started by learning theory and watching videos. Our instructors were very safety-conscious and wanted to be certain that we could cope before we tried any serious diving. The initial in-water instruction was provided in the lagoon, which a Japanese guest said was so much better than learning the basics in a swimming pool, as it meant we adjusted to the sea immediately.

We had our first dive on the third day of the course. My log book records: 'Hanna's Reef, 12 metres for 40 minutes in dive of 41 minutes.' I noted: 'Landed on the sand bottom to start with. Lots of fish.' The next day we dived at the Club Med reef (15m) with more theory and a simple written test afterwards.

To my delight, I passed the final written test and, on the fifth day, was allowed to do two dives; one in the morning to Banana Reef (17m) ('green turtle, white shark') and in the afternoon to Magiri Caves (19m) ('good visibility').

That night, the five members of our group of six (one lady withdrew halfway through) were presented with our log books and certificates. Two days later, I went on my first dive with experienced divers, to Bandos Reef (21m) ('two sharks, one with pilot fish').

I have learned that diving gives a different insight to the Maldives, with its fascinating community of fish and living coral just a few feet under water from the island resorts. Diving can also improve your social life, as you can meet your underwater buddies and swap stories in the bar at night.

instructors. All offer introductory lessons on diving, as well as dives to house reefs and further out for experienced divers.

All diving has to be supervised by an instructor, assistant instructor or diving guide. In order to take part in diving excursions, a person must at least be certified as a basic diver by PADI/NAUI or be a CMAS one-star diver. If not, the diver is considered a trainee.

Before signing up for a diving course, you should be able to guarantee that you have had a recent medical examination and were found fit for diving, and that you do not suffer from any chronic diseases such as organic heart disease or diabetes.

Always tell the truth about any previous diving experience (or lack of it) and be prepared to follow the orders of your diving instructor. Never dive on your own or under the influence of medicine or alcohol, and **don't dive within 24 hours of a flight**. Make sure, too, that your travel insurance covers you for diving, since

Sunset on Kudabandos Island (PLL/PCL) page 151

above **Aerial view of Male'** (P/Tips) page 131
below left **Calligraphy in Male's main mosque at the Islamic Centre** (GA) page 145
below right **The Islamic Centre in Male'** (GA) page 145

above **Transporting fruit in Male'** (CS/PCL)

left **On some islands breadfruit is an important part of the diet** (GA) page 8

below **Male' waterfront** (GA)

above left **Smoking *gudu-guda*, Alifushi, Raa Atoll** (GA) page 98

above right **Hammering coconut fibre to make coir rope** (GA) page 87

below **Playing chess, dried fish market, Male'** (GA) page 126

above **Drying fish on the beach of a village island** (GA) page 30

right **Young Maldivians at play on the beach** (GA) page 126

below **Maldivian fishermen** (GA) page 28

above left **Crescent-tail bigeye** (RD/Tips) page 15

above **A heron looking for lunch from the bow of a *dhoni*** (P/Tips) page 11

left **Whale shark** (P/Tips) page 15

below **Green sea turtle** (RD/Tips) page 11

the diving centre's insurance may not cover the boats, the diving equipment or the course participants. Just as you are likely to have a better vacation at a well-run resort, so, too, are you more likely to have better diving facilities (even if they cost more) at such a resort.

Each resort diving instructor will know the reefs in the locality that are suitable for experienced divers or for beginners. The theory is that resorts furthest from Male', being new, have reefs which are less dived and thus of greater interest. However, even in North Male' Atoll, within 30 minutes by speedboat from the airport, there are at least two dozen recommended diving places. For the beginner, the chance to watch fish under water and to see natural coral gardens is a delight, even close to Male'.

A TYPICAL DIVING SAFARI

VOYAGES MALDIVES

1st day	Welcome on board at airport – sail to Laguna Maldives Resort – light meal on the trip – diving certification and log book – briefing – visit resort – dinner on board – visit resort bar.
2nd day	Breakfast – departure to Rasdhoo Atoll (4–5 hours) – morning dive – lunch on board – afternoon dive – anchorage in lagoon (fishermen's village or resort, according to weather conditions) – visit island – dinner – visit resort bar (only if anchored nearby).
3rd day	Breakfast – departure to Ari Atoll (2 hours) – morning dive – lunch in Maayafushi lagoon – afternoon dive – anchorage in Maayafushi lagoon – visit resort – dinner on board – visit resort bar.
4th day	Breakfast – morning dive – barbecue on uninhabited island – afternoon dive – anchorage in Halaveli lagoon – dinner on board – visit resort bar.
5th day	Breakfast – morning dive at Shark-Point – departure to South Ari Atoll – lunch on trip – afternoon dive – anchorage at Mandhoo (fishermen's island) – visit island – dinner on board.
6th day	Breakfast – departure to Dhangethi – morning dive – anchorage at uninhabited island – lunch on board – afternoon at leisure – tea and biscuits – night diving – dinner on board.
7th day	Breakfast – morning dive – lunch on board – visit to Male' – afternoon dive – anchorage in Farukolhufushi resort lagoon (Club Med) – dinner on board – visit resort bar.
8th day	Breakfast – depart to airport.

This itinerary is only a suggested programme. It may be adjusted according to the wishes of any particular group. A competent tour guide will assist you in making new itineraries. Weather and tidal currents can require adjustments to anchorage and dive sites.

DIVING RATES US$88 per person per day

If a group size is fewer than four paying divers, a minimum charge of US$352 per day applies. The above rates include two day dives per day per person, inclusive of weights, tank, air, services of dive master and dive *dhoni* with a crew of three, in addition to the cost of chartering a safari vessel. Extra dives: US$40 per day dive; US$50 per night dive.

Other dive equipment is available at extra cost. Only qualified divers can take part. Rates vary according to the class of vessel.

There is actually a diving school in Male'. **Sea Explorers Associates** (*Asfaamn Bodufungandu Magu;* ✆ *3316172;* f *3316783;* e *seaexplo@dhivehinet.net.mv; www.seamaldives.com.mv*) is the capital's first diving school. It offers PADI dive courses, fun dives, night dives, wreck dives, underwater photography, diving safaris, equipment servicing and equipment rental.

The school uses *dhonis* from the waterfront to take Male'-based divers to a selection of over 25 dive locations in North and South Male' atolls. The school is very popular with expatriates working in Male', as well as with travellers staying in town guesthouses, and Maldivians who also want to explore their own underwater world. Because the school's overheads are lower, and everything is included, a dive course works out cheaper than at one of the resort dive schools.

Sea Explorers offers various all-inclusive courses, with a PADI Open Water Diver starting at US$450, a PADI Advanced Open Water Diver for US$220 and regular dives at US$35–40.

Prices vary around the resorts for diving and diving courses. As a rule, the more expensive a resort is, the higher the rates are. However this is not a hard rule; some resorts geared to diving may offer a wider range of courses and be good value.

As an example, a typical resort course (theoretical and practical) of four lessons, including training in shallow water and a fun dive at the resort's house reef, costs from US$150 to US$220. A PADI Open Water Diver or VIT certificate, including a course of nine practical and three theoretical sessions along with the relevant examination, might cost US$400 to US$500, plus an additional US$45 for the certificate. Boat charges are extra, as is any equipment hire. A beginner's course would take from four to six days. For the open water dive courses you ought to be thinking of six to nine days, to allow for sufficient dives and theory classes.

There is no need to go to the expense of buying a special camera to take your own photographs under water as these can be hired from a dive school. Disposable underwater cameras to take fish snaps are available in hotel gift shops at about US$30, or try in your home country.

Insurance Dan Europe is a 'Divers' Foundation' that offers specialist medical cover. It has offices in Italy, Malta and the UK (*Dan Europe UK, Unit 11, The Courtyard, Whitwick Business Pk, Stenson Rd, Coalville LE67 4JP;* ✆ *0870 872 8888;* f *0870 872 5555;* e *uk@daneurope.org*).

Diving safaris Diving safaris are popular among enthusiasts. A qualified and knowledgeable dive master goes on each safari, with a dive *dhoni* carrying the diving equipment. This enables easy access to difficult dive spots. Those joining a dive safari should already be qualified, to get the most benefit from the trips. Divers may want to bring their own personal gear, wetsuits, masks, etc, but tanks and weights are normally provided. And see box on page 123.

Diving-boat standards A diving boat must have a crew of at least three. It must also have a functioning walkie-talkie, a spare dive bottle and a regulator on board. Boats should have oxygen as standard, as well as radio. When divers are under water, the diving boat should have the international diving flag hoisted and the boat must be stationed in the vicinity of the divers. This flag should not appear if divers are not under water.

SNORKELLING Beginners of all ages can discover a new dimension in swimming with flippers, mask and snorkel. If you have not brought your own, resorts will have snorkelling equipment from US$10 per day for a set. A course costs from US$50. Equipment can be bought at shops in Male'.

SNORKELLING SURPRISES

Siân Pritchard-Jones and Bob Gibbons

Having been mountain trekkers and overland lovers for years, we feel a certain trepidation about jumping into a sea full of strange and exotic fish. Curious crabs and slimy rocks at the reef-edge jetty don't make this plunge into the unknown any more attractive. We retreat to the lagoon, safe in the knowledge that no currents and hazards lurk below the placid turquoise water on the other side of the island.

Managing to float in the shallow water is easier said than done. There must be a way to get those fins on without scooping huge amounts of sand into the shoe. With water barely 2ft deep, you need to wade some distance from the shore to get sufficient depth below your personal Plimsoll line. Going backwards is easier, but somewhat ungainly. Don't you just know that all those dozing sunbathers aren't really asleep, but watching you totter about beyond the shore like a drunken clown?

Well, this is better. We are floating, horizontal at last, and gasping for air through the claustrophobic mouthpiece. The water is swirling about at eye level. In the shallow lagoon we see brightly coloured fish of all sizes, and there is dead coral barely half a metre below. The reef is still miles away, but, having quickly mastered the breathing, we zoom off. The fish are simply amazing, and this is still only the lagoon. The waves are not big here, but not small either. These new snorkels seem to keep the water away, despite the crash of water over our heads. Better get back to the main house reef and the crab jetty, then.

Literally 1 metre off the jetty we are into a wonderworld of corals. It's perhaps a relief that they are all bleached here; at least there are no sharp or spiny things below. Massive brain corals, giant cauliflower things and nodular corals lie just below. Suddenly the reef plunges to murky depths, like a dramatic cliff dropping into an abyss. We are totally surrounded by a shoal of iridescent blue, red-toothed triggerfish – the most incandescent of blue colours and barely bigger than a hand. Below we can see angelfish with stripes of yellow hugging the reef. Down in the depths are shadowy outlines of bigger fish. Here and there dart the parrotfish, decked out in their finest colours of blue, turquoise and purple.

A rope used for training divers is a good anchor point from which to watch the underwater variety show. Suddenly a large slippery flat object glides by not five feet away, a spotted eagle manta ray heading out. The show goes on. And then a wave sends water rushing into the snorkel, but still it's not intimidating and the moment of panic passes. The show is just too spectacular to stop. Against our better judgement we stay on, knowing that we should nip back to the room to get some sun-protecting T-shirts. We are only here for the day, so there's no time to waste.

The sun is already low in the skies, but there is time to swim off along the reef edge, seeking out new gullies and hiding places in the wall of coral for other fish. Countless varieties are here, intent on finding nutrients. A cloud of white mist pours forth ahead; it's probably the coral dust being ejected from fish's digestive filters in the shoal ahead. An Indian butterflyfish slips by as we head for the jetty. The crabs are no longer skulking about on the slimy rocks and the heat of the sun dies, with lengthening shadows. A cooling balm settles over the island. A fiery sunset engulfs the skies and lights begin to twinkle across the channel on the distant resort.

We have seen only the tip of the reefs with our snorkels. Below and further on are countless new dimensions waiting to be explored here in the underwater world of the Maldives.

Even if you are a strong swimmer, it is advisable to wear a life jacket when snorkelling, especially if far from shore, because currents can carry away the unwary. To avoid sunburn during a long swim, a T-shirt is also a good idea.

Resorts that attract divers, as well as those suited to keen snorkelling enthusiasts, are noted in the general resort listings. Beginners wanting to snorkel will be given rudimentary instructions by dive centres. Some will provide lessons. Many people bring their own equipment. Modern snorkels have a system that allows water to drain out, so getting huge mouthfuls is less likely. Waves are sometimes choppy at reef edges. Beginners should practise and gain confidence in the shallow lagoons, where a remarkable variety of fish can sometimes be found in even half a metre depth of water. The reef edges are simply stunning for fish, and snorkellers should head for these as soon as sufficient confidence is established. Don't miss them!

Snorkelling expeditions by *dhoni* are also organised to take snorkellers beyond the resort lagoon, or simply to better waters. Where these trips depend on a minimum number of people, and there are not enough, it is usually possible to negotiate a price for the whole boat.

WINDSURFING With a very few exceptions, all resorts offer windsurfing. This normally costs extra and there is usually a separate windsurfing school (not part of the diving school) on the beach. It would be possible to try your potential skill as a windsurfer in an introductory session from US$20. A full course for beginners, with eight or more sessions of an hour each, could be had from US$200, certificate included. Private lessons are available and surfboards can also be rented by the hour. Instruction is usually by expatriates.

The Ministry of Defence and National Security has issued rules relating to windsurfing which require a watchman to be on the beach to observe the windsurfer, and a boat to be available if needed. Windsurfers wanting to go beyond the watchman's range of vision have to make special arrangements. Windsurfing at night is not permitted.

SAILING Sailing by catamaran or local sailing *dhoni* can be arranged at some resorts, either with a skipper or solo. Typical rates for an hour/day are from US$30/130, with private lessons at US$45.

Voyages Maldives has introduced the concept of sailing cruises using three of its vessels at a cost during 2008 of US$330–440 per day, depending on the season, for a minimum of four guests, with US$70–80 per day per each extra person. The itinerary is flexible; the box opposite is a suggestion.

WATERSKIING Where this is possible, expect to pay from US$5 a minute.

SURFING

Male' Atoll There are a number of surfing areas in the atolls, with Male' Atoll being the most convenient (surfers are even to be seen at the southwest corner of the capital). All are close to the airport, and a surfing competition has been organised to make Maldives surfing more widely known. The best months for surfing are April–October which, apart from August, coincides with the off-season from May, which is when room rates are lower. Waves are commonly 2m high.

Three good swells come each month, lasting a couple of days, and the best thing is they are offshore. Some of them are Himafushi (Jail break), Thamburudhoo left and right (aka Honkys and Sultans), Thulusdhoo Point (Colas), Kuda Vilingili (Chickens) and Airport.

Two resorts on the east side of the atoll are particularly noted for their surfing. These are Chaaya Dhonveli and Adaaran Hudhuranfushi (formerly Lohifushi).

1st day	Welcome on board the *dhoni* at the airport or at Male', the capital. Sail to Waagali Island (uninhabited) or to a resort island. Lunch aboard. Swimming/snorkelling. Night at anchorage.
2nd day	After breakfast depart to Felidu Atoll (4–5 hours). Lunch on the way. Visit a fishing village, Fulidhoo or Felidhoo. Walk through the island, meet the local people, observe their crafts like boatbuilding, and their lifestyle. Night at lagoon.
3rd day	After breakfast depart to a beautiful uninhabited island, Vashugiri or Fotheyo or Ambara. Relax on the beach. Snorkelling/swimming. Beach barbecue if there is a good catch and weather permits. Night at anchorage or camped on the beach.
4th day	Day at leisure – early morning fishing, swimming/snorkelling or just relaxing on the beach.
5th day	After breakfast sail to another inhabited island, Felidhoo or Keyodhoo. Meet the islanders. Night at anchorage. Local traditional entertainment of *bodu beru* on the island. (*Bodu beru* means 'big drum' where a group sits around and sings to a rhythmical beat of drums till it reaches a crescendo and stops abruptly.)
6th day	After breakfast depart to Male' Atoll. Lunch on the way. Visit Male'. Shopping and sightseeing – the Islamic Centre, museum, local fish and fruit markets, etc. Late afternoon depart to a close-by resort island. Snorkelling on the reef. Night at anchorage.
7th day	After breakfast depart to the airport.

The large island of Himafushi, just south of Dhonveli, offers surfers the waves named as 'Jail break'. North of Hudhuranfushi resort is the big island of Thulusdhoo, which has good surf between April and October. Not far from here is Kuda Villingili, the best 'left hander' in the North Male' Atoll. For further details it is best to contact specialist surf operators, like Voyages Maldives.

Sun Travels and Tours Pvt Ltd (*www.sunholidays.com*) also has surfing holiday packages, basing its surfing guests at Hudhuranfushi, Full Moon and Paradise resorts. All surfing is organised using a boat to visit the surf places around those resorts.

Surf areas and nearby islands

Sultan	Kanu Huraa	Arifs	Hudhuranfushi
Monkey	Full Moon	Nickys	Club Med Kani
Tiger	Thulusdhoo	Shyams	Kuda Villingili
Kamana	Than'burudhoo	Jumbo	Paradise

Outer Atolls In the far south, Laamu and Gaaf Alif/Gaaf Dhaal Atolls (also known as Huvadhu) are separated by the significant One and Half Degree channel. As there is not much land mass to the south of these atolls, swells generated by the roaring forties (a weather phenomenon created in the far south of the Indian Ocean) hit the islands of these atolls, creating the best waves in the country.

Laamu Atoll works in the same conditions as North Male' Atoll. The best times to visit the region are March to April and August to November.

The best time to visit Huvadhu Atoll is in northeast monsoon, January to March and also November to October. Although there are waves to ride throughout the season, swell is most consistent during January to March.

Vessels are available for charter to the surfing areas through Voyages Maldives, whose rates for a ten-day surfing voyage in Laamu or 14 days surfing in Huvadhu, living aboard the boat, start at US$120 per person per day for a minimum of four passengers, with fuel surcharge (US$20 per day) and airfare from Male' to the regional airports extra.

DEEP-SEA FISHING Maldivians do not go deep-sea fishing, as this would mean remaining at sea for several days and their fishing boats are not powerful or equipped for long voyages. But the big fish are there and big-game fishing has been introduced for guests at the major resorts. Lagoon fishing is not allowed.

One of the main operators is the Universal Big Game Fishing Centre based at Full Moon. They use a boat especially constructed for deep-sea big-game fishing. It has a special radar system for finding fishing areas, plus echo sounder, fish finder and radio transmitter set.

NIGHT FISHING

Royston Ellis

'You must go night fishing,' the manager of the island resort told me. His tone implied that not to go 'night fishing' while in the Maldives was the equivalent of not going to the theatre while in London or New York. 'We will barbecue your catch on the beach afterwards. There is nothing better than grilled freshly caught fish.'

I agreed ... reluctantly.

You see, I had been night fishing once before. It was when tourism in the Maldives was in its teenage years, and so were the boat crew who took us. We headed out to sea at nightfall and the boys enthusiastically baited every line they could find. I was given one and, caught up in their enthusiasm, eagerly chucked it in the sea.

While all around me fish were snapping greedily at the bait and my companions hauled in fish galore, I got nary a tickle. I waited and waited. Then suddenly there was a great tug on the line, which nearly pulled me overboard. 'I've got one!' I shouted to roars of encouragement from the boat crew.

Hurriedly I pulled in the line, not noticing at the time that it seemed to be rather short. Then there it was, breaking out of the water and swung over onto the deck, my first fish. As it lay gasping, I looked around for the congratulations of the crew. They were falling about with laughter.

Frankly, their behaviour at my moment of triumph and conquest deflated me somewhat. Then my companion told me the awful truth. One of the boys had pulled in my line without me seeing. He had hooked a fish on it that he had caught himself, just to make me feel happy.

Night fishing on my latest trip was rather more organised, perhaps because the resort manager had warned the boatmen not to bring me back without at least one fish. It was certainly more placid, too; an ideal exercise for calming nerves jaded by too much sunbathing or snorkelling.

I just sat there with my line in my fingers, waiting for it to jiggle suddenly, and then pulled the line in as quickly as I could. I actually caught two! Then I baited up, plopped the line and the weight back into the sea and waited for the next bite ... and waited ... and waited.

After half an hour, while my companions were whooping with delight at their catches, I gave up hope. I pulled in my line to change the bait, only to discover that I had been dangling a line that did not even have a hook on it.

Our catch was quickly barbecued afterwards on the beach and, as promised, the gutted, freshly caught fish tasted great, even if I didn't catch it myself.

Records of game-fish catches are recorded in association with the International Game Fishing Association (IGFA). European anglers lead the fishing expeditions, supported by experienced Maldivian crew.

Fishing is year-round for sailfish, blue and black marlin, yellow-fin tuna, barracuda, dogfish tuna, wahoo, jack fish, and a variety of sharks and dorado. All fish caught are the property of the boat, though sailfish and blue marlin are tagged and released.

Costs are from US$500 for six hours (05.30–11.30) or US$350 for four hours (14.00–18.00), for a maximum of four fishermen.

FISH FEEDING On some resort islands manta ray feeding takes place at sunset every evening. Huge flat rays glide into where the crystal-clear water laps against the white, coral-sand beaches. Guests stand on the jetty while a boy feeds the rays and swims with them in the surf.

Some environmentalists say they are not very happy with regular feeding of fish, since this interrupts the cycle of life under water and could upset the ecological balance. In the case of rays, it could lead to them reacting violently, since they could expect people at the water's edge at sunset to have food for them, or want divers to feed them. An awareness of human interference with the underwater world is spreading, and many dive masters emphasise observation rather than making performances out of dives.

WHALE- AND DOLPHIN-WATCHING TRIPS According to the tourist board literature, Maldives is home to 21 species of whale and dolphin. Since May 1993 they have been protected species. During a survey carried out in March and April 2003, more than 14,000 whales and dolphins of 16 species were sighted, in 356 separate encounters. The major Maldives travel agents or tour operators listed in *Chapter 2*, pages 49–50, will arrange specialist boat-based excursions and longer trips by request. For up-to-date information contact the Maldives Tourist Promotion Board (↘ *3323228;* f *3323229;* e *mtpb@visitmaldives.com*).

GLASS-BOTTOMED BOAT TRIPS An effortless way to view the underwater world is through the transparent deck of a glass-bottomed boat. Passengers sit on seats running the length of the fibreglass boat, peering into a well in the centre of the boat that reveals everything the vessel is cruising over. It is an amazing experience for the sedentary, not only to glimpse the brilliant-hued fish and the gardens of coral, but also to experience the dramatic plunging of a reef into the apparently infinitely deep ocean.

WHALE SUBMARINE Based in Male' is the submarine which takes visitors to a depth of 40m. They stop at various levels below the surface. More common fish to be seen include lionfish, yellow boxfish, snappers and even turtles. Dives at night may encounter manta rays. They run up to eight trips a day depending on demand. Bring a camera. Because the submarine is pressurised, it is quite safe to do this just before your flight home or if you have time to spare at the airport after arriving early from a distant resort (↘ *3333939;* e *sales@submarinesmaldives.com.mv;* *www.submarinesmaldives.com.mv*).

ACTIVITIES ON LAND

SOCCER Soccer is the game Maldivians identify with more than any other. In many cases, 'game' translates as 'passion'! It is the only sport where they have challenged other countries successfully and have won regional tournaments. There are 30–40 soccer clubs in Male', and villagers also play soccer on their islands almost as a ritual every afternoon, as long as there is space enough for a pitch. On resort islands, there are soccer games not just for the staff, but for guests to join in, too.

There are three divisions in the nation's soccer league, with six teams in the first division, about a dozen in the second and around 18 in the third. Three main tournaments are held every year and in one, the President of the Maldives Invitation Soccer Cup, foreign teams take part. Some club players are professionals, and do nothing else but play soccer.

The main matches are held at the National Stadium in Male'. They are televised and broadcast to enthusiastic viewers and listeners throughout the atolls. The Football Association of Maldives was founded in 1982; its base is at the National Stadium (*G Banafusaa Magu, Male'; ✆ 3317006*). At the time of the World Cup, a giant screen is set up in Jumhooree Maidan for the public to watch televised matches live. The website of the national team is www.famaldives.com.

VOLLEYBALL Volleyball is gaining in popularity, especially as it is played in practically every resort island as a form of relaxation for the staff. (Guests are welcome to join in, too, but are usually too sluggish for the energetic Maldivians.) Championship matches are held between resorts and the standard of play is high, disciplined and gentlemanly. Basketball and netball are also played.

TENNIS The Tennis Association and the Table Tennis Association of Maldives are governed by the Ministry of Youth and Sports (*www.youthsports.gov.mv*). Several of the larger resorts have tennis facilities, some with floodlit courts. The Tennis Association of Maldives has two tennis courts in Male' in what was once part of the gardens of the Sultan's Palace, adjoining Sultan's Park.

CRICKET Cricket is popular; there is a cricket ground in Male', and President Gayoom, who loves the game, sometimes takes part. International matches have been played against Malaysia, Saudi Arabia and the UAE. Inter-schools tournaments are also held. Cricket in Maldives is encouraged, promoted and developed by the Cricket Control Board, based at the Male' Sports Complex in Maafiythakurufaanu Magu. Expatriate teams occasionally hold cricket tournaments, too.

BASHI In open spaces you will see young women engaged in a curious sport which seems to consist of bashing a ball over a net while facing backwards to the opposing team. *Bashi* is an ancient game played only in the Maldives and is a favourite throughout the country. Traditionally, it was played with a hand-woven *bashi* (made from coconut palm leaves) as the bat, by two teams of about 11 women. Now a tennis racket and ball are used.

GOLF Golf used to be played in Gan, the former British Royal Air Force base. There, near the airport, the golf course survives, but it is overgrown and the former clubhouse is not to be seen (if it is still there) for the tropical tangle. Kuredu Island Resort in Lhaviyani Atoll added a golf course to its attractions in 2004 – the first of its kind in Maldives, with six golf greens (each about 13.7m x 9m) and a practice putting green. See www.kuredu.com and www.huxleygolf.co.uk. The lease on the island of Hondaafushi in Haa Dhaal Atoll to turn it into a resort is conditional on a golf course being built there, too.

CHESS Chess in Maldives is a fast game using pieces (of lacquerwork) that vaguely resemble those of ordinary chess. Like many introductions from overseas, the game has been adapted with a Maldivian flair to local circumstances. You will often see games being played in the shade of a tree or outside a shop in villages. Some of the moves will baffle a conventional chess player, especially since it may be difficult to know which piece is which.

FITNESS Some resort islands have gymnasiums equipped with the machinery necessary for a workout. Bandos provides aerobics classes in its well-equipped and air-conditioned sports centre and some other resorts have gym facilities. In Male', the energetic and dedicated work out at the gym in the street beside the new Presidential Palace. Women-only sessions are also held there. Fitness Centres include:

Heat-Health and Fitness Blue Grass, Keneree Magu; ✆ 3322383
Male' Fitness Club H Colesium, Janavaree Hingun; ✆ 3328722
Muscle Load Aaburuzu Higun; ✆ 7773588

Sheri H Rabe'ee Manzil Sosun Magu, Male'; ✆ 3310310; f 3315414; e sheri@dhivehinet.net.mv; ☻ 05.30–08.30 & 12.30–21.00 daily except Fri; special sessions for women only from 21.00–23.00. Yoga, gym & aerobics classes are available.

Also see *Health and beauty* in *Chapter 5*, page 142.

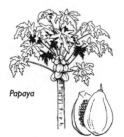

Papaya

4

Clown triggerfish

Part Two

THE GUIDE

Emperor angelfish

5

Male'

FIRST IMPRESSIONS

Male' has always been the political and business as well as cultural centre of the country. Your first sight of Male' may be from the air if you're sitting on the right side of the plane, which may be the left side depending on its approach. It's a small island, packed with tall buildings, and just a few open spaces; there are a few green trees in the Sultan's Park and around the SAARC conference centre in the south of the island.

Otherwise, your first sight will be as you approach by sea from the airport – or from your resort, if on a day trip. Arriving from the airport by *dhoni*, you first of all pass the fuel island, where the country's fuel is stored, away from the airport and the city in case of fire. Male' is not far away, its high (well, ten-storey) buildings impressive along the shoreline. Docking at the airport jetty, you will then be approached by taxi drivers, but Male' is such a small place that it is really not far to walk to anywhere if you know where you're going. If you're on a tour, you will dock at jetty number 1 or 2, next to the Presidential Jetty, and will probably go from there to the tourist shops on Chandhanee Magu.

Either way, Male' is a pleasant city to walk around with no hassles from touts or beggars. Indeed, Maldivians rarely initiate an approach to tourists. However, while a few old coral walls remain, most of the town is being relentlessly revamped to meet the demands of modern, sophisticated residents. The roads are busy with vehicles but there is none of the gridlock and traffic chaos of other Asian cities. But watch out for motorbikes; they come at you unexpectedly from around blind corners.

This chapter aims to give you full details of what to see in this small island capital, where to stay and what to eat. A few days will give you a much truer picture of what life is really like for Maldivians (and their guest workers) than any number of weeks in a resort. Staying in Male' is a good way to get a feel for the country, but it doesn't offer much in the way of a relaxing tropical island holiday.

ORIENTATION

On the map, Male' is easy to understand. It faces north; its important streets go inland north to south (Sosun Magu and Chandhanee Magu), form the waterfront road girdling the island (Boduthakurufaanu Magu), or bisect the island east to west (Majeedhee or Majeedee Magu). With the addition of two other major roads (Orchid Magu and Fareedhee Magu), which cut across the informal grid pattern by running northeast to southwest, and two more main roads (Ameer Ahmed Magu and Medhuziyaarai Magu), you have all the significant streets.

Although the island is not much more than a single square mile (2km²) in area, it has such a confusion of streets, most of which are much shorter than they appear from the map, that you could easily spend days discovering the mysteries of every one.

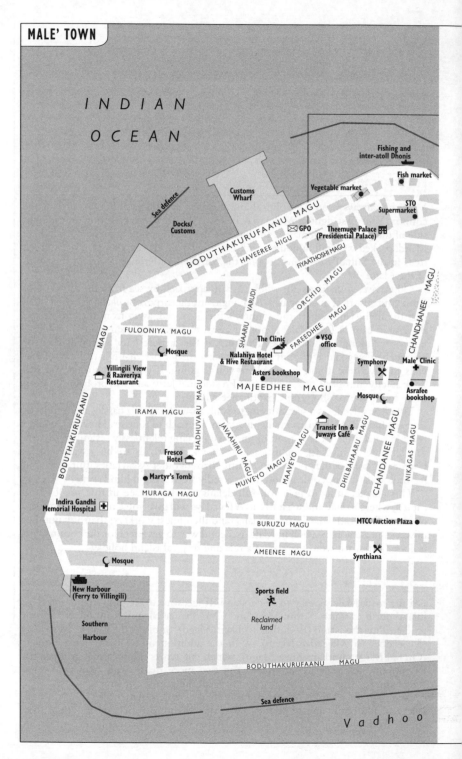

INDIAN

OCEAN

Fishing and
inter-atoll Dhonis

Fish market

Customs
Wharf

Vegetable market

STO
Supermarket

Sea defence

Docks/
Customs

BODUTHAKURUFAANU MAGU

HAVEEREE HIGU

GPO

Theemuge Palace
(Presidential Palace)

FIYAATHOSHI MAGU

ORCHID MAGU

VARUDI

CHANDHANEE MAGU

FULOONIYA MAGU

SHAARIU

FAREEDHEE MAGU

The Clinic

VSO
office

Mosque

Nalahiya Hotel
& Hive Restaurant

Symphony

Male' Clinic

Villingili View
& Raaveriya
Restaurant

Asters bookshop

HADHUVARU MAGU

MAJEEDHEE   MAGU

Mosque

Asrafee
bookshop

IRAMA MAGU

JAVAAHIRU MAGU

Transit Inn &
Juways Café

DHILBAHAARU MAGU

CHANDANEE MAGU

NIKAGAS MAGU

BODUTHAKURUFAANU

MAGU

Fresco
Hotel

MUIVEYO MAGU

MAAVEYO MAGU

Martyr's Tomb

MURAGA MAGU

Indira Gandhi
Memorial Hospital

BURUZU MAGU

MTCC Auction Plaza

Mosque

AMEENEE MAGU

Synthiana

New Harbour
(Ferry to Villingili)

Sports field

Southern

Harbour

Reclaimed
land

BODUTHAKURUFAANU   MAGU

Sea defence

Vadhoo

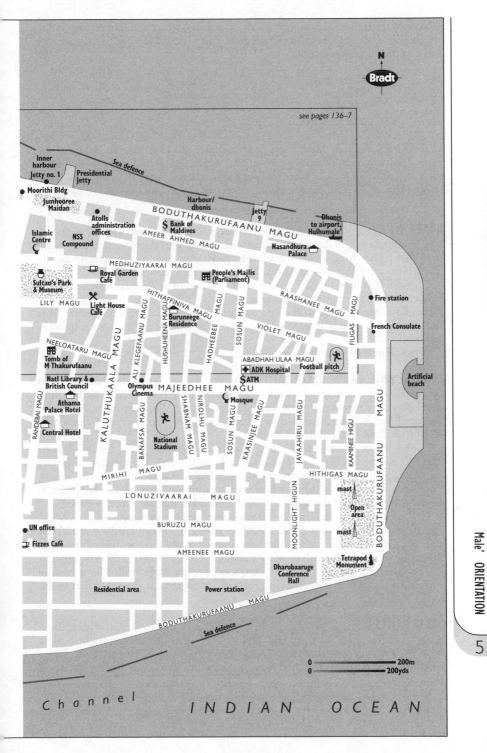

N

Bradt

Inner
harbour
Jetty no. 1

Presidential
Jetty

Moorithi Bldg

Sea defence

Jumhooree
Maidan

Harbour/
dhonis

BODUTHAKURUFAANU MAGU

Jetty
9

Dhonis
to airport,
Hulhumale'

Atolls
administration
offices

Bank of
Maldives

AMEER AHMED MAGU

Nasandhura
Palace

Islamic
Centre

NSS
Compound

MEDHUZIYAARAI MAGU

Royal Garden
Café

People's Majlis
(Parliament)

RAASHANEE MAGU

Fire station

Sultan's Park
& Museum

LILY MAGU

Light House
Café

HITHAFFINIVA MAGU

Buruneege
Residence

SOSUN MAGU

VIOLET MAGU

FILIGAS MAGU

French Consulate

NEELOATARU MAGU

KALUTHUKAALA MAGU

ALI KLEGEFAANU MAGU

HUSHUHEENA MAGU

HADHEEBEE MAGU

ABADHAH ULAA MAGU

Football pitch

Artificial
beach

Tomb of
M Thakurufaanu

ADK Hospital

Natl Library &
British Council

RAHDEBAI MAGU

Olympus
Cinema

MAJEEDHEE MAGU

ATM

Mosque

Athama
Palace Hotel

Central Hotel

BANAFSA MAGU

SHABNAM MAGU

NIROLHU MAGU

National
Stadium

SOSUN MAGU

KAASINJEE MAGU

JAVAAHIRU MAGU

KAAMINEE HIGU

MIRIHI MAGU

LONUZIVAARAI MAGU

HITHIGAS MAGU

MOONLIGHT HIGUN

mast

Open
area

BODUTHAKURUFAANU MAGU

BURUZU MAGU

UN office

Fizzes Café

AMEENEE MAGU

mast

Residential area

Power station

Dharubaaruge
Conference
Hall

Tetrapod
Monument

BODUTHAKURUFAANU MAGU

Sea defence

0 ——— 200m
0 ——— 200yds

Channel

INDIAN OCEAN

WARDS Male' is divided into four wards or districts, which roughly correspond to the following areas. (The abbreviation given first is how addresses in each area are listed in the telephone directory.)

H	Henveiru	northeast
M	Maafaanu	northwest
G	Galolhu	centre
Ma	Machchangolhi	south

In their book *Say it in Maldivian*, J B Disanayake and H A Maniku state that the name Maafaanu is in fact composed of two words: *maa* meaning 'large' and *faanu* meaning 'shore' or 'beach', since this ward used to have a large shoreline. They also suggest that Male' itself gains its name from *maa* (large) and *le* meaning 'blood' in Sinhala.

ROADS There are no longer any unpaved streets. Surfaced roads are laid with grey tiles interlocked in a herringbone pattern, rather like cobblestones but much smoother. This makes them resemble pedestrian-only malls which, as the motorbikes careering around corners make quite clear, they are not.

Footballers will be pleased to hear there are lots of *goalhis* here. These are the smaller lanes connecting the *magus* or main roads. Often they are not named, or the names have been eroded to become unreadable, but it doesn't really matter that much; you are unlikely to become totally lost for long, as the seafront is in every direction.

Higun signifies a walk or drive.

ZONING AND LAND RECLAMATION While the government has initiated decentralisation policies, including the setting up of satellite islands and development of regional growth centres, migration to Male' continues. As part of the need for housing, multi-storey complexes have been erected, including apartments built with aid from China.

Zoning has been introduced as part of the policy to make Male' a more pleasant island to live in, with expansion of open and green spaces. Opportunities for this are arising as the islands constituting Greater Male', that is Villingili (or Viligili); formerly a resort, now a thriving residential community expected to have 15,000 residents by 2010) and the reclaimed land named Hulhumale', are developed.

Hulhumale' is an ambitious project which will create a land area, between Male' and the airport, three times the size of Male' Island. It will be zoned for residential and commercial purposes as a permanent solution to Male's space limitations. The first phase of the project will provide housing space for 36,000 to 50,000 people.

The government hopes that the expanded Greater Male' will offer a healthy environment that is in every way as green and as pleasant as any other part of the idyllic Maldives.

HOUSE NAMES In the 14 years since the first edition of this book was written, there has been an incredible change in the skyline of Male'. Construction is obviously a booming industry with high-rise (a relative term, 30m in height is the limit) buildings sadly replacing the coral stone cottages that were so fascinating just a few years ago.

Very few of those cottages, with colourful doors set in street-side walls and with deep inner courtyards, remain, as the demand for housing and office space means that more and more are succumbing to the modernisation of Male'. Even so, each residence and office building has a name, often ending with the letters *ge*, (pronounced 'gay') which means house, as in *Esjehige*. Many houses have names in English, some bizarre enough to remember, such as *Corunet Peak*, *Gold Flint*, *Jelly Fish*, *Snow Flakes*, *Merry Dream* and *Rinso*.

Many names have survived, while the house itself has changed; they may refer in Dhivehi to the original owner or his profession, such as *Silversmith*, or to the name of a flower or fruit (*Mango Haven*) or any characteristic the owner fancies, such as *Neep Tide* (*sic*).

Residents are proud of the names of their houses and rarely change them. There is a story that an old man was asked by the municipal authorities to change the name of the cottage he had lived in for years. It was named *Wind House* because of its location on a draughty corner, but there was another house with the same name. The officials were worried that the man would refuse and begged him not to be upset but to think about the request.

'Don't worry,' said the man, with a philosophical shrug. 'If you don't want *Wind House*, I'll call it *No Wind House*.'

GETTING AROUND

TAXIS You could probably run around the whole island in 40 minutes and walk around in well under two hours, so it's hard to see how there can be much need for taxis. However, they are obviously useful if it's pouring with rain, which happens even during the high tourist season, or if you are carrying a lot of baggage. It may also be necessary if you're not sure where you're going, as the maze of unmarked backstreets can be very confusing. Because the taxis are air-conditioned, Maldivians as well as visitors use them to escape the heat rather than take even a short walk.

Taxis wait at the waterfront by the Presidential Jetty for passengers arriving by speedboat or *dhoni*. They also wait at the airport jetty, on the waterfront opposite the Nasandhura Palace Hotel, where a shelter has been provided for queuing passengers. This is more frequently used by the drivers to sleep, since there tend to be more drivers than waiting passengers, except when a couple of *dhonis* drop their passengers at the same time.

The staff in any shop, hotel or restaurant will happily telephone for a taxi, since they do not ply for hire. Taxis are the new cars with yellow number plates. The T in the registration number denotes Male'. There are also taxis in Gan but they are beat-up cars which set their own price according to where you want to go.

In Male', the fares start at Rf20 , depending on baggage. An hourly rate can be negotiated. Tipping is not expected. Taxi companies include:

- **Dial Cab** Orchid Magu; ☏ 3323132
- **Fine Taxi** Dhanburuh Magu; ☏ 3321414
- **JR Taxi** Buruzu Magu; ☏ 3321919
- **Kulee Dhuveli** Sabdheli Magu; ☏ 3322122
- **Regal Taxi** Handhuvaree Higun; ☏ 3321313

SELF-DRIVE/RIDE Drivers have to pass a test and apply to the Ministry of Transport for a licence. Although the roads are limited and speeding impossible (no road is long enough), accidents do occur. The sharp right-angle corners on Male' streets are potentially hazardous for pedestrians. Driving is on the left, where the streets are wide enough for there to be a left.

There are occasional traffic jams in Male', particularly when school sessions start or finish. As a sign of Male's growing traffic problem, traffic lights and dedicated traffic police have been introduced. Parking has become difficult, with parking zones invariably filled. Illegal parking is checked, with a note on the windscreen requiring the offender to pay a fine of Rf50.

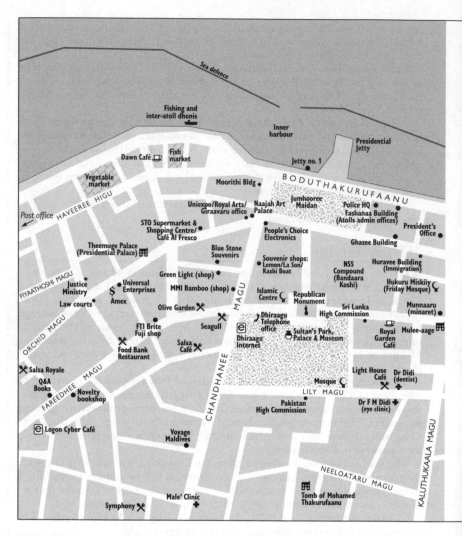

HIRE CARS There are no self-drive cars available for hire anywhere in the Maldives.

MOTORBIKES Motorbikes can sometimes be hired on an informal basis (but make sure you check the validity of your international or national driving licence with the Ministry of Transport first). Ask a local travel agent for help in arranging it. If you do take to two wheels, either hiring a motorbike or bicycle, check that your travel insurance policy covers you, in case of a mishap.

BICYCLES By pedal bike is a good way to discover Male', but there is no company offering them for hire, so you will need to borrow from a friend or a guesthouse. There are nearly 50,000 bikes in all the islands. Bikes are parked in all the busy parts of Male' during the day, carefully padlocked. Some resorts (such as Gan's Equator Village) have bicycles for hire; others (such as Island Hideaway) include a couple of bikes with each villa.

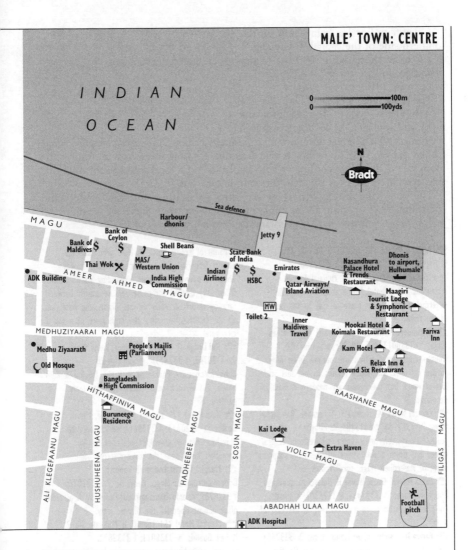

INDIAN
OCEAN

Bradt

N

0 — 100m
0 — 100yds

MAGU

Harbour/
dhonis

Sea defence

Jetty 9

Bank of
Ceylon

Bank of
Maldives $

$

Shell Beans

State Bank
of India

Dhonis
to airport,
Hulhumale'

MAS/
Western Union

Thai Wok

Indian
Airlines

$ $

Emirates

Nasandhura
Palace Hotel
& Trends
Restaurant

AMEER

AHMED

India High
Commission

HSBC

ADK Building

MAGU

Qatar Airways/
Island Aviation

Maagiri
Tourist Lodge
& Symphonic
Restaurant

MW

Toilet 2

Inner
Maldives
Travel

MEDHUZIYAARAI MAGU

Mookai Hotel &
Koimala Restaurant

Fariva
Inn

Medhu Ziyaarath

People's Majlis
(Parliament)

Kam Hotel

Old Mosque

Relax Inn &
Ground Six Restaurant

Bangladesh
High Commission

RAASHANEE MAGU

HITHAFFINIVA MAGU

Buruneege
Residence

HADHEEBEE MAGU

SOSUN MAGU

Kai Lodge

FILIGAS MAGU

ALI KLEGEFAANU MAGU

HUSHUHEENA MAGU

VIOLET MAGU

Extra Haven

Football
pitch

ABADHAH ULAA MAGU

ADK Hospital

🏠 WHERE TO STAY

Hotels in Male' vary from small unadorned guesthouses aimed at expatriate Asian workers, mostly from India and Sri Lanka, to tourist-class hotels near the jetty for the airport ferries.

Male' is a clean place, with none of the dodgy areas with littered streets associated with other parts of Asia, so the cheaper guesthouses away from the waterfront are fine to stay in, though they may be lacking in facilities if not in atmosphere.

HOTELS AND GUESTHOUSES These are listed here in alphabetical order. The lower-price guesthouses are taken over in their entirety by expatriates working in Male' so this list does not include them. All the hotels (but not all guesthouses) have air conditioning, fans, satellite television and showers as standard; the more expensive have fridges (with soft drinks) and safes.

A new city hotel is being built on the southern side of the capital. It is planned as a five-star hotel with 300 beds in the first stage, and 15 storeys. It is expected to be open by 2010.

The price range indicated here is based on a double room with breakfast, for one night, and applies to Male' hotels only, not to the resorts which have a different price grading (see box, *Accommodation price coding*, *Chapter 3*, page 108). Some hotels give discounts for long stays. As with resorts, the room rate is flexible according to who books it, and a local travel agent might be able to secure a room at less than the walk-in rack rate.

The following list is correct at the time of writing, but new hotels and guesthouses are opening all the time, or may change their name or location. An inclusion or exclusion here is no guarantee of quality or lack of it.

Athama Palace (15 rooms) G Dhivehi Atha, Majeedhee Magu; 3313118; f 3328828; e athamapalace@yahoo.com. Mugalai Indian restaurant below hotel. Not exactly a palace, but nevertheless a pleasant place to stay in the centre of the town. $

Buruneege Residence (10 rooms) Hithaffinivaa Magu; 3330011; f 3330022; e burunee@frontline.com.mv; www.frontline.com.mv. Silver Ring garden cafeteria. The lobby retains its old feel, with lots of wood, but the rooms are modern & simply decorated. $

Central Hotel (41 rooms) G Sanoraage, Rahdhebai Magu; 3317766; f 3315383; e info@centralmaldives.com; www.centralmaldives.com. Central indeed but down a side street off the main shopping street of Majeedhee Magu; small rooms. $$

Extra Haven Guest House H Halaveligasdhoshuge, Dhunburi Magu; 3327453; f 3325362. A small, low-priced guesthouse in a backstreet in the east of town. $

Fariva Inn Boduthakurufaanu Magu; 3337611; f 3315413; e amsha@dhivehinet.net.mv. On the northeast corner of the island, conveniently close to the airport jetty. At the low end of the price range. $

Fresco Hotel (38 rooms, 1 suite) Naseemee Higun, Maafanu; 3348833; f 3348822; e reservations@hotelfresco.com; www.hotelfresco.com. It takes 5mins by taxi from the jetty to this hotel which is on the western, residential side of town. Rooms & suite created out of a block of apts. $$

Hulhule Island Hotel (85 rooms) PO Box 20118; 3330888; f 3330777; e sales@hih.com.mv; www.hih.com.mv. Faru coffee shop & Gadhoo grill restaurant. Not in Male' at all but on the airport island & with a bar open to non-Maldivians that is a haunt of expats stuck in Male' who take the airport ferry to get there. At press time it was about to open a new wing, expanding its 85 rooms. Often fully booked for passengers in transit between faraway resorts & early or late flights, the hotel has all the facilities, including the high price of a top city hotel. $$

Kai Lodge H Mandhuedhuruge, Violet Magu; 3328742; f 3328738; e kailodge@dhivehinet.net.mv. Partnered with the Mookai & Kam hotels, this is in a quiet backstreet with leafy gardens. $

Kam Hotel (29 rooms) H Roanuge, Meheli Goalhi; 3320611; f 3320614; e kamhotel@dhivehinet.net.mv; www.kamhotel.com.mv. An upmarket hotel near the airport jetty. $$

Maagiri Tourist Lodge (5 rooms) Boduthakurufaanu Magu, Henveiru; 3322576; f 3328787; e info@maagirilodge.com.mv. A pleasant place almost opposite the airport jetty. $

Mookai Hotel (51 rooms) H Maagala, No 2 Meheli Goalhi; 3338811; f 3338822; e mookai@dhivehinet.net.mv; www.kaimoo.com. Rooftop pool. Koimala Restaurant on 9th floor. Near the airport jetty. $$

Nalahiya Hotel (42 rooms) Majeedhee Magu; 3346633; f 3345533; e info@beehivehotels.com; www.beehivehotels.com. Opened in 2007 & located at a busy junction where Orchid Rd meets Majeedhee Magu, its glass-walled, timber-floored lobby is wonderful for people-watching. Astute reception staff, efficient housekeeping, & a good b/fast buffet in its rooftop restaurant. Built as block of apts, rooms in each apt are let individually, or whole apts can be booked at discounted rates. Each of its smallish bedrooms has en-suite shower/toilet & is comfortably furnished with deep beds, oodles of pillows, live orchids & Wi-Fi facility. Rooms also available for day use. $$ plus 10% service charge.

⌂ **Nasandhura Palace Hotel** (31 rooms) Boduthakurufaanu Magu; ✆ 3323380; f 3320822; e nasandhura@dhivehinet.net.mv; www.nasandhura.com. Trends open-air garden restaurant. A popular, long-established hotel opposite the airport jetty, unfortunately scheduled for demolition as it has outlived its sell-by date. $$

⌂ **Relax Inn** (30 rooms) Ameer Ahmed Magu, Henveiru; ✆ 3314531; f 3314533; e relaxin@dhivehinet.net.mv; www.relaxmaldives.com. Ground Six Restaurant on top floor. Less expensive than its neighbours but near the airport jetty. $$

⌂ **Transit Inn** (7 rooms) Ma Dheyliaage, Maaveyo Magu; ✆ 3320420; f 3313174; e transit@dhivehinet.net.mv; www.transitmaldives.com. Juways Café (✆ 3316969) outdoors with fans & lots of trees nearby. A favourite with Siân & Bob when they were updating the 3rd edition of this book in 2004. A reader (thanks, Andy) who stayed there in 2007 reports: 'It's great. They now have free Wi-Fi in the lobby & restaurant.' $

⌂ **Villingili View Inn** (14 rooms) M Raaverige, Majeedhee Magu; ✆ 3321135; f 3325213. Raaveriya Restaurant; pleasant garden with shady trees. An atmospheric place built with old wood, upstairs too; the only quality guesthouse on the west coast. $

✖ WHERE TO EAT

Eating out in Male' is very good value almost anywhere. Even the more upmarket places are not very expensive. Restaurants are closed every Friday morning and lunchtime, when everyone goes to the many mosques around the city; they don't reopen until around 15.30. Maldivians are Muslim so no restaurants are open during the daylight hours of Ramazan. Beware of eating on the streets during Ramazan; non-Muslim foreign guest workers are not allowed to do so, and can get into serious trouble. Tourists are advised to act with restraint during Ramazan and eat only in their resorts.

While resorts close to Male' (like Kurumba, Full Moon, Paradise and Bandos) have splendid à-la-carte dining rooms and can be visited by non-residents with prior permission, getting there and back at night from Male' could add a few hundred dollars to a meal that would itself cost around US$100 for two without wine. For a night out off Male', many expat residents go by ferry to the airport island and dine at Hulhule Island Hotel (from US$25 per head).

Restaurants in Male' can be split into four categories: local cafés or tea shops used mostly by local men only; snack bars and cafeterias serving coffee and ice creams, etc; reasonable restaurants frequented by local families and young people on a day out; and, finally, more upmarket restaurants which are reasonably priced. Some are air-conditioned, others have delightful gardens with shady trees. The tea shops are where the local men meet socially. Women are rarely seen in them but visitors, male or female, can use them and meet local people.

A typical menu includes various omelettes, chips, Indonesian rice and noodle dishes, Italian pasta and pizza, chicken, beef, lots of dishes including tuna (of course), curries, prawns and lobster, with fresh fruit and ice cream for dessert. Lobster is always the most expensive, being Rf225–350, while a cup of tea ranges from Rf1 to Rf10, coffee Rf10 to Rf15 and soft drinks Rf12 to Rf15. Most main courses cost from Rf25 to Rf45 in the mid-range restaurants; prices are higher, from Rf70, in the more expensive ones.

There are lots of cafés attracting young Maldivians in the evenings at the northern end of the artificial beach (beyond the Hulhumale' ferry terminal) and around the Southern Harbour plaza. The following list of a few eating places is correct at the time of writing, but new tea

RESTAURANT PRICE CODES	
Based on average cost of main course	
$	Under US$5
$$	US$5–15
$$$	above US$15

shops, cafés and restaurants are opening all the time, or they may change their name or location. An inclusion or exclusion here is no guarantee of quality or lack of it.

⊑ **Café Al Fresco** Trade Centre Bldg, Orchid Magu. An open-air courtyard in the centre of the STO multi-storey shopping centre & office block. **$**

⊑ **Fizzes** Ameenee Magu; ✆ 3337887. Clean, cool & bright self-service cafeteria & ice-cream parlour; outside terrace upstairs. Popular with young people & anyone who wants to escape the heat & humidity outside. **$**

✗ **Hive Restaurant** Nalahiya Hotel, corner of Orchid Magu & Majeedhee Magu; ✆ 3346633. On the rooftop floor (take lift to 8th floor then walk up 1 flight & enter the door straight ahead; the side door is the kitchen), this restaurant has seats on the balcony as well as in the air-conditioned room. An original menu (spinach crêpes, peppered lamb) as well as standard fish dishes & snacks prepared with flair; huge portions at good prices. **$$** (Dinner for 2 with soft drinks cost less than US$25 in 2007.)

⊑ **Hut Cuisine Café** Near ADK hospital. Fast-food-style food. **$**

⊑ **Ice Cone** Sikka Goalhi; ✆ 3321702. Small café for tea & cakes etc. A cool spot near all the tourist sites. **$**

✗ **Juways Café** At the Transit Inn; ✆ 3320420. It serves the usual dishes, & is set in a pleasant open-air shady part of the hotel. A popular spot for locals. **$**

✗ **Light House Café** Lily Magu; ✆ 3310900. Pleasant 1st-floor restaurant with exciting menu; reservation essential. **$$$**

✗ **Olive Garden** Fareedhee Magu; ✆ 3312231. AC downstairs, open terrace upstairs. An especially good medium-priced restaurant offering a wide choice of food. Families & local business clientele as well as independent visitors. **$$**

⊑ **Royal Garden Café** Medhuziyaraiy Magu; ✆ 3320822. Formerly called Esjehi Café, this is located in the garden patio & air-conditioned interior of the old Esjehi Villa by Sultan's Park, behind the fort. Good for a coffee break or a snack away from the waterfront traffic. **$**

✗ **Sala Thai** H Orchid, Ameer Ahmed Magu; ✆ 3345959; www.salathaimaldives.com. The newest Thai restaurant in town with Thai décor & ambience & super Thai-owner-cooked Thai food. **$$$**

✗ **Salsa Café** M Melaa, Keneree Magu; ✆ 3310319; f 3330022. A good restaurant in a nice open garden, but no AC. Very popular but more expensive than some. Serves continental, Maldivian, Mexican & Italian food. **$$**

✗ **Salsa Royale** Orchid Magu (previously known as Twin Peaks); ✆ 3327830. More upmarket than its sister Salsa, with a Thai menu as well as continental cuisine. Cool & smart. Attracts local business people & sightseeing tour groups. **$$$**

✗ **Seagull** Fareedhee Magu; ✆ 3323332. A popular restaurant in a pretty walled garden, with an extensive selection of expensive ice-cream dishes. **$$**

⊑ **Shell Beans** Boduthakurufaanu Magu; ✆ 3333686. Excellent cafeteria on seafront, good choice of cakes & sandwiches as well as great coffee. **$**

✗ **Symphonic Restaurant** Boduthakurufaanu Magu; ✆ 3328696; f 3314350. Cool & dark main restaurant with good food. Also small outdoor section & part of the Maagiri Tourist Lodge Hotel. **$**

✗ **Symphony Restaurant** Athamaa Goalhi; ✆ 3326277; f 3314350. Excellent food in this cool & darkly lit mid-priced restaurant. Good fish dishes. **$**

✗ **Synthiana Restaurant** Ameenee Magu; ✆ 3315055; f 3314350; e info@symtravel.com. Bright pink paintwork. Sister restaurant of Symphony & Symphonic. Sympathetically designed in bright colours! **$**

✗ **Thai Wok** 1st Floor, Athireege Aage, Ameer Ahmed Magu; ✆ 3310007; f 3329020. A smart & popular restaurant specialising in Thai food. Items from its menu have been copied by other restaurants; genuine Thai food at a reasonable price. **$$$**

SHOPPING

On day trips from resort islands, visitors are crocodiled from the quay to see Male' sights and then led to the souvenir shops. During this time, a few local lads will attach themselves to those most likely to buy, and steer them to the shops that employ them. Since Male' is such a safe, hassle-free town there is no need to fear leaving the crocodile, shaking off the escorts, and looking at the shops by yourself.

The best time to explore the shops is at night, when the sun has gone down, the air is cooler, and lots of people are promenading, turning Male' into a fun city, Maldives-style. One's personal safety while strolling the streets at night is not the problem it is in other Asian, or indeed worldwide, cities.

Shop hours range from 06.00 to 23.00, with closing periods at prayer times. To be certain, check at your hotel or resort reception for the day's times so that you do not get frustrated – like the tourist who told her friend that she discovered the time for prayers was whenever she wanted to go into a shop.

SOUVENIRS AND CLOTHING As you stand facing inland with your back to the sea, the main shopping street, Chandhanee Magu, leads from the right side of the waterfront park. At its head, on the left, is the **People's Choice Electronics** showroom. Part of the State Trading Organisation (STO) enterprise, this shop has a wide range of electronic goods. Visitors can benefit from some low prices which, as part of STO's policy of keeping prices within the reach of Maldivians, are the equivalent of duty-free prices elsewhere. **Lemon** in Chandhanee Magu is renowned for T-shirts 'exclusively hand painted in bright sunny colours', and there are many other good souvenir shops in this area, including **Kaashi Boat**, **La Son** and **MMI Bamboo** (see also *Bookshops* below). **Walton Jewels**, **Green Light**, **Blue Stone Souvenirs**, **Uniexpo**, **Divegear** and **Dive Sports** are also nearby.

Across the road on the right, at the head of Orchid Magu, is the **Naajah Art Palace** souvenir shop. The owner started his career in a small way selling hand-painted T-shirts and now has shops at the airport as well as another in the STO shopping plaza further down Orchid Magu. This is the ideal place to shop for any kind of souvenir as well as for snorkelling equipment, and a large selection of books on the Maldives that are unobtainable elsewhere. It is air-conditioned.

A few doors further down Orchid Magu, the small **Royal Arts** shop specialises in postcards and T-shirts with Maldivian images. They also stock the biography by Royston Ellis of President Gayoom, *A Man for All Islands*.

A few paces westwards, past the **Reefside** shop on the left, which sells upmarket brand-name watches, and some hardware shops, there is the **STO shopping plaza**. Male's main supermarket is here and its shelves give a fascinating insight into what the resident of Male' buys. A visitor will be amazed not only at the range of goods (from sarongs to stationery) but at the superior quality and variety of the imports. There are also local bargains, such as canned Maldive tuna, to be found at low prices. Great for taking home.

By continuing along Chandhanee Magu inland from the waterfront, you will pass through a selection of souvenir and T-shirt shops before reaching the area where Maldivians themselves do their shopping. In Majeedhee Magu, which intersects Chandhanee Magu and runs east to west the length of Male', there are dozens of fashion boutiques, shoe shops and pharmacies. Majeedhee Magu is the longest street in Male'; perhaps that's why there are so many shoe shops there.

Maldivians are fashion-conscious and like to look good, so you will find the shops reflect the current trends in their stocks. A lot of items are imported from Singapore. Although it is a small island in the Indian Ocean, Male' can offer the keen shopper an amazing selection of up-to-date and well-priced goods, including the latest in computer equipment and electronics.

BOOKSHOPS None of the shops in Male' sells only books; they mostly sell stationery and postcards, posters, souvenirs and sometimes T-shirts as well.

The selection of imported books is limited, so bring your own favourites for beach reading. On the resorts, gift shops will have a very small selection of paperbacks but will have a choice of photographic coffee-table books on the

Maldives. Pricewise, the **Novelty Bookshop** is best for locally produced books, since they do not add the usual gift-shop mark-up. Also they have published many specialist books on the Maldives that are unavailable elsewhere.

Asrafee Bookshop 1/44 Chandhanee Magu; ⟍ 3323424; f 3328846

Asters Fareedhee Magu; ⟍ 3335505; f 3331759; e books @ asters.com.mv; www.asters.com.mv

Kaashi Boat 20 Chandhanee Magu; ⟍ 3322634. Souvenirs & postcards, etc; also sells brightly painted wooden fish.

MMI Bamboo 11 Chandhanee Magu; ⟍ 3322354, 3310040; f 3327872; e bamboo @ avasmail.com.mv. A construction company that also produces 3 fine plastic diving charts of all the colourful fish in the seas (Island Breeze publications at MMI Bamboo; US$6 in town & US$7 at resorts).

Najaah Art Palace Various shops at top end of Orchid Magu & Chandhanee Magu; ⟍ 3310551, 3322372, 3314171, 3322481; f 3313035

Novelty Bookshop Fareedhee Magu; ⟍ 3318899; f 3318811; e bookshop @ novelty.com.mv, www.novelty.com.mv. The business started in 1965 & has since published a wide variety of unique books on the Maldives, many unavailable elsewhere.

Q and A Books and Stationery Fareedhee Magu; ⟍ 3314090; f 3336800. A broad selection of secondhand paperbacks in English.

FILM On Fareedhee Magu, look for Kodak and Fuji **film shops**. They also stock digital camera essentials.

OTHER PRACTICALITIES

CINEMAS

⛵ **Athena** 3rd Floor, Aiminarani Bldg, Boduthakurufaanu Magu; ⟍ 3338998

⛵ **Olympus** Mheedhee Magu; ⟍ 3322497

Plenty of shops sell or rent DVDs and home video-watching has replaced cinema-going for Male' residents. There is a minute local film-making industry engaged in making tele-dramas for local television exposure.

HEALTH AND BEAUTY

Salon Jingles Chandhanee Magu; ⟍ 3325175. Hairdresser.

Sheri H Rabe'ee Manzil, Sosun Magu; ⟍ 3310310; f 3315414; e sheri @ dhivehinet.net.mv. For herbal medicine, yoga, gym, aerobic classes, massage, beauty products, etc.

NATIONAL LIBRARY The National Library is on Majeedhee Magu and incorporates the **British Council office**. It also has newspapers and books available for visitors to read within the premises. See Male' Town map on pages 132–3 for location.

MEDICAL TREATMENT There are two hospitals: the Indira Gandhi Memorial Hospital on the southwest corner of the island, and the ADK Hospital in the centre (see the enlarged Male' map on pages 136–7). At the southern end of Fareedhee Magu is a clinic served by several doctors, and at the junction of Chandhanee Magu and Majeedhee Magu is a complementary medicine clinic. There are also dentist and eye-clinic facilities. See the Male' map for locations, and *Chapter 2* (*Health*, pages 64–5) for more information.

TOILETS The best advice is for visitors to use the toilets of the main hotels (unfortunately they are all at the extreme ends of Male', not in the shopping district) or try at restaurants or souvenir shops. In emergencies, you could try the airline offices, or travel agents. There are toilets on every floor of the STO shopping complex in Orchid Magu. There are now several public 'Pay Toilets' marked around the city. Toilet number 2 is down a narrow street off Boduthakurufaanu Magu; see enlarged Male' map on pages 136–7.

WHAT TO SEE AND DO

The skyline of Male' as seen on the approach to the northern inner harbour, either from the airport or from a resort island, is undergoing a metamorphosis that will probably last until 2020. (Already *2020 Vision* is promoted as the theme for development of the Maldives.) Then the bright new Male' of high-rise apartments and office buildings currently being built will be complete, making it a miniature Singapore in appearance, and perhaps in personality, too.

Male' is not a huge island, and it is easy to see the main sights within an hour or so. If you have longer, you can walk around the entire island in less than two hours, but allow more time for sightseeing along the way. The old coral buildings are rapidly disappearing, swallowed up by new development. But it still retains some attractive corners and is definitely worth a stroll. Every street and lane yields unexpected sights: a goldsmith at work, a carpenter's workshop, a glimpse of an inner courtyard, a quartet of standpipes for domestic water supply, a dignified mosque. City residents will talk and help if you ask questions, but otherwise they take no notice. It is a fascinating combination of village, town and city, compact and convenient, an experience to enjoy.

MALE' MUSEUM (⊕ *08.00–18.00 daily, except 16.00–18.00 Fri; closed government holidays; admission free. Smoking & photography are prohibited*) Two new museum buildings are being built in Sultan's Park as a gift from China, so by the time you read these notes, their relevance and value – like the old museum building itself – may be purely historical.

Even if you make only one visit to the town, don't forget to call in at the Male' Museum. It gives an instant insight into a wealth of history most visitors never suspect existed. Little else remains of the Maldives' ancient culture.

Outside on the veranda, apparently stacked on display without much thought for its theme or conservation, are some priceless wooden chests, a few torpedoes and ancient stone figures. These sandstone and coral items are said to be pieces of Buddhist temples found in some islands in the 11th century AD.

The building is Edwardian colonial-style with three storeys, and arched windows with wooden shutters and bars on them instead of glass. An old man sits selling tickets at a table on the veranda and his companions of equal vintage turn out to be amiable (but only Dhivehi-speaking) custodians who follow visitors around to see they do not touch the exhibits. Since most items are laid out on open shelves this is a temptation. It makes you wonder if any have ever disappeared.

Inside are some even more fascinating Buddhist exhibits, some up to 1m high, including a five-faced coral stele and various Buddha heads made of coral. These are said to have links to Tantric Buddhism (see *Religion*, pages 40–2). The heads and other Buddhist exhibits were found in various places throughout the islands, many of them in what is now Ameer Ahmed Magu, in the northern part of Male'. In particular, there is a striking Buddha head with moustache and long ears, which was discovered in Orchid Magu as recently as 1976. Some 10th-century heads were found on Horubadhoo Island in Baa Atoll when excavating the Royal Island resort. At the Mundoo school in Laamu Atoll, a 10th-century Buddha head and monkey head were found. And in Thaa Atoll a beautiful box was found, with Buddhist engravings both inside and outside. Warlike and dragon figures and coral elephants, as well as multi-level stupas, are among the fascinating objects on display here.

5

The mixture of objects on display near the entrance gives a hint of the pleasures in store. There is the ancient throne of Abdul Majeed Ranna, who was proclaimed king in 1943, as well as a motorbike riddled with bullet holes; on an ancient bed someone had left a pot of glue which a tourist inspected profoundly.

The thrones, or royal chairs, are broad and ornately carved, covered with cloth and with inscriptions in English about their use and user. On display is the chair used by Sultan Mohamed Shamsuddeen III (1903–34) when he came down to the Gulhakulheyfasgan'du – the open space fronting the palace – to watch the *Kulhi Jehun* (innocuous lance, sword and buckler play).

In the next chamber, a gorgeous palanquin is the Dholhi Dhaankolhu used by the same sultan to be borne away in if it should rain during his attendance at the ceremonies of Hithi, an Eid prayer, in the month of Ramazan. There is another bullet-ridden motorbike in front of it, recalling the failed invasion by Tamil mercenaries in 1988.

In a corner is the first printing press used in the Maldives, manufactured by Waterlow & Sons of London in 1912. An intricately carved desk and chair were a gift to one of the sultans by the British governor of Ceylon.

Each small chamber leads to another packed with equally astonishing exhibits. A notice attached to a miniature sofa bed refers to the significance of the three pillows on it, but does not elaborate. On top of a typewriter (was it an exhibit or not?) a notice refers to the chest on which it was placed, saying the chest carried gunpowder for a sultan (1759–66). A stone massage bed dates from 1721. I was surprised to see a collection of old British money still in its presentation case.

You get the feeling of wandering through a wonderful antique shop or someone's memento-cluttered cottage, not a museum in part of a sultan's palace. It is so cosy, aided by the two custodians who wordlessly draw a visitor's attention to items perhaps missed, like bits of the moon brought back by astronauts and the flag of the Maldives carried with them.

There are cloth envelopes with the address embroidered in gold, an 18th-century bed, turbans belonging to several sultans, a sultan's broad and appliquéd umbrella, ancient brass and pottery and, incongruously, an autographed photo of Franklin Roosevelt.

By the royal umbrella is a sign saying: 'The inner side of this huge royal umbrella or *haiykolhu* is of embroidered pattern of dark and bright colours. Sultans used this when they went for various customary and official functions.'

By a collection of royal antique water-pipes is an explanation of how they were carried by a special attendant in the Hithi procession to the Hithige: 'It is similar to hookahs used in north and south India. A touch of aristocracy is added to its appearance by the decorating on the clay pot on top of it and by the beautifully designed art work on top of this clay pot… It is used by the sultan when he finishes his grand supper of the *Hithi* night at the *Hithige*.'

A large lacquer wooden box was used for carrying the sultan's official dress in the Hithi procession. A round, deep wooden tray with yellow, black and red lacquer designs turns out to be the cover for the sultan's supper. There are lacquered walking sticks and a collection of 18th-century brass kettles.

There are two more floors reached by wooden staircases. The close intimacy that can be achieved with the objects on display (no barrier ropes, few showcases) makes history seem real rather than distant or irrelevant.

One chamber containing various weapons and an old typewriter (this one definitely an exhibit) is quite revealing about the past with its descriptions in English. A cane, it says, was designed for use by a husband to punish his wife's lover. And there is a gruesome kind of knuckleduster on display with two spiked horns sticking out of a central cluster of spikes. Another item, like a large spatula, was a wife-beater, if I correctly understood the gestures of the guardian accompanying me.

The museum is a highlight of a visit to Male', and inspires the curious visitor to know more about the island's people.

SHORT WALK: THE MAIN SIGHTS Here follows a list of the main sights, which are all relatively close to the Presidential Jetty.

Jumhooree Maidan This public square opposite the jetty was created in 1988 with lawns and benches placed around it, which are popular with both locals and foreigners to sit and watch the passing parade or wait for resort *dhonis*. (*Maidan* is an Anglo-Indian word for open space in a town.)

Islamic Centre (☉ *09.00–17.00, except at prayer times*) A few paces inland from the waterfront with its striking golden dome, this was built in 1984, an eye-catching symbol of the island's faith. It is the island's most vivid architectural landmark, with spotlessly white walls, tall arched windows and a spectacular gold-coloured dome. The building is not only the main mosque, named after Sultan Mohamed Thakurufaanu Al A'z'am; it is also an Islamic library, a conference hall and classrooms. The main prayer hall has a capacity of 5,000 people; it displays beautiful wood carvings and Arabic calligraphy executed by Maldivian craftsmen. While one-storey villas and coral chalets are being torn down to be replaced by office and apartment blocks, the mosque and its elegant tiered minaret are like beacons guiding the nation as well as seafarers.

It is possible to visit the inside of the centre by climbing the steps that lead to a broad gallery with a view of the carpeted central area. A section is roped off for women. The gold dome is hollow with a white ceiling. Light is reflected on the shiny marble floor of the gallery, screened shutters creating a delicate play of shadows in the sunlight. Sometimes guides solicit tips from tourists but it is not necessary to oblige. Leave your shoes at the foot of the grand steps; they will be safe.

Republican Monument (Jumhooree Binaa) This is a stylistic aluminium sculpture forming the centre of the roundabout near the entrance to Sultan's Park. It was unveiled in July 1999 on the 34th anniversary of independence to commemorate the 30th anniversary of the Second Republic in 1998. Designed by Ahmed Fairooz, it was sculpted by students of the Maldives Institute of Technical Education under the direction of the National Security Service. It stands as a poignant and contemporary contrast to the traditional beauty of the nearby Islamic Centre and Sultan's Park.

Sultan's Palace and Sultan's Park (Medhuziyaarai Magu) Enter the park through the half-open wrought-iron gates. The park itself is a popular meeting place on Friday afternoons, when it is open 16.00–18.30. The mosque set in the corner has a less settled past than its tranquil appearance suggests. It was moved piece by piece to Bandos and reassembled there until it was decided to return it to Male', when it was dismantled, transported back and reassembled again. The palace was demolished when the Second Republic was created in 1968. Only one three-storey building remains, and this houses the **museum** (see page 143).

Munnaaru (Medhuziyaarai Magu) This short stocky minaret is a monument of classic proportions. The round tower is so well preserved it does not look its age, yet it was built in 1675 by Sultan Ibrahim Iskandhar. It was used from early times for calling prayers, a function taken over in 1984 by the minaret in the Grand Mosque at the Islamic Centre.

Hukuru Miskiiy Also known as Friday Mosque, this is behind the Munnaaru. It dates back to 1656, built during the reign of Sultan Ibrahim Iskandhar. Inside it radiates an atmosphere of deep reverence. It has heavy wooden doors that slide open to inner sanctums glimpsed through ancient latticework, lamp hangings of wood and panels intricately carved with Arabic writings. The ceiling is built with the original carved timbers while the walls are hewn and filigree-carved from coral. The floor is now carpeted and the mosque is used for contemplation and prayer. Permission can be obtained from the Ministry of Justice to visit the interior.

Much of the exterior and the roof is protected by corrugated iron sheets which give no clue to the grace and beauty inside. The mosque is set in a cemetery with a legion of headstones guarding it. Those with rounded tops are of women and those with a tip at the top indicate a man's grave. Children's graves are marked with smaller headstones. There are several sepulchres with sliding wooden doors which, when opened, reveal the coral stone tomb of a royal personage or nobleman buried within.

Mulee-aage (Medhuziyaarai Magu) With wrought-iron gates and fretwork friezes on its roof edges, the building shows Sinhalese influences and was built in 1906 for Sultan Mohamed Shamsuddeen III, replacing a house dating back to the mid-17th century. It was intended for his son but the sultan was deposed.

Mulee-aage was used for administrative offices instead; then, at the end of World War II, vegetables were grown in its garden to help relieve food shortages. In 1953, when the country first became a republic, it became the president's official residence. In 1994 President Gayoom moved into a newly built but traditionally styled handsome palace, almost Georgian in appearance, in Orchid Magu.

While the new office for the president was being constructed on the waterfront in the late 1990s, Mulee-aage again served as offices, this time for the president and his various directorates.

Medhu Ziyaarath (Medhuziyaarai Magu) This blue-and-white shrine is a memorial to the Moroccan Abu Barakaath Yoosuf Al-Barbari, who is credited with converting the country to Islam in 1153.

People's Majlis (House of Parliament) (Medhuziyaarai Magu) The parliament now meets in the magnificent new building east of Mulee-aage. This was a donation from the government of Pakistan and it dominates the surrounding buildings with its soaring simplicity. Here the members of the Majlis meet in an atmosphere inspiring calm deliberation.

Dharumavantharasgefaanu Miskiiy Found on the quiet backstreet of Dharumavantha Magu, this little mosque is a real gem. Siân and Bob were invited in on our last day in Male'. Beautiful wooden beams, red lacquerwork and an attractive central dome are its main features.

OTHER SIGHTS The **tomb of Mohamed Thakurufaanu**, the Maldivian hero who defeated the occupying Portuguese and restored the country's independence, is situated in the compound of the **Bihuroazu Kamanaa Miskiiy** (Neeloafaru Magu).

The new **Presidential Palace**, also called Theemuge, is in Orchid Magu. This is a tastefully designed building, a symphony of white and blue. Other government buildings in the same street include the new and modern-looking Ministry of Justice and Islamic Affairs in the next block, and Hilaaleege, the Government Guesthouse next to it.

At the junction where Fareedhee Magu and Orchid Magu meet, there used to be a clock tower, of a vaguely Moorish design in three tiers. It was erected on 22

November 1990 by the prime minister of Sri Lanka 'to serve as an enduring symbol of the close and traditional ties of friendship and co-operation between the people of the Maldives and the people of Sri Lanka', but it is no longer there.

LONGER WALK: AROUND THE ISLAND If you have enough time, you can walk around the whole island, and a description, again starting from the Presidential Jetty, follows.

Opposite the **Presidential Jetty** is the **Jumhooree Maidan**, the town square with its gigantic flagpole. Perhaps a forerunner of things to come, the **MTCC building** is to the right of the Maidan as you face inland. It has an exterior elevator with glass sides, which gives a super view of the waterfront drive and the *dhoni*-filled harbour as it glides to the top floor. To the east of the square is a charming high-rise building with a wall of tinted glass presenting an attractive backdrop to the town square. This is the police headquarters. At the southern side of the square (photography forbidden) is the **Bandaara Koshi**, the old fort headquarters, surrounded by a high wall.

Eastwards, following **Boduthakurufaanu Magu** (which goes right round the island and keeps the same name all the way) along the waterfront, are various government buildings, including that of the **Atolls Administration**. The new building for the **President's Office** commands a superb view of the harbour and islands and presents an image of security and permanence.

The vessels of the **Coastguard** are moored in front of the building and the impressive blue-and-glass building of the coastguard with its lookout tower occupies the corner of the adjacent block. The new **Bank of Maldives** building has a contrasting façade of polished marble-like slabs.

The **Ministry of Foreign Affairs** building fills a street block, while other buildings lining the waterfront boulevard are a contrast; a few squat single-storey shops remain but most have been transformed into buildings with six or eight storeys housing travel agents and airline offices.

Dhonis for hire tie up at **the waterfront** along this stretch. The steel piling for the sea wall was done in 1994 with assistance from the Australian government; there is a new waterfront park there.

It is pleasant to stroll along the eastern coast road, even walking the top of the retaining wall, like an ancient rampart defending the town from the sea. Open space for sports (soccer, basketball and even cricket) has been reclaimed from the sea and an **artificial beach** and swimming area created.

At the southern corner where the waves break onto a patch of sand, daring boys body-surf. The open square by the sea serves as a recreation area. A **tetrapod** on a plinth serves as a monument to the massive reclamation of land along the southern side of Male'.

A boulevard begins here along the Male' breakwater, which is actually a long rampart of tetrapods. These four-spar objects each weigh three tons and are made out of marine cement and rock. Twenty thousand of them have been interlocked together in ten different blockades, with a gap between each unit, to reduce wave force. They were placed there between 1988 and 1990 with Japanese aid, following the high tidal swells of 1987, which flooded a third of the town.

It is a hot walk along the reclaimed southern side, where the **Dharubaaruge conference hall** graces the area. The lush gardens here are very beautiful, providing some much-needed greenery on a built-up island. The hall was built for the 1990 meeting of **SAARC** leaders and extended for the 1997 summit. Official functions often take place here; it has several meeting rooms as well as its huge main hall. Construction started here in 2007 on the new five-star, 15-storey city hotel. In this area of the capital are the electricity board's plant and a water storage tower. Further along are new residential blocks and a large sports ground.

At the end of the south coast boulevard lies the **southern (new) harbour**. This was built to ease congestion in the old harbour, and it is used by *dhonis* and inter-atoll vessels staying for a few days tied up to the quay. It has become a fascinating, bustling port, with busy trading and lots of local-style sidewalk cafés.

Continuing the circuit of the island, you come to the impressive 200-bed **Indira Gandhi Memorial Hospital** built with aid from India. Further northwards, at the western end of Majeedhee Magu is the new **Maldives Centre for Social Education**. This serves as a multi-purpose sports hall, and has a fully equipped language laboratory and classrooms.

Now there is a chance to discover a historical site not marked on maps of Male' since it originally was not in Male' but offshore: the spot where **Ali Rasgefaanu** – Ali the Martyr – died defending Male' against the Portuguese in 1558. He was buried where he fell and, with the reclamation of land from the sea, his Martyr's Tomb is now inland, behind the Indira Gandhi Memorial Hospital in a road, Shahid Ali Higun, running parallel to it. It is marked by a green door set in a wall, next to a house called (in English) Thinfiya. However, there may be nothing to see, unless (unlike me) you can find someone to let you in and show you what's behind the green door.

At the northwestern corner, you come to the western end of the northern waterfront road, with the squat blocks of warehouses and administrative buildings remaining from pioneering days. New buildings are replacing the old though and after the commercial docks and the **Customs** is the new **GPO**.

Along the waterfront there is a lot to see. Inter-atoll boats are tied up at the quay, men pull carts carrying cargo or fish, shops are stacked with everything village islanders need and the sidewalk is busy with islanders shopping and greeting old friends. Facing the sea on a jetty is the **vegetable market**. The doors into the market are kept closed so you have to push one open to enter. There is a tranquil atmosphere inside, induced by the light filtering through green screens, and the calm pace of business; no vendors shouting. Bunches of bananas hang on coir ropes from ceiling beams and, while there may not be many different kinds of vegetables, every stall is fascinating. There are packets of sweetmeats, nuts and breadfruit chips on sale; the vendors will let you sample and will chat a little if you show an interest.

The **fish market** on the other side of the main road is to be relocated to its own jetty. In the meantime, visit in the afternoon and you are sure to get in the way of fish being unloaded at great speed from *dhonis* as they land their catch. The fish are dragged into the open-sided area with a tiled floor, where they are swiftly gutted and cleaned. As fast as fish are brought in, they are sold and taken away by men pulling carts or hanging a whole tuna from a bike's handlebars. The market is kept scrupulously clean, washed down each day and disinfected. Upstairs above the original fish market on the land side of the road are some shops and the Fishmarket Café, which is just what you would expect it to be: noisy and fast-paced. Short eats and meals with fresh fish are prepared on the premises and are delicious and cheap.

The **northern inner harbour** is separated from the outer harbour by a coral stone breakwater first built between 1620 and 1648. There are no manmade boundaries for the outer harbour. This is the roadstead defined by three islands: Funadhoo, Dhoonidhoo and Villingili. Ships anchor there while their cargo is unloaded and ferried by towed lighter to the wharf in Garaabu Thundi, which also houses the Male' Customs. The building of a wharf there enables small container ships to tie up alongside to load and unload containers of cargo.

The terrace of shops on the left as you walk south along Chandhanee Magu, after the **People's Choice electronic showroom**, is devoted to tourist knick-knacks.

The **Islamic Centre** is behind this row, with the minaret peeping out where it is visible (and photographable) from the other side of the road. After passing several souvenir shops, you come to a crossroads, with Fareedhee Magu on the right and Medhuziyaarai Magu on the left.

Turn left here, with the Islamic Centre on your left and **Dhiraagu teleshop** and the **Sultan's Park** on your right. Left again brings you to the main entrance of the Islamic Centre with its broad three-sided flight of marble steps.

Now you are almost back at the jetty, for the boat ride back to the resort. There is a low wall and a few concrete bench seats around the Jumhooree Maidan where tired tourists sit to await the transfer boat.

AROUND MALE'

Male' has two islands as its suburbs and both are open to visitors and are especially interesting for those who want to see more of how Maldivians live. These are Villingili (also spelt Viligili) and Hulhumale'.

VILLINGILI This inhabited island lies just 15 minutes, and only a Rf3 *dhoni* ride, west of Male'. It was one of the first resort islands but has since been developed as an overspill residential area for Male'. *Dhonis* for the island leave from New Harbour, not far from the Indira Gandhi Memorial Hospital. On arrival, a walk along the beach towards the south, where locals often picnic, is interesting for the view. From there Male' looks as if it's floating, with its new higher-rise blocks dominating the horizon and seemingly trying to sink the whole island. At the far end of the beach a fence blocks the area, so head to your right to join the road. Following this and heading right (westward) takes you past a Muslim college and the new residential blocks.

At the next junction, if you head left, you come back to the beach. Eventually around the shoreline you will come to a *dhoni* repair yard facing westwards. Be careful if you choose to explore the yard, in case of falling wood. The boatbuilders seem happy to see visitors. Heading into the centre of the island, you come to a café called Randhaan and then the open football-pitch area. On the west side of the open area is an attractive mosque with shady cover. Going ahead (north now) you reach the beach once more. Following the road you come to Café Point and then the post office, before seeing the jetty ahead. The whole walk takes half an hour or more, depending on whom you meet.

HULHUMALE': THE RESIDENTIAL CAPITAL OF THE FUTURE A grey-green lizard, about 20cm long, its tail erect, darted across the broad highway that runs around the coast of Hulhumale' Island. Its presence was remarkable since, just a few years ago, the island was a lagoon where the only wildlife was fish. Now birds come to nest in the bushes, coconut palm trees are flourishing, and children play cricket in the crimson-flowered scrub.

Colour, whether the sheer blue of the sky or the bleached white of land reclaimed from the sea, characterises Hulhumale'. Apartment blocks have balcony railings painted in different pastel shades, the administration building is a glorious red, the hospital roof a healthy green, and the power station an electric blue. But Hulhumale' is more than a work of art: it is the creation of visionaries concerned about the congestion of living conditions in Male'.

An unusual solution to the overcrowding problem was chosen in 1997 – to dredge the waters of the shallow Hulhule-Farukolhufushi lagoon to the northeast of the airport island and 1.3km away from Male'. This would create a purpose-built island to meet the capital's need for extra residential accommodation, as well as industrial and commercial space.

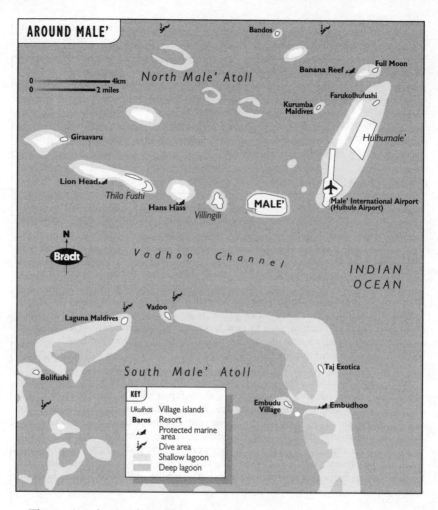

The project began sluggishly, only accelerating to completion of 188ha of reclaimed land in 2002, at a cost of US$33 million. A highway was constructed to the airport where future expansion (to take the newest long-haul jets) will add a further 305ha. With an extension to embrace the island of Farukolhufushi (formerly the Club Med resort) another 204ha will be added. The entire reclaimed area has been named Hulhumale' to identify its link with the capital and the airport.

There is a gleaming new building on the Male' waterfront (close to Nasandhura Palace Hotel) serving as the ferry terminal for motorised passenger boats leaving every 30 minutes for the embryonic residential capital. The voyage to Hulhumale' is one of the world's cheapest, at only Rf5, the equivalent of 40 US cents, for the 20-minute crossing. The ferry holds a hundred passengers, either pioneering Hulhumale' residents or other islanders in a party mood as they make an outing to inspect the new island.

The pioneering spirit takes over the minute the ferry docks at the jetty in front of the new, mirror-walled terminal. Passengers shake off the confines of Male' and revel in the wide-open space of this manmade island. Trees have been planted along the shore and beachfront housing lots are staked out with survey markers.

Highways, with neat borders filled with plants on either side, defining where the pavements will be laid, stretch into the distance. A sense of freedom and of challenge – of being on the verge of the future – fills the air.

There is a bus service on the island (Rf1 to any destination) and passengers board the bus to visit the shopping centre and the apartment blocks. Huge numbers are painted on each block for easy identification, and the different-coloured balconies help individualise each apartment.

These were the first buildings in phase one of the project, and housed the first 2,000 residents. The rent of apartments is about 40% less than rents in Male' and freehold in the apartments and building lots can be purchased over a 20-year period. Foreigners are not permitted to own land in the Maldives, but they can sub-lease property.

The basic infrastructure and municipal facilities have been completed, with electricity, water, sewerage, waste disposal and telecommunications services. There is a school with 400 pupils, a 50-bed hospital and a mosque. Subsequent phases will see the development of private houses on beach lots, the opening of a commercial and industrial area and a port, playing fields and all the amenities of a thriving city. The building of a 500-bed five-star hotel is planned under a lease agreement between STO and government. Funding has also been approved for the construction of a bridge linking Hulhmale' and Male'. If all goes well, eventually it will be possible to drive from Male' to the airport, by the bridge to Hulhumale', and then on the causeway of reclaimed land linking Hulhumale' with the airport island of Hulhule.

The problem of congestion in Male' is not confined to the land. Boat owners lack proper mooring facilities for their vessels and already they are seeing the advantages of this new island. Scores of safari vessels used for tourist cruises around the atolls now anchor offshore, and the new harbour provides security and bunkering for boats.

Although the island has been reclaimed from the sea, it hardly suffered during the tsunami. At 2m above sea level it is higher than natural islands in the archipelago. Some of those who lost their dwellings in other islands were temporarily re-housed in Hulhumale' after the tsunami. The presence of experienced construction crews and the new infrastructure enabled shelters to be erected within seven days of the disaster.

While the target population for the first phase is 53,000 inhabitants, there are expected to be 100,000 residents by 2020 as the next two phases are completed.

NEIGHBOURING RESORT ISLANDS The neighbouring resort islands in North Male' Atoll, such as Kurumba, Full Moon, Paradise, Giraavaru, Bandos and its satellite of Kudabandos, can all be visited independently. However, prior permission should be obtained in advance (by telephoning the resort) in case the resort is not open to non-residents when you want to visit. Their facilities can be utilised for a fee but visitors to Kurumba, Full Moon and Paradise usually go to them to sample the classy restaurants.

Access would be by *dhoni* hired from those tied up along the jetty in front of the former Nasandhura Palace Hotel, or by speedboat from an operator such as Inner Maldives Holidays (see page 50). The cost is based on period of hire plus fuel charge and could cost a few hundred dollars for the return trip. Access is easier to the airport island of Hulhule by public ferry (cost Rf10) where the Hulhule Island Airport Hotel (✆ 3330888) is open to non-residents who want to use the pub-like bar or its two restaurants.

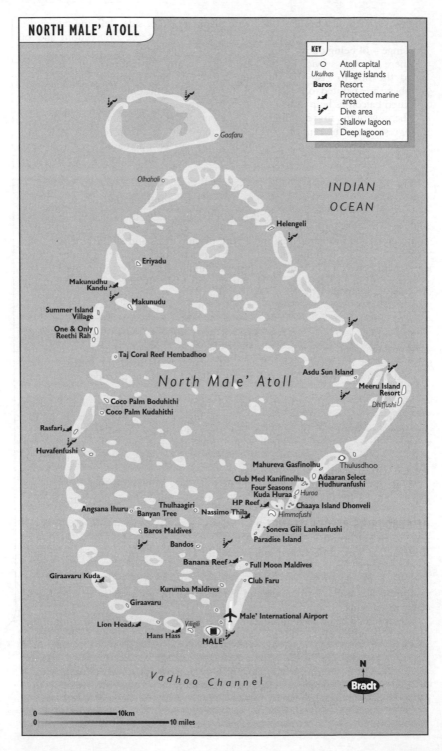

NORTH MALE' ATOLL

KEY

○	Atoll capital
Ukulhas	Village islands
Baros	Resort
	Protected marine area
	Dive area
	Shallow lagoon
	Deep lagoon

INDIAN OCEAN

Gaafaru

Olhahali ○

Helengeli

Eriyadu

Makunudhu Kandu

Makunudu

Summer Island Village

One & Only Reethi Rah

Taj Coral Reef Hembadhoo

North Male' Atoll

Asdu Sun Island

Meeru Island Resort

Dhiffushi

Coco Palm Boduhithi

Coco Palm Kudahithi

Rasfari

Huvafenfushi

Mahureva Gasfinolhu

Thulusdhoo

Club Med Kanifinolhu

Adaaran Select Hudhuranfushi

Four Seasons Kuda Huraa

Huraa

Angsana Ihuru

Thulhaagiri

Banyan Tree

Nassimo Thila

HP Reef

Chaaya Island Dhonveli

Himmafushi

Baros Maldives

Soneva Gili Lankanfushi

Bandos

Paradise Island

Banana Reef

Full Moon Maldives

Giraavaru Kuda

Club Faru

Kurumba Maldives

Giraavaru

Lion Head

Viligili

Male' International Airport

Hans Hass

MALE'

Vadhoo Channel

N

Bradt

0	10km
0	10 miles

6

North and South Male' Atolls

RESORTS ON MALE' ATOLLS

There are 27 resorts on North Male' Atoll and 17 on South Male' Atoll.

H MALE' (KAAF) Male' Atoll is known by its traditional name (Male') and *not* its alphabetical code name (Kaaf). If you find the naming and numbering of the islands confusing, *Appendix 2*, page 200, is helpful. Four geographical atolls, as well as the nation's capital, make up the administrative atoll of Male'. The island atoll of Kaashidhu and Gaafaru Atoll are east of the Horsburgh Channel and north of two atolls – Male' north and Male' south. Kaashidhoo (H-1) is 91km from Male', while the capital of the atoll is Thulusdhoo (H-4). There are nine inhabited islands in total. The atoll stretches for some 130km from north to south, and 48km east to west.

Ever since anything about Maldives has been recorded, Male' has been its centre of administration, economy and culture and gave its name to the atoll. However, according to H A Maniku, from evidence in Isdhoo Loamaafaanu, written in 1194, South Male' Atoll was called Biyaidhuvu Athelhe (*atholhu*), which suggests that Biyadhoo (now a resort) may have been an important centre.

The most heavily populated islands are Kaashidhoo in the north, and Guraidhoo (H-13), which is the southernmost inhabited island.

Kaashidhoo is known for toddy tapping, but agriculture is not of major concern in the atoll, with only 19ha identified as being suitable for cultivation. The best fishing islands are Dhiffushi (H-3), Gulhi (H-11), Maafushi (H-12) and Guraidhoo. The reef off Dhiffushi has caused many wrecks; a children's reformatory was opened in Maafushi in 1979.

Thulusdhoo has become a major industrial island. There is a soft-drinks bottling plant there and it is a trans-shipment point for dried, smoked and salted fish for export. There is so much fish that discarded dried fish is sometimes used to fill in pot-holes in the mud roads.

Of the 72 uninhabited islands, 44 have been converted to tourist resorts. The island of Dhoonidhoo, officially listed as uninhabited but used for special banishment, was the residence of the British representative in Maldives until 1964. The closest island to Male', Villingili was inhabited until 1961 and was a resort from 1973 until 1990. It is now a flourishing residential community. The island of Funadhoo is used for fuel storage.

Hulhule, now dedicated to the airport, has a long history. Ibn Battuta, the noted 14th-century Arab traveller, was one of the first foreigners known to have gone there; he landed on his second visit to Maldives in 1346. The island was also a royal holiday resort for a time, another harbinger of things to come. It was planned to settle the urban overspill of Male' there, but a temporary runway was built in 1960, following a survey done by the British, and the first aircraft landed at 13.55 on Wednesday, 19 October 1960. More land was gained in 1968 by spanning the

477.6m between Hulhule and Gaadhoo to make one island. The island became Male' International Airport 21 years after the first plane landed.

It now shares with Male' the distinction of being a cornerstone for the development of Hulhumale' as part of the future Greater Male'.

RESORTS ON NORTH MALE' ATOLL These island resorts in North Male' Atoll are all within a speedboat ride of the airport. They are listed by the resort brand name with the original island name, if different, included in the text.

🏠 **Adaaran Select Hudhuranfushi** (137 beach villas, 40 water villas) ☏ 6641930; f 6641931; e info@hudhuranfushi.com.mv, www.adaaran.com. Formerly known as Lohifushi, this island has been branded as an Adaaran Select resort of the Sri Lankan Aitken Spence hotel group, hence nearly 50% of the staff are Sri Lankans, as is the holiday ambience. The island, a coconut plantation until it became a resort in 1979, is lush with mature vegetation including huge banyan trees; it also has a large football field. The 40 overwater villas (opened in 2007) line a central jetty. They have attractive palm-thatched roofs & brightly upholstered rooms where the clothes closet can also be accessed from the bathroom, which has its own balcony & steps to the lagoon. Beach villas are densely packed together with bland décor & small, open-air bathrooms. Meals are buffets in a vast sand-floored restaurant where wine costs as much as in a 5-star resort. There is a pool with a swim-up bar & a lounge with banal evening activities like crab racing. The best snorkelling is by boat while surfing is good from the southern beach area. Transfers: speedboat 30mins. $(HB)–$$(all-inclusive)

🏠 **Angsana Ihuru** (45 rooms) ☏ 6643502; f 6645933; e ihuru@angsana.com; www.angsana.com. Angsana, which opened in 1979, is close to – & associated with – Banyan Tree but with a simpler ambience. This is a picture-postcard paradise island, with an encircling reef & pretty beaches. The island is small & lush, with access to some parts restricted in order to protect the environment. It has won awards for its attention to environment & nature. It has thatched cottage-type units with a swing seat on each patio. The interiors are designer-smart. Meals are mostly buffets in an open-sided restaurant. The biggest plus here is the reef. It is one of the best in the country & is literally a couple of metres offshore; ideal for snorkelling. The reef drops off sharply, with abundant varied fish; its coral was excellent before bleaching. For good diving there are many sites within an hour's ride by *dhoni*. The resort is popular with independent travellers & repeat clients, who like its easy-going atmosphere. Transfers: speedboat 30mins. $$$

🏠 **Asdu Sun Island** (30 rooms) ☏ 6645051; f 6640176; e info@asdu.com; www.asdu.com. Asdu Sun Island is one of the few original Maldivian-style resorts. It is on the eastern side of the atoll & was opened in 1981. Some of the rooms are in blocks of 2 or 3 with shared ceilings of *sataa* & coir rope. Rooms have louvred wooden windows, no glass, & are pleasantly rustic in style & that's what attracts its loyal repeat guests. Its restaurant is pavilion-style, with columns braided with coir rope. Beaches are varied & the snorkelling is good, too. Diving is low-key but good value. The clientele is mainly Italian, Swiss & French, with smaller numbers from other countries. This is a resort for those in search of simple magic. It is a very relaxed, lazy place where one might spot staff happily asleep by the jetty at 10.00. Transfers: fast boat 95mins. $ (plus 5% service charge)

🏠 **Bandos** (225 rooms) ☏ 6640088; f 6643877; e info@bandos.com.mv; www.bandos.com. Bandos is one of the larger islands (178,900m²) & was opened in 1973. In the 1960s it was an orphanage. The island has good beaches all around, with well-developed vegetation. Bandos is particularly good for the wide range of sporting activities it offers, such as tennis, badminton, squash, aerobics & gym, etc. Children are well looked after here. There is a new walkway around the resort, making access to its natural attractions easier. There is a conference centre, too. It also has an excellent house reef just 40–60m offshore. The diving is top rate, with perhaps one of the best in-house set-ups in the country, including new decompression chambers. The bar has a nautical theme; there is a beachside coffee shop; & a new over-sea restaurant terrace. Big-game fishing is available. It has become a favourite of British visitors, although there's an overall mix of nationalities. Those wanting an intimate quiet retreat might look elsewhere. Bandos is one of the few resorts to attract day visitors, being close to Male'. Transfers: *dhoni* 45mins, speedboat 25mins. $–$$$

🏠 **Banyan Tree Vabbinfaru** (48 rooms) ☏ 6643147; f 6643843; e vabbinfaru@banyantree.com;

Following the tsunami of December 2004, the staff of Banyan Tree Resorts played an energetic part – in collaboration with the United Nations Development Programme (UNDP) – in the repair and reconstruction of Naalaafushi Island in Meemu Atoll, which was badly damaged. As the Banyan Tree website (www.banyantree.com) explains, 'continual high exertion rates produced impressive results, rivalling any professional construction company'. Teams from Banyan Tree and Angsana resorts travelled by boat to Naalaafushi, where they worked alongside the islanders to rebuild shattered homes and to repair the doors, windows, toilets, kitchens and boundary walls of others. Construction materials were provided by the UNDP.

'We have lived and worked among these communities for many years,' explained the leader of the recovery team. 'I see our role in recovery efforts as something much larger than simply handing out a cheque. We are directly involved in the assessment of damage, transportation of materials, and construction. We've worked closely with UNDP to see these dreams come true.'

Similar energy and enterprise have been shown in rebuilding tsunami damage throughout Maldives. Now that the Naalaafushi homes have been restored, Banyan Tree Resorts plan to remain in contact with the island and to offer continued support. For more information see the Banyan Tree website (above), also the box Naalaafushi Rebuilds on page 186 and the UNDP website (www.mv.undp.org/adopt/banyantree.htm).

www.banyantree.com. Banyan Tree is to the north of Baros, in the middle of the atoll. It opened as Vabbinfaru in 1977 & was transformed in 1995 into the 5-star Banyan Tree. The beaches are good & there is a definite attempt to make the resort eco-friendly. The architectural style is Indonesian, with rustic thatched-roofed cottages right on the beach. They open on all sides to the lushness of their surroundings; guests glancing from their 4-poster beds feel they are all at sea. Many rooms now have a jacuzzi as standard. Meals are taken on a FB basis. Its special spa treatments are an attraction, with Thai masseuses (US$20–50). The emphasis here is on a low-key restful experience. Its literature claims it is 'a sanctuary for the senses'. That is not to say there aren't excellent activities under water. Most of the house reef, some of which overhangs, offers good snorkelling & is reached by a walkway, but the best diving is a little way offshore. The resort offers free night fishing, canoeing, windsurfing & sailing. It's the attention to detail & the little touches, like a constant flow of cold towels, that make this intimate island special. Transfers: speedboat 25mins. $$$$

🏠 **Baros Maldives** (75 rooms) 🕾 6642672; f 6643497; e info@baros.com.mv; www.baros.com. Baros has been a favourite holiday resort ever since it opened in 1973. No-one who stayed there then

would recognise it now as it has recently been transformed into one of the most in-demand, top-end resorts. It has, however, retained its island atmosphere accompanied by seamless service & a great camaraderie among guests, with the addition of being a treat for gourmets. There are 30 overwater villas with sun decks for private lounging & on-land spacious beach cottages with garden bathrooms. Unusual features in each room include a TV hidden in an ottoman at the foot of the bed, & a mini wine cellar as well as a minibar. Amazing *degustation* menus with wines included are a speciality of its overwater Lighthouse Restaurant, as are fusion-inspired dishes. Another à-la-carte restaurant, the Cayenne Grill, concentrates on seafood or meats cooked to guests' command. Even the b/fast buffet is a foody's thrill. Baros is a lush semicircular island with good beaches along most of its shoreline located in the centre of the atoll. Its lagoon offers good water activities & the reef has good snorkelling; the diving school has a reputation as one of the leading ones of the Maldives. Transfers: speedboat 35mins. $$$$

🏠 **Chaaya Island Dhonveli** (24 rooms, 60 bungalows, 36 water bungalows, 24 overwater suites) 🕾 6640055; f 6640066; e resorts@keells.com.mv; www.chaayahotels.com. Rebranded as a Chaaya property by its new Sri Lankan operators, John

6

Keells Hotels, Dhonveli has benefited from its fame (as Tari Village on Kanuhuraa) as the island for surfers, when it became known for its activities & good value. With swathes of beach for sunbathing, an exciting bar viewpoint at Pasta Point to watch surfers (many are families with fathers & teenage children surfing happily together), the island caters for all budgets. Older rooms are standard but the new 24 overwater suites are stunning, not just because of their vibrant blue walls under thatched roofs but for their butterfly-shape layout. The entrance opens into a broad lounge with balcony & lagoon steps beyond glass-panelled doors. The bedroom, with glass walls, is in one wing, the bathroom with jacuzzi in the other. There is a dedicated restaurant, with varnished thatched ceiling, for suite guests & another inland for the other rooms, each of which has plenty of extras, like tea/coffee maker & bathroom amenities. It's a short walk from the landing jetty to reception & rooms; diving is excellent with many sites within easy reach. Transfers: speedboat 30mins. $–$$$

⌂ **Club Faru** (152 rooms) ✆ 6642903; f 6643803; e fiha@dhivehinet.net.mv; www.clubfaru.net. This resort was started as Club Med Maldives in 1978 & operated successfully until Club Med transferred to another island in anticipation of the island, called Farukolhufushi, becoming part of the Hulhumale' development. Until that happens it is being run on similar lines with all inclusive holidays, even including a free excursion to Male'. The island is 1,200m long & 450m at its widest & provides guests with lots of activities on land & in the sea. Rooms are brightly furnished in 2-storey blocks in 8 units. It is only 2km from the airport & close to Male'. Transfers: *dhoni* 15mins. $ (FB)

⌂ **Club Med Kanifinolhu** (208 rooms) ✆ 6643152; f 6644859; e kanccre01@clubmed.com; www.clubmed.com. Club Med took over Kanifinolhu to maintain its presence in the Maldives when its original island, Farukholhufushi, was relinquished for eventual inclusion in the Hulhumale' development scheme. The resort suffered in the tsunami & bounced back a year later after a US$15m refit, giving it beach bungalows in Polynesian style & spacious suites (where bathtubs have a sea view) spread out over the lagoon. With the usual all-inclusive Club Med action & activities & enticing buffets, its guests mostly come from continental Europe. Transfers: *dhoni* 35mins, speedboat 15mins. $$ (FB)

⌂ **Coco Palm Boduhithi** (103 rooms) ✆ 6641122; f 6641133; e boduhithi@cocopalm.com.mv; www.cocopalm.com. This resort opened as Coco Palm

Boduhithi in Nov 2006 after being remodelled. It now has a beach & overwater villas & residencies as well as a spa, all designed to appeal to the discerning guest who wants luxury laid onto a beach escape. There are beaches on both sides, & the coconut palms remaining on the island are said to be descended from those planted by ancient sultans. It originally became a resort in 1979 although it bears little resemblance to its simple start. Even so it has less appeal for dedicated divers than other resorts & the snorkelling potential is limited. Transfers: speedboat 1hr. $$$$

⌂ **Coco Palm Kudahithi** (1 room) ✆ 6648866; f 6648877; e sunland@dhivehinet.net.mv; www.cocoplam.com. Coco Palm Kudahithi is a sister island to the nearby Boduhithi & a northern neighbour of Huvafenfushi. It began as an exclusive 7-villa resort that has been remodelled into 1 residence catering for the upper echelon of big spenders. The island is very small, with a beach only on one side. It is a resort for those seeking to get away from the world, rather than for those seeking an active vacation. Transfers: speedboat 1hr. $$$$$

⌂ **Eriyadu** (57 rooms) ✆ 326309; f 330884; e info@innermaldives.com; www.innermaldives.com. Eriyadu is out on its own in the northwest quarter of the atoll. It is an oval-shaped island surrounded by beaches & a lagoon. The island has good shade, although there are few coconut palm trees. Following major rebuilding & refurbishment, the resort has retained its simple, easy-going atmosphere. Rooms are in semi-detached units & single-storey blocks along the beach. They feature hardwoods from Malaysia in particular. The reef can be accessed from walkways & is excellent for snorkelling. The island is especially popular with divers since it has relatively under-utilised sites close by, such as the Makunudhoo Kandu Marine Reserve. Guests are varied in nationality, many being repeat visitors. The island makes up for what it lacks in size & luxuries with personal attention that creates a friendly atmosphere. Transfers: speedboat 50mins. $

⌂ **Four Seasons Resort Kuda Huraa** (96 rooms) ✆ 6644888; f 6644800; e reservations.maldives@fourseasons.com; www.fourseasons.com. The Four Seasons Resort on Kuda Huraa was transformed with massive amounts of money, energy & brilliant ideas, from a resort that first opened in 1977. It suffered in the tsunami & while it was being rebuilt employees, many of them born in the neighbouring village island of Little Huraa, were seconded to other Four Seasons resorts in the USA, UK, France & China.

This has resulted in an international, & mature, standard of service now the resort has reopened. An extension to the island has been created with long jetties leading to overwater villas, so it can be quite a trek in the hot sun from the villas at one end & the infinity swimming pool & restaurants at the other. However, some of the beach villas have their own swimming pool while the lagoon serves as the pool for the others. All the rooms are designer lavish with lots of tropical-themed knick-knacks. To the ambience of competence is added cuisine of gourmet standard. The residential island of Little Huraa is a coconut's throw away, enabling guests to discover a little of island life, & how the success of the resort has led to massive improvements in the islanders' lifestyle. Transfers: speedboat 25mins.
$$$$$

🏠 **Full Moon Maldives** (156 rooms) ☎ 6642010; f 6641979; e sales@fullmoon.com.mv; www.fullmoonmaldives.com. Full Moon was formerly called Furanafushi & it opened in 1993. The island is quite large, with good beaches for about two-thirds of its shoreline. A number of groynes protect the more vulnerable sections, but these are well out in the lagoon. The resort pitches its appeal to those wanting a familiar, well-run tropical island atmosphere. Accommodation spans various types with 1 water suite, 4 water villas, 52 water bungalows spaced along 1 side of the long island, 55 beachfront cottages & 44 deluxe rooms. A natural look created by an extensive use of timber & thatch for the rooms enhances the island image. Added to the high standard of the rooms are some of the smartest restaurants & bars in the islands. There is a bar with a deck over the sea on 1 side (with a view of Male') & a magnificent free-form swimming pool on the other. It has live entertainment nightly, & there is a piano bar with karaoke. Fine dining in style is possible at the Casa Luna Restaurant, with top-class Thai & Chinese cuisine in another restaurant. Seafood & pizza are served in the beachside Atoll Grill, & there is an elegant coffee shop. The sports complex includes 2 floodlit tennis courts, a gym, an outdoor whirlpool & a bar. There is a spa built on its own private island. The diving school is on the jetty, which is where a customised big-game fishing boat is based. Full Moon has the ambience of a well-run resort. It is promoted as a romantic island for honeymooners, but it caters for families, too, with a children's pool & free babysitting service. It is the kind of island the whole family can enjoy without any worries. Transfers: speedboat 20mins. $$$–$$$$

🏠 **Giraavaru** Giraavaru is one of the smallest resort islands & is conveniently located west of Male'. It was inhabited before becoming a resort. It has 2 good beaches & offshore is the Giraavaru Kuda Haa marine area & Lion Head marine area, so the diving is spectacular. The resort was very popular with independent travellers because of its low room rates. However, at press time it was closed & being reconstructed to emerge in the top half of the price range. Transfers: speedboat 20mins.

🏠 **Helengeli** (50 rooms) ☎ 6644615; f 6642881; e info@helengeli.net; www.helengeli.net. Helengeli is the northernmost resort on the eastern side. The island is about 800m long, & narrow. It looks like a village island, with plenty of jungly vegetation & a large sand spit at one end. A 3rd of it is left untouched, inhabited only by flying foxes. The middle is the staff area. Rooms are tastefully appointed beachfront bungalows with open-air bathrooms & outdoor seating, spread the length of the island. Guests tend to be active, as it's the diving that brings the visitors. The lagoon is small & coral-filled, so there are no watersports, as such, but the snorkelling is superb. Even with only mask & snorkel, it is possible to see shoals of banner fish, turtles & sharks. The house reef is one of the best in the atoll. The ocean currents touch the reef, so there is a wide variety of corals & fish. There are 40 dive sites in the vicinity, seldom visited by divers from other resorts, which are too far away. The inhabited island of Gaafaru is across a channel about 25km to the north & can be visited by groups. Transfers: fast boat 2hrs. $

🏠 **Huvafenfushi** (44 cottages) ☎ 6644222; f 6644333; e info@huvafenfushi.com; www.huvafenfushi.com. Huvafenfushi was previously called Nakatchafushi Island & is about 12km northwest of Angsana. Huvafenfushi means 'dream island' in Dhivehi, which gives a clue as to the resort's romantic themes. The earlier resort was completely demolished & in its place is an amazing spa island (the spa is set under water so guests get to know what it's like being in an aquarium, except the fish are outside looking in). Accommodation is in 44 timber beach, lagoon & water cottages, each with a private plunge pool & sleek furnishings & fittings. Food fit for gourmets is complemented by a choice of 6,000 wines from the underground wine cellar that doubles as private dining room. The lagoon area offers good swimming & windsurfing. Fast boats now offer diving some way out; also on offer are sunset fishing, sandbank

6

snorkelling & big-game fishing excursions. As if that weren't enough, a 21m luxury cruiser, *Sensuelle*, is an added attraction. According to the resort, this partners the rooms with 'super-sexy, super-luxurious cruising – perfect for guests seeking exploration & adventure on water, combined with an indulgent island paradise'. You'll need an indulgent bank manager too since the cruiser starts at US$8,000 a night, double BB, 2-night minimum, or US$3,500 for an afternoon. Transfers: speedboat 30mins. $$$$$

⌂ **Kurumba Maldives** (180 rooms) ☎ 6642324; f 6643885; e kurumba@kurumba.com.mv; www.kurumba.com. Kurumba was the 1st resort to be opened in the Maldives, on 28 October 1972. Close to Male', this is still the 1st choice of many, since it has matured into a hotel of class & style. It is the island equivalent of a Grand Hotel. An electric car will take you to your room. The welcome begins at the jetty with a uniformed receptionist who will escort new arrivals to their rooms. A steward offers a cold towel & a welcome drink as you sit in the elegant lobby to register. There is even a fountain in the lobby garden. Rooms are in all categories. The presidential suites are like town houses with an upstairs bedroom; most rooms are cottage-style, each with its own small garden leading to the beach. Many have private outside showers, baths & pools. The sports centre offers floodlit tennis courts as well as jacuzzi, sauna, swimming pool, billiard room & bar. The swimming pool close to the open-sided main bar is one of the prettiest in the Maldives. Inland there is a beautiful spa based on a water theme offering aromatherapy, Maldives sand massage & extensive exotic treatments. The public areas grouped close to reception include the main deck bar with views of Male', a pizza counter & a popular sushi/sashimi bar. Top-class dining (expect to pay about US$150 for dinner for 2) is available at the Arabian, Chinese, Indian & Mediterranean restaurants, all of which have extensive wine lists with New World as well as French wines, at reasonable prices. There is also the main restaurant, a coffee shop & a beach grill terrace. As well as the usual watersports, Kurumba has a glass-bottomed boat & offers big-game fishing. It is also popular with business travellers (there is a fully equipped conference hall & business centre). It is a sophisticated resort, best enjoyed on a B&B basis so that you can sample all there is to offer at the various restaurants. Transfers: speedboat 15mins. $$–$$$$$

⌂ **Mahureva Gasfinolhu** (40 rooms) ☎ 6642078; f 665941; e mahureva@valtur.it; www.valtur.com/villaggio/mahureva. Beginning resort life as Gas-Huri-Finolhu in 1980 & dedicated to camping, Gasfinolhu crept upmarket with an inclusive club concept marketed solely in Italy. It is a small island, shaped like a banana with a length of 350m & only 70m at its widest. The accommodation consists of 36 bungalow-style rooms with small veranda, & 6 larger 'sunshine' rooms at the tip of the island. Access is by a long jetty. It is still operated on a club concept with dashing young animators to encourage guests to party. Transfers: speedboat 40mins. $$ (FB)

⌂ **Makunudu** (36 rooms) ☎ 6646464; f 6646565; e makunudu@sunland.com.mv; www.makunudu.com. Makunudu was opened in 1983 & revamped in 1994 when it was a pioneer in the rustic luxury concept. The compact island (only 6 acres in area) is lush, offering peace & some privacy to guests. The rooms are Maldivian cottage-style, with doors opening directly onto the beach. The interior décor tastefully captures a rustic feel; the high ceiling is of *sataa*, with natural wooden beams & rugged mangrove posts lashed together with coir rope as a room divider. Even the minibar & AC units are disguised by rattan, the object being to have no plastic or metal visible. There are various water activities. Visitors are mixed, from most European countries & Japan. Transfers: speedboat 50mins. $$ (HB)

⌂ **Meeru Island Resort** (284 rooms) ☎ 6643157; f 6645946; e reservations@meeru.com; www.meeru.com. Meeru Island Resort is sometimes referred to as Meerufenfushi. It is on a long island with pretty, lush vegetation &, being fertile, part has been utilised for growing some fruit & vegetables. It takes about 45mins to walk around. The beaches are good on the west side & vary with the seasons on the east. Rooms are in long lines of chalets by the sea on either side & there are timber & thatched overwater bungalows. The 2 overwater honeymoon suites are huge. The resort attracts families & there is a children's pool. Meeru also attracts divers because it has access to so many good areas. Big fish, sharks, tuna & barracuda are common sights. There are day-dive trips further afield, some as far as Helengeli. The house reef is some way out, so a shuttle boat operates throughout the day for snorkelling. The inhabited island of Dhiffushi to the south is close by, but notices warn against swimming or windsurfing to it. A minimum stay of 6 nights is stipulated by this resort, which describes itself as offering 'no fuss comfort'. A genuine lack of urgency characterises the place. Transfers: speedboat 60mins. $$ (FB)

⌂ **One & Only Reethi Rah** (130 rooms) ℘ 6648800; f 6648822; e reservations@ oneandonlyresorts.com.mv; www.oneandonlyresorts.com. Reethi Rah is aptly named since *reethi* means 'pretty'. The island, called Medhu Finolhu, is indeed long & pretty. The only One & Only luxury island resort remaining in the Maldives (the other was Kanuhura), Reethi Rah's prettiness has been enchanced with beachside guest villas, many with a deck over the lagoon, & some with private swimming pool. Villas are large (130m²) with high ceilings & high-tech equipment including a plasma TV screen. The publicity boasts that it is a 'chic all-villa resort', thereby capturing its flamboyant essence, much loved by celebrities. The lagoon is large, & one side of the island is edged by beaches in coves. Swimming is good but snorkelling disappointing. For divers there are a number of attractions not far away, particularly the Makunudhu Kandu protected area. Transfers: speedboat 45mins. $$$$$

⌂ **Paradise Island** (260 rooms) ℘ 6640011; f 6640022; e info@paradise-island.com.mv; www.villahotels.com. Paradise Island is a long thin island; it is now 2½ times larger than it used to be when it was the rustic resort of Lankanfinolhu. A vast amount of cement must have been used to construct its 200+ island rooms & semi-detached villas over the lagoon. The effect is stunning; a resort built with the 21st century in mind, & to compete with holiday hotels worldwide. This version of Paradise means big city glamour & glitter; it even has 3 bars that never close, as well as a vast karaoke lounge/piano bar. Piped music wafts guests along covered walkways. Rooms are large & modern, with TVs that receive a score of satellite channels. There is a conference hall with the latest gadgetry & attached committee rooms. The harbour has enough space for 10 boats to come alongside at once. There are speciality restaurants at either end of the island, with an open-sided one by the main jetty, great for people & boat-watching. There is also a Japanese restaurant (many of the guests come from Japan), a huge open-sided main restaurant where all the meals are buffets, & a coffee shop. Every conceivable recreational activity is available. Landscaping has not been forgotten, with new vegetation being integrated. Soil has been imported from India & there is a nursery of 10,000 plants. Snorkelling is by boat & there is a diving centre. This is a large glitzy place for action lovers yearning for a Bahamas-style resort. Transfers: speedboat 20mins. $$

⌂ **Soneva Gili Resort Lankanfushi** (45 rooms) ℘ 6640304; f 6640305; e reservations-gili@ sixsenses.com; www.six-senses.com. Soneva Gili Resort is on the island of Lankanfushi & was formerly a low-budget resort called Hudhuveli. Its newest reincarnation could not be more astonishing. The island has dazzling white beaches & has been transformed with the addition of mature palm trees. Accommodation is in amazing wooden villas on stilts over the lagoon; the villas are so long it takes ages to find the toilet from the bedroom. The eco-friendly touches are resolutely designer-fashionable. Its ultimate accommodation is called the Private Reserve, consisting of 6 overwater structures housing 2 master suites plus accommodation for guests, & extensive leisure areas. A private spa features a sauna & steam room, as well as a chill shower, plus a massage pavilion & an AC gym. A personal Mr & Mrs Friday are on call at all times – with their own on-premises quarters. There is a waterslide into the lagoon as an additional flight of fantasy in this resort: one which guests either love or loathe. Guests can eat à la carte in their open lounges or terraces. Top-class fresh food is on offer in the sand-floored restaurant, or there is the option to eat out under the stars at the beach BBQ. With so many diving attractions close by, there is no shortage of activities for those seeking to add to their total relaxation experience. The Six Senses Spa makes sure guests can sink back into restful lethargy. Transfers: speedboat 20mins. $$$$$

⌂ **Summer Island Village** (108 rooms) ℘ 6641949; f 6641910; e siv@summerislandvillage.com.mv; www.summerislandvillage.com. Summer Island, formerly called Ziyarafushi, was a cheap & cheerful diving resort that has been remodelled with the addition of 16 overwater bungalows to complement the beach & rooms that are simple with extra 3rd beds. Sandy floors are a feature of the resort. Meals are buffets & guests stay on an all-inclusive plan. A disco & cosy bars provide relaxation after a hard day's diving. Diving is a big plus, with an amazing variety of sites close by. The house reef is not accessible here, though, so boats are provided to reach good snorkelling areas. The lagoon is large & perfect for watersports. The windsurfing conditions are excellent, being some of the best in the Maldives. The majority of the guests are German. Transfers: *dhoni* 90mins, speedboat 1hr. $ (FB)

⌂ **Taj Coral Reef Resort Hembadhoo** (65 villas) ℘ 6641948; f 6643884; e coralreef.maldives@ tajhotels.com; www.tajhotels.com. Taj Coral Reef Resort is on the small island of Hembadhoo. It is run with the panache expected of a resort that is part of the renowned Taj Group of India. The small but beautiful island is triangular in shape with good vegetation cover. It has good beaches on 2 sides. The resort has 65 villas comprising 30 beach villas & 35 over-lagoon villas. Rooms have satellite TV, & tea- & coffee-making facilities. Meals are often theme-based, Maldivian, Mexican, Indian, etc. There has been a conscious attempt to provide many recreational activities, such as photo-flights, stingray feeding, glass-bottomed boat rides & *bodu beru* cultural shows as well as pools, tennis & spa. The house reef drops in stages & offers snorkelling. There is a house wreck for divers. Overall this resort attracts a wide range of visitors. Transfers: speedboat 45mins. $$

⌂ **Thulhaagiri** (72 rooms) ☏ 6645930; f 6645939; e reserve@thulhaagiri.com.mv;

www.thulhaagiri.com.mv. Thulhaagiri is near the centre of the North Male' Atoll. This attractive island is very lush, compact & surrounded by a large lagoon. The beach on one side is excellent, but on the other it is lined by protecting groynes. The exotic thatched building style is very attractive, & there are 17 new overwater villas. The resort has acquired a reputation for good food, particularly its buffets. The lagoon offers great swimming, windsurfing, waterskiing & messing about in boats & the watersport & diving centre is well equipped. The dive school is a 5-star PADI instruction centre. The house reef is a mixture; some parts are good for snorkelling. In any case there are plenty of nearby reefs & dive sites. Germans make up about half the guest list. Transfers: *dhoni* 70mins, speedboat 25mins. $

Olhahuli Not a resort but a tiny uninhabited island occasionally visited by tour groups to picnic. A scheduled destination of one of the world's most luxurious cruise liners, *Silver Wind*, in February 2009, for passengers to enjoy a day on the beach and in the lagoon.

RESORTS ON SOUTH MALE' ATOLL

It takes at least 15–30 minutes longer to reach islands in South Male' Atoll from the airport, because you have to cross the Vadhoo Channel separating the two halves of Male' Atoll. The distance is 3.6km and the journey can sometimes be choppy. Most of the resorts are on the eastern side of the atoll, which has a total of nine inhabited islands and 17 holiday resorts.

⌂ **Anantara Maldives Dhigufinolhu** (160 rooms) ☏ 6644100; f 6644101; e maldives@ anantara.com; www.anantara.com. This exquisite, Thai-inspired resort embraces the long island of Dhigufinolhu &, from 2008, its satellite islet of Bodu Huraa. The main complex of 5 acres has 68 beachfront villas & 4 pool suites onshore, & 38 offshore teak-timbered suites with infinity edge bathtubs & sun deck with lagoon access. Bodu Huraa added another 50 overwater bungalows to the complex. With a swimming pool that sparkles with underwater lights at night, a choice of 7 restaurants with delectable cuisine (inc a Thai one reached by boat), an offshore spa, a fitness centre & a kids' club, fusion cookery classes & obliging, exotically clad staff, this new resort has everything to satisfy holiday craving. Even the diving is excellent with a wreck, a cave & a manta point to visit. Transfers: speedboat 30mins. $$$–$$$$$

⌂ **Adaaran Club Rannalhi** (116 rooms) ☏ 6642688; f 6640235; e front@rannalhi.com; www.adaaran.com. Opened in 1996 as a completely rebuilt resort on a compact island with good vegetation cover & plenty of palms for shade. Sandy

beaches encircle the island, although they are generally not very wide. There are 100 rooms on the island, in attractive, thatched 2-storey mansions, & 16 semi-detached overwater lodges set in the lagoon. This is a very active resort with energetic animators & all the sports & entertainment as well as lively evenings young-at-heart guests could want. The dive school is popular & the reef edge is very close. The resort is justly called a club for its chummy character. The majority of the guests are Italian. Transfers: *dhoni* 2hrs 30mins, speedboat 95mins. $$ (HB)

⌂ **Biyadhoo** Under new leaseholders & undergoing reconstruction.

⌂ **Bolifushi** (55 rooms) ☏ 6643517; f 6645924; www.bolifushi.com, www.eonresorts.com. Bolifushi is a small, compact island to the northwest of the atoll. It has good beaches most of the way round, particularly on the east & west sides. Vegetation is dense. It is being redeveloped by Eonresorts, a company marshalling 'Elements of Nature' as developers & operators of luxury boutique spa resorts. Open 2008/9. Transfers: speedboat 30mins. $$$$

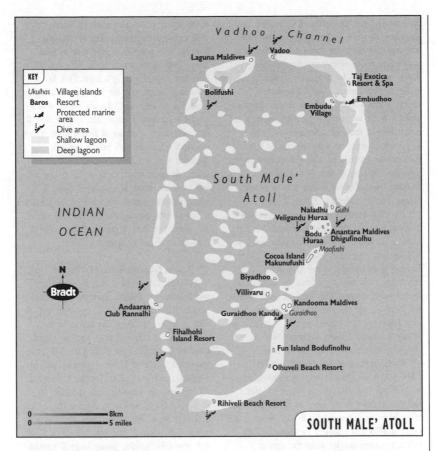

Vadhoo Channel

Laguna Maldives | Vadoo

KEY

Ukulhas	Village islands
Baros	Resort
	Protected marine area
	Dive area
	Shallow lagoon
	Deep lagoon

Bolifushi

Taj Exotica Resort & Spa

Embudhoo

Embudu Village

South Male' Atoll

INDIAN OCEAN

N

Bradt

Naladhu | *Gulhi*
Veligandu Huraa
Bodu Huraa | **Anantara Maldives Dhigufinolhu**
Maafushi

Cocoa Island Makunufushi

Biyadhoo

Villivaru

Andaaran Club Rannalhi

Kandooma Maldives

Guraidhoo Kandu | *Guraidhoo*

Fihalhohi Island Resort

Fun Island Bodufinolhu

Olhuveli Beach Resort

Rihiveli Beach Resort

0		8km
0		5 miles

SOUTH MALE' ATOLL

⌂ **Cocoa Island Makunufushi** (35 rooms) ✆ 6641818; f 6641919; e res@cocoa-island.como.bz; www.cocoaisland.como.bz. Cocoa Island is the resort name for Makunufushi, a long & narrow island with shady vegetation & no accommodation since all the units are offshore, served by a long, curving boardwalk. The history of the resort is fascinating since Eric, a young beachnik settled on it in 1980, eventually creating a do-it-yourself haven for the incognito famous with 8 A-frame rustic cottages. Now everything is done with style including the service & cuisine, which is a blend of Indian & Sri Lankan with gourmet touches. Some of the rooms resemble *dhonis* & some have lofts for sleeping; all have access to the lagoon. The extensive use of wood, Maldivian-style, in the room construction blends well with delicate interior decoration. Many rooms have wooden whirlpools, glass fronts & verandas. The Shambala Spa offers yoga & holistic treatments & all guests have complimentary use of the hydrotherapy pool, steam

room, gym facilities & treatment services. For divers there are over 20 dive sites nearby. The resort exudes discretion & understated elegance & seems extremely well run. Transfers: speedboat 40mins. $$$$–$$$$$ (with HB or FB option extra)

⌂ **Embudu Village** To reopen 2008/9. Embudu (also spelt Embudhu & Embudhoo) is a small island with narrow beaches & ample shade & vegetation. The ambience was one of simplicity & comfort but the resort is undergoing change from its laid-back formula as it is redeveloped. Some of the best dive sites in the country are very close; one is the Embudu Kandu Marine Area, which has the famous drift dive of the Embudu express plus the coral gardens of the Embudu Thila & a shark-watching point.

⌂ **Fihalhohi Island Resort** (150 rooms) ✆ 6642903; f 6643803; e fiha@dhivehinet.net.mv; www.fihalhohi.net. Fihalhohi is on the western rim of the atoll & was opened in 1981. The large, open island is also known as Lhohi Faru. It supports very luxuriant vegetation with large shady palm trees, many swaying over the beaches & coves. Birds find this island attractive. The main beaches face west with super-fine sands. The rooms are classified as standard to deluxe, with water bungalows, too. Buffets are the rule for meals with themed cuisine in the evenings such as Chinese, Mongolian, Sri Lankan, Italian & BBQs. All the usual watersports are available & the snorkelling is good for beginners as is the diving & there are some good sites within easy reach. However, the main emphasis at this Maldivian-run resort is on families & children are particularly well looked after. It is marketed in Germany, France, England & Italy & often heavily booked. Transfers: speedboat 95mins. $ (HB)

🏠 **Fun Island Bodufinolhu** ➘ 6640033; f 6640044; e info@fun-island.com.mv; www.villahotels.com. Fun Island is the resort name for Bodufinolhu Island, a long low-lying resort that suffered from the tsunami & closed so that timely, as well as essential, renovations could take place. Given the thoroughness of the owning company, Villa Hotels, in construction, redevelopment was still underway at press time with some fascinating new features planned. It is likely to be utterly modern & lively, in keeping with the group's other resorts, such as Paradise Island.

🏠 **Kandooma Maldives** (160 rooms) ➘ 6640511; f 6645948; e info@kandooma.com; www.kandooma-maldives.com. Kandooma, on the rim of the atoll near the inhabited fishing island of Guraidhoo, used to be known as Kadoomaafushi. It was opened as a resort in 1985 & is scheduled to reopen in 2008 with a brand-new concept under the aegis of a Singaporean hotel group (which also runs Rihiveli). The accommodation in its long 32 acres consists of semi-detached beach & garden villas, duplex & family villas, & top-notch water villas. Décor accentuates nature's colours with lots of white, including whitewashed wooden floors, & the ambience is very spic & span. The public areas have unusual domed thatch roofs resembling gigantic beehives; cuisine is described as 'Med-Asian'. Wi-Fi broadband covers the island & pre-programmed iPods are available. Lots of activities, including classic black-&-white movie-watching on the beach under the stars, & visits to Guraidhoo. Transfers: speedboat 50mins.
$$$–$$$$

🏠 **Laguna Maldives** (132 rooms) ➘ 6645903; f 6643041; e sales@lagunamaldives.com; www.lagunamaldives.com. Laguna Beach Resort opened in 1974 & was transformed in 1991 to the elegant resort it is today. The island takes at least 10mins to walk around & has plenty of shady palms, particularly on the south side. Good beaches & the lagoon extend all around the island. It is a neat, orderly island distinguished by attractive buildings with a wealth of good taste in room design. Some rooms are in blocks, 65 rooms are individual cottages with split levels. Each has an entrance & lounge with the bed area on a higher plane. The 17 overwater villas are superb, with a private beach area. 4 restaurants, a coffee shop & 3 bars offer plenty of choice of food & drink. With a top-notch spa, a children's pool, a free-form swimming pool, & a free gymnasium, plus tennis courts, the resort offers plenty to do on land as well as at sea, where fully equipped diving & windsurf centres provide the activities. The client mix is international. Laguna combines charming service with modern facilities & represents good value & good quality. Transfers: speedboat 20mins.
$$–$$$

🏠 **Naladhu Veligandu Huraa** (19 'elite dwellings') ➘ 6641888; f 6644188; e stay@naladhu.com; www.naladhu.com. Naladhu is unique not because it costs over US$1,000 a night to stay there, but for what it delivers 'for those who appreciate the sophistication & charm of times past' on a coral island in the tropics. Each of its 6 beach & ocean houses has a colossal 300m² of gorgeous, perfectly designed, stylish living space. Completely private & self-contained, the accommodation is perfect to enjoy on a rainy day as well as on a sunny one. Entrance is through an ancient wooden door into a walled garden from where a glass door opens into a hall with wine cellar, goodies pantry, fridge & espresso machine. On one side is a walk-in closet before sliding doors that open to reveal a sumptuous bathroom with massage couch, outdoor garden with waterfall shower, separate toilet, an indoor shower, a dedicated sauna chamber, a sunken glass bathtub & an irresistible full-sized mosaic-tiled swimming pool. It flows to a teak deck with teak sun loungers & a sala for in-house dining, with ocean beyond. The bedroom has a king-size bed smothered in silk cushions & soft pillows & sheets. Curtains hide a flat screen TV, & there is a bookcase with coffee-table books, an iPod & other gadgets, a writing desk, & Wi-Fi facility. A 'House Master' is on call 24hrs a day to perform the duties of a major-domo. There is fine dining in-house on demand or in the island's bar/restaurant called the Living Room & in the Thai restaurant reached by private boardwalk jetty & shared with the parent resort of Anantara. There is a 17m lap pool & snorkelling, surfing & watersports available but this resort seems to be designed more for guests who want to spoil themselves doing nothing very much in grand style. Transfers: speedboat 30mins. $$$$$

⌂ **Olhuveli Beach Resort** (129 rooms) ☏ 6642788; f 6645942; e info@olhuveli.com; www.olhuveli.com. Olhuveli Beach Resort began with 36 beds in 18 rustic rooms in 1979. This small island has been vastly improved with the addition of more vegetation & planting. The beaches cannot be faulted; there is a large sandbar & the shallow clean lagoon is fairly extensive. The resort was redeveloped & repositioned in the market place after the tsunami & now has 8 beach villas, 32 jacuzzi villas (the jacuzzi is on the sun deck), 63 deluxe rooms with either terrace or balcony, 21 deluxe water villas with swim-up sun deck, & 5 honeymoon water villas that each have a large living room as an extra. Transfers: speedboat 55mins. $$–$$$ (HB)

⌂ **Rihiveli Beach Resort** (48 rooms) ☏ 6643731; f 6640052; e info@rihiveli-maldives.com; www.rihiveli-maldives.com. The southernmost resort in the South Male' Atoll. Rihiveli means Silver Sand, but the island's original name is Mahaana Elhi Huraa & it is also called Fenboahuraa. The resort actually has 2 uninhabited islands set within its vast shallow sandy lagoon. The style here is rustic; paths are sand & grass & rooms are simple, set under palm trees, each with an individual garden. There is no AC or TV, but hot water is on tap, & there's a rustic ambience the guests, mostly French, seem to like as the resort thrives on repeaters. B/fast & lunch are served as buffets with a table d'hôte menu for dinner in a restaurant, sitting over the lagoon. The all-inclusive rate covers some watersports & excursions, snorkelling trips are organised & there is diving although no house reef. Transfers: speedboat 45mins. $$ (all inclusive)

⌂ **Taj Exotica Resort & Spa** (62 villas) ☏ 6642200; f 6642211; e exotica.maldives@tajhotels.com; www.tajhotels.com. Formerly the down-market Embudhu Finolhu until magnificently transformed after the tsunami to raise it to the standard of the Taj Group. It offers classic grand-hotel-style accommodation with a tropical touch in thatched beach villas (the deluxe versions each have a private pool) & lagoon villas with sun deck. There is a pan-Asian restaurant & an overwater Mediterranean one as well as a wine room (& Cuban cigars). The island is narrow, 780m long, with an extension created by the arc of jetties serving the offshore villas. It is set in a huge lagoon for safe, effortless swimming down steps from each overwater villa. Transfers: speedboat 20mins. $$$$–$$$$$

⌂ **Vadoo** Closed in 2007 for redevelopment as an all overwater bungalow resort. Vadoo opened in 1978 as Vadoo Diving Paradise. The island is very small but quite green. Similarly, the beaches are compact & a 5min walk will display the joys of the island. The house reef is superb & some of the best dive sites in the country are not far away. 5 are designated marine reserves. The adjoining Vadhoo Channel offers an amazing variety of underwater life & dolphins are often seen sporting in it. Transfers: speedboat 20mins.

⌂ **Villivaru** Under new leaseholders & undergoing reconstruction.

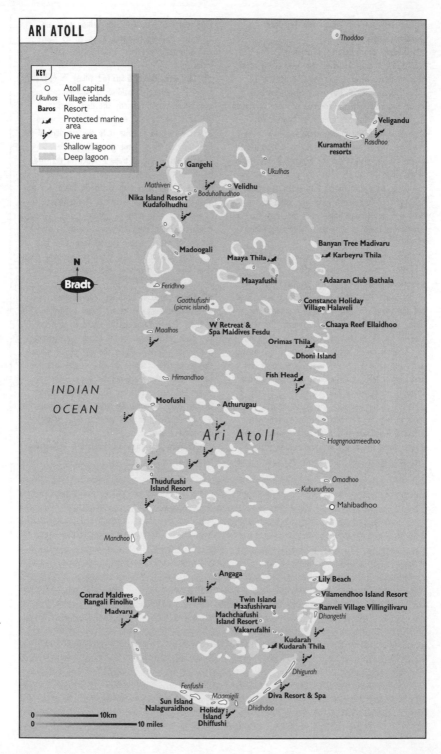

ARI ATOLL

KEY

○ Atoll capital
Ukulhas Village islands
Baros Resort
Protected marine area
Dive area
Shallow lagoon
Deep lagoon

○ Thoddoo

Veligandu

Kuramathi resorts
Rasdhoo

Gangehi

Ukulhas

Mathiveri
Velidhu
Boduholhudhoo
Nika Island Resort
Kudafolhudhu

Banyan Tree Madivaru

Madoogali
Maaya Thila
Karbeyru Thila

Maayafushi
Adaaran Club Bathala

Feridhno
Constance Holiday Village Halaveli

Gaathufushi
(picnic island)

Maalhos
W Retreat & Spa Maldives Fesdu
Chaaya Reef Ellaidhoo

Orimas Thila

Dhoni Island

Himandhoo
Fish Head

N

Bradt

INDIAN OCEAN

Moofushi
Athurugau

A r i   A t o l l

Hagngnaameedhoo

Thudufushi Island Resort
Omadhoo
Kuburudhoo

○ **Mahibadhoo**

Mandhoo

Angaga
Lily Beach

Conrad Maldives Rangali Finolhu
Mirihi
Vilamendhoo Island Resort

Madvaru
Twin Island Maafushivaru
Ranveli Village Villingilivaru
Dhangethi
Machchafushi Island Resort
Vakarufalhi
Kudarah
Kudarah Thila

Dhigurah

Dhiidhoo

Fenfushi
Diva Resort & Spa

Maamigili

Sun Island Nalaguraidhoo
Holiday Island Dhiffushi
Dhidhoo

0 ———— 10km
0 ———— 10 miles

7

Ari Atoll

RESORTS ON ARI ATOLL

There are 30 resorts on uninhabited islands in Ari Atoll and its near neighbour (ten minutes away by *dhoni*), Rasdhoo Atoll. None was closed because of tsunami damage and, apart from the few that have changed hands and are remodelling, they have matured into quality holiday resorts. A surprising number are marketed only in Italy and Germany, for whose nationals they cater exclusively.

I ARI (ALIF) Ari Atoll is generally known by its traditional name (Ari) and *not* its alphabetical code name, Alif.

Lying to the west of Male' Atoll, the district of Alif is made up of the inhabited island atoll of Thoddoo (I-1) all on its own in the north, the small Rasdhoo Atoll and the long Ari Atoll. From north to south, the distance is 76.5km and 28km east to west. The capital is Mahibadhoo (I-13) situated on the east side, 91km from Male'. Eighteen islands are inhabited. Even with only 73ha for cultivation, Thoddoo has a reputation for agriculture, especially watermelons. The ruins of a Buddhist temple were excavated there and a report on it published in 1958. A huge statue of Buddha was discovered hidden in a chamber. Also found were a chest, a silver bowl, a gold cylinder, perhaps a prayer wheel and some Roman minted coins. The coins were dated to around 90BC. The Hukuru Miskiiy was built in the 17th century and is now renovated. Rasdhoo (I-2), the only inhabited island in its small atoll, was the chief island of Ari Atoll before the shift of responsibility to Mahibadhoo. The new capital is also the best fishing island in the atoll. The inhabitants of Maamigili (I-3) and Fenfushi (I-17) are renowned as suppliers of sand and coral for building.

Fenfushi has an old, renovated mosque, as has Mathiveri (I-5), whose mosque was built by Sultan Ibrahim Iskandar I (1648–87). The curiously named Hagngnaameedhoo (I-10) has the tomb of Sultan Ibrahim Kalaafaanu, who reigned from 1585 to 1609. The island was inundated by high waves in December 1964. Omadhoo (I-11) on the east, near the capital, is a fishing island.

Resorts Resorts are listed alphabetically.

🏠 **Adaaran Club Bathala** (46 rooms) ☎ 6660587; f 6660558; e bir-front@aitkenspace.com.mv; www.bathala.com. Bathala is the 1st resort down the eastern rim of the atoll, & was opened in 1983. Most of the island is attractive. It is quite small with a reasonable amount of shade, although few of the trees are palms. The beaches are excellent with a smallish lagoon surrounding them. Accommodation is in what the resort describes as 'rustic cabana-style cottages' but some are not on the beach. Guests stay on a FB basis, so the public areas for eating & drinking are compact. Because it is located at the edge of the channel, there is constant underwater activity to appeal to divers. Karibeyru & Maaya *thilas*, 2 of the most famous protected marine zones in the Maldives, are close & provide superb diving opportunities. The house reef also attracts snorkelling fans. The island, one of several Adaaran properties under the management of the Sri Lankan group, Aitken Spence Hotels, was popular with repeat guests, who like its informal style, very much in keeping with the island's natural environment. At press time, its rooms were under contract to an Italian company. Transfers: plane 20mins. $ (FB)

⌂ **Angaga** (70 rooms) ☏ 6680510; f 6680520; e angaga@dhivehinet.net.mv; www.angaga.com.mv. Angaga was the 1st resort to open (in 1989) in the new Ari Zone tourist area. There are 50 thatched bungalows & 20 newer overwater villas with private sun deck. Furnishings are rustic with bamboo-framed beds & screwpine weave ceilings. There is an *undhoali* wooden swing bed on the veranda of the beach villas. The bar & restaurant is thatched, with an appearance like an upturned *dhoni*. All holiday packages are FB, with meals as buffets, but a coffee shop offers extra goodies. The island is quite small, with lush cover & plenty of palm trees. The beaches are magnificent, encircling the island, while the lagoon extends on one side, with the reef close on the other. The snorkelling & diving are excellent along the house reef & further out around the Angaga Thila. Fishing trips are advertised & evening entertainment is tailored to visitors' whims. Transfers: plane 30mins. $$ (FB)

⌂ **Athurugau** (51 rooms) ☏ 66880508; f 6680574; e info.athuruga@planhotel.com; www.planhotel.com. Athurugau is about 15km northeast of Thudufushi (see below), but the islands are very similar in geography as well as in image & management. Everything is tiled & comfortable, with rattan fittings & brown the predominant colour; rooms are basic & compact. As well as the spacious public areas, there is a stage for animators & entertainers. The resort's publicity carries the intriguing note: 'singer with pre-lunch, after lunch, pre-dinner & after dinner singing'. The beaches are good & the small island is lush with palms. The lagoon, ideal for both watersports & snorkelling, is large on one side & on the other the attractive reef is close in. All-inclusive resort dedicated to Italians. Transfers: plane 25mins. $$ (all-inclusive)

⌂ **Banyan Tree Madivaru** (6 rooms) ☏ 6660760; f 6660761; e reservations-madivaru@banyantree.com; www.banyantree.com/madivaru. This beautiful tiny island was originally used as a picnic destination & was a popular call for the small, Scottish cruise liner, *Hebridean Spirit*. It was a real wilderness with thatched huts for picnickers & a long sand bank for strolling into the lagoon. It has been agreeably transformed by Banyan Tree into 'an exclusive island sanctuary' with accommodation in freestanding tented

pool villas. There are 6 units (the island is too small for more) each consisting of 3 individual tents, 1 each for living, sleeping & bathing, grouped around a pool. They have timber floors, rattan & teak furniture, 'inspired island décor' & 'luxurious tent canopies' as well as conventional hotel fittings. The bath tent has a pair of spa beds for intense, in-tent treatment. Meals & scheduled excursions are all-inclusive & guests are cared for by Island Hosts who are available 24hrs a day. Sandbank dining is a diversion. This is the 1st resort of its kind in Maldives, & combines the high degree of comfort associated with the Banyan Tree group with the excitement of being a holiday castaway. Transfers: plane 20mins. $$$$$ (FB)

⌂ **Chaaya Reef Ellaidhoo** (112 rooms) ☏ 6660586; f 6660514; e ellaidhoo@chaayahotels.com.mv; www.chaayahotels.com. Ellaidhoo, also called Kadoogadu, is a smallish island but has quite lush vegetation & avenues of coconut palms. In January 2008 it reopened after a major makeover as one of the Sri Lankan hotel group, John Keells, properties. It is a villa-style hotel with new overwater villas. It takes its new name from the house reef right by the shoreline where there is an opportunity for superb snorkelling. This resort has always been one of the most devoted to the diving cause & continues to cater for dedicated divers. There are an incredible number of diving attractions close by, with caves & a very high, steep reef wall. Maaga Island, part of the resort, has a larger lagoon & is just 10mins away. Transfers: plane 25mins. $$

⌂ **Conrad Maldives Rangali Finolhu** (150 rooms) ☏ 6680629; f 6680619; e maldivesinfo@ conradhotels.com; www.maldivesconrad.com. This resort came into existence in December 2007 with the rebranding of the Hilton, the 1st major hotel chain to set up in Maldives. Locally known as Rangali Finolhu, it is at the western rim of Ari Atoll, the furthest west of any Maldivian resort. The resort actually consists of 2 islands, linked by a long wooden bridge. The seaplane passenger lounge is in the centre. One island is circular with a lot of shady greenery, & the other is very narrow & long. The beaches are truly inviting. This has never been a traditional city-style Hilton hotel but the exemplary high standard remains even with the name change, since it's still part of the same family. The resort opened in 1994 & evolved into a classy place to stay. Both its stylish overwater bungalows (on the long peaceful island) & beach rooms have a wholesome quality, enhanced by the use of tidy wood, some coral, traditional materials & fabrics. The overwater villas are large, built in wood & have glass floors. There are 2 spas, I with a glass-floored treatment room. As one would expect, there is a variety of fine food & wine served in 7 restaurants, including the famous world-first all-glass underwater restaurant (think US$500 for 2). The lagoon is shallow with a reef accessible for snorkelling. There is a dive centre, but most guests are looking for comfort & pampering in a memorable manner in a superb setting. Transfers: plane 35mins. $$$$

🏠 **Constance Holiday Village Halaveli** (86 rooms) ↘ 6660559; f 6660564. Halaveli is tucked inside the eastern rim of the atoll & first opened in 1982 with 15 units. It is a lush, palm-covered, half-moon-shaped island, about 275m long with excellent beaches & an extensive lagoon with a spectacular reef created from a specially installed shipwreck. At press time it was closed for redesigning with 86 suites, both beachfront villas & villas on stilts in the middle of the lagoon. Open 2008. Transfers: plane 20mins. $$

🏠 **Dhoni Island** (5 *dhonis*, I motor yacht, 6 land rooms available) ↘ 6660751; f 6660727; e reservations@blackgoldresorts.com; www.dhoni-island.com. Dhoni Island (Mushimas Migili) is south of Ellaidhoo in the centre of the atoll. Accommodation is actually offshore in 5 super-deluxe *dhonis* with AC & luxury modern facilities, & in I motor yacht; each boat is served by dedicated crew & a butler. The boats can cruise on demand for fishing, diving, deck picnics & to neighbouring islands. There are also 6 stylish, thatched cottages hidden in the lush vegetation by a white-sand beach for guests who want to sleep ashore. With an open-sided, sand-floored restaurant for exquisite meals & a bar made out of a dhoni, this tiny archetypal tropical island never has more than 12 guests, & children are banned. The emphasis is on personal service & guests are treated warmly by the island's young Maldivian owners & their amiable staff. It's a tranquil, private natural retreat with none of the pretentions of brand-name, up-market resorts. Meals & drinks, including champagne, as well as non-motorised watersports are included in the cost; diving is available with an experienced Maldivian dive master & there is a spa. The whole island (with *dhonis*) can be rented from US$12,000 a night. Transfers can be arranged by *dhoni* (4hrs); speed boat (about 90mins) or sea plane (25mins). $$$$$

🏠 **Diva Resort & Spa** (93 rooms) ↘ 6660513; f 6660512; e diva@naiade.com; wwww.naiade.com. Diva Resort & Spa has a long holiday lineage, having begun life in 1988 as Ari Beach with Dhidhoo Finolhu & then becoming White Sands

Resort until 2007. With beaches totalling about 1km in length, the resort is ideal for holiday fun, both onshore & offshore & there are plenty of dive sites close to the island. As befits a diva, the resort has moved upmarket to offer a classier deal with water villas, beach pool villas, beach villas & junior suites. There are Oriental, Italian & Japanese speciality restaurants with a main buffet restaurant built on stilts over the lagoon. There are 3 bars & evening entertainment with singers, guitarists & DJs. Open 2008. Transfers: plane 30mins. $$$

🏠 **Gangehi** (25 rooms) ↘ 6660505; f 6660506; e gangehi@clubvacanze.com.mv; www.clubvacanze.com. Gangehi is the northernmost resort of the Ari geographical atoll & opened in 1987. The small island is very densely foliated & a nature trail allows access to this typically Maldivian paradise. The beach is mostly on one side, but quite extensive for the island's size. The Maldivian theme is carried over to the large rooms & there are 8 overwater villas. This is an all-inclusive resort for Italian clientele. The lagoon is shallow, good for swimming & canoeing, & the diving is good value as, being on an isolated island, the dive sites are not much frequented. Transfers: plane 20mins. $$ (all-inclusive)

🏠 **Holiday Island Dhiffushi** (142 rooms) ↘ 6680011; f 6680022; e info@ holiday-island.com.mv; www.villahotels.com. Holiday Island is a sister of Sun & Paradise Island resorts. The island's real name is Dhiffushi. Most of the rooms are functional chalets with composition roofs. For families, there are 18 with adjoining doors. The main restaurant serves buffet meals, & there is a karaoke bar as well as a beach bar & a billiard room. Holiday Island is big, very green, with excellent wide beaches. The lagoon is large, so the reefs are more distant. The watersports & dive centres are at each end of the resort. There are usually 4 trips a day to the reef for snorkelling but diving, although good, is not the main activity here. Fishing, day or night, is popular. Italians, Swiss & Germans tend to form the majority of guests. This resort is not a quiet retreat, & offers plenty of fun & action. The inhabited island of Maamigili is close by. Transfers: speedboat 2hrs 30mins, plane 35mins. $ (HB)

🏠 **Kuramathi Blue Lagoon** (56 rooms) ↘ 6660527; f 6660556; e info@kuramathi.com.mv; www.kuramathi.com.mv. Blue Lagoon can be reached by minibus from Kuramathi Village if it seems too far to walk. The trip is worth it for contrasts. Blue Lagoon is also aptly named, especially as it has 20

Kuramathi is unique in being an island with three separate and quite different resorts, Kuramathi Village, Kuramathi Cottage and Blue Lagoon. Each is open to residents of the others, which means there is somewhere else to go when you want a night out. The island is shaped like a hockey stick, with Kuramathi Village at the handle end in the southeast. It is actually about 1.6km long and 550m at its widest. It is narrowest at the curved end, which embraces the charming resort of Blue Lagoon. Kuramathi itself was inhabited until 1970 when the population had dwindled, so the residents moved to Rasdhoo. The resort opened in 1977.

Guests at all three resorts may also use the facilities of the Kuramathi Sports Club, set in the middle of the island. This has a large freshwater pool, with a children's section, a gym, bar, coffee shop and other facilities and services. The lagoon is well suited to those wanting to learn all the different watersporting activities; nearly all except parasailing are catered for. The well-organised diving professionals provide an excellent and varied programme. There is a decompression chamber and the hammerhead shark point is close by. If the lagoon and beach should get boring, there is the wilderness of the interior of the island to explore or the well-populated village island of Rasdhoo only ten minutes away by *dhoni*.

lagoon overwater villas, wooden cabins built right over the water & approached through gardens bright with bougainvillaea & hibiscus. With trimmed thatched roofs & exteriors darkened to protect them from the weather, these overwater lodges were the first of their kind to be built in the islands. They are neat with tiled floors, separate toilet & bathroom. There are also 36 beach bungalows hidden in the flower gardens beside the beach. There is a deck bar overlooking the trim jetty, where manta rays are fed at the water's edge as the sun goes down. Transfers: speedboat 1hr 45mins, plane 15mins. $$

🏠 **Kuramathi Cottage & Spa** (83 rooms) ↘ 6660527; f 6660556; e info@kuramathi.com.mv; www.kuramathi.com.mv. Kuramathi Cottage is located midway down the island. It has retained its air of exclusivity, even with the addition of 50 wooden suites built in the lagoon. These are furnished to a high standard, the best in the whole island. Dining options include the elegant Siam Garden Thai Restaurant & the Palm Court Grill. Guests tend to be older than at its sister resorts. Transfers: speedboat 1hr 45mins, plane 15mins. $$

🏠 **Kuramathi Village** (151 rooms) ↘ 6660527; f 6660556; e info@kuramathi.com.mv; www.kuramathi.com.mv. Kuramathi Village has an undeniably holiday atmosphere. Development has been kept to a minimum to satisfy the fantasies of island lovers, while ensuring the latest in creature comforts. Because it is at the tip of a long island, Kuramathi Village offers spaciousness & the chance to explore in solitude. Accommodation is in 3 different categories, but all rooms have many modern features expected by today's clientele. The restaurant provides perfectly adequate food, reflected in the prices, & there is an Indian restaurant as a dining option as well as speciality restaurants in the adjoining 2 hotels. Kuramathi has been very popular with independent travellers from around the world & is good value for money, but with nothing cut-price in service & ambience. This resort tends to attract a younger party set of many nationalities. Transfers: speedboat 1hr 45mins, plane 15mins. $–$$

🏠 **Kudarah** (60 rooms) ↘ 6660549; f 6660550; www.yachttoursmaldives.com. Kudarah was opened in 1991 & marketed as a restful resort for Italian guests. Under new management, it opened again in 2007 after renovation & with the addition of 30 water bungalows to its 30 beach bungalows. The resort has a swimming pool & spa. The island is small but has a good covering of shady trees. Its beaches are not extensive & vary in size from year to year. The encircling lagoon is also small, but this means the house reefs are very close in. The building style is very Mediterranean, to suit the Italian guests, & somewhat suburban. The tennis courts are excellent, unlike in most resorts. It has superb snorkelling & the Kudarah Thila Reserve is nearby for diving enthusiasts. Transfers: plane 25mins. $$

🏠 **Lily Beach** The island is long & fairly narrow, with bulbous beaches at each end. The house reef is just 10m from the shore, so snorkelling is excellent

& the diving is good. Closed for redevelopment. Transfers: plane 25mins.

🏠 **Maayafushi** (60 rooms) ☎ 6660588; 📠 6660568; 📧 maaya@dhivehinet.net.mv. Maayafushi is to the west of Bathala & should not be confused with the stylish Maafushivaru (Twin Island) further south. Maldivian-style rooms are fairly basic. Meals of fresh fish are a special feature. The island is small with fairly lush cover, & can seem a little crowded at times. The beaches are good & so is the house reef. The diving is the main attraction, & most of the usual water activities are available. The Maaya Thila marine area is practically a house feature. The island has been called Ruhindhifushi & Jamuyyaafushi in the past. Most guests come from Germany on FB packages. Transfers: plane 25mins. $ (FB)

🏠 **Machchafushi Island Resort** (74 rooms) ☎ 6686868 📠 6686869; 📧 machchafushi@dhivehinet.net.mv; www.machchafushi.com. Machchafushi was opened in 1993. The established vegetation, with a shady palm grove at one end of the island, is being helped along to increase cover. Upgrading is planned to feature split-level rooms on the beachfront as well as overwater suites & paradise villas, as well as a spa & swimming pools. Meals are buffets & this is an all-inclusive resort much favoured by Germans. The star attractions are the snorkelling & diving. The many offshore *thilas*, including the Kudarah Thila, together with the house reefs, provide some of the most exciting & varied diving in the Maldives. Transfers: plane 30mins. $$ (all-inclusive)

🏠 **Madoogali** (56 rooms) ☎ 6660611; 📠 6660554; 📧 madugali@dhivehinet.net.mv; www.skorpiontravel.com. Madoogali is on the western rim of Ari Atoll & is a long-established resort in the traditional Maldivian mould of coral stone cottages with *sataa* (screwpine weave) ceilings & simple fittings in a garden setting. The island has lots of shady thick greenery, with an obvious effort being made to enhance nature's gifts. The house reef is quite good for snorkelling, & the dive centre can provide trips into less-frequented waters. Nearly 50% of Madoogali's guests at any one time have been to the resort before. Italians form the majority, but other Europeans are discovering this well-run, beautiful island resort's attractions. Transfers: plane 20mins. $$

🏠 **Mirihi** (36 rooms) ☎ 6660500; 📠 6660501; 📧 info@mirihi.com; www.mirihi.com. Mirihi is a tiny (300m long by 70m wide) island in the southern central part of the atoll. Along the other shoreline are 30, thoroughly modern, overwater villas & some

have balconies overlooking each other. 3 are designed with families in mind. There are also some beach bungalows. The restaurant is the centre of island life; it is circular & built around a clump of bougainvillaea with alcove seating. Although the island has quite a lot of shade, it does not offer complete cover. The beaches are its star attraction, with 3 sides well endowed. The house reef is particularly gifted by nature & the dive centre is top class. There is a spa. A convivial atmosphere prevails in this resort, which happily combines a touch of the romantic with good diving. Most of the guests come from Germany & Austria. Transfers: speedboat 2hrs, plane 25mins. $$$

🏠 **Moofushi** (62 rooms) ☎ 6680517; 📠 6680509; 📧 moofushi@dhivehinet.net.mv; www.moofushi.com. Moofushi opened in 1990 & is on the western side of the atoll. Accommodation is in simple, thatched, concrete huts & in 17 overwater bungalows that have easy access to the reef. While meals are buffets or from a set menu designed to appeal to the resort's majority Italian guests, there is an à-la-carte restaurant. With the emphasis on relaxation rather than adrenalin activities, watersports are low-key. Reflecting the style of the resort, a note says: 'Staff consist of a perfectly integrated international community' which, in this case, means Asians & Italians. The island is small with plenty of vegetation & shade & an extensive lagoon with the house reef close to the shore. Beaches are good but limited. The snorkelling & diving offer chances to see big fish & explore the caves. Transfers: plane 25mins. $

🏠 **Nika Island Resort Kudafolhudhu** (37 rooms) ☎ 6660516; 📠 6660577; 📧 nika_htl@dhivehinet.net.mv; www.nikaisland.com. Nika Island Resort on Kudafolhudhu is a legend, not just for being a pioneer of high room rates, but for its unique transformation in 1983 of an uninhabited island into a Maldivian-style village. Timber & thatch overwater villas have been added to the 27 villas; each are set in a dedicated large garden with access from a sandy lane defined by coral walls, just like the roads in a fishing village island. Each villa is over 70m² in area & has rooms shaped like a shell, with coral stone décor & walls hung with timber objects, such as a *dhoni*'s polished rudder. 12 of the bungalows & the 2-bedroom suite have AC, while 14 have fans. Reception, coffee shop & the cocktail bar are at one end of the island with the restaurant at the other. Meals vary from buffet to grand table-d'hôte presentations. The island is well endowed by nature, with masses of trees in a canopy of green. A large banyan tree is a feature of the central area.

The beaches are small, seclusion for each villa created by vegetation. Guests are asked not to walk around the island's outer edge so that beach privacy is preserved. Those seeking some activity can swim & snorkel in & beyond the lagoon. Windsurfing, canoeing, tennis & badminton are included. Divers are not ignored either, with a long walkway direct to a large platform at the reef edge. The resort also offers overnight shark fishing, as well as visits to nearby uninhabited islands. The philosophy behind the creation of Nika is undeniably romantic, designed for the discerning of all nationalities. Transfers: plane 25mins. $$$$ (FB)

🏠 **Ranveli Village Villingilivaru** (56 rooms) ✎ 6680828; **f** 6680823; **e** sales@ranvelivillage.com; www.ranveli-maldives.com. Ranveli Village is on the island of Villingilivaru & is so called to reflect the island's golden sands which in Dhivehi could be rendered as 'ranveli'. It opened in 1991 & the accommodation is reminiscent of the rather austere style in vogue then, although thatch roofs soften the lines. There are 56 beach-facing superior rooms, some in 2-storey blocks which, because the island is small, sometimes seem to overwhelm the vegetation, although there are abundant coconut palms. Its beaches are very narrow in the main, but sand has been relocated to provide an excellent beach at one end. The lagoon is wide & shallow & the house reef is very close; snorkelling is excellent. Fishing trips are popular & there are a number of uninhabited islands nearby providing excursion destinations. There is a large overwater pier-style complex for eating & entertainment, dedicated to the demands of the resort's exclusively Italian clientele. Transfers: plane 25mins. $ (FB)

🏠 **Sun Island Nalaguraidhoo** (350 rooms) ✎ 6680088; **f** 6680099; **e** info@sun-island.com.mv; www.sun-island.com; www.villahotels.com. Sun Island, set on Nalaguraidhoo Island near to Holiday Island, has been transformed by the same owner (Villa Hotels). With so many rooms, it is fortunate that the island is large (1.6km long, 380m wide) & luxuriant. The beaches are wide & broad for the most part, as is the vast lagoon. The philosophy of the developers seems to be to show that every convenience can be found in the Maldives. There are bicycles for hire & even golf buggies to transport visitors around on mini roads. There is a putting green, too. Everything about the rooms is state of the art. There are 72 overwater villas, of which 4 are 'presidential', on concrete pillars over the lagoon. There are numerous bars (10 at the last count) & 5 different restaurants: Thai, Italian, Japanese, seafood & grills.

Every conceivable facility & activity has been provided, night & day. Snorkellers, however, may find the lagoon is not ideal. Diving is enthusiastically run & the sites nearby are interesting. With composition roofs to the buildings & a small-town atmosphere, Sun Island is probably as far from a traditional Maldivian resort as it is possible to find. It is the attention to detail & the variety, that make it a popular choice for all nationalities. Transfers: speedboat 2hrs 30mins, plane 35mins. $ (HB)

🏠 **Thudufushi Island Resort** (49 rooms) ✎ 6680583; **f** 6640515; **e** info.thudufushi@planhotel.com; www.planhotel.com. Beach & garden bungalows provide the accommodation on this small picture-postcard island with luxuriant vegetation, palm trees & super beaches. Composition roofs & screwpine-weave ceilings with tiled floors & half-open-air bathrooms set the character of this basic, all-inclusive holiday resort. Buffets, lots of animation, a free island excursion & some watersports. The snorkelling is some of the best in the area & there are some exciting dive sites nearby as the island is almost completely surrounded by a superb house reef. Exclusively marketed in Italy. Transfers: plane 25mins. $$ (all-inclusive)

🏠 **Twin Island Maafushivaru** (47 rooms) ✎ 6680596; **f** 6680524; **e** maafushivaaru@tclub.com; www.tclub.com. Maafushivaru is called **Twin Island** because it has a sister isle; it opened in 1990. The island is semicircular & small. It has very good broad beaches protected by fairly inconspicuous walls further out. The island is quite built-up with clusters of houses (with blue roofs), but this resolves into an orderly resort with muted luxury. Beachfront cottages have style & spaciousness & there are also 10 semi-detached houses of white with blue roofs built on pillars over the water. All meals are buffet-style with lots of Italian dishes. Near the reception area is a stage theatre. The reef is wonderful for variety & accessibility. The diving is also excellent, although the resort does not pitch itself towards diving. Fishing is popular, though. This is a resort sold entirely to Italian clients. Transfers: speedboat 2hrs 30mins. $$ (all-inclusive)

🏠 **Vakarufalhi** (50 rooms) ✎ 6680004; **f** 6680007; **e** reservations@vakaru.com; www.vakaru.com. From the sea, Vakarufalhi looks like an archetypal tropical island retreat. The thatched roofs of the buildings peep out from under the coconut palms, which cluster & shade the island. It is fringed with glistening white sand & has a long jetty as its entrance. There are 42 detached cabana-style rooms & 8 family-style rooms with inter-connecting doors. The bar doubles as a coffee shop & there is 1 restaurant. The lagoon & house reef offer superb snorkelling, but windsurfers & other watersports enthusiasts need to wait for high tide for their activities. With so many exciting dive sites nearby, the diving is excellent, although the resort is, surprisingly, not a dive-focused place. Management from 2008 is by the group operating the Mount Lavinia Hotel in Sri Lanka. Transfers: plane 25mins plus *dhoni* ride 30mins. $$

⌂ **Velidhu** (100 rooms) ☏ 6660551, in Male' 3313738; f 6660630; e velidhu@dhivehinet.net.mv; www.velidhoo.com.mv. Velidhu is towards the northern centre of the atoll & began as Avi Island. It was improved beyond recognition & run successfully for many years by the Sri Lankan hotel group, John Keells. However, it was scheduled to change hands in March 2008. There were garden & beach rooms & 20 suites in 10 cottages over the lagoon. The lagoon is sheltered & extensive, with good diving sites to the east & west. Transfers: plane 25mins. $$

⌂ **Veligandu** (74 rooms) ☏ 6660519; f 6660648; e reservations@veliganduisland.com; www.veliganduisland.com. Veligandu began operations in 1984 with the newest version opening in Dec 2007. It has plenty of jacuzzis: 54 water villas & 10 beach villas each with its own jacuzzi as well as 10 basic water villas. Rooms are thatched tropical style & have king-size beds, wood floors & a patio or sun deck, with steps to the lagoon. There is a swimming pool with a wooden deck, too. It's a rectangular island, not quite as lush as other islands, but with a great L-shape spit of sand protruding into a shallow lagoon. The fabulous sands & beaches are a prime feature, ideal for sunbathing (there are *cadjan* parasols) & novice swimmers. With such excellent beaches, the resort attracts those in search of an easy-going holiday. Recreational activities are not the main incentives, although there is windsurfing & canoeing & visits to neighbouring Rasdhoo village island. There is an all-inclusive option available upon checking-in as an add-on to the FB room rate. Transfers: plane 20mins. $$–$$$ (FB)

⌂ **Vilamendhoo Island Resort** (141 rooms) ☏ 6680638; f 6 6680639; e sales-vilamendhoo@ pch.com.mv; www.vilamendhoomaldives.com. This resort is winning rave reviews from its guests, even from those who do not usually like the 'all-inclusive' concept, since the choice of food is so good. All meals are buffets. The resort promotes itself as

having rooms in the style of 'classic, early 1980s resorts' thereby cannily appealing to those who want a good old-fashioned holiday without the frills of designer-inspired interiors. There are 131 beach bungalows with an extra 10 deluxe ones. Guests from many nationalities bond easily, especially after meeting in the bar at 16.00 to watch the sunset. The island itself is large with a lushness of vegetation that smaller islands don't have. There is a beautiful sandbank at the western end, but around much of the resort the beaches are narrow. The resort boasts 'superb recreational facilities: parasailing, waterskiing & scuba diving', which is pretty accurate. The house reef is good for snorkellers & accessed easily via channels. Some of the corals here have escaped the bleaching & the nearby *thilas* are interesting, making it one of the best areas within Ari Atoll. Vilamendhoo is constantly evolving & so are its visitors. Transfers: plane 25mins. $ (all-inclusive)

⌂ **W Retreat & Spa Maldives Fesdu** (78 private retreats) ☏ 6662222; f 6662200; e wmaldives.welcome@whotels,com; www.whotels.com/maldives. Built on what was formerly the picturesque island retreat of Fesdu, this resort amazingly contrives to make guests forget they are on an island; the beach & the sea become incidental to the fervour of holiday bliss. This is inspired by thatched retreats (much more than rooms) with elaborate interiors & all with plunge pools. The majority (46) are in the overwater Ocean Oasis category with 146m² including lounge, by jetties fanning out a long way from the island into the lagoon. On the island there are 22 Beach Oasis rooms of 188m² area with BBQ as well as lounge. 2 retreats have private swimming pools. In-villa dining is popular & there are 2 fine-dining restaurants (1 specialises in caviar & oysters) & 1 with delectable buffets, as well 3 bars including an underground one dedicated to vodkas served in glasses made of ice. There are help-yourself soft drinks & ice-cream stations at strategic points around the 10-acre island. The spa is overwater. The island is centred in the northern half of Ari Atoll & originally opened in 1982. Eco diving & watersports are available for guests who can tear themselves away from self-indulgence in keeping with the W theme of 'Whatever you want, whenever you want it — that's W'. Transfers: plane 25mins. $$$$

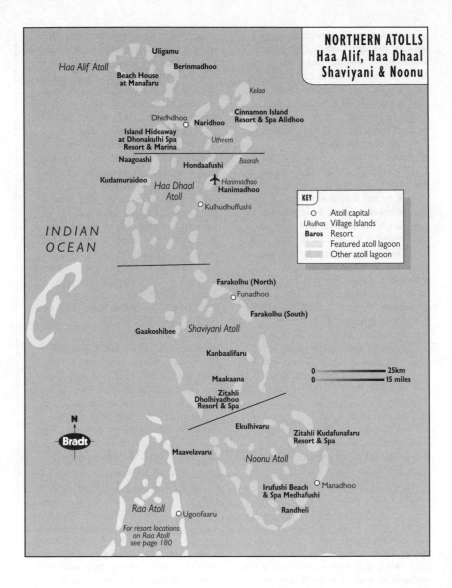

Uligamu

Haa Alif Atoll

Berinmadhoo

Beach House
at Manafaru

Kelaa

Dhidhdhoo   Cinnamon Island
Naridhoo   Resort & Spa Alidhoo

Island Hideaway
at Dhonakulhi Spa   *Utheem*
Resort & Marina

Naagoashi   *Baarah*

Hondaafushi

Kudamuraidoo   *Haa Dhaal*   ✈ *Hanimadhoo*
Atoll   **Hanimadhoo**

Kulhudhuffushi

INDIAN
OCEAN

KEY

○	Atoll capital
Ukulhas	Village Islands
Baros	Resort
	Featured atoll lagoon
	Other atoll lagoon

Farakolhu (North)
Funadhoo

Farakolhu (South)

Gaakoshibee   *Shaviyani Atoll*

Kanbaalifaru

0 ━━━━━━━ 25km
0 ━━━━━━━ 15 miles

Maakaana

Zitahli
Dholhiyadhoo
Resort & Spa

N   Ekulhivaru

Bradt   Zitahli Kudafunafaru
Resort & Spa

Maavelavaru   *Noonu Atoll*

Irufushi Beach   ○ Manadhoo
& Spa Medhafushi

Raa Atoll   Ugoofaaru   Randheli

*For resort locations
on Raa Atoll
see page 180*

8

Northern Atolls

RESORTS ON NORTHERN ATOLLS

Most of the resorts in the northern and southern atolls are newly developed, or still under construction. The thrust of the government's plan to expand tourism throughout the archipelago will take visitors to areas they were not previously allowed to visit, bringing benefits directly to those areas as well as expanding the tourist horizon. The decision to convert far-flung uninhabited islands into tourist resorts is a recent one so, at press time, many of the 40 or so resorts expected to be functioning in 2010 are still on the drawing board or at the negotiating table, as Maldivians lucky enough to have secured a lease are looking for investors. Two government corporations, Maldives Tourism Development Corporation (MTDC) and Airport Investments Maldives Pvt Ltd (AIM), are undertaking resort and hotel projects parallel to private-sector developments. A review of the resorts open at press time and of those planned appears below.

A HAA ALIF (NORTH THILADHUNMATHI) The northernmost island in the Maldives is **Thuraakanu** (A-1), one of the 16 inhabited islands of this atoll. As an administrative unit, the atoll consists of the whole of the natural atoll of Ihavandhippolhu and the northern part of Thiladhunmathi, separated from it by the Gallandu Channel. The atoll is 600km southwest of India. The area is 30km north to south and 43km east to west.

The capital was **Dhidhdhoo** (A-10) from 1958 to 1977 and again from 1980. The people were renowned for being adept at making sails from coconut leaves. **Utheemu** (A-14) is the birthplace of Sultan Mohamed Thakurufaanu; a memorial centre with a hall and library and an annexed school was opened here in 1986. The wooden house where he lived in the 16th century is beautifully preserved. Mat weaving is done and the bamboo grown there is in demand for fishing rods.

There was a British base from 1934 until the end of World War II at **Kelaa** (A-8), which is also where yams are grown and *cadjan* made. It is estimated that 364ha in the atoll could be used for agriculture; fishing is the main industry. One island, **Huvarafushi** (A-6), the atoll's capital from 1977 to 1980, thrives on fish processing for export. Another island, **Baarah** (A-16), is said to have people showing evidence of Portuguese ancestry.

There is a regional airport on the inhabited island of **Hanimadhoo** in the next atoll. This serves the resorts in the area with speedboat transfers from a jetty close to the airport. The flight to Hanimadhoo from Male' takes about 50 minutes, the speedboat transfer from 20 minutes.

Resorts

⌂ **Beach House at Manafaru** (68 rooms)
📞 6500400; f 6500444; e pr.maldives@beachhousecollection.com;

www.beachhousecollection.com. Opened in Dec 2007 on a 35-acre island of which only 4 acres have been utilised for the resort, leaving the rest wild.

With glass-panelled floors, infinity plunge pools & sun decks leading straight out to sea, 38 of the villas are built over water. Beachfront villas have open-air rain showers & lounge cabanas by the lagoon. Each villa & suite has a private pool, complete privacy & 'a personal butler to pre-empt & exceed expectations'. There are 3 restaurants, I over water, as well as a spa whose 10 treatment rooms, for coconut oil with white sea salt & sand massages, are linked by footbridges through the undergrowth. As well as a dive centre, the resort, according to its publicity, boasts a 'sorbet butler', bungee trampolines & a 'Gentlemen's retreat' with golf simulator & game consoles. The resort is in the centre of Ihavandhippolhu Atoll, across the Gallandhoo Channel from the airport. Transfers: plane 55mins, plus speedboat. $$$$

🏠 **Berinmadhoo** Planned. A 100-bedroom hotel on this inhabited island on the eastern rim of the small Ihavandhippolhu Atoll.

🏠 **Cinnamon Island Resort & Spa Alidhoo** (100 rooms) ⚊ 6501111; f 6501234; e fom.alidhoo@cinnamonhotels.com.mv; www.cinnamonhotels.com. A round, newly developed island of 35 acres that opened as a resort in late 2007. Although buggies are available, walking anywhere on the island is easy & pleasant in the lush vegetation. Its 100 rooms (served by butlers) are on the periphery either on the beach or offshore in 45 overwater villas, 7 of which are duplex with a large parlour & upstairs bedroom. The villas over the sea have interiors painted a glorious green, to match the sea, while the beach villas are decorated with hues reflecting the golden sand. The beach villa interiors are spacious with an entrance hall, a bedroom more like a homely apt than a hotel room, & an amazing bathroom with twin washbasins, twin hand showers & a central rain shower. There is a jacuzzi tub on the wooden deck by the sea. The island has a reputation for shifting sands with the beach changing sides at different times of the year. Since there are free snorkelling & sand-bank safaris by boat every day, & a huge swimming pool, it makes little difference when the beach pops around to the other side of the island. Meals are taken as buffets in the jungly Village Restaurant & there is a speciality restaurant too as well as a disco. A nice touch: b/fast is served in the villas 24hrs a day. Alidhoo's tropical vegetation has remained intact & even the dive centre, which is only 5 paces from the beach, is out of sight of the sea. The spa is under a banyan tree. Part of the Sri Lankan John Keells hotel group, this is a real value-for-money

resort. Transfers: plane 55mins, plus speedboat 15mins. $$–$$$$

🏠 **Island Hideaway at Dhonakulhi Spa Resort & Marina** (43 villas) ⚊ 6501515, 6501616; e sales@island-hideway.com; www.island-hideaway.com. Opened in Aug 2005, this was the 1st ultra-luxury resort to be created so far away from the capital & the 1st to capitalise on its exclusivity. Despite being 1.4km long, & with a beach around it that is 3.2km long, under 5% of the island has been developed. This preserves privacy since the 43 guest villas are scattered around the island, with a maze of paths linking them. (Bicycles are available & buggies can be summoned so guests don't have to hike to the restaurants.) The variety of accommodation means there is something for everyone. Natural finishes, finely grained timber (inc Merbau, teak & coconut), satin-finished linen & oversized cushions set the sophisticated tone; & every villa has a dedicated butler who meets guests at the airport, tends them exclusively throughout the stay & escorts them back when the time comes, unfortunately, to leave the resort & return to normal life. There are 7 Funa Pavilions (176m²) on the beachfront, 7 rustic Raamba Retreats (385m²), 2 spa villas built over the lagoon close to the island's spa & with extra wide daybeds & sun loungers. The majority of the villas (20) are on the beach & are called Dhonakuulhi Residences & have jacuzzi splash pools. The 5 Jasmine Garden Villas are also on the beach & have their own infinity swimming pools. There are also 2 Hideaway Palaces with several infinity swimming pools. The finesse of the accommodation is matched by fine cuisine either served in the restaurants (Gaafushi serving Asian delicacies is over water, Matheefaru for international & grills by the beach) or in guest villas. The Meeru Bar hosts the largest malt whisky collection in the Indian Ocean.

There are 25 berths, with full bunkering facilities, for visiting yachts. The diving is to newly discovered sites, there is a kids' club for children to be left in safety & with over 200 staff motivated by the slogan of 'The Answer is Yes, what is the question?' hiding away at Island Hideaway is a chance to relish tropical isolation in style. Transfers: plane 55mins then speedboat 15mins. $$$$–$$$$$

🏠 **Naridhoo** Planned as a 50-bedroom resort. When open this will form the apex of a triangle of resorts (the others being Island Hideaway & Alidhoo) within 15mins or so by speedboat from the airport at Hanimadhoo.

🏠 **Uligamu** An MTDC project planned as a 50-bedroom city hotel. This inhabited island in the natural atoll of Ihavandhippolhu has a busy harbour & the construction of a so-called city hotel is in anticipation of both local & visitor demand. This will be the northernmost hotel in the archipelago (& thus the closest to India about 600km away).

B HAA DHAAL (SOUTH THILADHUNMATHI) One of the highest islands in the Maldives, Faridhoo (B-1), about 2.5m above sea level, is in this atoll. It is difficult to land there and its population is not much more than 100. The administrative atoll is part of the natural atoll of Thiladhunmathi and includes the small Makunudhoo Atoll lying to its south. There are 17 inhabited islands. The total area is 38km north to south and 47km east to west. The former capital is Nolhivaranfaru (B-7), which is 285km from Male'. *Cadjan* is produced here and the island has a good anchorage.

There are an estimated 344ha of land suitable for agriculture, and the island of Vaikaradhoo (B-15) specialises in agricultural produce. According to Mohamed Farook's *The Fascinating Maldives*, the inhabitants of Kulhudhuffushi (the capital, B-12) are renowned throughout the Maldives as being strong and hard-working. The Northern Regional Hospital and the Northern Secondary School, opened in 1998, are here. The island is one of the most developed and benefits from money sent by islanders working in Male' or as seamen on foreign vessels. Toddy is plentiful in Kuburudhoo (B-11), where landing is difficult, in Kumundhoo (B-13), which has some ruins about which little is known, and in Maavaidhoo (B-16).

Resorts

🏠 **Hanimadhoo** (B-3) A 100-bedroom regional airport hotel is planned for this inhabited island in the north of the atoll. This is an island already used to visitors & has administration buildings, roads & cars & a gentle, small-town atmosphere. There is a neat airport served by planes of Island Aviation & TMA & the flying time from Male' to the airport is around 50mins for the 250km distance. The airport has a refreshing charm after the bustle of the international airport at Male'. There is a short walk across the tarmac to the single-storey terminal building which has a small hall where luggage is unloaded from a trolley. Outside the doors the representatives of the resorts in the area wait with name boards for their passengers. They are then taken by car for the 5min ride to the other side of the island to the small jetty where speedboats (or chartered safari live-aboard boats) are waiting.

Departure from the airport involves checking-in at a small counter, & being weighed & then going out again to wait in the small café selling soft drinks & local snacks which is across the road. A few mins before departure, passengers are collected & re-enter the building to undergo a friendly search before being allowed to board the aircraft. With the opening of new resorts in the atoll, including the building of an airport hotel with all facilities on Hanimadhoo, the laid-back atmosphere of being a holiday pioneer enjoying frontier flying will surely become more hectic.

🏠 **Hondaafushi** Planned as a 100-bedroom resort with 25 water suites, & 75 beach suites & a golf course. This is the closest uninhabited island to the airport.

🏠 **Kudamuraidoo** Planned as a 125-bedroom resort. Tucked just inside the western rim of the atoll, reached by crossing the interior lagoon by speedboat from the Hanimadhoo airport.

🏠 **Naagoashi** An MTDC project planned as a 300-bedroom resort. In the southern part of the atoll, on the western rim, this is a long island with the western end known as Bodunaagoashi & the eastern end as Kudanaagoshi. It is a little isolated with only uninhabited islands for neighbours.

C SHAVIYANI (NORTH MILADHUNMADULU) The island of Narudhoo (C-8) in this atoll is a picturesque one because of its inland lakes. The atoll is geographically part of Thiladhunmathi Atoll and includes 15 inhabited islands, but there are at present only planned and developing resorts. It is 50km from north to south and 42km east to west. The capital since 1968 is Funadhoo (C-15, formerly known as Farukolhufunadhoo), which is 228km from Male' and has a good harbour.

Utheemu is small, hard to find on a map of the Maldives, but from this island came one of the greatest heroes the Indian Ocean has ever known. In 1573 Portuguese invaders were on the verge of putting to death all Maldivians who refused to renounce Islam and become Christians. On the fateful night before the planned mass execution, a man from Utheemu, Mohamed Thakurufaanu, sailed secretly into Male', leading a band of freedom fighters. He shot the Portuguese tyrant who was governor, routed the occupying forces and restored the islands to Islam and independence.

Facts passed down by word of mouth over four-and-a-quarter centuries have become embroidered by different narrators, but there is no gainsaying the triumph of this dedicated man from Utheemu. In the Maldives, he is a national hero and, because of his respect for religion, he continues to be held in the highest esteem. For Maldivians, a visit to Utheemu has the awe of a pilgrimage. For foreigners, this small northern island is a quiet contrast in a country more often regarded as one glorious holiday resort.

Landing at Utheemu is not easy. I arrived by launch and had to wait for a ladder to be brought so I could clamber down it onto the beach instead of wading ashore. Tourists come by safari boat or by *dhoni* from the nearest airport (on Hanimadhoo) or from their new holiday resorts in the northern atolls. There are helpful government-licensed guides on hand to explain the history of the island and to talk about the artefacts on display. There has been constant erosion of the island over the years so it is now much smaller than it was in the 16th century. At that time, Mohamed Thakurufaanu and his two brothers, Ali and Hassan, were the scions of a well-respected family. The graves of his grandfather and father, an island chief, are still to be seen at the abandoned mosque in what is now the uninhabited part of the island.

The graves of men in the Maldives are marked with a pointed headstone, those of women with a rounded one. There were fears that the Portuguese, angry with Mohamed and his brothers for their prolonged guerrilla activities, would try to disturb the grave of their father. To mislead them a rounded headstone was placed on it so

The main fishing island is Komadhoo (C-13) but the atoll is mainly agricultural, producing various vegetables. Maakadoodhoo (C-9), known for its production of *jaggery* (coconut-palm candy), is the most heavily populated of the islands. On the island of Kaditheemu (C-1), a door frame of the main mosque contains the oldest-known written Thaana script and gives the date the roof was put on the mosque as more than 500 years ago.

Feevah (C-5) is known for *jaggery* production, as are other islands in this atoll, and has a mosque, which was built at the end of the 17th century. Severe storms struck the islands of this atoll in 1812 and 1821. The now-uninhabited island of Nilandhoo is where the vessel *Kalhuoffummi*, used by the Thakurufaanu brothers in the guerrilla-style liberation battle against the Portuguese, was hidden in a creek (*koaru*).

Resorts

⌂ **Gaakoshibee** Planned as a 100-bedroom resort. Of the resorts planned for this atoll, only this one is on the western rim, the furthest from the proposed airport at the other side of the atoll.

⌂ **Farakolhu (North)** An AIM project for a 100-bedroom tourist resort. This will be built on the uninhabited island of Farakolhu, which is north of the inhabited capital island of Farukolhufunadhoo.

⌂ **Farukolhu (South)** An AIM project for a 100-bedroom airport & transit hotel. The airport to be built here will serve the 5 new resorts in the atoll.

⌂ **Kanbaalifaru** Planned as a 100-bedroom resort. This resort will be the closest to the new airport.

⌂ **Maakaana** (35 rooms) www.maakanaa.com (under construction at press time). Created on the tiny island of Vagaru in the lower centre of the outsiders would think it was a woman's grave. A pointed headstone was buried below the round one.

The house where this hero of the Maldives used to live is well preserved, and open to visitors (fee payable). It is a profound experience to visit because it is constructed in traditional style, while most houses in the Maldives are simple coral cottages or new buildings of cement blocks. It is known as a palace since Mohamed Thakurufaanu became sultan, founding a dynasty that endured for 121 years. It stands in a compound of buildings surrounded by a low white wall from which white flags placed by worshippers can be seen fluttering outside its veranda. This is low-roofed; wooden posts, whose base is painted bright blue, support the overhang.

The interior of the palace is hung with white flags and contains relics of the past, including wooden sandals of different eras. Items of furniture, such as antique beds and large wooden chests, are preserved for their connection with the hero who lived there. A modern monument has been built on the other side of the vast, sand-covered open area that forms Utheemu's public square. This is the Bodu Thakurufaanu Memorial Centre and serves as a place of study for scholars, as well as having a library devoted to religious and historical books on the Maldives.

There is an air of tranquillity about Utheemu. Like many of the inhabited islands, there seems to be very little happening by day, because the men are either fishing or have migrated to holiday resorts or Male' for work, and the women stay in their homes out of the sun.

It is possible to wander freely around Utheemu, imagining how the island must have been over 425 years ago. Legend has it that, as a boy, Mohamed Thakurufaanu would go to the beach and trap birds with his bare hands. He would talk softly to them, warning them to be more careful and not let themselves be so trusting as to get caught. Then he freed them. He was regarded as a romantic dreamer but, after his father sent him to India to study, he returned as a brilliant seaman and an inspiring natural leader.

To visit Utheemu is to experience a link with history that makes time disappear.

atoll, this resort is being developed by the innovators (Per Aquum) behind the successful spa resort of Huvafenfushi in Male' Atoll. It offers land & water villas with private plunge pools. According to Per Aquum, 'each villa will evoke the graceful shape of the native Maakanaa bird with naturally modern furnishings & hip, state-of-the-art design & technology throughout. 3 venues for dining will offer a vast range of options from teppanyaki, cocktails, live music, seafood, pizzas, tapas & destination dining of the guests' choice. Among the many activities, guests will be able to enjoy sandbank snorkelling, a young adventurers' zone, morning yoga, spa treatments at Lime, watersports & diving.' Transfers: plane 45mins. $$$$–$$$$$

🏠 **Zitahli Dholhiyadhoo Resort & Spa** (100 rooms) ➘ 3316131; f 3341885; e reservation@ zitahlidholhiyadhoo.com; www.zitahlidholhiyadhoo.com. A new resort with 56 deluxe beach & 44 stand-alone Aqua water suites of several different types, each with an individual pool. 3 restaurants with fine food, including 1 featuring Asian fusion cuisine, & a cigar lounge & library as well as a champagne & wine bar. This island is crescent shaped. 2km from tip to tip & 500m at its widest. Open 2008. Transfers: plane 55mins. $$$$

D NOONU (SOUTH MILADHUNMADULU) In this atoll the island of Kedhikulhudhoo (D-3) has 37ha of undulating land suitable for millet cultivation, out of an atoll total of 116ha. The atoll forms the southern end of the Thiladhunmathi geographical atoll. There are 14 inhabited islands, and almost 60 uninhabited ones. The atoll is 35km north to south and 37km east to west. Its capital is Manadhoo (D-12), which is a fishing island and was affected by a big storm in 1955, as were other islands in the atoll. It is 180km from Male'.

Landhoo (D-7) is a source of yams and timber, and has an ancient mound. Lhohi (D-9) has an 18th-century mosque. At Magoodhoo (D-11) there are some old shade trees and much of the island is jungly. Holhudhoo (D-13) and Velidhoo (D-15) are the most populated, with over 1,000 inhabitants in each. The Noonu Atoll Education Centre is at Velidhoo and safari boats are made and repaired on the island. Five resorts are in the planning stage for this atoll.

Resorts

⌂ **Ekulhivaru** An MTDC project for a 90-bedroom resort.

⌂ **Irufushi Beach & Spa Resort Medhafushi** (100 rooms) ⊐ 6560591; f 6560592; e info@irufushi.com; www.irufushi.com. On the island of Medhafushi set in 210,000m² of tropical lushness, this new resort has oval-shaped beach villas with conical thatched roofs, 5 of which have pools in their courtyards. There are also 45 water villas, 35 jacuzzi water villas & 5 water suites with private pool. The main bar is the hub of the island with beach bars & a coffee shop, plus a main restaurant, a speciality one & a grill. The Sun Spa has 15 treatment pavilions & there is a gym, a kids' club with its own pool &, for evening entertainment, a karaoke corner. Open 2008. Transfer: plane 45mins. $$

⌂ **Maavelavaru** A 50-bedroom resort is planned on this large island on the western rim of the atoll.

⌂ **Randheli** (50 rooms) With 9 beach suites & 41 water suites curving out in spurs from the half-moon-shape island in the interior of the atoll. Under development.

⌂ **Zitahli Kudafunafaru Resort & Spa** (50 rooms) One of the new Zitahli properties (see above). The island is 1km long & 300m wide with 20 overland & 30 overwater villas & a spa with 6 treatment rooms. Transfers: plane 45mins.

E RAA (NORTH MAALHOSMADULU)

E RAA (NORTH MAALHOSMADULU) The chain of islands opens into a garland with this atoll, which lies to the west of and parallel to its neighbours Noonu and Lhaviyani atolls. It contains one of the most densely populated islands, Kadholhudhoo (E-8), overcrowded because of its proximity to the bountiful western sea-fishing grounds. There are 17 inhabited islands. A new inhabited island, called Hulhudhuffaaru, was declared officially inhabited in 1995. It had been settled by people from two other islands in the atoll, Ugulu (E-6) and Gaaudoodhoo (E-5). North to south, the atoll (which actually consists of two natural atolls) measures 63km, with 26km east to west. The capital, Ugoofaaru (E-7), is 174km from Male'. There is a regional hospital there.

The northernmost inhabited island, in its own atoll, is Alifushi (E-1), famous for the government boatbuilding yard, opened there because of the skill of the atoll's carpenters and boat builders. Although some agricultural land use is apparent – there is said to be 234ha suitable for cultivation – fishing brings prosperity to the islands, and Raa is among the best atolls for fishing. Rasgetheemu (E-3) on the eastern side is where, according to legend, an exiled Sinhalese princess and her husband are said to have landed (see *History*, page 18). Raa is one of the more interesting atolls because of its fishing and boatbuilding industries.

Resorts

⌂ **Adaaran Select Meedhupparu** (215 rooms) ⊐ 6587700; f 6585500; e res@meedhupparu.com.mv, info@adaaran.com; www.meedhupparu.com, www.meedhupparu.com. Run to the standards of the Sri Lankan hotel group Aitken Spence, whose resorts in the Maldives are branded as Adaaran, this resort & its associate Water Villas (see below) has been created on a large island (43 acres) catering for over 400 guests. Only 16% of the island has been built on to preserve the jungly atmosphere &, since it was opened in 2000, the C-shape clusters of rooms built around the island have had time to blend in with the natural environment. Meals are buffets in the main restaurant, since all guests are on HB, FB or all-inclusive packages. There is a fine-dining restaurant & a disco bar, a swim-up bar by the swimming pool, & a grill bar. The day's activities are carefully programmed; this is an active resort with animators, watersports & dive centre & even (rare in Maldivian resorts) a hairdressing salon. $$

⌂ Adaaran Water Villas Meedhupparu (20 rooms) ✆ 6580126; **f** 6580127; **e** watervillas@ meedhupparu.com.mv; www.thewatervillas.com. The exclusive part of Meedhupparu, sharing all the facilities & management, but restricted to 20 overwater villas near the forested shore. They are bright with timber floors & walls, teak furniture & a sun deck with jacuzzi, daybed & glass fish-viewing panel. Another exclusive part of the island is dedicated to an **Ayurveda Village** (www.ayurvedamaldives) with its own restaurant & treatment rooms. This specialises in the herbal & oil therapy practised in Sri Lanka. Transfers:, plane 45mins. $$$

⌂ Lundhufushi Planned as a 20-bedroom resort. This will be the closest resort to Ugoofaru, the capital.

⌂ Maanenfushi Planned as a 75-bedroom resort on this island in the north-central part of Raa Atoll.

F BAA (SOUTH MAALHOSMADULU) Baa Atoll is interesting because of its various handicrafts and also through its proximity to the capital, which gives its residential islands a more developed look. It is separated from Raa Atoll by the Moresby Channel, and its neighbour across the sea to the south is Ari Atoll. There are 13 inhabited islands. The atoll is 53km long and 39km east to west. The capital, Eydhafushi (F-10), some 119km from Male', is a thriving town with a new harbour, and is one of the most developed islands in all the atolls. The atoll consists of the smaller half of the geographical Maalhosmadulu Atoll and the small Goidhoo-Falhu (Horsburgh) Atoll.

There is not much organised agriculture, with only 77ha of arable land. The uninhabited island of Maarikilu has 24ha available for cultivation; there is the ruin of a mosque on it. Kihaadhoo (F-4) has a tradition of weaving from coconut leaves and the weaving of *feyli* (a long wraparound skirt for women) was practised in Eydhafushi. The 19th-century mosque here has been renovated to modern standards for the needs of this heavily populated island. Thulhaadhoo (F-12) is famed for lacquerwork, although fishing is its main industry, as it is on the islands of Kendhoo (F-3) and Dharavandhoo (F-8), and the mainstay of the atoll. Its small southern atoll with the three inhabited islands of Fulhadhoo (F-14), Fehendhoo (F-15) and Goidhoo (F-16) played its part in Maldives' history, accommodating people exiled from Male' in 1962. The *Corbin* was shipwrecked on Fulhadhoo in 1602 with French explorer François Pyrard on board. Goidhoo's claim to fame is

---

NEWS FROM EYDHAFUSHI

Eydhafushi, capital of Baa Atoll, has around 2,000 inhabitants and is one of the main fishing islands in Maldives. The Baa Atoll Education Centre on it was the first one to be established in Maldives, 50 years ago. It teaches grades one through 12 and is one of the schools that was selected for UNESCO's Small Islands Voice Youth Forum. Small Islands Voice (SIV) activities started in Maldives in June 2003 (www.unesco.org and follow Small Islands Voice links).

The main function of the SIV committee is to discuss and organise activities concerning current environmental, developmental and social issues. On Eydhafushi, a particular concern is the management and disposal of waste. This was discussed at a meeting in February 2004. The committee were keen to build a waste dump site on the island, and had prepared an outline and cost estimate. However, the Environment Ministry felt that a waste characterisation survey should first be carried out; with the support of the Ministry, the students of the education centre undertook this in their homes and on the island reef and lagoon.

Also under the SIV scheme, computer equipment and furniture were provided to three Maldives schools (including the Baa Atoll Education Centre) in 2004, and a schools' poster competition on destructive fishing practices and marine pollution was organised.

NORTHERN ATOLLS
Raa, Baa & Lhaviyani

Shaviyani Atoll

Noonu Atoll

Maanenfushi

Manadhoo

N

Raa Atoll

Lundhufushi

Ugoofaaru

0 — 20km
0 — 10 miles

Kuredu Island Resort
Keredu Express — Kanuhura

Komandoo
Island Resort

Adaaran Select Meedhupparu/
Adaaran Water Villas/
Ayurveda Village

Fushifaru Kandu
Palm Beach Island
Madhiriguraidhoo

Naifaru

Lhaviyani Atoll

Kanifushi

Hudhufushi

Kihavah Huravalhi

Four Seasons at
Landaa Giraavaru

Reethi Beach Fonimagoodhoo

Baa Atoll

Kihaadhuffaru Fonimagoodhoo

Royal Island Horubadhoo
Dhigali Haa

Soneva Fushi Kunfunadhoo

Coco Palm
Resort
Dhunikolhu

INDIAN OCEAN

Eydhafushi

KEY

O	Atoll capital
Baros	Resort
	Protected marine area
	Dive area
	Shallow lagoon
	Deep lagoon

the landing of nearly four million flying fish on it in 1963. A 1m-high mound in the centre of the island has never been investigated.

Resorts There are six resorts in Baa Atoll, with one other planned for the future.

⌂ **Coco Palm Resort Dhunikolhu** (98 rooms)
☎ 6600011; f 6600022; e dhunikolhu@
cocopalm.com.mv; www.cocopalm.com. In the southwest corner of the atoll, Coco Palm Resort is on the Dhunikolhu Island. It features beach & deluxe villas & lagoon villas & suites with local-style furnishings of wood, rattan & cotton; some have open-air garden bathrooms, splash pools with private terrace & sunken & spa baths. A couple of restaurants & bars provide top-quality international or seafood menus. There is a spa built over the lagoon which has shallow areas & a house reef quite close on the other side. Swimming is good & snorkelling off the reef is fine for novices, but diving is not big here although there is a professional dive centre. The resort's emphasis is on romance, with

champagne b/fasts & sunset cocktails on isolated sandbanks. One unusual trip is for couples to have a BBQ dinner on an uninhabited island close by & to be left there overnight. Transfers: plane 30mins.
$$$–$$$$

⌂ **Four Seasons Resort at Landaa Giraavaru** (102 rooms) ☎ 6600888; f 6600800;
e reservations.maldives@fourseasons.com; www.fourseasons.com. The northernmost resort in Baa Atoll, this is unique in its design. With enough space (44 acres) to spread out, a Maldivian-style village has been created with thatched beach & water bungalows & villas. Permission was received from the government to recycle coral used from a redevelopment project & this has been incorporated into external walls. Particularly striking are the coral

walls around each compound, complete with turquoise entrance gate, just like traditional village island properties. The accommodation includes beach bungalows & beach villas, each with plunge or lap pool & some have outdoor dining pavilions. 10 of the 38 overwater villas also have a pool. The elegant accommodation is complemented by 4 fine-dining restaurants & 3 bars. There is a Spa & Ayurvedic Retreat set in nearly 3 acres stretching down to the sea, incorporating a beauty salon & juice bar. There are 3 swimming pools including one that cantilevers over the sea, with a swim-up bar & private gazebos. There is a health club, a young adults' club, a library & a kids' club. Shallow waters team with marine life attracting snorkellers while the efficient dive-school team lead divers to new sites for sightings of manta rays & whale sharks. A marine research centre is located on the island as part of the Four Seasons' environmental projects. The island is fringed by a 1km white sandy beach on both its northern & southern shores, ending in stunning sand spits on its eastern & western tips. The taming of the environment has been a gentle process resulting in a memorable amalgamation of holiday sophistication & tropical island renaissance. Transfer: plane 50mins. $$$$$

⌂ **Kihaadhuffaru Fonimagoodhoo** (100 rooms) ↘ 6606688; f 6606633; e kihaad@valtur.it; www.valtur.com/villaggio/kihaad. Located south of Reethi Beach, Kihaadhuffaru is sometimes referred to as Kihaad Maldives Resort & is marketed in Italy. The D-shaped island is very attractive, with good vegetation, beaches & lagoon. Palm trees sway over some beach areas. Buildings are in typical Maldivian style with thatching. Rooms are intimately decorated with white walls & wooden ceilings. The deluxe villas have whirlpools. A walkway leads visitors out to the house reef for snorkelling. There is a freshwater swimming pool suitable for children. Transfers: plane 30mins. $$

⌂ **Kihavah Huravalhi** An MTDC project for a 55-bedroom resort to the west of the Four Seasons resort.

⌂ **Reethi Beach Fonimagoodhoo** (100 rooms) ↘ 6602626; f 6602727; e info@ reethibeach.com.mv; www.reethibeach.com.mv. Reethi Beach is on the island of Fonimagoodhoo, which sits in a wide, beautiful, turquoise, sandy lagoon, with both clear shallow zones & a narrow band, allowing the house reef to draw in close. The island has been well blessed by nature, with a cooling canopy & lots of greenery. Some care has been given to preserving this gift, with a leafy path providing access across

the island. The beaches are very good & broad for much of the shore, although some sections are inaccessible. Accommodation is in standard, deluxe & 30 overwater bungalows of basic design with few frills, catering for a rustic-style of holiday in keeping with the beach theme. As well as the main restaurant there is a Chinese restaurant & a grill for special functions. With swimming pool, sports complex, spa, diving school & watersports there's lots to do. The house reef is excellent for snorkelling, & the lagoon is ideal for swimming, waterskiing, jet skiing, parasailing & windsurfing. Because of the channels around the resort larger fish are enticed closer to shore which adds to the attraction of dives & the dive centre organises up to 4 dives a day. This is a resort for active people & outdoors lovers on a modest budget. Transfers: plane 35mins. $

⌂ **Royal Island Resort & Spa Horubadhoo** (150 rooms) ↘ 6600088; f 6600099; e info@ royal-island.com.mv; www.villahotels.com. Royal Island, located on Horubadhoo, opened in 2001 as an ultra-modern, comfortable resort with a design that is tasteful & blends with nature. Rooms are airy & wood is used extensively. There are 148 beach villas & 2 suites with main restaurants offering a wide range of international fare, usually as buffets. The spa provides a variety of holistic treatments in a Maldivian village-style setting. The island is long & very lush, with plenty of coconut palms & large banyan trees amongst the dense vegetation & narrow, pristine beaches. With the Dhigali Haa Marine Reserve nearby, the dive centre has access to many sites. When construction was under way, some ancient Buddhist relics were uncovered & are now in the museum in Male'. This has a reputation as a good-value-for-money resort in the typical Villa Hotels mould. Transfers: plane 30mins. $$ (HB)

⌂ **Soneva Fushi Resort Kunfunadhoo** (65 rooms) ↘ 6600304; f 6600374; e reservations-fushi@ sixsenses.com; www.sixsenses.com. Soneva Fushi Resort on Kunfunadhoo has become legendary for its transformation of a large, 1.5km long, forested island into a resort of excellence & exclusivity. Back-to-nature style is taken to the ultimate, turning the resort into a natural treasure, with its archetypal tropical paradise image. With extravagantly made timbered villas in a lush wilderness, it is like a woodland fantasy, ecologically over-the-top (bamboo strapped together to make armchairs, incoming faxes delivered in bamboo tubes). Natural materials like coir, coral & clay are used for fittings. There are 2 superb restaurants on opposite sides of the island.

Much of the island's magnificent vegetation is easy for guests to explore & find quiet corners & hidden beaches. There is a large lagoon & all popular watersports are available. The diving is good & the centre offers full-day trips to some of the 30 sites around the atoll. This is the kind of resort that wins rave reviews in fashion magazines & colour supplements & offers a complete holiday compatible with its exclusive image. Many clients are happy simply to chill out over a champagne b/fast, laze on the beach, then take a romantic sunset cruise for 2. Transfers: plane 30mins. $$$$–$$$$$

G LHAVIYANI (FAADHIPPOLHU) Geographic and administrative atolls coincide in this atoll to the east of Baa Atoll. It has only four inhabited islands (and over 50 uninhabited). It is 56km long and 57km at its greatest width. Naifaru (G-2) is the capital, 143km from Male', and is noted for indigenous medicine. The most populated islands are Naifaru and Hinnavaru (G-1), both dedicated to fishing. Naifaru has a new government power house provided with assistance from Japan, as well as a branch of the Bank of Maldives.

The uninhabited island of Felivaru has been turned into a tuna-fish canning factory, first built in the 1970s and reopened as a modern fish-processing plant in 1986. The project includes refrigeration plants, cold storage, quay and slipways. The island of Maafilaafushi is being settled with government encouragement. Another uninhabited island, Kuredhu in the north of the atoll, became a camping resort in 1978 but has now been upgraded into a holiday village complex. It took 21 years for more resorts to be opened in the atoll. There is a new airport on Madivaru, north of Naifaru on the western rim.

Resorts

🏠 **Hudhufushi** An unusual, V-shape island on the eastern rim, long-earmarked for development as a 200-bedroom resort.

🏠 **Kanifushi** Planned as a 150-bedroom resort, this long island lies on the southwest corner of this rectangular shaped atoll.

🏠 **Kanuhura** (100 rooms) ☎ 6620044; f 6620033; e info@kanuhura.com.mv; www.sunresorthotels.com. Developed to provide a high standard of self-indulgence & good living this resort has tastefully appointed villas & suites dotting its beach fringe, where landscaped gardens add a sense of individuality. There are also thatched timbered overwater villas with steps down to the enticing lagoon. The main restaurant features themed buffet meals & another specialises in Mediterraean cuisine. Facilities include a kids-only club, AC squash court, aerobics studio & spa with sauna & steam room & cold plunge pools. The beaches are superb all around the island, which is quite long & narrow. Conditions on the large lagoon are ideal for windsurfing & catamaran sailing. It does not lend itself to snorkelling, but divers can easily go further afield to find some interesting unfrequented sites. Transfers: plane 40mins. $$–$$$

🏠 **Komandoo Island Resort** (60 rooms) ☎ 6621010; f 6621011; e info@komandoo.com; www.komandoo.com. Komandoo Island Resort is located in the northwest of the atoll. All the rooms are built in wood, inside & out & sit on the beachfront. The main buildings are in Maldivian style & most guests are on all-inclusive deals taking meals in the buffet restaurant. The modest-sized island does not have dense cover, but there are plenty of shady palms. Its beaches are superb & its lagoon is shallow with a close house reef. The snorkelling is great, with a variety of fish to be seen including mantas & dolphins. With so many channels, *thilas* & other underwater attractions the diving is rewarding & specialist dives include shark & ray sorties, underwater photography & drift dives. Despite all the frenetic activities below the water, the ambience is one of calm, peace & tranquillity. Guests visit mostly from Germany, the UK & elsewhere in Europe. A 6-day minimum stay is required & children under 12 are not allowed. Transfers: plane 40mins. $$ (FB)

🏠 **Kuredu Island Resort** (330 rooms) ☎ 6620337; f 6620332; e reservations@kuredu.com; www.kuredu.com. Kuredu is located on the northern tip of the atoll & is one of the pioneers of less-expensive holidays in the Maldives, having started as a camping resort. Guests now have a choice of 2 resorts & 4 room types. The Sangu Resort on the eastern end has jacuzzi beach villas & sunset water villas, whereas the original Kuredu resort has accommodation in beach bungalows & beach villas more in keeping with the 'holiday as party' atmosphere. There are 2 main restaurants for FB guests & 3 à-la-carte restaurants & 5 bars. There is a swimming pool & a 6-hole golf course set in this large, green island with 3km of beaches. Most guests stay on special packages & this has diversified activities so it's no longer nothing to do but dive or snorkel. Adding to the diversity & vibrancy of this resort, young-at-heart guests come from all over Europe. Transfers: plane 40mins. $–$$

⌂ **Palm Beach Island Madhiriguraidhoo** (104 rooms) ✆ 6620084; f 6620091; e reservations@ sportingholiday.com.mv; www.palmbeachmaldives.com. Palm Beach Island is on the large, triangular-shaped island of Madhiriguraidhoo in the northeast of the atoll, south of Kanu Hura. The rooms are big & well designed, if a little solid looking, & the public facilities are sumptuous & large. Visitors stay on an FB plan but there is an option of an à-la-carte restaurant as well. The island has vast swathes of shady palms & some areas of more open & lower bushy vegetation. As the beaches have been left to nature, occasional shifts in sand can vary the layout, but on the whole they are wide & excellent. The lagoon is also extensive. Watersports are included for all-inclusive guests, as are many excursions. The diving is extra, but with the Fushifaru Kandu marine area & other sites nearby, this is a delight. A wide range of nationalities come to seek the casual laid-back atmosphere, but Italians are the majority. Transfers: plane 35mins. $$ (FB)

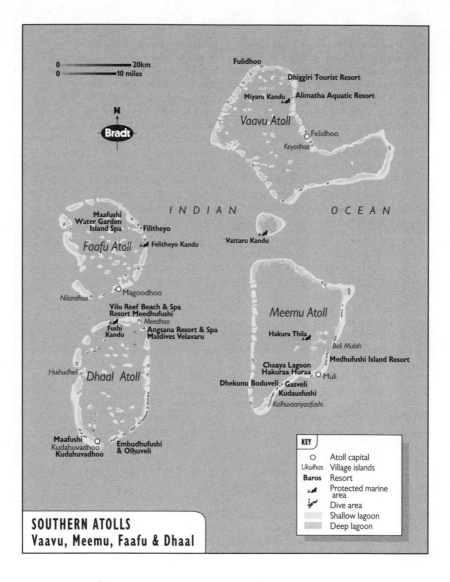

SOUTHERN ATOLLS
Vaavu, Meemu, Faafu & Dhaal

0 ——— 20km
0 ——— 10 miles

N
Bradt

Fulidhoo
Dhiggiri Tourist Resort
Miyaru Kandu — Alimatha Aquatic Resort
Vaavu Atoll
Felidhoo
Keyodhoo

INDIAN   OCEAN

Maafushi
Water Garden
Island Spa   Filitheyo
Faafu Atoll   Felitheyo Kandu   Vattaru Kandu

Nilandhoo   Magoodhoo

Vilu Reef Beach & Spa
Resort Meedhufushi
Fushi   *Meedhoo*
Kandu   Angsana Resort & Spa
          Maldives Velavaru

Meemu Atoll
Hakura Thila
Boli Mulah
Medhufushi Island Resort
Chaaya Lagoon
Hakuraa Huraa   Muli
Dhekunu Boduveli Gasveli
          Kudausfushi
          Kolhuvaariyaafushi

Huihudheli   *Dhaal Atoll*

Maafushi
Kudahuvadhoo   Embudhufushi
Kudahuvadhoo   & Olhuveli

KEY
○   Atoll capital
Ukulhas   Village islands
Baros   Resort
         Protected marine
         area
         Dive area
         Shallow lagoon
         Deep lagoon

9

Southern Atolls

RESORTS ON SOUTHERN ATOLLS

With the opening of Gan International Airport in the deep south of the archipelago and of new resorts close to Gan, the southern atolls will see a surge in development and progress during the next few years as tourism penetrates further south. For tourists this brings a chance to see parts of the Maldives, both above ground and underwater, and beyond the Equator, as yet unexplored by visitors.

J VAAVU (FELIDHU) This is the least populated atoll, and the population is spread over five inhabited islands. The atoll, which actually consists of two natural atolls – Vatturu (uninhabited) and Felidhu – is 35km north to south and 47km wide. The capital, Felidhoo (J-3), is 78km from Male'. There is some fishing, but no agriculture. Vaavu Atoll is 61km from Male' Airport.

Resorts

🏠 **Alimatha Aquatic Resort** (102 rooms)
🕿 6700575; f 6700544; e alimatha@
dhivehinet.net.mv; www.alimatharesort.com. Alimatha Aquatic Resort is south of Dhiggiri on the eastern rim of the atoll. It was opened with 10 rooms in 1975 & has gone through several transformations since then. It now has 102 rooms including overwater lodges. The island has a shallow lagoon, lots of palms & a beach that extends right around it. The accommodation has retained traces of the local style it began with & it is still basic tropical-island rustic. It is favoured by aquatic enthusiasts from Italy who stay on all-inclusive packages. Transfers: speedboat 1hr 40mins, plane 30mins. 💲

🏠 **Dhiggiri Tourist Resort** (45 rooms) 🕿 6700593; f 6700592; e dhiggiri@dhivehinet.net.mv; www.dhiggiriresort.com. Dhiggiri in the north of the Vaavu Atoll is isolated, which is part of its attraction. It began in 1982 with 50 beds, adding another 10 a year later. It now has 45 rooms, which include overwater lodges. The island is small & compact. It has a good accessible house reef. A brochure candidly described it as the 'most primitive resort in the Maldives', but now the rooms have AC, hot water & most of the extras (except TV) expected by today's clientele. Primarily an island for watersports fans, it caters mainly for Italians; its style & marketing reflect this. Transfers: speedboat 1hr 30mins, plane 25mins. 💲

K MEEMU (MULAKATHOLU) Lots of islets and islands form this administrative and geographical atoll south of Vaavu Atoll, also known as Mulaku. There are nine inhabited islands. The capital, Muli (K-5), is on the eastern side of the atoll, 138km from Male'. In size, the atoll is 41km long but only 27km wide. There is barely any agricultural land and most of the population are engaged somehow in fishing, but the catch is not exceptional. Some yams are grown.

The atoll's name is derived from that of Mulah (K-4), which was formerly the chief island. Raiymandhoo (K-1) became uninhabited between 1969 and 1975 and is still not heavily populated. A 17th-century mosque is on the island of Veyvah (K-3), which used to be called Ve-oh. The island of Kolhufushi (K-7) is also known as Kolhuvaariyaafushi. A sword believed to have been used by Sultan Mohamed Thakurufaan was deposited in its mosque. Dhiggaru (K-8) and Maduvvari (K-9) were part of Vaavu Atoll until included in Meemu Atoll, where they belong geographically, in 1959.

Resets

🏠 **Chaaya Lagoon Hakuraa Huraa** (70 overwater bungalows, 10 beach rooms) ➘ 313738; f 326264; e jkmr@dhivehinet.net.mv; www.chaayahotels.com. Operated by the Keells hotel group of Sri Lanka, the resort of Hakuraa Huraa has been branded as a Chaaya property & appropriately includes 'lagoon' in its name because that's where the accommodation is. 70 detached suites, perched on pillars over the lagoon, are accessed by a long boardwalk running parallel to the island's shore with 7 piers linking to the rooms. Room 101 is the closest to the public areas located on the island, 170 is the furthest away. With a 500m-long jetty from landing point to reception, this resort is made for walking. The long, rectangular over-lagoon rooms each have a white, tent-style roof, wooden floors with glass fish-viewing panel & bright white & glass walls, complemented by curtains fringed with traditional black-&-white stripes, chunky wooden furniture, colourful art & real (not plastic) potted plants. Lots of amenities like spare toothbrushes, bath robes & slippers, & extra pillows. Huge buffet feasts in the main restaurant with à-la-carte coffee shop & bar. No swimming pool but access down balcony steps from each room to the vast lagoon where a *dhoni* takes guests out to the reef platform for snorkelling. One of the best value-for-money (all-inclusive) & friendliest of the

lower-priced resorts. Transfers: plane 45mins, then 5mins by *dhoni*. $–$$ (all-inclusive)

🏠 **Dhekunu Boduveli, Gasveli, Kudausfushi** 3 slips of islands in the south of the atoll, planned as a 30-bedroom resort.

🏠 **Medhufushi Island Resort** (120 rooms) ➘ 6720026; f 6720027; e medhu@aaa.com.mv; www.aaaresortsmaldives.com.mv. Medhufushi is set on a long, narrow, well-endowed island with dense vegetation & plenty of palm trees. It is south of Naalaafushi. The superb sweeping beaches are excellent & palms sway invitingly across many of them. The lagoon is fairly extensive & there are small sand-spits. It closed for redesign to give it better facilities, with 44 water villas & 2 honeymoon water villas, 58 beach villas & 7 2-bedroom beach suites, all with soft furnishings for a more romantic image. The thatched rooms, although not large, are top-notch with all the latest extras. Many have verandas & French windows, giving an airy feeling of back-to-nature. There is a beautiful & intimate restaurant beside the pool. The watersports are well served with an inviting lagoon. There is a dive centre, which has opened up the attractions of the atoll. The resort sees itself as 'the idyllic barefoot luxury island'. Not a place for those looking to party as the accent's more on tranquillity. Transfers: plane 45mins. $$

L FAAFU (NORTH NILANDHE) On the western side of the garland, opposite Vaavu and Meemu atolls, this is a geographical atoll, south of Ari Atoll. It has only five inhabited islands. Its capital is Magoodhoo (L-4) in the south of this neat circular atoll. It is 131km from Male'. The atoll, which is 27km long and 23km broad, takes its name from one of its islands, Nilandhoo (L-2), where there are ancient ruins indicating its former importance. This island has the most inhabitants in the atoll. It fascinated Thor Heyerdahl, who wrote about it in his book *The Maldives Mystery*. The mosque here was originally built during the reign of Sultan Mohamed Ibn Abdullah (1153–66). Known as the Aasaari Miskiiy, it is the second-oldest mosque in the Maldives and has well-crafted stonework. It retains some other impressive features, like the ornamented scrollwork of its interior. Some evidence can be found on the islands here of a large Hindu temple with characteristic Shiva phallic symbols. Buddhist friezes from pre-Islamic structures have also been discovered.

There are said to be 12ha available for cultivation, most of them on Dharaboodhoo (L-5), which is the least populated and where turtles are accustomed to laying their eggs. The atoll is not a good fishing region and is inhabited only on its eastern islands. On the western side is the island of Himithi, whose inhabitants, having dwindled to 48, left in 1968. A French ship was wrecked on its reef in 1777.

Resorts

🏠 **Filitheyo** (125 rooms) ➲ 6740025, in Male' 3316131; f 6740024; e fili@aaa.com.mv; www.aaaresortsmaldives.com. Filitheyo was opened in 2000. This is a large, picture-postcard island with dense palm trees covering almost the whole area. Thatched roofing adds to the charm of the light & airy rooms which are top class, most with open-air bathrooms. There are 16 overwater villas set some way out in the lagoon. There are 2 restaurants, 2 bars & a pool bar as well as a dedicated spa. The beaches are particularly good & the lagoon is shallow with a close house reef. Channels have been cut in the lagoon bed to aid access. The house reef offers exciting snorkelling, with a big drop-off & lots of fish. The diving offers a variety of channels, *thilas* & sites nearby. It is the main attraction on

this island & the evening ambience is low key. Germans seem to be in the majority, but there are other Europeans & some Japanese. Transfers: plane 35mins. $$

🏠 **Maafushi Water Garden Island Spa** (6 rooms) ➲ 6740555; f 6740557; e info@ raniaexperience.com; www.raniaexperience.com. Officially Maafushi, set alone in the eastern centre of the atoll, is a small picnic island that can accommodate 12 guests in sublime luxury with exclusive spa facilities. It is offered as part of the Rania Experience, which is actually a private 26m yacht with the entire island, butlers, personal chefs, delectable food, spa treatments, diving & almost everything included from US$12,000 per night for 2, minimum of 3 nights stay. Transfers: plane 35mins. $$$$

M DHAAL (SOUTH NILANDHE) Almost a mirror image of its close northern neighbour, this is a single atoll opposite Meemu with eight inhabited islands and as many as 50 uninhabited ones. The nation's silver and goldsmiths come from this atoll. It is hardly surprising that there is a profitable craft here when the fishing is not up to much, nor is there much land (about 20ha) good for agriculture. The capital, with the majority of the atoll's inhabitants, is Kudahuvadhoo (M-8) in the south. It is 176km from Male'; the complete atoll, a regular oblong, is 35km north to south and 24km east to west.

Ribudhoo (M-3) is renowned for the skill of those of its inhabitants who make gold jewellery. It is interesting to speculate that this skill arose as a result of salvaging gold from a vessel that sank in the nearby Faafu Atoll in the 18th century. However, another suggested reason is that a sultan's goldsmith was exiled here and taught his skill to others. Its southern neighbour (also on the western rim of the atoll) of Hulhudheli (M-4) boasts silversmiths. These islands have also been the site of several shipwrecks.

Resots

🏠 **Angsana Resort & Spa Maldives Velavaru** (84 rooms) ☎ 6760028; f 6760029; e velavaru@angsana.com; www.angsana.com. A super new place with a very attractive island as its base, south of the inhabited island of Meedhoo. Accommodation comprises 48 beach bungalows, 16 island bungalows & 20 deluxe beach bungalows, all with exquisite interiors. All the rooms & the buildings have thatched, conical roofs that help them blend in with the vegetation, mostly palm trees. The beaches are dazzling & the lagoon has much variety of depth & fish, but the house reef is some way out. This is a sister property of Angsana Ihuru & Banyan Tree Vabbinfaru, both in North Male' Atoll. Transfers: plane 40mins. $$$$–$$$$$

🏠 **Embudhufushi & Olhuveli** 2 neighbouring islands in the south of the atoll near the capital island. An MTDC project for a 110-bedroom resort is planned.

🏠 **Kudahuvadhoo** The atoll's capital island for which there is an AIM project for a 100-bedroom airport & transit hotel.

🏠 **Maafushi** The neighbouring island to the northwest of the capital with an AIM project for a 100-bedroom resort in the planning stage.

🏠 **Vilu Reef Beach & Spa Resort Meedhufushi** (101 rooms) ☎ 6760011; f 6760022; e info@vilureef.com.mv; www.vilureef.com. Vilu Reef Resort is on Meedhufushi & is a small, compact retreat with swaying palms over sun-drenched beaches. There are 65 beach villas hidden amongst the lush vegetation, & built in the lagoon & reached by a long oval-shaped extension are 35 jazuzzi overwater villas, 5 honeymoon water villas & a presidential suite with pool. There are 2 restaurants, 3 bars & an infinity swimming pool by the beach as well as the health spa. Diving is a big attraction with some interesting sites although the swells & currents can sometimes be strong. There is a good mix of clients; most from Europe, with Germans in the majority. Transfers: plane 40mins. $$ (HB)

N THAA (KOLHUMADULU)

This is another circular atoll, which actually closes the garland, leaving only the pendant of atolls hanging down to Addu. In its near-circle (38km long and 47km wide) are 13 inhabited islands. The capital is Veymandhoo (N-11), which is 222km from Male'. For fishing, the atoll is supposed to be among the best; it also has some agriculture with potential for 59ha of cultivation. H A Maniku suggests that the atoll's name could be derived from *kolhuvan*, meaning the dry whole coconut leaves used for roofing by the first inhabitants.

The northernmost island is Buruni (N-1), devoted to fishing, while the women do mat weaving. The uninhabited islands of Kalhufaraa, Fahala and Rakeefushi combined make up one of the larger islands in the archipelago: Kalhufahalafushi. There is a cluster of inhabited islands on the eastern side of the circle. Among them, the best fishing islands are said to be Vilufushi (N-2), Guraidhoo (N-5) with a 17th-century mosque, and Thimarafushi (N-10), which suffered two devastating fires at the beginning of the 20th century; it is one of the most populated islands in the atoll. Kadoodhoo (N-6) is reputed to have good carpenters. On Dhiyamigili (N-4) there are traces of the 18th-century palace of the founder of the Dhiyamigili dynasty of sultans, which ended when the Malabars of south India occupied Male' for three months (see *History*, page 20).

Resorts

🏠 **Elaa** With an easier name to remember than most islands, Elaa is south of the capital island of Veymandhoo, which should be interesting for guests to visit. It is planned as a 140-bedroom resort.

🏠 **Kalhufahalafushi** (100 rooms) Planned as a resort of 36 water suites & 64 suites on the long island that runs along the eastern rim of the atoll.

🏠 **Maalefushi** (50 rooms) This small island is close to the inhabited island of Guraidhoo & is being developed as one of the Regent Hotels & Resorts. It has 23 beach & 27 overwater villas, all with private

plunge pools & expansive timber decks. There is a spa with 8 private treatment rooms open to the sea breeze. Open 2008. Transfers: plane 50mins. $$$$$

🏠 **Olhugiri** An island in the northern part of the atoll for which an AIM project for a 100-bedroom tourist resort is planned.

🏠 **Thimarafushi** An AIM project for a 100-bedroom airport & transit hotel is planned for this island, which lies in the south of the atoll, northeast of the capital.

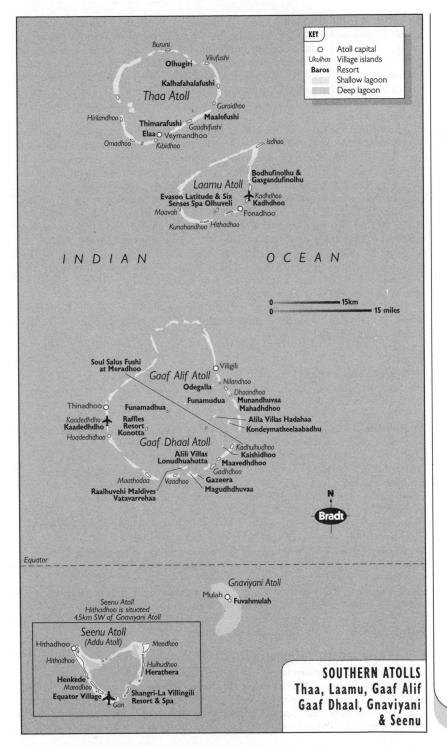

KEY
○   Atoll capital
Ukulhas   Village islands
Baros   Resort
    Shallow lagoon
    Deep lagoon

Buruni

Vilufushi

Olhugiri

Kalhafahalafushi

Thaa Atoll

Guraidhoo

Hirilandhoo

Maalefushi

Thimarafushi Gaadhifushi
Elaa ○ Veymandhoo

Omadhoo   Kibidhoo

Isdhoo

**Bodhufinolhu &
Gasgandufinolhu**

Laamu Atoll

**Evason Latitude & Six
Senses Spa Olhuveli**   Kadhdhoo
Kadhdhoo

Maavah   Fonadhoo

Kunahandhoo Hithadhoo

I N D I A N   O C E A N

0   15km
0   15 miles

**Soul Salus Fushi
at Meradhoo**   ○ Viligili

Gaaf Alif Atoll   Nilandhoo

Odegalla   Dhaandhoo

Funamudua **Munandhuvaa**
Mahadhdhoo

Thinadhoo ○ **Funamadhua**

Kaadedhdho ✈ **Raffles**
Kaadedhdho   **Resort**
    Konotta

Hoadedhdhoo

Alila Villas Hadahaa
Kondeymatheelaabadhu

Gaaf Dhaal Atoll

Kadhulhudhoo

Alili Villas **Kaishidhoo**
Lonudhuahutta **Maavedhdhoo**

Gadhdhoo

Maathodaa Vaadhoo **Gazeera**
Raalhuvehi Maldives   **Magudhdhuvaa**
Vatavarrehaa

N

Bradt

Equator

Gnaviyani Atoll

Mulah ○ **Fuvahmulah**

Seenu Atoll
Hithadhoo is situated
45km SW of Gnaviyani Atoll

Seenu Atoll
(Addu Atoll)

Hithadhoo ○   Meedhoo

Hithadhoo

Hulhudhoo
Herathera

Henkede
Maradhoo
Equator Village ✈ **Shangri-La Villingili**
Gan   **Resort & Spa**

SOUTHERN ATOLLS
Thaa, Laamu, Gaaf Alif
Gaaf Dhaal, Gnaviyani
& Seenu

9

O LAAMU (HADHDHUNMATHI) Laamu Atoll has good fishing and good agriculture, 12 inhabited islands including Gan, also known as Gamu (O-6) – one of the largest in the archipelago – and over 70 uninhabited islands. It is shaped a bit like an upturned horseshoe, and is 34km at its longest and 34.6km at its widest. Its former capital, Hithadhoo (O-11), is 269km from Male'. The people are known for growing yams and breadfruit. An estimated 434ha of land is good for agriculture, much of it on Gan, which has rich, black peaty soil and is the most populated. Gan has three villages.

The former capital is in the south and has ancient ruins, as does Gaadhoo (O-9), with some of the most imposing to be found anywhere in the Maldives. A very large Buddhist stupa, known as the Vadiyaamagu Hawitta, once stood here. In its prime it must have been an incredible sight, its white dome rising proud against the lush green vegetation around it. The new capital, Fonadhoo (O-8), has a small population spread over three villages. In 1922, archaeologist H C P Bell investigated ruins on Gamu, Mundu (O-4) and other islands in the atoll, finding traces of Buddhist monuments. There have been several wrecks in the atoll at Maavah (O-7) and Isdhoo (O-1), where a Chinese vessel, *Yuang Haing*, ran aground in 1969 and was named *Isdhoo Muli* when re-floated. Isdhoo, on the northeastern tip of the atoll, has a Friday Mosque which is more than three centuries old. Its interior crafted rafters, fine lacquered supports and calligraphy indicate the quality of workmanship that existed in the islands.

There has been an airport since 1981 on the uninhabited island of Kadhdhoo, which is between Hithadhoo and Fonadhoo. It was built because of the development potential of the atoll.

Resorts

⌂ **Bodufinolhu & Gasgandufinolhu** 2 tiny islands immediately north of the long, populated island of Gan on the eastern rim of the atoll. There are plans for an MTDC project for a 100-bedroom resort.

⌂ **Evason Latitude & Six Senses Spa Olhuveli** (100 rooms) www.sixsenses.com/evason-laamu. On a small island in the south of the atoll, near the capital island of Hithadhoo, this fantasy island is the newest resort by Sonu & Eva Shivdasani, the creative geniuses behind the Sonevafushi & Soneva Gili resorts. Their company, Six Senses Resort & Spa group, comprises the luxury Soneva & Evason resorts of which there are 11 worldwide, the Six Senses Spa brand, & Soneva Kiri, a new residential development in Thailand, so guests at this new resort know they are in good hands. The resort consists of beach pool villas & overwater villas, which feature outdoor rain showers, water gardens, private sun decks & outdoor seating areas. Several overwater duplex villa suites offer indoor-outdoor bathrooms & water slides into the lagoon from the upper level. These suites are detached from the main island & are linked by jetty. Other features are an underwater restaurant, which converts to a chill-out lounge with DJ, an above-water restaurant with cooking hut, ice-cream parlour, pastry shop & a Chef's Table, & a restaurant for organic dishes located above an organic vegetable garden. The duplex, overwater wine cellar has cheese & charcuterie rooms & offers wine tastings & *dégustation* dinners. The spa is located ashore, with the stilted treatment areas interconnected with rope & plank bridges. There is a kids' club with adventure activities in the wilderness, & great surfing nearby. Open 2008. Transfers: plane 45mins then speedboat 20mins. $$$$$

⌂ **Kadhdhoo** There is an airport serving the atoll on this uninhabited island, 45mins' flying time from Male'. A 100-bedroom regional airport hotel is planned.

P GAAF ALIF (NORTH HUVADHU) One half of the natural Huvadhu Atoll, this is separated from its northern neighbour by the Huvadhu Kandu, known as One and Half Degree Channel. There are ten inhabited islands and over 80 uninhabited ones; the majority of the population live in Viligili (Villingili) (P-2), the capital. This is 380km from Male', on the northeastern side of the upper part of the atoll. The atoll extends 109km from north to south and 60km at its widest.

Fishing is the main occupation, followed by agriculture. The island of Ko'nday (Kodey) (P-7) has 87ha of cultivable land out of an atoll total of 260ha. There are ancient *hawittas* (mounds) there, which might have been Buddhist stupas in the distant past. The capital, one of several islands in the Maldives called Viligili or Villingili, is the most populous in the atoll and has a tradition of quality mat making. The only inhabited island on the western rim, Kolamaafushi (P-1), was the scene of the wreck of the sailing vessel *Surat* in 1800. It is a fishing island, as is Maamendhoo (P-3). The island of Dhevvadhoo (P-6) is known for textile weaving and coir making and has some ruins, as well as mosques, dating back to the 16th and 17th centuries.

Resorts

⌂ **Alila Villas Hadahaa** (50 rooms) To the east of centre in this vast atoll, this island will be the home of the first Alila Villas resort in the Maldives & a sister resort to the one on Lonudhoohuttaa, further south in Gaaf Dhall Atoll. It is the brainchild of a small hotel group headquartered in Singapore. The concept has been approached as a 'testament to the architect's art' with the idea of melding the culture of place into structure. As an example of the developer's acknowledgement of environmental conditions, the island has 2 jetties to cope with tidal changes, with the villas positioned to give long vistas towards the sea. A further quote from the pre-opening publicity states that the resort will benefit from 'emerging trends in top tier luxury resort design, embracing several characteristics: ecological, spiritual, contemporary, boutique, cultural, luxurious – oases of indulgence & rejuvenation'. Promised is 'the best of contemporary lifestyle'. There are 36 beach villas, 10 with private pool & 14 overwater villas. Open 2008. Transfers: plane & speedboat. $$$$$

⌂ **Funamudua** (50 rooms) In the centre of this huge atoll, with access via Kaadedhdhoo regional airport. Planned as a resort called Summer Dream with 25 beach & 25 water bungalows & an à-la-carte restaurant as well as a main one. Flood-lit tennis court, a surf school & game fishing as extra attractions. Transfer: plane 45mins & speedboat 20mins. $$

⌂ **Kondeymatheelaabadhu** With a name that seems almost as long as the island, this is scheduled for an MTDC project for a 50-bedroom resort.

⌂ **Mahadhdhoo** A larger island than its neighbour Munandhuvaa, it is planned as a 50-bedroom resort.

⌂ **Munandhuvaa** Planned as a 24-bedroom resort, this island is on the eastern rim & a close neighbour to Mahadhdhoo.

⌂ **Odegalla** An AIM project for a 100-bedroom tourist resort on an island in the northern half of the atoll.

⌂ **Soul Salus Fushi at Meradhoo** (22 rooms) A soulistically inspired retreat managed by Per Aquum, the creators of the famous Huvafenfushi Resort in Male' Atoll. Located on 2 islands, the driving passion behind Soul Salus Fushi is transformation: a place devoted to body & soul, health, wellness & nutrition. Each pool villa has its own sanctuary, a peaceful & energising space designed with an emphasis on sensory & holistic elements. The 3 distinctive dining venues include a central retreat restaurant featuring meal planning with recipe analysis & nutritional assessment programmes, a lounge bar with organic drinks & spa cuisine & a live kitchen offering an additional range of fresh, healthy food. Spa treatments include traditional Chinese medicine, vibration & sound healing, acupuncture, shiatsu, spa rituals, Ayurveda, energy & meridian healing, naturopathic & homeopathic consultations & high performance skin-care treatments. Open 2008/9. $$$$$

Q GAAF DHAAL (SOUTH HUVADHU) The bulbous lower half of the onion-shaped Huvadhu Atoll has ten inhabited islands and over 150 uninhabited ones. It is 42km long and 51km wide. The capital is Thinadhoo (Q-10) on the western rim, not far from the airport on the uninhabited island of Kaadedhoo. The capital, the most populous island in the atoll, is 404km from Male'.

Like many islands, the capital has gone through changes of settlement. It was depopulated in 1962 and the chief's office transferred to Gadhdhoo (Q-4), but it was moved back and the island resettled in 1969. It is one of the atoll's major fishing islands. The uninhabited island of Gan has some ancient mounds, investigated by Thor Heyerdahl, and is farmed for coconuts and firewood by people from Gadhdhoo, which is next to it.

There are 291ha of potential agricultural land in this atoll. Taro is grown on Gadhdhoo, which is also a fishing island but used to be renowned for mat weaving, as was Fiyoari (Q-7). There is a *hawitta* at Vaadhoo (Q-6) and a 17th-century mosque built by a sultan who came from the island. Maathodaa (Q-8) was joined to its neighbour Fares (Q-9) by a causeway in 1981. One authority says that the people of Huvadhu Atoll used to speak a dialect that people of the northern atolls found difficult to understand.

Resorts

⌂ **Alila Villas Lonudhuahutta** (50 rooms) A sister property to the Alila Villas resort on Hadahaa Island to the north in Gaaf Alif Atoll, created with the same architectural & holiday philosophy. There are 20 beach villas & 16 water villas each with a pool as well as 14 overwater villas. Access is via a flight from Male' to Kaadedhdhoo regional airport to the west. Open 2008. Transfers: plane & speedboat. $$$$$

⌂ **Gazeera** On this small island in the south of the atoll, plans are in hand for a 22-bedroom resort.

⌂ **Kaadedhdho** A regional airport hotel of 100 bedrooms is planned for this inhabited island on the western rim of the atoll.

⌂ **Kaishidhoo** A small 30-bedroom resort has been approved for this island to the north of the inhabited island of Gadhdhoo.

⌂ **Maavedhdhoo** An uninhabited island on the atoll's eastern rim with a plan for an AIM project for a 200-bedroom airport & transit hotel.

⌂ **Magudhdhuvaa** This island is close to the resort planned for Gazeeraa & is to be the site for an MTDC project for 100-bedroom resort.

⌂ **Raalhuvehi Maldives Vatavarrehaa** A resort of 75 bedrooms is planned for this resort, said to resemble a manta ray from the air.

⌂ **Raffles Resort Konotta** (49 rooms) A range of duplex villas from 116m² to 350m² feature in this new resort in the centre of the atoll. The beach villas (27) have plunge pool & rooftop sun deck as well as a spa pool, while the 21 overwater villas boast a glass-panelled floor, rooftop sun deck & spa treatment beds with a jacuzzi & a private plunge pool. The presidential water villa is appropriately grand. There are 4 speciality restaurants & a spa. The resort is reached by speedboat from Kaadedhdhoo Airport, which is a 50-min flight from Male'. Open 2008. Transfer: speedboat 15mins. $$$$

R GNAVIYANI (FUVAH MULAH) Across the Equator, administrative and geographical atolls combine here in one island, measuring 4.4km north to south and 2.8km east to west. It consists of only one island, called Fuvah Mulah or Mulah (R-1), and the atoll is also known as Fua Mulaku. H A Maniku has written that it is probably called Fua (meaning areca nut) Mulah to distinguish it from Mulah in Meemu Atoll. The distance from Male' is 496km.

This is a wooded, fertile and industrious island, with two large freshwater lakes. Cultivators produce grains, yams, mangoes, oranges, pineapples, bananas and vegetables, some of which are shipped to sell in other parts of the Maldives. Some 81ha have been identified as cultivable. Since there was no harbour until 2003 and a constant swell surges around the island, fishing is not much practised except during calm days. This is one of the oldest inhabited islands, and the largest, in the Maldives.

History records a 70-day stay on it by Ibn Battuta in 1344 and the arrival of two French brothers, Jean and Paul Parmentier, in 1529. Archaeologist H C P Bell investigated its ruins in 1922, as did Thor Heyerdahl some 60 years later. They were as impressed with the island as all other foreign visitors have been. Among the sites are the ruins of a Buddhist stupa. The Kedeyre Mosque and its baths are very well constructed, with superb workmanship and finely carved tombstones. It sits quietly near the beach. The Dhiguvanu Mosque is another site worth seeing. Access is by flight to Gan and then a 57km boat ride to land at the solidly built new harbour.

Resort

Fuvahmulah (Foammulah) A 60-bedroom city hotel is planned for this large, inhabited island.

S SEENU (ADDU) Ask a good steward in a resort where he comes from and the answer will often be Addu/Seenu Atoll. It is the southernmost atoll, the tip of the garland's dangling pendant, a croissant of islands surrounded by a reef with a deep lagoon. It is the most densely populated atoll (although Kaaf has more people if Male's population is included). There are officially six inhabited islands in an area extending 13km from north to south and 17km east to west. The capital is Hithadhoo (S-2), 536km from Male'. The name of the atoll, Addu, is said to come from an island of that name since eroded away, or is an amalgam of the Dhivehi *ah* (eight) and *dhoo* (islands), except there are more than eight islands, even though some of them have been joined by a causeway to make a single one.

Gan The islands include one, Gan, that is now officially uninhabited, but in the past was twice taken over by the British with far-reaching consequences. With no jobs when the British left in 1976 and a strong tradition of spoken English, many people from this atoll looked to the tourist industry for their future. This is why it is not hard to find someone from Addu Atoll in a resort. Gan's ancient history bequeathed ruins, investigated by H C P Bell in 1922, and six mosques, one of them dating from the 17th century.

The British landed in 1941 on the large island of Villingili (Viligili), also uninhabited and open in 2008 as a resort. A Royal Air Force base with a long runway was set up on the neighbouring island of Gan, to where the British moved. The inhabitants were resettled on Maamendhoo, part of Hithadhoo. When the RAF left at the end of World War II, the people returned.

In 1956, another RAF staging facility was used at Gan and the inhabitants again moved, this time to Feydhoo (S-4) where they stayed, even though the British left after 20 years. Development since includes the improvement in 1981 of the link from Gan to Feydhoo, and on to Maradhoo (S-3), Hankede, Rajjeheraa and Hithadhoo, on the causeway built by the British in 1970. This has now been surfaced and become a major road, a Maldivian version of a super corniche.

The islands of Meedhoo (S-1) and Hulhudhoo (S-6), on the east of the croissant, joined together to form one, adopting the name Hulhumeedhoo in 1969, but were designated as separate islands again in 1975. On Meedhoo there is an ancient cemetery known as Koaganu. Local people make a living from fishing and agriculture. Many of the male population of the atoll work elsewhere in Maldives, remitting their earnings, which lends an air of incipient development to the islands. This is becoming more noticeable as Addu expands into tourism and people return after working in resorts in the north, to secure lucrative employment in their home atoll.

The atoll is linked to Male' by daily flights by both Island Aviation and TMA and the the old military runway has been reconstructed, with the addition of immigration and customs buildings, for international long-haul jets to land. A new terminal complete with luggage carousel and trolleys, as well as a smoking room and a prayer room in the new departure lounge, has been added. As Addu Gan International Airport, it welcomed its first charter passenger flight from Europe in December 2007.

Around Gan There is no sign to say you have crossed the Equator when you land at Gan Airport, but it is easy to sense something is different. Even 30 years after the British abandoned Gan, what they did to the island is not only visible; it can be felt in the atmosphere, too. There is an air of desolation about the place, curiously so, because in fact it is very well cared for, with neat lawns and flower borders, buildings closed but well preserved, sturdy British steel manhole covers, and then the final legacy: no inhabitants.

Of course, people do stay in Gan, either for work or at the Equator Village, but no-one actually lives there. Home now, even for those born on the island, is Feydhoo or somewhere else.

While there have long been plans to promote Gan as a holiday destination, its future is more as a transit point for guests bound for the island resorts in the atoll. Enthusiasts believe a holiday in Gan could appeal to the nostalgia market, particularly to servicemen. They may have a point, since it seems stuck in the 1950s with its high-eaved barrack buildings, officers' quarters (now administrative buildings) and a disciplined air. Sightseeing excursions are arranged, whether by coach or alone on a hired bicycle, touring the islands linked by the super new highway.

Gan is an island whose marine environment has not suffered through exploitation; turtles are said to thrive and there are reported to be great diving spots at wrecks. Big-game fishing could be big indeed, because of the depth of the ocean close to shore. The birdlife is different from the rest of Maldives; there are no crows. Nor are there any snakes. Fruit and vegetables are grown. Its difference and history make its supporters believe Gan could be the answer for the vacation visitor who wants more than a beach holiday.

In the early 1990s I strolled down to what used to be the NAAFI social club, where a notice called it Cola Fihaara. It was located at a quiet crossroads with shady trees over its forecourt where metal sunshades left by the British topped outside tables. A metal sculpture which, when studied carefully, resembled a graceful woman bearing a water jug at her hip, served as a sign of refreshments. The shopkeeper, born on Gan but living on one of the linked islands, remembered the British. He recalled how the barrack-like huts close by used to be the Blue Lagoon Hotel for transit passengers from the many flights that touched down in Gan during RAF days.

Less than a minute's walk along the broad avenue that is Gan's main thoroughfare is a memorial garden and a plaque saying 'Royal Air Force, Gan, 1956–1976'. A war memorial lists the many Indian army regiments that served there, such as the Royal Bombay Sappers and Miners and the 13th Frontier Force Rifles, commemorating those 'who died in the service of the country. The mortal remains of some were committed to fire and others lie buried elsewhere in Addu Atoll.' Two big guns mounted by the memorial in 1972 formed part of the defences of Addu Atoll in World War II.

The Seenu Gan Branch of the Bank of Maldives ($\oplus$ *09.30–13.30*) is opposite. There is a post office in the same block with a post box in its wall. In a shopping complex near the hotel (Equator Village) are a pharmacy, a gift and clothes shop and a branch of the STO.

There are taxis in Gan, and a long road linking the island with its neighbours over the causeway. The residential islands of Feydhoo and Maradhoo and, further away, Hithadhoo, add interest to a visit to Gan. This is a chance to discover a little of the lifestyle of Maldivians at home, at work and at play, since all you really need is a bicycle (borrow from Equator Village) and a sunhat. Although the only place to stay in Gan is the Equator Village, there are tea shops for socialising on the islands now joined together by road. Hithadhoo, at the northern point, is the main port and is like a pioneering frontier town.

The Southern Secondary School is at Hithadhoo, with over 400 students studying in English. It has a thriving cadet force, whose members train on the beachfront, and an eager brass band which parades on state occasions. At the end of Hithadhoo, the harbour is being developed and there I saw *Nitaz*, one of the inter-island cargo ships shaped like a cross between a junk and an ark, which I had seen in Male' a few days before.

Foreign travellers are not allowed passage on such vessels as there is no provision for payment or collection of the nightly head tax payable by every foreigner without a residence visa.

In his listing of the islands of Maldives, H A Maniku records that Hithadhoo was known for its 'fishing, blacksmiths and jewellers'. Now, as the atoll capital, it is more memorable as an island waiting for things to happen as the infrastructure is developed. Dhiraagu has set up a telecommunications base in the atoll and there is a school bus service. Houses are well developed and roads are wide.

There is a checkpoint at the entrance to Gan from the causeway and there the relaxed atmosphere of the causeway islands gives way to Gan's strange stillness. A jeep with NSS men cruised slowly past me. It was easy to imagine the tread of marching feet on the barrack square, a sergeant's bark of command, and the other ranks downing beers in the setting sun outside the NAAFI. Not really what one expects after crossing the Equator, but it is part of the Gan experience, which makes a visit there intriguing for the independent traveller.

Resorts

Equator Village (78 rooms) ℘ 6898721; f 6898020; e equator@dhivehinet.net.mv; www.equatorvillage.com. Equator Village was formerly known as the Ocean Reef Club. Unlike the typical Maldives resort, Equator Village is more of a hotel on an island. None of the infrastructure beyond its walls has anything to do with the hotel, & guests are free to roam wherever they like. The beach here is not picture-postcard, but the beaches elsewhere, the variety & the space more than counteract this. The hotel is built on the site of the sergeants' mess, with basically furnished rooms, in blocks of 4 & 6. With large verandas facing the sprawling lawns shaded with frangipani trees, the rooms have refrigerator, AC, & hot water in the shower. There is a large swimming pool in the hotel's garden.

The drive to the hotel from the airport is short, but gives an instant impression of Gan's immediate past, with everything neatly laid out. The gardens of the Equator Village are mature, such as you would find in the Caribbean, not dependent on imported soil as in the resort islands. It is a great improvement from its previous existence when it tried to flourish as the Gan Holiday Village in the 1980s.

The reception area of the hotel is a delightfully painted pillared lobby leading to a vast bar. This gives access to the restaurant overlooking the swimming pool & garden, with some huge old trees, & the sea. There is a separate billiard room, whose ancient marker board seems to have been used for dart practice. Dhoni trips are organised to inhabited & uninhabited islands close by, where snorkelling is good. As for diving, the big plus is the lack of bleaching of the corals. This is the place to see the glories of Maldivian coral banks. Just to add a final touch, all the big fish are found in the channels nearby. With bicycles for hire & easy access to real villages & settlements, this is a good place, apart from Male', to see normal Maldivian life. Transfers: plane 70mins, taxi 5mins. $

Henkede One of the small islands in the centre of the group linked by main highway from Gan to Hithadhoo. An 80-bedroom hotel is planned by the beach. Promoters believe Gan could be the answer for the vacation visitor who wants more than a beach holiday.

Herathera (300 rooms) ℘ 6897766; f 6897733; e reservations@herathera.com; www.herathera.com. As the first guest to swim (in Nov 2007) in this resort's vast 50m-long pool beside the full-length bar & restaurant facing the beach, My comments on Herathera are tinged with pride. First, what to call this wonderful value-for-money, all-inclusive resort? The list of islands for development issued by the Ministry of Tourism calls it Herethere, which is apt for a long island with so much to do as guests go here & there. The map calls it Heretere & it is, in fact, pronounced as Hairy-terra. It means 'hideaway' or 'sanctuary' in Dhivehi. The island has 4km of beach & has been developed in record time by the government-owned corporation, MTDC, with 180 beach villas & 120 larger jacuzzi beach villas (the jacuzzi is in a private wooden-deck compound at the back of each room) down both sides. The rooms are comfortable chalets with a pleasing décor of bright fabrics to complement the natural tones of the wooden floors, veranda decks, exterior walls & exposed beam ceilings. There are 2 main restaurants, with sand floor & thatched roof, for the 2 different categories of rooms & both feature 'all-you-can-eat' buffets for b/fast, lunch & dinner. There are 2 optional restaurants with a choice of either a grilled seafood menu or Asian cuisine, & 3 bars. There are in fact 3 swimming pools, as well as a children's wading pool, & stacks of activities including 2 floodlit tennis courts, & scuba, windsurfing & sailing centres & a glorious spa as well as evening entertainment. All-inclusive is an option & includes a night fishing & a sunset cruise as well as 'all you can drink'. The island itself is rich in birdlife with a mini-wilderness surrounding a natural lake &, being the first resort in the area, has exciting diving possibilities. It opened in Dec 2007 & looks set to become a new destination (via the new international airport at Gan) for travellers in search of a complete, inexpensive & fascinating holiday experience. Transfers: plane 70mins (from Male') plus speedboat 20mins. $ (all-inclusive)

🏠 **Shangri-La Villingili Resort & Spa** (142 rooms) www.shangri-la.com. Villingili, also spelt Viligili, is a large island a few kilometres east of Gan. It was long earmarked for the creation of an upmarket resort but there were many delays. At press time construction, which had been speeded up, was almost complete. The resort has been designed with 5 different villa concepts (& pricing). A total of 142 villas each feature a private terrace & some infinity pools. One-bedroom villas have a minimum of 132m². Set along the treeline, 16 tree villas perched on stilts offer a special perspective of the island through lush foliage. 60 water villas with terraces extend over the lagoon. The rest of the island is dotted with 29 beach villas, 15 water-pool villas, 20 twin villas & 2 presidential suites. A selection of bars & restaurants serves a wide range of international, as well as local, cuisine. This is an eco-oriented resort with lagoon beaches on one side & a surf beach on the other. Construction has been carefully carried out in order to preserve large trees, including some towering old banyans. Nature lovers can enjoy over 5km of picturesque coastline including nearly 2km of beaches. Sporting activities include scuba diving, snorkelling, windsurfing, game fishing, wind sailing & boating. There is an indoor & outdoor kids' club. The wild, rugged natural beauty of the island is exciting &, unusual for the Maldives, the island has 3 freshwater lakes. Open 2008. Transfers: plane 70mins to Gan from Male' & then by speedboat. $$$–$$$$$

Appendix I

LANGUAGE

PRONUNCIATION Providing you can master the pronunciation guides, phrasebooks are a wonderful help in asking questions. (For some words and phrases in Dhivehi see below.) However, they are useless when you hear the answer, as it will be a jabber of extraordinary sounds. If the person you are trying to communicate with actually reads Roman script, they might be able to find an answer in the phrasebook and point to the English equivalent, but since most Maldivians who do not speak English cannot read Roman script, you are stuck.

Whenever I have tried to speak Dhivehi using phrases from the phrasebooks available in Male' (see *Further information*, page 209), I have been faced with stares of incomprehension. Perhaps it was my pronunciation, since in Dhivehi the accent is put on the first syllable of a word.

LANGUAGE USE Some expressions with which English-speakers pepper their conversations are not used much in Dhivehi. For instance the word for 'Thank you' (*shukriyya*) is a recent introduction from Arabic. Instead of some words, a simple smile or gesture is often enough.

One linguist explained that Maldivians don't regard saying 'Thank you' as necessary and the person being thanked could be demeaned by being thanked if they are doing an expected thing; a clue here to the nature of the Dhivehin.

'Hello' has actually become part of the modern Maldivian's vocabulary. More formal is the version of the traditional Arabic greeting: *assalaamu alaikum*. The reply is *va-alaikumussalaam*. Shorter and more commonly used is *kihineh*, as though you are saying simply, 'How?'

Farewell is cut short to *dhanee*, which literally means 'going', used where in English 'See you' might suffice instead of 'Goodbye'. *Ran'galhu* can be used for 'good' or 'OK' and in answer to the question *kihineh*? Avoid *baraabaru* which appears to serve the same purpose but doesn't; Maldivians use it only to foreigners.

In the first edition of this book I wrote that Maldivians do not use an equivalent of Mister, even when addressing a Maldivian who is a stranger, perhaps a result of island informality. Mariyam Zulfa, a Maldivian editor and journalist, has since pointed out that:

> However close someone is to a person, if the English language is to be used in conversation, it is customary to use 'Mr' before a name, especially in a third-person reference. This is not indicative of an unequal relation or denoting of someone worthy of higher respect, but just a mark of courtesy. Also, 'Mr' is often used with the informal or first name. For women, 'Miz' may be used but more not than often.

Mariyam Zulfa also adds:

> It is not uncommon for Maldivians to use their second names as the so-called first name. For example: Ibrahim Hussain Zaki is referred to by friends and associates as 'Zaki'. Hussain Afeef is 'Afeef', never 'Hussain'. The same goes for women who rarely take on the husband's name. For instance, my name remains as Mariyam Zulfa, whatever my marital status.
>
> And, like for many men, it is usual for me to be referred to as 'Zulfa' and not 'Mariyam', which would be the first name in a western system.

Commenting on the apparent 'non-expressiveness' of Maldivians, Zulfa warns against taking this lack of emotion as impoliteness. She writes:

> Maldivians do not habitually greet one another; a greeting of say 'Good morning' from a visitor may be met with a smile or a nod from a Maldivian. This is not to be understood for impoliteness or ignorance, far from it!

Also, there are simply no words in Dhivehi that depict 'Please' or 'Thank you', or for greetings for times of day. These sentiments are expressed in a genuine smile and it is generally understood that these emotions are inherent in the demeanour and disposition of one's associates or by those deemed fit to partake of one's society.

The phrases listed here may be helpful to break the ice, but, if you are lucky enough to be on a village island without a guide to translate for you, sign language, personality and quick-wittedness will soon have you conversing with more satisfaction than any list of useful phrases. Then, of course, you will find that you are really learning the language.

USEFUL WORDS AND PHRASES

Hello (formal)	*Assalaamu alaikum*
Hello (informal)	*Kihineh*
How are you?	*Haalu kihineh?*
What is (your) name?	*Nama kee kobaitha?*
My name is...	*Aharen ge namakee...*
How old are you?	*Umurun kihaa varehtha?*
My age is...	*Aharen ge umurakee…*
Where do you work?	*Kon thaneggatha masai kai kuranee?*
What is your job?	*Vazee faa akee kobaitha?*
Where do you live?	*Dhiri ulhenee kon thaneh gai?*
Can I visit your house?	*Thige yah ziyarai kurevidhaa netha?*
May I take your photo?	*Photo eh negi dhaa netha?*
Good	*Ran'galhu*
Yes	*Aan*
No	*Noon*
Thank you	*Shukriyya*
Excuse me (sorry)	*Ma-aafu kurey*
Lover	*Loabiveriyaa*
Mother	*Mamma*
Father	*Bappa*
Brother	*Bey be*
Sister	*Dhath-tha*
Which island are you from?	*Kon rasheh tha?*
How much does it cost?	*Agu kihaa vareh?*
Where can I find ...	*Kon thana kun tha ...*
a *dhoni*?	*dhoni eh libe nee?*
a doctor?	*doctereh?*
a shop?	*fihaara eh?*
the mosque?	*miskiy theh?*
the post office?	*post office eh?*
the island chief?	*rashu bodu katheebu?*
Goodbye (informal)	*Dhanee*

NUMBERS

0	*sumeh*	3	*thineh*	6	*hayeh*
1	*ekeh*	4	*hathareh*	7	*hatheh*
2	*dheyh*	5	*faheh*	8	*asheh*

9	nuva-eh	16	soalha	50	fansaas
10	dhihayeh	17	sathaara	60	fasdholhas
11	egaara	18	ashaara	70	haiydhiha
12	baara	19	navaara	80	addiha
13	theyra	20	vihi	90	nuvadhiha
14	saadha	30	thirees	100	satheyka
15	fanara	40	saalhees	1,000	eh haas

THE CALENDAR
Days of the week

Sunday	adheeththa dhuvas	Thursday	buraaffathi dhuvas
Monday	hoama dhuvas	Friday	hukuru dhuvas
Tuesday	angaara dhuvas	Saturday	honihiru dhuvas
Wednesday	budha dhuvas		

Months (lunar calendar)

1	Muharram	7	Rajah
2	Safar	8	Shaaban
3	Rabeeu al-Awwal	9	Ramazan
4	Rabeeu al-Akhir	10	Shawwal
5	Jumada al-Oola	11	Zul Qaidaa
6	Jumada al-Akhira	12	Zul Hijjaa

Hawksbill turtles

Appendix 2

ATOLL AND ISLAND NAMES

Each atoll has two names, its traditional geographical one (given first in the listing below) and its code name which is actually a letter of the Dhivehi alphabet. See box below for a list of atoll names. In conversation, atolls are referred to by their code name when it is easier than the long traditional name. Exceptions are Male' Atoll (Kaaf in alphabetic code) and Ari Atoll (Alif in code). Islands in this list total more than the 198 (200 for administrative purposes) inhabited islands, as it is a list of designated code numbers for boats belonging to the various islands. In March 1995 Hulhudhuffaaru in North Maalhosmadulu was declared an inhabited island. Asterisks (*) denote the atoll capitals.

NORTH THILADHUNMATHI/HAA ALIF

A-1	Thuraakanu	A-7	Ihavabdhoo	A-13	Thakandhoo
A-2	Uligamu	A-8	Kelaa	A-14	Utheemu
A-3	Berimmadhoo	A-9	Vashafaru	A-15	Muraidho
A-4	Hathifushi	A-10	Dhidhdhoo*	A-16	Baarah
A-5	Mulhadhoo	A-11	Filladhoo		
A-6	Huvarafushi	A-12	Maarandhoo		

ATOLL NAMES

CODE LETTER	TRADITIONAL NAME	CODE NAME
A	North Thiladhunmathi	Haa Alif
B	South Thiladhunmathi	Haa Dhaal
C	North Miladhunmadulu	Shaviyani
D	South Miladhunmadulu	Noonu
E	North Maalhosmadulu	Raa
F	South Maalhosmadulu	Baa
G	Faadhippolhu	Lhaviyani
H	Male'	Kaaf
I	Ari	Alif
J	Felidhu	Vaavu
K	Mulakatholu	Meemu
L	North Nilandhe	Faafu
M	South Nilandhe	Dhaal
N	Kolhumadulu	Thaa
O	Hadhdhunmathi	Laamu
P	North Huvadhu	Gaaf Alif
Q	South Huvadhu	Gaaf Dhaal
R	Fuvah Mulah	Gnaviyani
S	Addu	Seenu

SOUTH THILADHUNMATHI/HAA DHAAL

B-1	Faridhoo	B-7	Nolhivaranfaru	B-13	Kumundhoo
B-2	Hodaidhoo	B-8	Nellaidhoo	B-14	Neykurendhoo
B-3	Hanimadhoo	B-9	Nolhivaram	B-15	Vaikaradhoo
B-4	Finey	B-10	Kuribi	B-16	Maavaidhoo
B-5	Naivaadhoo	B-11	Kuburudhoo	B-17	Makunudhoo
B-6	Hirimaradhoo	B-12	Kulhudhuffushi★		

NORTH MILADHUNMADULU/SHAVIYANI

C-1	Kaditheemu	C-6	Biliyfahi	C-11	Lhaimagu
C-2	Noomaraa	C-7	Foakaidhoo	C-12	Firubaidhoo
C-3	Goidhoo	C-8	Narudhoo	C-13	Komadhoo
C-4	Feydhoo	C-9	Maakadoodhoo	C-14	Maaugoodhoo
C-5	Feevah	C-10	Maroshi	C-15	Funadhoo★

SOUTH MILADHUNMADULU/NOONU

D-2	Hebadhoo	D-7	Landhoo	D-12	Manadhoo★
D-3	Kedhikulhudhoo	D-8	Maafaru	D-13	Holhudhoo
D-4	Tholhendhoo	D-9	Lhohi	D-14	Fodhdhoo
D-5	Maalhendhoo	D-10	Miladhoo	D-15	Velidhoo
D-6	Kudafari	D-11	Magoodhoo		

NORTH MAALHOSMADULU/RAA

E-1	Alifushi	E-7	Ugoofaaru★	E-13	Iguaraidhoo
E-2	Vaadhoo	E-8	Kadholhudhoo	E-14	Fainu
E-3	Rasgetheemu	E-9	Maakurath	E-16	Meedhoo
E-4	Agolhitheemu	E-10	Rasmaadhoo	E-17	Kinolhas
E-5	Gaaudoodhoo	E-11	Innamaadhoo		
E-6	Ugulu	E-12	Maduvvarie		

ALPHABETICALLY BY TRADITIONAL NAME

Addu	Seenu
Ari	Alif
Faadhippolhu	Lhaviyani
Felidhu	Vaavu
Fuvah Mulah	Gnaviyani
Hadhdhunmathi	Laamu
North Huvadhu	Gaaf Alif
South Huvadhu	Gaaf Dhaal
Kolhumadulu	Thaa
North Maalhosmadulu	Raa
South Maalhosmadulu	Baa
Male'	Kaaf
North Miladhunmadulu	Shaviyani
South Miladhunmadulu	Noonu
Mulakatholu	Meemu
North Nilandhe	Faafu
South Nilandhe	Dhaal
North Thiladhunmathi	Haa Alif
South Thiladhunmathi	Haa Dhaal

SOUTH MAALHOSMADULU/BAA

F-1	Kudarikilu	F-8	Dharavandhoo	F-14	Fulhadhoo
F-2	Kamadhoo	F-9	Maalhos	F-15	Fehendhoo
F-3	Kendhoo	F-10	Eydhafushi★	F-16	Goidhoo
F-4	Kihaadhoo	F-12	Thulhaadhoo		
F-7	Dhonfan	F-13	Hithadhoo		

FAADHIPPOLHU/LHAVIYANI

G-1	Hinnavaru	G-3	Kurendhoo
G-2	Naifaru★	G-4	Olhuvelifushi

MALE' ATOLL/KAAF

H-1	Kaashidhoo	H-4	Thulusdhoo★	H-11	Gulhi
H-2	Gaafaru	H-5	Huraa	H-12	Maafushi
H-3	Dhiffushi	H-6	Himmafushi	H-13	Guraidhoo

MALE' ISLAND (NATIONAL CAPITAL)

T-10   Male'

ARI/ALIF

I-1	Thoddoo	I-7	Feridhoo	I-13	Mahibadhoo★
I-2	Rasdhoo	I-8	Maalhos	I-14	Mandhoo
I-3	Maamigili	I-9	Himandhoo	I-15	Dhangethi
I-4	Ukulhas	I-10	Hagngnaameedhoo	I-16	Dhigurah
I-5	Mathiveri	I-11	Omadhoo	I-17	Fenfushi
I-6	Boduholhudhoo	I-12	Kuburudhoo	I-18	Dhidhdhoo

FELIDHU/VAAVU

J-1	Felidhoo	J-3	Felidhoo★	J-5	Rakeedhoo
J-2	Thinadhoo	J-4	Keyodhoo		

MULAKATHOLHU/MEEMU

K-1	Raiymandhoo	K-4	Mulah	K-7	Kolhufushi
K-2	Madifushi	K-5	Muli★	K-8	Dhiggaru
K-3	Veyvah	K-6	Naalaafushi	K-9	Maduvvari

NORTH NILANDHE/FAAFU

L-1	Feeali	L-3	Biliydhoo	L-5	Dharaboodhoo
L-2	Nilandhoo	L-4	Magoodhoo★		

SOUTH NILANDHE/DHAAL

M-1	Meedhoo	M-4	Hulhudheli	M-7	Maaeboodhoo
M-2	Badidhoo	M-5	Gemendhoo	M-8	Kudahuvadhoo★
M-3	Ribudhoo	M-6	Vaani		

KOLHUMADULU/THAA

N-1	Buruni	N-6	Kadoodhoo	N-11	Veymandhoo★
N-2	Vilufushi	N-7	Vandhoo	N-12	Kibidhoo
N-3	Madifushi	N-8	Hirilandhoo	N-13	Omadhoo
N-4	Dhiyamigili	N-9	Gaadhiffushi		
N-5	Guraidhoo	N-10	Thimarafushi		

HADHDHUNMATHI/LAAMU

O-1	Isdhoo	O-5	Kalhaidhoo	O-9	Gaadhoo
O-2	Dhabidhoo	O-6	Gamu	O-10	Maamendhoo
O-3	Maabaidhoo	O-7	Maavah	O-11	Hithadhoo
O-4	Mundu	O-8	Fonadhoo★	O-12	Kunahandhoo

NORTH HUVADHU/GAAF ALIF

P-1	Kolamaafushi	P-5	Dhaandhoo	P-9	Gemanafushi
P-2	Villingili★	P-6	Dhevvadhoo	P-10	Kaduhulhudhoo
P-3	Maamendhoo	P-7	Ko'nday		
P-4	Nilandhoo	P-8	Dhiyadhoo		

SOUTH HUVADHU/GAAF DHAAL

Q-1	Madaveli	Q-5	Rathafandhoo	Q-9	Fares
Q-2	Hoadedhdhoo	Q-6	Vaadhoo	Q-10	Thinadhoo★
Q-3	Nadallaa	Q-7	Fiyoari		
Q-4	Gadhdhoo	Q-8	Maathodaa		

FUVAH MULAH/GNAVIYANI (FUA MULAKU)

R-1   Mulah★

ADDU/SEENU

S-1	Meedhoo	S-3	Maradhoo	S-5	Maradhoo
S-2	Hithadhoo★	S-4	Feydhoo	S-6	Hulhudhoo

Appendix 3

RESORTS AT A GLANCE

For an explanation of price-range coding, see the inside-front cover of this guide. The resorts in North and South Male' are within speedboat distance of the airport, while resorts in other atolls are reached by a combination of plane and speedboat, or seaplane and *dhoni*. Transfers by plane can entail a waiting time of two to three hours after arrival by international flight before take off from the seaplane terminal or domestic airport. Information on transfer times can be found with the resort listings.

★ *Resort under construction or reconstruction.*

RESORT	ATOLL	PRICE BAND	NO OF ROOMS	PAGE
Adaaran Club Bathala	Ari	$	46	166
Adaaran Club Rannalhi	South Male'	$$	116	160
Adaaran Select Hudhuranfushi	North Male'	$–$$	177	154
Adaaran Select Meedhupparu	Raa	$$	215	178
Adaaran Water Villas	Raa	$$$	20	179
Alila Villas Hadahaa★	Gaaf Alif	$$$$$	50	191
Alila Villas Lonudhuahutta★	Gaaf Dhaal	$$$$$	50	192
Alimatha Aquatic Resort	Vaavu	$	102	185
Anantara Maldives	South Male'	$$$–$$$$$	160	160
Angaga	Ari	$$	70	166
Angsana Ihuru	North Male'	$$$	45	154
Angsana Velavaru	Dhaal	$$$$–$$$$$	84	188
Asdu Sun Island	North Male'	$	30	154
Athurugau	Ari	$–$$$	51	166
Bandos	North Male'	$–$$$	225	154
Banyan Tree Madivaru	Ari	$$$$$	6	166
Banyan Tree Vabbinfaru	North Male'	$$$$	48	154
Baros Maldives	North Male'	$$$$	75	155
Beach House at Manafaru	Haa Alif	$$$$	68	173
Berinmadhoo★	Haa Alif		100	174
Biyadhoo★	South Male'			160
Bodufinolhu & Gasgandufinolhu★	Laamu		100	190
Bolifushi★	South Male'	$$$$	55	160
Chaaya Island Dhonveli	North Male'	$–$$$	144	155
Chaaya Lagoon Hakuraa Huraa	Meemu	$–$$	70	186
Chaaya Reef Ellaidhoo	Ari	$$	112	166
Cinnamon Resort Alidhoo	Haa Alif	$$–$$$$	100	174
Club Faru	North Male'	$	152	156
Club Med Kanifinolhu	North Male'	$$	208	156
Cocoa Island Makunufushi	South Male'	$$$$–$$$$$	35	161

Coco Palm Boduhithi	North Male'	$$$$	103	156
Coco Palm Dhunikolhu	Baa	$$$–$$$$	98	180
Coco Palm Kudahithi	North Male'	$$$$$	1	156
Conrad Maldives	Ari	$$$$	150	166
Constance Holiday Village★	Ari	$$	86	167
Dhekunu Boduveli, Gasveli, Kudaufushi★	Meemu		30	186
Dhiggiri Tourist Resort	Vaavu	$	45	185
Dhoni Island	Ari	$$$$$	6	167
Diva Resort & Spa★	Ari	$$$	93	167
Ekulhivaru★	Noonu		90	178
Elaa★	Thaa		140	188
Embudhufushi & Olhuveli★	Dhaal		110	188
Embudu Village★	South Male'			161
Equator Village	Addu	$	78	195
Eriyadu	North Male'	$	57	156
Evason Olhuveli★	Laamu	$$$$$	100	190
Farakolhu North★	Shaviyani		100	176
Farakolhu South★	Shaviyani		100	176
Fihalhohi Island	South Male'	$	150	161
Filitheyo	Faafu	$$	125	187
Four Seasons Kuda Huraa	North Male'	$$$$$	96	156
Four Seasons Landaa Giraavaru	Baa	$$$$$	102	180
Full Moon Maldives	North Male'	$$$–$$$$	156	157
Fun Island★	South Male'			162
Funamudhua★	Gaaf Alif	$$	50	191
Furahmulah★	Gnaviyani		60	192
Gaakoshibee★	Shaviyani		100	176
Gangehi	Ari	$$	25	167
Gazeera★	Gaaf Dhaal		22	192
Giraavaru★	North Male'			157
Hanimadhoo★	Haa Dhaal		100	175
Helengeli	North Male'	$	50	157
Henkede★	Addu		80	195
Herathera	Addu	$	300	195
Holiday Island	Ari	$	142	167
Hondaafushi★	Haa Dhaal		100	175
Hudhufushi★	Lhaviyani		200	182
Huvafenfushi	North Male'	$$$$	44	157
Irufushi Beach Medhafushi	Noonu	$$	100	178
Island Hideaway Dhonakulhi	Haa Alif	$$$$–$$$$$	43	174
Kaadedhdho★	Gaaf Dhaal		100	192
Kadhdhoo	Laamu		100	190
Kaishidhoo★	Gaaf Dhaal		30	192
Kalhufahalafushi★	Thaa		100	188
Kanbaalifaru★	Shaviyani		100	176
Kandooma	South Male'	$$$–$$$$	160	162
Kanifushi★	Lhaviyani		150	182
Kanuhura	Lhaviyani	$$–$$$	100	182
Kihaadhuffaru	Baa	$$	100	181
Kihavah Huravalhi★	Baa		55	181
Komandoo Island Resort	Lhaviyani	$$	60	182
Kondeymatheelaabadhu★	Gaaf Alif		50	191

Kudahuvadhoo★	Dhaal		100	188
Kudamuraidhoo★	Haa Dhaal		125	175
Kudarah	Ari	$$	60	168
Kuramathi Blue Lagoon	Ari	$$	56	167
Kuramathi Cottage & Spa	Ari	$$	83	168
Kuramathi Village	Ari	$–$$	151	168
Kuredu Island Resort	Lhaviyani	$–$$	330	182
Kurumba Maldives	North Male'	$$–$$$$$	180	158
Laguna Maldives	South Male'	$$–$$$$	132	162
Lily Beach★	Ari			168
Lundhufushi★	Raa		20	179
Maafushi★	Dhaal		100	188
Maalefushi★	Thaa	$$$$$	50	188
Maakaana★	Shaviyani	$$$$–$$$$$	35	176
Maanenfushi★	Raa		75	179
Maavelavaru★	Noonu		50	178
Maayafushi	Ari	$	60	169
Maafushi Water Garden Island Spa	Faafu	$$$$$	6	187
Maavedhdhoo★	Gaaf Dhaal		200	192
Machchafushi Island Resort	Ari	$$	74	169
Madoogali	Ari	$$	56	169
Magudhdhuvaa★	Gaaaf Dhaal		100	192
Mahadhdhoo★	Gaaf Alif		50	191
Mahureva Gasfinolhu	North Male'	$$	40	158
Makunudu	North Male'	$$	36	158
Medhufushi Island	Meemu	$$	120	186
Meeru Island	North Male'	$$	284	158
Mirihi	Ari	$$$	36	169
Moofushi	Ari	$	62	169
Munandhuvaa★	Gaaf Alif		24	191
Naagoashi★	Haa Dhaal		300	175
Naladhu Veligandu Huraa	South Male'	$$$$$	19	162
Naridhoo★	Haa Alif		50	174
Nika Island Resort Kudafolhudhu	Ari	$$$$	37	169
Odegalla★	Gaaf Alif		100	191
Olhugiri★	Thaa		100	188
Olhuveli Beach	South Male'	$$–$$$	129	163
One & Only Reethi Rah	North Male'	$$$$$	130	159
Palm Beach Island Madhiriguraidhoo	Lhaviyani	$$	104	183
Paradise Island	North Male'	$$	260	159
Raalhuvehi Vatavarrehaa★	Gaaf Dhaal		75	192
Raffles Konatta★	Gaaf Dhaal	$$$$	49	192
Randheli★	Noonu		50	178
Ranveli Village Villingilivaru	Ari	$	56	170
Reethi Beach	Baa	$	100	181
Rihiveli Beach	South Male'	$$	48	163
Royal Island Resort & Spa	Baa	$$	150	181
Shangri-La Villingilli★	Addu	$$$–$$$$$	142	196
Soneva Fushi	Baa	$$$$–$$$$$	65	181
Soneva Gili Lankanfushi	North Male'	$$$$$	45	159
Soul Salaus Fushi, Meradhoo★	Gaaf Alif	$$$$$	22	191

Summer Island village	North Male'	$	108	159
Sun Island Nalaguraidhoo	Ari	$	350	170
Taj Coral Reef	North Male'	$$	65	159
Taj Exotica	South Male'	$$$$–$$$$$	62	163
Thimarafushi★	Thaa		100	188
Thudufushi	Ari	$$	49	170
Thulhaagiri	North Male'	$	72	160
Twin Island Maafushivaru	Ari	$$	47	170
Uligamu★	Haa Alif		50	175
Vadoo★	South Male'			163
Vakarufalhi★	Ari	$$	50	170
Velidhu	Ari	$$	100	171
Veligandu	Ari	$$–$$$	74	171
Vilamendhoo Island	Ari	$	141	171
Villivaru★	South Male'			163
Vilu Reef Beach & Spa Resort	Dhaal	$$	101	188
W Retreat & Spa Fesdu	Ari	$$$$	78	171
Zitahli Dholhiyadhoo★	Shaviyani	$$$$	100	177
Zitahli Kudafunafaru★	Noonu		50	178

Appendix 4

FURTHER INFORMATION

BOOKS

Abdulla, Ismael *Maldives Impressions*

Allen, Dr Gerald R and Steene, Roger *Indo Pacific Coral Reef Field Guide* Tropical Research, Singapore

Amin, Mohamed, Willetts, Duncan, & Marshall, Peter *Journey Through Maldives* Camerapix Publishers International, Nairobi, 1992. Coffee-table book of photographs and text.

Anderson, Charles *Diver's Guide to the Sharks of the Maldives* Male'

Anderson, Charles *Living Reefs of the Maldives* Male'

Anderson, Charles and Hafiz, Ahamed *Common Reef Fishes of the Maldives* Parts One, Two & Three, Novelty Books, Male'

Atoll Editions *Divers' and Travellers' Map*

Atoll Editions *Malways: Maldives Island Directory* Australia, 1996

Battuta, Ibn *In Maldives and Ceylon* Asian Educational Services, New Delhi, 1996 Reproduction of the *Journal of the Royal Asiatic Society*, Ceylon Branch, 1882.

Bell, H C P *Excerpta Maldiviana* Asian Educational Services, New Delhi, 1998. Bell's collection of documents on Maldives, first published 1922–35.

Bevan, Stuart and Greig, Virginia *Maldives via Sri Lanka* Other People Publications, Australia, 1982

Camerapix *Spectrum Guide to Maldives* Camerapix International, Nairobi, 1993

Coleman, Neville *Marine Life of the Maldives* Atoll Editions

Cuthbertson, Lydia J *Guide to the Maldives* Immel Publishing, London, 1994

Debelius, Helmut *Indian Ocean Tropical Fish Guide*

Department of Information *History* Male'

Department of Information *Constitutional History* Male'

Edwards-Jones, Imogen *Beach Babylon*, Bantam Press, London, 2007. A riveting exposé of life at a tropical resort. The stories are true, the resort fictitious, but from the clues (a Muslim country, alcohol confiscated from arriving passengers, proximity to Colombo), it could only be the Maldives. Fun and informative to read before staying – or working – in the islands.

Ellis, Royston *A Maldives Celebration* Times Editions, Singapore, 1997. To commemorate 25 years of tourism in the Maldives, with photographs by Gemunu Amarasinghe.

Ellis, Royston *A Man For All Islands: A Biography of Maumoon Abdul Gayoom, President of the Maldives* Times Editions, Singapore, 1998

Ellis, Royston *A Hero In Time* Times Editions, Singapore, 2000. A historical novel based on the life of Mohamed Thakurufaanu.

Farook, Mohamed *The Fascinating Maldives* Novelty Press, Male', 1985

Farook, Mohamed *The Story of Mohamed Thakurufaanu*, Novelty Press, Male', 1986. A retelling in English of the story in Dhivehi by Hussain Salahuddeen.

Friel, Bob *Underwater Maldives* Male', 1989

Gayoom, Maumoon Abdul *Maldives: A Global View* Department of Information & Broadcasting, Male', 1990. Excerpts from speeches, 1979–89.

Gayoom, Maumoon Abdul *The Maldives: A Nation in Peril* Ministry of Planning, Human Resources & Environment, Male', 1998. An inspiring collection of speeches by the President of the Maldives appealing not just for the protection of the environment, but also for ways to save people whose lives and homes could be destroyed by an environment in turmoil.

Geiger, Wilhelm *Maldivian Linguistic Studies* Asian Educational Services, New Delhi, 1996. Reproduction of the Journal of the Royal Asiatic Society, Ceylon Branch, 1919.

Ghisotti, Andrea *Fish of Maldives* Bonechi Publications

Godfrey, Tim *Atlas of the Maldives* 4th edition, Atoll Editions, Australia

Habeeb, Habeeba Hussain *Muhammad Thakurufaan the Great* Privately published, Male', 1989

Hussain, Mustag and Gunaratna, Rohan *The Maldives: Home of the Children of the Sea* Male', 1987

Innes, Hammond *The Strode Adventurer* Fontana Books, 1968. A strange novel with vague Maldivian connections.

Kuiter, Rudie H *Fishes of the Maldives* Atoll Editions

Laroque, Toni de, with Ellis, Royston *Toni, The Maldive Lady* Times Editions, Singapore, 1999. The biography of a British woman who promoted tourism to the Maldives in England.

Maldives Tourism Promotion Board *Maldives, Resort/Hotel Guide* (produced annually) Male'. Information provided by the resorts and hotels.

Maloney, Clarence *People of the Maldive Islands* Orient Longman, India, 1980

Maniku, H A and Disanayake, J B *Say It in Maldivian (Dhivehi)* Lake House, Colombo, 1990

Maniku, Hassan Ahmed *The Islands of Maldives* Novelty Printers & Publishers, Male', 1983. A list of all the islands with some historical notes.

Maniku, Hassan Ahmed *Dhevi (in Vanavaru)* Male', 1988

Mojetta, Angelo, Ferrari, Andrea and Ferrari, Antonelle *Wonders of Coral Reefs* White Star publishers

Nasheed, Mohamed *Maldives Historical Overview, 1800 to 1900* Oriental Academic Centre, Male'

Neville, Adrian *Male': Capital of the Maldives* Novelty Books, Male', 1995. A photographer's view of the capital.

Neville, Adrian *Dhivehi Raajje: Portrait of the Maldives* Novelty Books, Male'

Neville, Adrian *Resorts of the Maldives* Novelty Printers & Publishers, Male', 1998. A photographic guide to each resort.

Pyrard, François (translated and edited by Grey, Albert and Bell) *The Voyage of François Pyrard of Laval to the East Indies, the Maldives, the Moluccas and Brazil* Hakluyt Society, London, 1887. A swashbuckling history by Pyrard who was shipwrecked in the Maldives; written in 1611.

Shafeeq, Mohamed and Abdulla, Ismail *Through Maldives* Novelty Press, 1984. Photographs of resorts as they used to be.

Vitharana, V *Sri Lankan-Maldivian Cultural Affinities* Academy of Sri Lankan Culture, Sri Lanka, 1997

Yapa, Vijitha *Papineau's Travel Guide to the Maldives* MPH Publishing, Singapore, 1987

Zuhair, M *Practical Dhivehi* Male', 1991

WEBSITES

www.visitmaldives.com The most useful website with which to begin a search for information about the Maldives is that of the Maldives Tourism Promotion Board (MTPB) (e *mtpb@visitmaldives.com*).

www.maldivesinfo.gov.mv Official website of the Republic of Maldives with lots of links.

www.eveningweekly.com.mv With news in English taken from the website of the daily Maldivian paper *Haveeru* (*www.haveeru.com*).

For the websites of tour operators, travel companies etc, see under the relevant headings in *Chapter 2*. Websites and email addresses for the resorts can be found under their descriptions in *Chapters 5–9*.

Bradt Travel Guides
www.bradtguides.com

Africa

Africa Overland	£15.99
Algeria	£15.99
Benin	£14.99
Botswana: Okavango, Chobe, Northern Kalahari	£15.99
Burkina Faso	£14.99
Cape Verde Islands	£13.99
Canary Islands	£13.95
Cameroon	£13.95
Congo	£14.99
Eritrea	£15.99
Ethiopia	£15.99
Gabon, São Tomé, Príncipe	£13.95
Gambia, The	£13.99
Ghana	£15.99
Johannesburg	£6.99
Kenya	£14.95
Madagascar	£15.99
Malawi	£13.99
Mali	£13.95
Mauritius, Rodrigues & Réunion	£13.99
Mozambique	£13.99
Namibia	£15.99
Niger	£14.99
Nigeria	£15.99
Rwanda	£14.99
São Tomé & Principe	£14.99
Seychelles	£14.99
Sudan	£13.95
Tanzania, Northern	£13.99
Tanzania	£16.99
Uganda	£15.99
Zambia	£17.99
Zanzibar	£12.99

Britain and Europe

Albania	£13.99
Armenia, Nagorno Karabagh	£14.99
Azores	£12.99
Baltic Capitals: Tallinn, Riga, Vilnius, Kaliningrad	£12.99
Belarus	£14.99
Belgrade	£6.99
Bosnia & Herzegovina	£13.99
Bratislava	£6.99
Budapest	£8.99
Bulgaria	£13.99
Cork	£6.99
Croatia	£13.99

Cyprus see North Cyprus	
Czech Republic	£13.99
Dresden	£7.99
Dubrovnik	£6.99
Estonia	£13.99
Faroe Islands	£13.95
Georgia	£14.99
Helsinki	£7.99
Hungary	£14.99
Iceland	£14.99
Kiev	£7.95
Kosovo	£14.99
Krakow	£7.99
Lapland	£13.99
Latvia	£13.99
Lille	£6.99
Lithuania	£13.99
Ljubljana	£7.99
Macedonia	£14.99
Montenegro	£13.99
North Cyprus	£12.99
Paris, Lille & Brussels	£11.95
Riga	£6.99
River Thames, In the Footsteps of the Famous	£10.95
Serbia	£14.99
Slovakia	£14.99
Slovenia	£12.99
Spitsbergen	£14.99
Switzerland: Rail, Road, Lake	£13.99
Tallinn	£6.99
Ukraine	£14.99
Vilnius	£6.99
Zagreb	£6.99

Middle East, Asia and Australasia

China: Yunnan Province	£13.99
Great Wall of China	£13.99
Iran	£14.99
Iraq	£14.95
Iraq: Then & Now	£15.99
Kyrgyzstan	£15.99
Maldives	£13.99
Mongolia	£14.95
North Korea	£13.95
Oman	£13.99
Sri Lanka	£13.99
Syria	£14.99
Tibet	£13.99
Turkmenistan	£14.99
Yemen	£14.99

The Americas and the Caribbean

Amazon, The	£14.99
Argentina	£15.99
Bolivia	£14.99
Cayman Islands	£14.99
Colombia	£15.99
Costa Rica	£13.99
Chile	£16.95
Dominica	£14.99
Falkland Islands	£13.95
Guyana	£14.99
Panama	£13.95
Peru & Bolivia: The Bradt Trekking Guide	£12.95
St Helena	£14.99
USA by Rail	£13.99

Wildlife

100 Animals to See Before They Die	£16.99
Antarctica: Guide to the Wildlife	£14.95
Arctic: Guide to the Wildlife	£15.99
Central & Eastern European Wildlife	£15.99
Chinese Wildlife	£16.99
East African Wildlife	£19.99
Galápagos Wildlife	£15.99
Madagascar Wildlife	£15.99
North Atlantic Wildlife	£16.99
Peruvian Wildlife	£15.99
Southern African Wildlife	£18.95
Sri Lankan Wildlife	£15.99

Eccentric Guides

Eccentric America	£13.95
Eccentric Australia	£12.99
Eccentric Britain	£13.99
Eccentric California	£13.99
Eccentric Cambridge	£6.99
Eccentric Edinburgh	£5.95
Eccentric France	£12.95
Eccentric London	£13.99
Eccentric Oxford	£5.95

Others

Your Child Abroad: A Travel Health Guide	£10.95
Something Different for the Weekend	£9.99

Index

Page numbers in **bold** refer to major entries, those in *italics* indicate maps
For the page numbers of all resorts, see *Resorts at a Glance*, pages 204–7